MASTERS OF THE UNIVERSE?

MASTERS OF THE UNIVERSE?

NATO's Balkan Crusade

Edited by

TARIQ ALI

VERSO

London • New York

First published by Verso 2000

Verso
UK: 6 Meard Street, London W1V 3HR
US: 180 Varick Street, New York, NY 10014–4606

Verso is the imprint of New Left Books

ISBN 1–85984–752–8
ISBN 1–85984–269–0 (pbk)

British Library Cataloguing in Publication Data
A catalogue record for this book is available from the British Library

Library of Congress Cataloging-in-Publication Data
A catalog record for this book is available from the Library of Congress

Typeset by M Rules
Printed in the USA by R.R. Donnelley & Sons Co.

CONTENTS

INTRODUCTION: AFTER THE WAR

Tariq Ali

Eric Hobsbawm, commenting on the recent conflict in the Balkans, has reminded us that despite the rhetoric, wars are rarely, if ever, actually waged for humanitarian reasons.[1] The assault on Serbia was no exception. Designed largely to boost NATO's credibility, the entire operation ended up a complete mess. Hence the muted triumphalism and a desire by its media-backers to forget the entire episode. In reality, the NATO crusade teetered on the edge of total disaster. When Michael Ignatieff, the London-based human rights warrior, asked General Wesley Clark why Milošević had withdrawn his forces when they remained undefeated, Clark offered no real explanation: 'You'd have to ask Milošević and he'd never tell you.'[2]

The answer is hardly a big secret. Senior officials in both Moscow and Belgrade are only too eager to explain why Milošević accepted the cease-fire. It was Moscow's brokerage that was decisive in preventing what could have been a major catastrophe for NATOland: Moscow's refusal, under US pressure, to provide the Serbs with sophisticated anti-aircraft weapons enabled the indiscriminate terror from the sky to continue unabated for several weeks. This was made clear by Ignatieff in the *New Yorker*:

> Devastating as the execution of the air campaign proved to be, particularly against Serbia's civilian infrastructure, it might have turned out very differently if the Russians had given the Serbs their latest technology. The air war was essentially a duel between seventies Soviet air-defense technology and state-of-the-art American precision-guidance systems. If NATO had been up against eighties Soviet technology, it might have lost twenty planes, and it is unclear whether NATO's electorates would have stood for such losses.

> Deputy Secretary of State Strobe Talbott has confirmed that the United States 'repeatedly and explicitly' warned Russia not to provide Yugoslavia with 'any military assistance – material, know-how, personnel'. As he put it, 'We didn't mince words' . . .
>
> Milošević had gambled that NATO would not hold together if it were faced with the aroused opposition of the Russians and their overt military assistance to Serbia. Russia could have split NATO in two, but for all their talk of Slavic brotherhood, the Russians ultimately decided that their national interest lay with America . . .[3]

In the end it was Moscow's threat to cut off oil supplies to Serbia that occasioned the cease-fire. On this front Washington reaped the benefit of supporting the corrupt and undemocratic Yeltsin clique in the Kremlin. Over ninety percent of the Russian population wished to defend Serbia. Only an authoritarian regime, completely insensitive to democratic pressures from below, could have preserved such a stance. Thus a so-called triumph for 'democracy and human rights' was only made possible by a de facto dependence on a venal and dictatorial administration in Moscow. Here, too, the story is far from over. Virtually every political current in Russia was alienated from the West as a result of NATO's war. The first consequences of this will be seen in the next presidential elections but, on a more fundamental level, the NATO offensive was used by the powerful military-industrial complex in Moscow to push through research, development and production of a new range of intercontinental ballistic missiles.

What made this war surreal was the way in which it was fought exclusively from the skies. NATO dominated the air space over the Balkans, but on a strictly military level it achieved very little. For the first few weeks every NATO politician spoke in semi-religious tones of 'degrading' the Yugoslav Army. This was stated to be a major war aim. It was a dismal failure. Despite seventy-eight days of continuous bombardment and more than thirty-six thousand sorties, the Yugoslav armour emerged from Kosovo virtually unscathed. The morale of the Serbian soldiers leaving Kosovo after the cease-fire appeared to be high. A first balance sheet of the war indicates that it went wrong on every level. There was no military victory. The Albright-led war party in Washington, which had decided to wage NATO's first war against a sovereign state in breach of all international regulations, was convinced that it would be, at best, a three-day affair. A short, sharp shock that would bring Milošević to his knees. This did not happen.

Serious divisions existed at the highest military levels of NATO even on the question of what was being targeted. The Supreme Commander, Wesley Clark, was constantly at odds with his Air Force chief, General Michael Short. Clark wanted to hunt down Serbian army units in Kosovo. Short wanted an easier option: he was for destroying the infrastructure within Serbia, which clearly included the Chinese Embassy. When NATO planes bombed Belgrade the following conversation took place between Clark and Short:

> SHORT: This is the jewel in the crown.
> CLARK: To me, the jewel in the crown is when those B-52s rumble across Kosovo.
> SHORT: You and I have known for weeks that we have different jewellers.
> CLARK: My jeweller outranks yours.[4]

On the political level, all that NATO achieved had already been on offer from the Serb leadership well before the beginning of the war. The provocative clauses in the Rambouillet Treaty (an open violation of Serb sovereignty), inserted at the last minute to prevent a Serbian signature and thus enable NATO to show its muscle, were not included in the cease-fire treaty.

Many liberal pundits find it difficult to believe that the war in Kosovo was fought for any other but the most profound moral and humanitarian reasons. They believe this not because it is true, but because they want it to be true. Having watched real massacres in Rwanda and unpleasant ethnic bloodbaths in Bosnia, the liberal warmongers wanted retrospective action in Kosovo. The United States played on this liberal guilt as much as they could, but they knew very well why they were waging war. The goals of US policy after the collapse of the Soviet Union were spelt out straightforwardly in a forty-six page Pentagon document entitled *Defense Planning Guidance* (see also chapter 4 in this volume). Excerpts appeared in the *New York Times* on 8 March 1992 and the report was never denied by any government official. It was the clearest indication of how the US intended to maintain its hegemony in the New World Order. The Pentagon paper stated that:

> Our first objective is to prevent the re-emergence of a new rival . . . First, the US must show the leadership necessary to establish and protect a

> new order that holds the promise of convincing potential competitors that they need not aspire to a greater role or pursue a more aggressive posture to protect their legitimate interests.
>
> We must account sufficiently for the interests of the advanced industrial nations to discourage them from challenging our leadership . . . Finally, we must maintain the mechanism for deterring potential competitors from even aspiring to a larger regional or global role.
>
> It is of fundamental importance to preserve NATO as the primary instrument of Western defense and security as well as the channel for US influence and participation in European security affairs . . . *We must seek to prevent the emergence of European-only security arrangements which would undermine NATO . . .*[5]

After the dust had settled it emerged that NATO had been bitterly divided throughout the conflict. The Germans, Italians and the French were trying to achieve a negotiated settlement from a very early stage. The Greek government feared a national insurrection if ground troops were landed in Salonika, since ninety percent of Greeks were opposed to the war. In these circumstances, NATO propagandists were correct in pointing out that preserving the unity of the military alliance counted as one of the victories of the war. This was Solana's real achievement: not that he led a war for Kosovan liberation, but that he kept a divided alliance together.

And what of the Kosovans in whose name this war was fought? It was argued by some that even if the real motives for the war were great-power interests, this was irrelevant if the end result turned out to be positive. For some this meant the overthrow of Milošević. Downing Street certainly believed this was possible. General Wesley Clark recalls how Blair came into his office 'and told him that the future of every leader in Europe depended on the outcome. "Are you in this to win?" Blair asked him. Clark said he was.'[6] Milošević certainly did not fall: but what has the victory achieved for the Kosovans themselves?

The war encouraged the Serbian leaders to drive the Kosovans out of their homes. It accelerated the casualties. The NATO powers' declared aims had been exclusively humanitarian: they were bombing Serbia to prevent Serb militias from attacking the ethnic Albanians; yet the bombing had exactly the opposite effect. Once NATO had gone to war (though not before) there was a systematic Serb drive to clear big swathes of territory of Albanians (of a kind very similar to Western counter-insurgency tactics used in Malaya,

Algeria, Vietnam, etc.). Hundreds of thousands of Albanians were driven out of their homes . This was an outcome which Pentagon chiefs had foreseen as likely well before the war was launched. As the *Washington Post* reported: 'Privately even the staunchest advocates of air power amongst the four-star commanders doubted that air power alone could do much to budge Milošević in the near term. They noted the challenges of sending planes against widely dispersed ground forces that were carrying out door to door terror.'[7] The Defence Secretary, William Cohen, also advised before the war started that there would have to be a long bombing campaign. The *Washington Post* explained: 'Aides say Cohen never counted on the operation being over quickly.'[8]

The declared aims thus clashed with the entire conduct and operation of the war. In reality, NATO was prepared to trigger a humanitarian disaster in order to achieve humanitarian goals, i.e. a NATO occupation of Kosovo. This may explain the earlier statements emanating from NATO sources which suggested that Milošević wanted the bombing in order to convince Serbian public opinion that Kosovo had to be occupied by the UN. But this argument was dropped when NATO leaders realised that it contradicted the suggestion that the bombing was necessary to stop Milošević terrorising Kosovo.

Instead, NATO's war has led to the destruction of the infrastructure of the entire region and the Kosovars have ended up with a de facto NATO Protectorate. It could be argued that the original deal on the table at Rambouillet, which Madame Albright provoked the Serbs to reject, would have allowed the Kosovars more real autonomy and more real democracy than they enjoy today:

1. Rambouillet envisaged a three-year transition in Kosovo towards a referendum on independence. The peace terms envisaged no referendum and a continuation of Serbian sovereignty over Kosovo, including the return of Serbian state personnel.
2. Rambouillet recognised the KLA and its leadership as the political representatives of the Kosovar Albanian majority and as a provisional government of Kosovo. The peace terms did not recognise the KLA as a political authority. Tensions between the supporters of Ibrahim Rugova and the KLA continued to exist. When KLA leader Hashim Thaqi turned up at a football match in Priština's football stadium in September 1999 the crowd greeted him with continuous chants of 'Rugova, Rugova'.

3. Rambouillet did not recognise any role for the UN Security Council in the affairs of Kosovo. The peace terms placed Kosovo and the NATO occupation force under UN Security Council authority and indeed did not explicitly acknowledge NATO as having any overall authority within Kosovo.
4. Rambouillet did not recognise any independent role for Russian forces within Kosovo. The peace terms gave Russia the right to an independent presence of Russian forces within Kosovo.
5. Rambouillet gave NATO forces the right to operate throughout Serbia proper. This was the Albright clause which the Serbs rightly rejected. The peace terms denied NATO military forces any right to enter Serbia proper.

Judged objectively, the mass of ethnic Albanians in whose name this war was fought have, so far, not got a better deal as a result of it. Indeed, some of them have found the 'ethnically pure' Kosovo not to their taste and have fled to cosmopolitan Belgrade, where prices of apartments in the Albanian districts are at an all-time high.

NATO unity could only be preserved by mounting a mega-propaganda offensive which set out deliberately to conceal the truth from the citizens of Europe. The British, experienced hands in the art of deception, played a major role in orchestrating the news-management. Editors were cajoled, bribed and flattered into believing that they were part of this noble war effort.

One of the first to comment on this English ability to manipulate the news was a former German corporal who had fought in the First World War. In *Mein Kampf*, Hitler noted with admiration the consistently effective British war propaganda during the First World War. He admired its 'psychologically correct' form:

> By displaying the German to their own people as a barbarian and a Hun, they were preparing the individual soldier for the horrors of war . . . In England there were no half-statements which might give rise to doubts . . . Enemy propaganda confined itself to a few points of view, was addressed solely to the masses and was pursued with untiring perseverance. Throughout the whole war use was made of basic ideas and forms of expression found to be right at the beginning and even the slightest alteration was never considered.

It was this tradition that Hitler's colleague Goebbels further developed and applied with single-minded ruthlessness during the Third Reich.

NATO's propaganda war was only made possible with the easy collaboration of the television networks and liberal newspapers. They consistently promoted the idea that Milošević was Hitler, that the Kosovan Albanians were the equivalent of wartime Jews and that the Serbian irregulars were engaged in genocide. Hence, war was necessary to defeat the beast and stop the genocide.

This was a barefaced lie but, paraphrasing the old German master of propaganda, the bigger the lie the better it works. Very few Western journalists stood up against the juggernaut. Those who did were denounced as traitors, appeasers and worse. In the realm of information, NATOland during the war reminded one of a one-party state. Dissident voices were occasionally permitted, but only as a token reminder that we live in a democracy. The only television networks that showed both Western and Serb footage and encouraged an independent view were those of Russia, China and India.

The big victory of the war has been the ethnic cleansing of Serbs, Romanies and Jews from the Kosovan protectorate. This was not NATO's desire, but rather the inevitable outcome of its adventurism. Yet another 'pure' state has been created in a part of Europe once known for multinational character. The liberal warmongers who once spoke of defending 'multiculturalism' have fallen silent. The Serbs (and it is worth remembering that they, too, had lived in Kosovo for centuries) were demonised so severely that their fate left liberal opinion in the West virtually unmoved. A British Cabinet Minister, Clare Short, referred to Serbs as 'scum'.

Much of the information now beginning to seep out of Kosovo – now that the international media has moved on elsewhere – indicates that the number of Kosovans killed by the Serbs is far removed from the grotesque holocaust analogies employed by war propagandists in the media all over Western Europe – analogies that were denounced by Claude Lanzmann, the director of *Shoah*, in the strongest terms:

> Intellectuals didn't use this reference to the Holocaust even in the worst periods of the Algerian war, when FLN combatants were being murdered in large numbers and tortured, and huge areas of the country were entirely emptied of their inhabitants. Same thing with the Vietnam war when hundreds of villages were being flattened by napalm along

> with forests, rice paddies and so on. Even during the Biafra war, which saw the birth of humanitarian ideology and practice, people did without the comparison with Nazism . . .
>
> With the failure of what they call the 'half-war', intrepid armchair warriors of both sexes are now demanding total war, a ground invasion with all its predictable and unpredictable (but surely frightful) consequences. I am revolted by this total lack of respect for the gravity of history . . . These perpetual references to the Holocaust are a way of muzzling all discussion. Talking forbidden! Argument over![9]

Thus the week before the war ended, a junior British Foreign Office minister, Geoff Hoon, stated that: 'According to reports we have gathered, mostly from the refugees, it appears that around 10,000 people have been killed.' Bernard Kouchner, the UN proconsul in Kosovo, claimed that 11,000 bodies had already been found in mass graves.

In fact, at the time of writing, the figures being released by war crimes investigators are in the hundreds rather than thousands. The Kosovan media had reported that 700 ethnic Albanians had been massacred and dumped in a mass grave in a mine shaft in the Trepča lead and zinc mine near Mitrovica. War crimes investigators, acting on behalf of the International Criminal Tribunal for the Former Yugoslavia (ICTY), eager to discover evidence that could indict Milošević, found nothing, despite special excavation equipment and forensic experts.[10] If this pattern continues as other 'mass graves' are investigated the consequences for NATO countries could be serious.

While there is no doubt that *after* NATO's bombing campaign began the violence against ethnic Albanians multiplied, there is still no evidence available to justify claims of genocide or even killings on the Bosnian scale. The FBI, for instance, conducted two investigations in June and August, 1999. In a total of thirty sites they discovered 200 bodies. A team of Spanish investigators were told that they were going into the real killing fields and should be prepared for the worst. They were warned they might have to prepare 2000 autopsies. They found no mass graves and only 187 bodies, all buried in individual graves. The Spanish team's chief inspector, Juan Lopez Palafox, was reported in *El Pais* as saying: 'In the former Yugoslavia crimes were committed, but they derived from the war. In Rwanda we saw 450 corpses (at one site) of women and children, on top of another, all with their heads broken open.'

During the war NATO released satellite images of what purported to be mass graves in Pusto Selo where the Serbs allegedly killed 106 men. No bodies were found at the site. In Izbica, refugees claimed 150 ethnic Albanians were killed in March 1999. No bodies, or traces of bodies being removed, were discovered at the site. Of course, it is possible that the investigators might yet discover a site where a large massacre took place, but the evidence so far is decidedly shaky.

Those who sought to justify the war as a moral crusade will have to explain how and why they manufactured the evidence needed to justify offensive action by NATO.

The war against Serbia was the first to be waged by NATO. It may well be the last for it is unlikely that the Germans, French, Italians and Greeks will be as easily dragged into another adventure. The future pattern might well be direct US action, aided by Britain, of the sort that is being carried out against Iraq.

One of the side-effects of NATO unilateralism has been to give the green light to other powers to behave in exactly the same fashion. The Russian assault on Chechnya is an appalling act on the part of an embattled government in Moscow; the coverage on the TV networks and in the Western press has been extremely restricted. Could it be that this is Moscow's reward for helping to end the war in Kosovo? Or is it the case that the Russian leadership feels that it can operate just like NATO in its own backyard? In the South Asian subcontinent, the clashes in Kashmir between India and Pakistan were ended only when the Indians began, in the words of Indian newspapers, a 'NATO-style bombardment' of Pakistani troop emplacements. Certainly the Chinese government now feels no constraint in dealing with its own internal or external problems (Tibet/Taiwan). Ironically, a war designed to assert US hegemony and NATO superiority, and to prevent other regional powers from exercising real independence on a military level, has had precisely the opposite effect; we have yet to see all the repercussions.

The essays collected in this volume share one common approach to the region: all regard the break-up of Yugoslavia as a major European disaster. It was not inevitable and could have been avoided if the major states of the European Union had not engaged in a gadarene rush to seek cheap advantages in the region. An EU reconstruction plan could have preserved Yugoslavia as a loose confederation, and the amount of money needed would have been a fraction of that spent on the war. The Serb, Slovene and Croatian elites would have found it difficult to resist an attractive package.

The volume consists of four different sections. In Part One, Peter Gowan, Giovanni Arrighi and Gilbert Achcar analyse the tensions between Europe and America and the latter's continuing struggle for mastery on a global scale after the end of the Cold War. In Part Two, Diana Johnstone, Robert Redeker, Alex Callinicos and Ellen Meiksins Wood unmask the traditional power politics of the United States at work behind the bluff of 'humanitarian warfare'. In Part Three, Susan L. Woodward, David Chandler and Michel Chossudovsky examine the tragedy of recent Balkan history in closer detail.

Part Four consists of various texts produced during the war itself by Régis Debray, Harold Pinter, Yevgeny Yevtushenko, Edward Said, Robin Blackburn, Oskar Lafontaine, Noam Chomsky, John Gittings and Dieter Lutz. They have stood the test of time somewhat better than the journalism of 'Third Way' warmongers. And, in conclusion, we have the moving voice of the exiled Albanian poet Gazi Kaplan who, like the demonstrators in Seattle, makes an unfashionable plea for a new internationalism.

December 1999

Notes

1. 'Global Order: a Roundtable', *Prospect*, August/September 1999.
2. Michael Ignatieff, 'The Virtual Commander: How NATO invented a new kind of war', *New Yorker*, 2 August 1999. The interview contains much that is of interest, but it is also a true masterpiece in the art of sycophancy. Ignatieff, on this front, can outshine most competitors.
3. Ibid.
4. Dana Priest, 'Strikes Divided Nato Chiefs', *International Herald Tribune*, 22 September 1999.
5. Quoted in *NATO in the Balkans: Voices of Opposition*, New York 1998.
6. Michael Ignatieff, op. cit.
7. Bradley Graham, 'Joint Chiefs Doubted Air Strategy', *Washington Post*, 5 April 1999, p. A1.
8. Bradley Graham, 'Cohen Wrestles with Mission Risks', *Washington Post*, 11 April 1999, p. A24.
9. Interview with Claude Lanzmann, *Marianne* no. 110, 31 May 1999.
10. *New York Times*, 13 October 1999.

PART I

How to Rule the World: Geopolitics after the Cold War

1

THE EURO-ATLANTIC ORIGINS OF NATO'S ATTACK ON YUGOSLAVIA

Peter Gowan

It is largely taken for granted inside the main NATO states that the Clinton administration was driven to launch the NATO air war against Yugoslavia on 24 March 1999 mainly as a result of its perceptions of developments within the Western Balkans. Yet there has been one dissenting voice on the Clinton administration's main motive for war. It is President Clinton's. Some may regard him as an unreliable witness. But this article will argue in support of Bill Clinton's public view as to what he was up to when launching the war.

Clinton explained his motive quite bluntly in his speech of 23 March, the day before he unleashed the US Air Force. He explained that the attack was needed mainly because of its wide Euro-Atlantic political effects. As the *Washington Post* reported, Clinton explained 'that a strong U.S.-European partnership "is what this Kosovo thing is all about".'[1] So he didn't just say that the war was *mainly about* the political relationship between Europe and the US rather than Kosovo's Albanians or Yugoslavia's government. He said it was *all about* the US relationship with Western Europe.

Clinton made a second important point about Washington's motives for the war. He explained in the same speech why a 'strong partnership' between the US and Europe was vital for the US: 'If we're going to have a strong economic relationship [with the world, PG] that includes our ability to sell around the world, Europe has got to be a key.'[2]

The Decision for War

Understanding a state leadership's motives for launching a war is a guide to its war aims and thus to understanding and judging the whole operation. But the leadership's public words are not always a good guide to its real intentions. And secondly, state leaderships are not unitary. In the US there is a whole array of actors with different concerns, often concerns in tension or conflict with each other. We must therefore probe, as far as we can, into that federal policy-making system to see who was for what and why.

A first guide is the Clinton speech. What, one wonders, could Clinton's words mean? The *Sunday Times* correspondent reporting the speech simply could not understand it. Noting that the speech did not seem to have been scripted by Clinton's media advisers, the correspondent considered that the President was off-message. This is, at first sight, a contradiction in terms: how can the President of the United States, the creator of the message, be off-message? But this contradiction remains intriguing. Could it be that the President was simply transmitting the message from the wrong set of advisers: he was telling us what the executive bureaucracy was telling him instead of what the media-management professionals would have told him to say?

This possibility is reinforced by another curious, even unique feature of the Washington war decision. Neither US public opinion nor its Congressional representatives in either House were pressing for war. There was no significant push from that direction on Clinton. Not only was US public opinion not prepared politically for the war: the leaders of US public opinion had not been politically prepared either. In that 23 March speech President Clinton felt bound to ask the American people to get out their family atlases and look up Kosovo since, as he said, large numbers of them would never have heard of it. The whole thing was new to them. And as the BBC's Alistair Cooke explained in his 'Letter from America' programme on Sunday18 April 1999, this war was unique in US history at least since Roosevelt's time in one central respect: in neither house of Congress was there any pro-war political leadership when the war was launched. Public opinion in the USA was, in other words, out of it at the start.

The drive for war came from within the federal executive. The Pentagon is a very important and powerful player in that bureaucracy, the guardian of US geostrategic interests. So if the Pentagon had been the lead force for war we could conclude that US strategic interests in the Western Balkans, South East Europe more generally or, perhaps, in relation to Russia, were engaged: Kosovo was important for US national strategy in the east.

Yet according to the *Washington Post*, the Pentagon had been against the war. The *Post* has reported:

> In the weeks before NATO launched its air campaign against Yugoslavia, U.S. military chiefs expressed deep reservations about the Clinton administration's approach to Kosovo and warned that bombing alone likely would not achieve its political aims, according to sources familiar with their thinking. The Pentagon's senior four-star officers, meeting in closed-door sessions in the Pentagon's secure 'tank' room, argued that the administration should use more economic sanctions and other non-military levers to compel Belgrade to make peace in the rebellious Serbian province before resorting to air strikes. They also complained about what they saw as the lack of a long-term vision for the Balkans and questioned whether U.S. national interests there were strong enough to merit a military confrontation. 'I don't think anybody felt like there had been a compelling argument made that all of this was in our national interest,' said one senior officer knowledgeable about the deliberations.[3]

The Pentagon thus feared US interests in the Balkan theatre could actually be damaged by the war. But they also warned Clinton that his war plan would not work militarily: 'Privately, even the staunchest advocates of air power among the four-star commanders doubted that air strikes alone could do much to budge Milošević in the near term. They noted the challenges of sending planes against widely dispersed ground forces that were carrying out door-to-door terror. They spoke about the difficulty of hitting Yugoslav troops and equipment without striking Albanian refugees mixed among them.' They knew it would be a long air war and 'They fret that the American public was not adequately prepared to accept a prolonged air operation.' But finally, the *Post* reports, the Joint Chiefs went along with the campaign because of one key argument: 'embracing the administration's view that U.S. leadership in NATO had to be preserved.'

This view from the military brass was evidently shared by Secretary of Defence Cohen and the civilian side of the Pentagon. 'Aides say Cohen never counted on the operation being over quickly. They say he did not subscribe to what one defence official called the "Milošević-is-just-a-bully theory" that was prevalent among some in the administration and that held the Yugoslav leader would retreat promptly once subjected to NATO air strikes.' The *Post* reported Cohen as warning: 'I would plan for the worst with Milošević, like with Saddam Hussein,' the Iraqi president.[4]

The CIA also warned beforehand that Milošević would very likely expel thousands of Kosovans when the war started. For military reasons, the Serbian army would flood into Kosovo and seek to clear out the KLA and villages near the border to secure their defences. The *Post* reported that CIA officials had been running over the scenarios as war started for no less than 14 months, looking at all the possible chain reactions to the bombing and considering each one.

All these major objections in terms of the likely negative military and political consequences for Kosovo, the Balkans and Eastern Europe of launching the attack were overridden by the one group within the federal bureaucracy that had been dead set on war for a full year: the *political* strategists in the State Department. These people are very bright conceptual thinkers. They plan meticulously for all the angles. They know the ABC of what happens when a superpower launches a local war anywhere: it sets off streams of chain reactions across the entire globe. They plan in detail for all the possible chain reactions in the main fields affected: the local war zone itself, in this case the Western Balkans; the chains of shock waves that would run through Eastern Europe, especially Russia and Ukraine; and the chain reactions, cleavages, swings in the elites and masses in the NATO zone itself. Their task is to seek to articulate the planning of these shock waves in such a way as to maximise the gains of objectives in each theatre of chain reactions. Any war is bound to produce some negative consequences for the superpower in at least one theatre. The trick is to try to contain or absorb these while maximising success in the strategically key sector for the superpower.

We can see from the comments of Cohen and others that what they called 'NATO credibility' was a key issue for them. Before the war was launched, on 23 March 1999, the *Washington Post* reported that it was 'the humiliation of NATO and of the United States, NATO's creator and main component' that was the key factor leading to war. But credibility with whom? The *Post* went on: 'Inaction "could involve a major cost in credibility, particularly at this time as we approach the NATO summit in celebration of its fiftieth anniversary," said a European diplomat. National security adviser Samuel R. "Sandy" Berger, speaking Sunday, listed among the principal purposes of bombing "to demonstrate that NATO is serious".'[5]

The suggestion from all this is pretty clear. NATO's credibility was at risk *with NATO members in Western Europe.* This might suggest that NATO's European partners had been pushing for war and the US had been resisting, and that the Partnership might break down because the Europeans would say, 'If you don't bomb them, we will and NATO will be dead.' But the reverse was the case. The European partners had been resisting the US's aggressive diplomacy for war. They would have been relieved if the US had backed off. So what was at risk was simply the US campaign to bounce its NATO partners into war.

As the *Post* again explained, Washington had been preparing diplomatically for this attack on Yugoslavia since February 1998: 'Some critics have seen a lack of resolve in the successive warnings Washington has issued since [February 1998]. But what critics see as vacillation is described by policymakers in Washington as orchestration of international backing for military force, much as they said they accomplished in Iraq.'[6] This is a very important statement. The drive for the Yugoslav war was being led by the State Department strategists. It was a drive to bring the West Europeans into line for war, lasting for over a year. 'The diplomacy that led up to yesterday's final warning was designed and built in Washington.'[7] The key final steps were: first, to get the West Europeans to agree that if there was no deal struck between the two sides at the Rambouillet conference, there would be war, whatever the Russians and UN said. Secondly, to insert into the draft agreement (written by Hill from the State Department) a clause for a NATO-led force creating effectively a NATO Protectorate in Kosovo, a demand the US government knew Milošević could not accept. Then at Rambouillet, just to be sure, the US insisted that these NATO forces would have the right to roam anywhere in Yugoslavia. And at the same time, the US would not allow negotiations between the Serbian government (which wanted them) and the Kosovar Albanians to take place, presumably for fear of some other kind of agreement emerging between the two sides. As the *Post* explained, the US government 'wrote up a model agreement between them and demanded that both sides sign before they had ever even laid eyes on one another'.[8]

So the US drove, over 14 months, for a war that it knew was in tension with US interests in the Balkans but was needed for the credibility of the US in being able to swing its NATO allies into war.

A naive, media-led version of liberal-democratic ideology leads many to imagine that war policy planning comes full-blown from the heads of elected leaders. In reality it comes 95 per cent from the policy professionals whose work is structured by their government agencies and inter-agency coordinators. The task of the strategy professionals is to tell the President 'the facts' of what the situation is, what his options are, what the consequences of each option are likely to be in all relevant theatres. These are absolutely central roles in the making of policy.

Those who consider that human rights concerns or even a strong human rights constraint played a part in the planning of this war may, of course, be right. The evidence shows that the President knew from the CIA that there would be a refugee exodus. He knew, also from the military, that the bombing campaign would not stop a huge Serb army operation in Kosovo: it would provoke one. He knew, also from the military, that it would be a long bombing campaign – the talk of Milošević caving in swiftly was spin. Another, more feeble bit of spin is the claim that Clinton launched the bombing on Wednesday, 24 March, after the Serbian army had flooded into Kosovo. The suggestion is that Clinton was *responding* to Milošević. But this is a false picture. Clinton announced that the bombing would start on Friday, 19 March, in unambiguous terms, telling the Serbian authorities that they had better get moving to shore up their positions. As the *Post* reported: 'Clinton declared Friday that "the threshold has been crossed" for bombing, a comment described by one U.S. official as "enormously significant." But by one accounting, Milošević crossed the threshold more than a year ago.'[9]

Let us then recapitulate on the war decision:

1. The political/diplomatic side of the Clinton administration, with Clinton's support, had been preparing a careful build up for a war against Yugoslavia for a full year. They wanted the war so that the US could pull its NATO allies under US leadership. They wanted to do it before the NATO summit in Washington scheduled for late April 1999. They prepared the build-up diplomacy very carefully through ensuring a Serbian rejection of Rambouillet which in turn would bounce the German, Italian and Greek governments into war, without UN sanction and against Russian hostility. In other words the Yugoslav war theatre was a lever for achieving political goals mainly within NATOland. Clinton even said the war was *all about that*.
2. The big gain was to be a 'strong partnership' between Europe and the US. In US official parlance, the phrase 'strong partnership' is code. In diplomatic language, it means strong US leadership over Euroland. More bluntly, it means US hegemonic leadership of Western Europe, the kind of 'strong partnership' that used to exist during the Cold War (and in the Gulf War).

3. This war as a step towards the return of US hegemonic leadership over Western Europe is vital because it is a key to a strong US economic relationship to the world economy, one that enabled the US to 'sell' all over the world. This is another way of saying that the basic rationale for this war had to do with assuring the international dominance of US capitalism, through bending Western Europe to accept US goals for the continuing reorganisation and management of the world economy.

The *Sunday Times* correspondent reporting Clinton's 23 March speech thought that Clinton's reference to economics was bizarre. He said that Clinton's mind was wandering back to his old campaign slogan – 'It's the economy, stupid.' But this is a misunderstanding of two things: Clinton's supposed economic obsession; and the uses of military power for political brigading.

Clinton has, throughout his presidency, been obsessed with rebuilding the global dominance of US capitalism. He has approached this as his central goal, indicating that it is the central *security* objective of the United States, focusing his intelligence agencies, the State Department, the NSC and other agencies on this goal. He has set up a National Economic Council alongside the NSC to coordinate the efforts of all US agencies dealing with external economic relations. But he has never seen this effort as a task that separates politics and economics. The strengthening of US capitalism relative to other capitalisms is, for the Clinton administration, as much about politics as economics.

Secondly, the *Sunday Times* correspondent seems to be ignorant of the various political feedback roles of the military statecraft of great powers. By waging a local war against a 'rogue' state a superpower can gain valuable political feedback on its relationship with allied powers. Or again, by identifying a potential challenge to state A from actor B and by applying its military power effectively against actor B, the superpower can change its relationship with state A in desirable directions. The end political result of the military operation might be to enable the superpower to brigade state A more firmly under the superpower's leadership. A classic example of this type of political-brigading effect on a grand scale can be seen in the construction of NATO in the early 1950s. Electorates in Western Europe came to perceive the existence of a Soviet military threat to their lands. The US then supplied military services to Western Europe to tackle this threat. As a result, Western Europe fell in behind US political leadership in world politics.

And with that leadership in place, the US could exert great influence over the internal political and economic arrangements within the region.

We will not examine here the global political-economy strategy of the Clinton administration.[10] We will concentrate our analysis on the meaning of Clinton's phrase about building US hegemonic leadership in Western Europe. Washington's campaign to achieve this during the 1990s has been focused upon one central task: transforming NATO, transforming its role in European affairs, and blocking West European attempts to build political forms which would deny the US hegemonic leadership. This exploration will take us into a rather shrouded and complex zone: the internal politics of the Western alliance.

PART 1. EXPLAINING INTRA-NATO POLITICS

Some matters are too difficult and sensitive to be discussed frankly in front of the children. One such, in the West, is open and frank discussion and theorising about how the NATO powers engage in *political conflict and compromise amongst themselves, and what the substance of these conflicts and deals is all about.*

During the Cold War it was considered very bad form for NATO governments to air and explain their differences openly and frankly in public; political conflicts within the Atlantic alliance were generally conducted behind the backs of electorates and, so to speak, behind closed doors. Outside of governments, only attentive communities of policy experts with the time and resources for meticulous detective work could follow the ebb and flow of political conflict and compromise between the Western powers. They would do so through careful analysis of the codes used in communiqués and in the public speeches of leaders. This was the science of what might be described as Atlanticology, a type of research akin to its eastern equivalent – Kremlinology. And those seeking a really successful career in this field would often find themselves having to relinquish their independence of analysis in order to acquire the inside information they craved.

Even worse form would have been to disclose the bottom-line concerns of the NATO states in their intra-NATO political processes. These concerns were as much about the various states' national capitalist strategies – strategies for assuring the political conditions for dynamic capital accumulation not only within Europe but more widely. For all these states, the military, political and economic dimensions of their national strategies were seamless webs, or ought to be. But for public consumption, the substance of intra-NATO politics was supposed to be about one thing only: how to cope with the Soviet threat to protect the shared values of the Western liberal democracies.

As for attempts to theorise the forms, dynamics and sources of such intra-NATO political conflict, there was very little in the mainstream literature. The dominant schools of thought in academic International Relations in the West, Cold War realism and Cold War liberalism, offered no adequate framework for explaining such conflict. Instead, they tended, in different ways, to explain it away.

Realism and liberalism explained intra-NATO politics overwhelmingly in terms of responses to a Soviet threat which would tend to suppress political differences between the NATO powers, reducing them largely to technical-managerial issues. For realists, the Western states were unified by the strategic power balance: Western Europe and the US unified in an alliance for power political reasons to counter-balance the power of the Soviet Union. Disagreements within NATO would be accommodated and suppressed because of collective power interests. In liberal International Relations, the unity derived more from the internal political characteristics of (most of) the NATO states: their liberal democratic orders and values (and, for some, their open, market economies and liberal international economic frameworks). Because of these characteristics, the NATO states united against the Communist totalitarian threat to their values. If the USSR had been a liberal democracy, there would or need have been no NATO and no Cold War.

One might have thought that with the collapse of the Soviet bloc, there would have been the swift development of new theorisations of West–West relations. After all, both realism and liberalism in their Cold War forms would have predicted the collapse of the Western Alliance after 1991: realism, because the collapse of the Soviet superpower would lead to a rebalancing against the United States; liberalism, because without a threat from any totalitarian/dictatorial enemy to the states with liberal values, there would be no need for any such military-political alliance: peace, liberal democracy and harmony would reign supreme. Thus, at the very least one would have thought there would be a puzzle for those working in these frameworks as to what on earth was going on as NATO showed no sign of disappearing.

Some NATO leaders have, of course, tried to claim that NATO has turned from being a military-political defender of states with liberal values into a liberal, norm-based, collective security regime itself. Yet in the run-up to all three of Europe's wars in the 1990s – the Croatian war, the Bosnian war and the current war against Yugoslavia – the NATO powers have flagrantly violated basic international norms: in the Croatian case by recognising Croatia in the face of its government's refusal to grant CSCE rights to its Serbian minority; in the Bosnian case by proclaiming that there was a Bosnian nation when there was not: there were four main self-identifying nations in Bosnia: the largest minority was the Bosnian Muslims, with the Serbs close behind numerically, followed by the Croatians and, lastly, the Yugoslavs. Both Yugoslav constitutional principle and the EC's International Commission of Jurists agreed that in such a republic all the constituent nations must in their majority each approve a secession from Yugoslavia. But the US proclaimed a 'Bosnian nation's' right to self-determination and to a unitary state, producing a civil war. And now NATO flouts a cornerstone of the UN Charter and the international legal order – one state does not launch aggression against another sovereign state – and kicks aside the international constitutional role of the Security Council. Whatever else NATO is, the claim that it is a norm-based collective security organisation will not do.

Yet, on the whole both realism and liberalism have managed to evade such issues, while much of the new theories in academic International Relations have taken our eyes off this ball altogether by suggesting that the discipline should spend less time focusing on the drives of powerful states and should devote its attention to other matters. One great interest in this context is 'non-state actors' such as multinational companies and NGOs; another is international or global institutions, with the supposed emergence of a global post-state system embracing both new institutions and even a new international 'civil society'. States, on this reading, are increasingly passé. Yet search though we may for such new trends, they do not seem to help us with explaining the intra-NATO background to this war. The war has generated great concatenations of chain reactions, both in the Western Balkans, across Eastern Europe and also across the NATO world. The political life of hundreds of millions of people is being thrown into a turmoil of new potential patterns and cleavages. And this is being done through the decisions of the NATO states. While non-state actors, such as mass political parties or anti-colonial movements, were certainly important in the Cold War, and while one is involved in the current conflict – the KLA – they do not seem to be driving the politics of NATO in taking their war decisions.[11] We must therefore search for some other framework for explaining the politics of NATO or , in other words, what President Clinton calls the US–European 'partnership'.

The continued existence of the NATO alliance throughout the 1990s, after the end of the Soviet Union, suggests that it has all along been held together by something other than an enemy threat to security, or values, or power-balancing. In other words, NATO has not been what either the realists or liberals have claimed. When we find out what the alliance *may actually have been about* we may gain an answer to the mystery of the real Western background to the NATO military campaign in the Western Balkans.

We can posit four constitutive elements in the Western Alliance missed by both realism and liberalism in much of the Western variants of these literatures:

1. Shared (capitalist) interests.
2. Tensions within from conflicting capitalist interests.
3. US hegemonic dominance and the use of military power for political feedback leading to economic pay-offs.
4. The cardinal political management principle: 'Not in front of the children': closed politics – plus the US's hegemonic privilege of leading by fait accompli when necessary.

All four of these elements were at the centre of the Atlantic Alliance from the start, but they were easy to miss during the Cold War itself because both realism and liberalism seemed to provide adequate cognitive frameworks for understanding what NATO was about.

1. Shared (capitalist) interests

A close look at NATO's formation would demonstrate that the domestic fear of Communism in Western Europe amongst capitalist classes seriously weakened by collaboration during the war was the biggest demand-pull on the continent, first for British, then for US, help, through the formation of an alliance (first the British-led Western Union, then US-led NATO). NATO then provided a framework for the revival and re-integration of German capitalism, and the strongly American-inspired formation of, first, the European Coal and Steel Community, and then the European Economic Community, built a new anchor for German revival within a West European and Atlantic economic division of labour. All these arrangements drew the West European and American capitalist classes together in both a common project of domestic management of social and political conflict and in shared arrangements for securing common international interests – in tackling a whole range of opponents, especially non-state actors in the disintegrating European empires; in common capitalist expansion; and, of course, in exerting pressure on the Soviet bloc while maintaining basic European stability.

2. Tensions within from conflicting capitalist interests

There were, nevertheless, always tensions and conflicts within the alliance right from the start of NATO and the West European integration process, and some of these would become very intense. In the early years these were often connected to battles in the imperial field between West European powers and the US: Suez was a prime example, as was Algeria for the French as well as a whole range of other such issues. There were also tensions on the German question, and intense tensions at times over US dollar policy, oil price manoeuvres, etc. And perhaps the most sensitive issue in the late 1970s, an issue that would appear again at the end of the 1980s, was the issue of Germany's – and more generally Western Europe's – relations with Eastern Europe. The United States, Britain and France worried that German capitalism might, in the context of the economic turbulence that began in the early 1970s, re-orient its accumulation strategy eastwards, using European detente for that purpose. This period also witnessed what was known as conflicts over industrial policy or conflicts of 'interdependence', conflicts which eased only through the European turn towards neo-liberalism in the early 1980s.

Such tensions over capital accumulation strategies were also combined with battles over political and military issues. De Gaulle's attempts to build a West European bloc under French leadership as a way of constructing what he might have called, à la Clinton, a 'strong Franco-German partnership' was one such political power battle. The long political struggle between Britain and the Franco-German axis in Western Europe was another. And of course there was a third political cleavage which became prominent on occasions: that between 'Europe' and the USA.

In all these conflicts within the NATO Alliance, all sides commonly used, for public consumption, the Soviet card. But this Soviet card was above all an ace in the hand of the United States. The US could shift the whole European agenda back and forth by altering the state of relations with the USSR. And one of the main ways in which it could engage in this political game derived from its overwhelming military capacity and military leadership of the alliance. To take one example: by deploying Pershing missiles in Germany, the US was able to break the Soviet-German détente and pull Germany firmly back under its political leadership in the early 1980s. But it also had other cards to assure its hegemony in Western Europe: its dollar dominance in the world economy, its effective control over world energy supplies, its capacity to play off its allies against each other – these were the main cards in a very strong hand.

3. A political system which, at its height, gave the US hegemonic sovereignty

At the same time, NATO was from the start the institutionalisation of US political dominance over the West European states. Much discussion of this US hegemony misses the specific *political form* that this dominance took and imagines that US dominance was anchored only in its preponderance of quantitative power resources – economic and military above all. Yet the hegemony acquired a political form which we could even describe as quasi-political sovereignty, when US dominance was at its zenith.

In liberal thought, sovereignty is usually defined in legal terms and it involves the notion of a highest legal authority to act, untrammelled by any other legal authority. But the German theorist Carl Schmitt furnished a non-liberal (indeed, an anti-liberal) concept of politics which provided a political concept of sovereignty. And Schmitt's thought was a powerful influence of some of the main intellectual organisers of American post-war foreign policy thinking, such as Hans Morgenthau and Henry Kissinger. When we deploy his concepts of politics and political sovereignty we can gain insight into the form of political power exercised by the US over the territory of the NATO alliance.[12] His concept of politics was that of friend-enemy relations. Political action thus consists of developing the capacity to decide, for a given community, who their friends are (and thus who they are) and who their enemies are (and thus, also, who they are). Using this concept of politics, we could say that the politics of NATOland in the Cold War were of a liberal-capitalist, anti-Communist political community, shaped by and under US leadership. Armed with this concrete friend-enemy politics, successive US administrations could maintain their political leadership over Western Europe.

But Schmitt also, from this definition of politics, offered a political definition of sovereignty, explaining that sovereign is he who can decide the state of emergency. Thus, for the US to have sovereign hegemony over Western

Europe, it would have to be able to impose a state of emergency upon the region if it wished: it would have, in other words, to be able to call the political community to order and to discipline it under its undivided leadership, untrammelled by restriction.

Time and time again, in the Cold War, the US demonstrated this ability to declare a state of emergency in Europe. It did so over the Berlin Blockade; it chose not to do so over the invasion of Czechoslovakia. It chose to do so over the Soviet deployment of SS20s, using the Soviet intervention in Afghanistan and the declaration of Marshal Law in Poland. It imposed a spectacular state of emergency over the Iraqi invasion of Kuwait in 1990–91. Herein lies one of the secrets of US hegemonic leadership: none of these interventions required the US to alter the juridical sovereignties of the states under its political command. Indeed, maintaining such juridical sovereignties strengthened US command capacities. The 'juridical empire' approach of the West European powers in the nineteenth and first half of the twentieth centuries was replaced by a radically new concept of imperial hegemony.

Through this political form, buttressed by the Soviet threat and the huge power resources of the USA, Washington effectively controlled the basic foreign policy orientations of the West European states and was able to secure the interests of US capitalism within Western Europe. In these ways, the US could negatively control the international orientations of West European capitalisms, ensuring that their international strategies for capital accumulation did not impinge upon the central US goals in this field. And it could ensure that US capital had favourable opportunities for growth in Western Europe. There were often occasions when one or more of the West European states felt threatened or seriously disadvantaged by US decisions and policies. But they would tend *not* to respond by breaking with NATO and entering into a confrontation with the USA – which could be very dangerous; instead, they coped with US threats mainly by bandwaggoning – rolling with the punches, adapting to whatever new drive came from Washington and attempting to find opportunities for themselves within the new direction of US policy.[13]

4. 'Not in front of the children': the bifurcated 'citizens' and institutions of the NATO political system

One of the most important constitutive elements in the whole NATO–EC ensemble was the establishment of a closed, state-elite, collective political system for resolving intra-capitalist conflicts behind the backs of electorates. Within NATO, this consisted of the structure of committees centred on the North Atlantic Council (NAC) and the core executives of member states. The personnel of these bodies, along with a periphery of networks of policy intellectuals, 'sound' journalists and business-linked think tanks, constituted the 'active citizens' of the NATO polity. We should also include the central institutions and central personnel within the EC: first the Council of Ministers (i.e. the same core executives of states) and, from the early 1970s, the European Council, as well as the political sides of the Council Secretariat and key personnel from the most important directorates of the Commission. All states entered into a basic understanding that they would restrict their political battles to within the walls of these institutional structures wherever possible, maintaining the secrecy of the deliberations of these committees and not trying to rouse electorates across the Alliance for their point of view against those of other states. The only state to which this did not necessarily apply was the United States. As the hegemonic leader, it was entitled to launch public campaigns for its policy objectives within the electorates of the Alliance.

By thus placing a diaphragm between the Alliance and EC elite political systems and the domestic, democratic systems, a number of very important gains could be made: the leaders of states defeated in the political process would not be humiliated publicly and could therefore accept defeat more easily; realpolitik and power-political goals and tactics could remain out of public view and thus electorates could imagine that harmony within the Alliance was the rule and that the Alliance was united solidly by 'shared values'. And finally, the real, overwhelming dominance of the US over its European allies could be concealed behind a façade of democratic consensus among equals, and even of what looked like West European collective political autonomy, in the EC.

To understand the intra-NATO politics of the West we must always bear in mind this bifiguration of institutions and personnel. When any one actor in intra-NATO politics acts politically, that actor is always addressing two audiences in two utterly different arenas: one is the elite audience in the closed elite arena; the other, the mass audience in the mass, open political arena. Handling this bifurcation discursively requires the use of linguistic codes. As any member of the elites of East Central Europe will explain, one of their urgent tasks after the collapse of the Soviet bloc was to learn Western languages: not so much English or German as the secret language of NATOland elite communication. To take a simple example, what does the word 'partner' mean for the elite citizens of NATOland?

But just as it is a mistake to fail to notice the centrality of the elite citizenship in the politics of NATOland – they are the political subjects in the system – it is equally a mistake to fail to recognise the importance of the second-class, mass citizenship: the electoral, public-opinion base. These masses could be a powerful tool or lever to be used by groups of elite citizens against each other. This lever could, for example, be exercised through instilling certain political values within the mass, which could serve long-term national strategy. Then, through linking together an elite objective with the mass values, powerful political leverage could be generated against other elite groups' positions on that objective. To take a simple example, the Reaganite turn in the second Cold War was extremely effective in redisciplining West European elites. But it was largely ineffective at the mass level in Western Europe, generating war fears and peace movements. With the arrival of Gorbachev to Soviet leadership, certain elite groups in Western Europe in the late 1980s were able to link their distinctive political objectives vis-à-vis West European–USSR relations with this mass peace and anti-Reagan sentiment in Western Europe. Bereft of the mass politics lever for operations in Western Europe, the Bush administration found itself constrained in the tactics it could employ in Europe in 1989. Gorbachev's peace offensive was combining with moves by West European elites and mass peace sentiment to beach the US.

There remains, of course, the issue of where the Soviet bloc threat fitted in. For Western Europe's main states, there were a number of discrete threats or problems that were coded as 'the Soviet Threat'. One was a domestic threat from Communist Parties in states such as Italy and France; another was the big problem of the division of Germany by the USA and the USSR in the late 1940s; and a third was the threat that the US–Soviet global rivalry could plunge Europe into a devastating regional war.

If this was indeed the nature of 'the Soviet Threat' to Western Europe, then we are led towards the conclusion that many of NATO's apparent preoccupations during the latter part of the Cold War were not what they were really preoccupied with at all. The NATO powers appeared to be overwhelmingly preoccupied with technical-military force issues of a defensive kind: how many war-heads do we need, what kinds of missiles, tanks etc., etc., to meet the Soviet threat? But in reality this constant military deployment debate was about politics more than defensive warfare: placing Cruise and Pershing missiles in Germany would have political effects: they would threaten the USSR and thus break the Soviet–German detente of the 1970s; and they would thus pull Germany more firmly under US leadership. Putting modernised Lance missiles into West Germany in the Spring of 1989, as Mrs Thatcher tried vainly to insist upon, would threaten the GDR and pull its population away from any dynamic towards German unity, remaining instead tied in to the Soviet alliance (which the Kohl government would not tolerate and thus insisted upon rejecting) and so on.[14]

But the collapse of the Soviet bloc had the effect of destroying this entire West European political framework. The entire shape of European politics and economics in the 1990s has been shaped by the battles amongst the main NATO powers over how to reshape the political framework in Western Europe after it was shattered by the Soviet bloc collapse.

This series of political battles over the political reshaping of Europe has proceeded in the same way as the West–West political battles of the Cold War period. The actual political conflicts have taken place very largely behind the backs of the electorates of Europe, within the largely closed contexts of the NAC, the European Council of the EU and state-to-state bilateral exchanges. The political coinage of these political interactions has been above all military/security moves: plans for changing the roles, capacities and decision-making authorities of military or potential military organisations, such as NATO, the WEU and the EU, or of security organisations such as the CSCE/OSCE. The political battles have been waged on a number of levels: partly through debates and coalition-building tactics within the Western institutions; but also through practical steps, attempted fait accomplis by the various key players – Germany, France and the United States. And throughout the 1990s, one very important zone in which various powers, especially the USA, have made big moves in this political conflict has been in the Yugoslav theatre. Military moves by the USA there have had a major impact upon the political battles within the West.

PART 2. NATOLAND PROGRAMMES AND POWER POLITICS AFTER THE COLLAPSE

A superficial view of the collapse of 1989–91 would be that Western Europe remained untouched. Both the key institutions, NATO and the EC, remained in place. Yet their political structure was shattered, and the future of their political economy thrown into question, by the radical transformation of Western Europe's geopolitical and geoeconomic context. The geopolitical context was transformed because the Soviet Union/Russia was no longer a threat or an enemy, or even an opponent. Cold War NATO, the chief instrument of US hegemony, was redundant, as were the services supplied by the US in exchange for its leadership – US military power. The USSR/Russia was threatening to become an included, legitimate player in West European politics, and hence transforming all the equations of that NATOland political system.

No less important was the transformed geoeconomic context. The East was opening for Western business to flood in, transforming the conditions for Western capital accumulation in the whole of Europe. The West-facing, East-blocked West European division of labour, institutionally anchored in the EC, faced a major challenge. Would its whole institutional form be battered down in capital's Eastward stampede, and through East Central Europe's beating against the doors of the EC trade regime, single market and accession procedures?

Thus the Soviet bloc collapse placed two questions before the Western powers. The first was an absolutely fundamental, interlinked challenge to the main Western powers: what was their new accumulation-strategy cum geopolitical strategy for the whole of Europe going to be? And in answering this, the main Western powers had to provide the answer to a second question: what new institutional forms for political-military arrangements and for political-economy arrangements for the whole of Europe would they advance, in line with and in pursuit of their answers to question one.

If no answers were given to these two questions then two spontaneous dynamics would be unleashed upon NATO and the EU. First, NATO would become a society for reminiscences of the good old days of the Cold War, since it had been established for territorial defence of its members against attack and for nothing more. But now there were no territorial threats to its members from anywhere for the foreseeable future (except for mutual threats between two members of the alliance, Greece and Turkey). Thus the West Europeans could produce NATO's effective death simply by insisting that it should *remain the same* in terms of its formal constitution and military posture. As a result, it would give the US no political leverage whatever over the political orientations of the West European states, since its military services would be redundant.

The second spontaneous dynamic would be for the West European states and business classes to start moving off in all different directions, pursuing their own, national, political and economic gains in the East, and thus pulling apart both NATO and the EC, neither of which had the institutional or political frameworks for preventing such a development: the EC had no joint foreign policy nor any form of federal government. NATO could impose a stop on the scramble for the East only when such a ban could be justified by an enemy threat. This problem of the scramble for the East would be most seriously posed in the case of Germany, whose expansion in that direction would take place quite spontaneously unless it was consciously reined in by itself or by others.

All the stories of the 1990s in Europe have been little more than sub-plots or spin-offs of one big central plot: the manoeuvres of the Western powers in the battles over the two questions outlined above. From the collapse of Yugoslavia through the various post-Yugoslavia wars, the Katastroikas in Russia and Ukraine, the blow-out in Albania and crises and impoverishments in other parts of East Central Europe – none of these events can be understood unless they are situated in a context shaped, above all, by the power struggles in the West and by the various available solutions to them. The peoples of East Central and Eastern Europe have been the big losers, both from these struggles and from the ways in which the Western powers have sought to manage or resolve them.

Some, of course, have taken different views, arguing that the reshaping of European politics and economics has been achieved by leaders of small Balkan states such as Slobodan Milošević. This is simply not serious. Others have argued that Europe has been 'whole and free', as US leaders like to say, since 1989, a world of peace, harmony and interstate equality occasionally interrupted by explosions in the Balkans. Yet this is precisely what has not been happening. The potential wholeness of Europe was already disappearing by 1991, and the re-division of Europe has been deepening ever since as the direct consequence of the power struggles in the West, and of the ways in which various Western powers have been attempting to resolve these power struggles. The 1999 NATO war against Yugoslavia is only the latest and most obviously dramatic of the steps along that path of division. Much of public opinion in Europe is blind to these power struggles in the West precisely because of the closed, elite character of the discursive side of these Western battles. Public opinion thus views developments such as the NATO campaign against Yugoslavia in a cognitive political void. Hence their commonsense idea that the war is only about NATO military-technical issues, the fate of the Yugoslav government and the fate of Yugoslavia's peoples – the Kosovo Albanians, the Serbs, the Hungarians and Muslims of Serbia, the Montenegrins and the populations of Macedonia and Albania.

To make sense of the main features of the post-Cold War political battles over Europe's future it is important to appreciate that some states have been more important than others in this series of political dances. Only four states have been capable of fighting for programmes for the whole of Europe: the United States, Germany, France and Russia. No other state had a structural role in any of the possible projects: Britain, for example, could play the role of a partial spoiler of some projects, but only at great potential cost to itself. It was not integral to any of the possible projects. And Russia faded, partly because it had swallowed some economic medicine, urged on its leaders by American economic specialists, which had turned out to be both narcotic and highly toxic for Russian power. All other, smaller states have had to attach themselves to programmes generated by these pivotal four. And none of the four have been able to gain victory for their own programme alone: they have had to forge alliances for victory – each set of alliances bringing forth, of course, countervailing pressures from the other key players.

The ensuing political dances have progressed through the main players making small demarches, in efforts to achieve a small advance. Sometimes they make their forward moves by seizing on shifts on the part of other states; sometimes by seizing on opportunities on the ground, using events, say, in the Western Balkans as an arena for making a larger move in the European political theatre as a whole.

The whole game is further complicated by the fact that the states themselves are not fully unitary actors: the German defence ministry under Volker Rühe, for example, was used as a valuable ally by the US administration to drag a reluctant German Auswärtige Amt and Chancellory behind a key US move – NATO enlargement into Poland. The French military have been desperately eager to be re-integrated into the NATO command, while the Quai D'Orsay has been much less so. Similarly the British MOD has been a bigger fan of US political strategy in Europe, on the whole, than the Foreign Office. And so on. But for the sake of simplicity we will tend to discuss the main players as if they were unitary actors.

A further complication lies in the fact that each of the programme-capable states has to advance a programme which embraces a very wide field, basically the following: how to organise the politics and economics of three zones – EU Europe, Eastern Europe and the EU–American partnership.

The three basic programmes on offer were, very schematically: 'One Europe'; West European–Russian balance (here there were two main variants of both path and form); and American hegemony, with Russian exclusion. (Of course, it could be argued that a fourth possible variant exists: that of renationalisation – in other words, the collapse of efforts to provide any new stable structure for European politics in the post-Cold War period and a consequent fluidity reminiscent of the nineteenth century.) To explore this fourth possibility would take us beyond the scope of this essay, so we will restrict ourselves to examining each of the first three projects in turn. But before we do so, we must understand the deep issues of what we might call the 'geopolitics of accumulation' for the key Western players: the US, Germany and France. Only through a grasp of these deep-structure issues can we gain an appreciation of the specifics of the three programmes.

Key Issues of the Geopolitics of Accumulation for the Major Western States

It is important to bear in mind that the USA, France and Germany all have accumulation strategies that involve their reach across the world; and that this world is mainly under the sway of the USA. This means that the European states must not push their battles with the USA too far, for fear of being seriously damaged by the USA in the global theatre. Such damage could be wreaked not only by Washington's use of military-generated political influence against European interests, but also by its use of economic statecraft – exploiting the global dominance of the dollar and US leadership of the IMF/World Bank or, indeed, the role of its huge financial market and dominant financial services operators. This panoply sets limits to West European ambitions, especially while it lacks a euro acting not only as a 'domestic' European currency but as a global challenger to the dollar, backed by united political and military power.

And, especially once Clinton had become president, it became very clear that the US administration was making the rebuilding of US global capitalist ascendancy in the international political economy its dominant, governing priority.

This emphasis in US global strategy in the 1990s derived only partly from an awareness among US elites that their operations in the Cold War had diverted their attention from tackling new competitive threats from other capitalist centres: not only Japan and Western Europe, but also East and South East Asia. This defensive concern was combined with a new offensive concept, forged by the Reagan Administration: the concept of 'globalization'. This involves using political leverage – not only military-political statecraft but, especially, economic statecraft – to radically transform the political economies of the rest of the world so that they 'converge' with the needs of US capitalism. Such convergence requires removing the right of states to control the free movement into and out of their territories of financial flows, financial service companies, and all kinds of other multinational enterprises; it also involves re-engineering their domestic institutions to facilitate profit-making by Atlantic capital within their territory.

This new imperial drive into the South, initiated in the Reagan years, required the US to establish a political alliance with European Union capitalisms in order to pursue this campaign effectively through the multilateral organisations: especially through the GATT/WTO but also through the OECD and the IMF/WB, the operations of the Bank for International Settlements and so on. Yet at the same time, these West European capitalisms had many particular interests which conflicted with US interests in its expansion into the South. To deal with this problem, the US had to plan a campaign to pressurise the EU states to re-engineer the EU political economy in ways that would achieve a convergence of the EU with the US programme for global capitalist expansion. This was a vital US interest. Yet with the Soviet bloc collapse, finding ways to exert pressure on Western Europe for these purposes was extremely difficult, since the use of US hegemonic leadership of Western Europe through NATO was disappearing.

And here was Washington's first big European problem at the end of the Cold War. The collapse of the Soviet bloc was destroying the US's hegemonic political leadership over its European allies. The leverage it had enjoyed over its allies' internal political economies, in return for its supply of military/security services, was withering. Samuel Huntington has explained how US tactics had worked during the Cold War:

> Western Europe, Latin America, East Asia, and much of South Asia, the Middle East and Africa fell within what was euphemistically referred to as 'the Free World', and what was, in fact, a security zone. The governments within this zone found it in their interest: a) to accept an explicit or implicit guarantee by Washington of the independence of their country and, in some cases, the authority of the government; b) to permit

> access to their country to a variety of US governmental and non-governmental organisations pursuing goals which those organisations considered important . . . The great bulk of the countries of Europe and the Third World . . . found the advantages of transnational access to outweigh the costs of attempting to stop it.[15]

And as David Rothkopf has added, in the post-war years 'Pax Americana came with an implicit price tag to nations that accepted the US security umbrella. If a country depended on the United States for security protection, it dealt with the United States on trade and commercial matters.'[16]

The efficacy of the tactic depended upon two conditions: first, the ability of the US to persuade the local dominant social groups that they faced an external threat; and secondly, the US's ability to persuade these same groups that the US, and only the US, had the resources to cope with the threat and the will to do so. The distinctive US organisational model of the giant corporation could thus enter foreign labour and product markets, spreading first to Canada, then to Western Europe (facilitated by the EC's rules and development) and then on to other parts of the world. In this way, rather than in the primitive militarist conceptions of realist theory, military power played a central role in post-war capitalist power politics.

In addition, the Soviet bloc collapse was accompanied by a new sense among European elites that they could build a strong European political entity through an EU resting on a social-democratic christian-democratic/social-liberal identity. In other words, European political construction would be carried out under a banner which implicitly challenged the whole American capitalist social model. This was a tendency expressed by European Commission President Jacques Delors but also by Chancellor Kohl and, indeed, by French elites. Only the leaders of British capitalism (supported to a great degree by the Dutch) were on message with the US line. Yet within the capitalist classes of Western Europe there was, potentially, a powerful social constituency that could be mobilised for a domestic social transformation of the EU towards the American social model. The heartland of this domestic EU constituency lay in Germany. Provided the leaders of the German capitalist business systems could be diverted from a main orientation of expansion eastwards into Russia, the US could offer them the possibility of a partnership with US business at a global level, opening opportunities for them in the UK and in the US and in other parts of the American-led world. But the price would be transforming their own domestic social model in the direction of the US model. This would be a very attractive offer not only for German capital, of course, but for all the most dynamic European multinationals, ready and eager for a race to capture markets all over the world and to position themselves strongly in the American market. But Germany was the key.

Thus, the US strategy for Europe would combine the drive to rebuild US leadership over Europe, through the campaign to reorganise NATO, with a parallel campaign to reorganise the political economy of the EU. This strategy has emerged ever more clearly since the Clinton administration arrived in power in 1993. A full analysis of the campaign would have to track both its prongs: not only the political battles over the military-political reorganisation of NATO and European security, but also the battles over the reorganisation of the EU and its domestic political economy. Tackling the latter would take us into US diplomacy over Maastricht, the Uruguay Round, the formation of alliances between big US and European capital through the Trans-Atlantic Business Dialogue, the switch of the biggest of German banks and businesses towards American alliances, and the growing strength of a radical neo-liberal coalition within the European financial sectors, Central Banks and parts of the EU European Commission.

The atmosphere in the United States when Clinton came into power was one suffused with a sense of great historical drama, a sense that the United States was facing a great world-historical Either/Or. There was the awareness of America's gigantic power in the military field and in the monetary-financial regime; on the other hand, there was the challenge of East Asia, and uncertainty about Europe. There was the sense that the United States was about to give birth to an entirely new set of global growth motors through the new information industries and a feeling that these could play the role of the motor car as a huge pathway to revived international accumulation which the US could hope to dominate; yet, after very large investments in this sector, its supposed transformative potential for US productivity has simply not materialised. And, finally, there was the triumph over the Soviet bloc and the international left; and yet, paradoxically, that collapse posed, as we have seen, a major question-mark over the means that the US could use for exerting political influence in the world and for consolidating that influence through institutions similar to the security zones of the Cold War.

Tremendous American intellectual energy was being devoted, therefore, to these strategic issues as Clinton came into office. As one policy intellectual put it, 'essentially, we have to erect a whole new conceptual basis for foreign policy after the Cold War'.[17] Others equated the tasks facing Clinton to those that faced Truman in 1945: Clinton, said one writer, is 'present at the creation' of a new epoch in world affairs and 'the next half century hangs in the balance'.[18]

The Clinton team itself was not, of course, going to spell out publicly how it conceptualised its strategic problem or its strategy and tactics for tackling it. The signs had to be read more indirectly: for example, through Clinton's appointments and institutional arrangements as well as through policy statements and initiatives.

Clinton's top foreign policy appointments – such as Warren Christopher (State), Anthony Lake (National Security), Madeleine Albright (UN), Lloyd Bensten (Treasury) seemed to be conventional, rather passive figures with links back to the Carter days.[19] Many observers wondered why Clinton had received a reputation for external activism when he made such personnel appointments.[20] But this perception was itself the product of old thinking whereby foreign policy meant what the Secretary of State or the NSC chief or the Secretary of Defence did. It ignored the instruments of economic statecraft; yet these were the instruments which Clinton placed in the hands of the dynamic activists.

The new team brought in to wield the levers of economic statecraft were a distinctive group: Robert Rubin, Ron Brown, Mickey Kantor, Laura Tyson, Larry Summers, Jeff Garten, Ira Magaziner and Robert Reich (as well as Vice President Al Gore) had distinctive general approaches to the defence of American power:[21] for them, it was about 'the economy, stupid'. And they believed that strengthening American capitalism was, above all, to be tackled through international political action. In line with this was their belief in the importance, even the centrality, of state political action in economic affairs: a conviction that the success of a national capitalism was 'path dependent', and that the path could be built of institutions, fashioned by states. There should be no barren counter-positioning of national states and market forces: they should work together, help each other, whether in technology, trade or finance. They were not classical national protectionists, but neither were they free traders. The term used to describe the school of thought represented by this team was 'globalists', promoters of a kind of global neo-mercantilism. The new concept was that competition among states was shifting from the domain of political-military resources and relations to the field of control of sophisticated technologies and the domination of markets.[22] The nature of the new game was also given a name: 'geoeconomics'. Lloyd Bensten may have been of a different generation and of a different background from the others, but he also shared a 'globalist' view.

The outlook of this new team was expressed in books like Laura Tyson's *Who's Bashing Whom* and by a host of other such works by those within or close to the administration.[23] The outlook was often expressed most bluntly by Clinton's new US Trade Representative, Mickey Kantor, who openly argued for a new kind of American Open Door strategy to ensure that the twenty-first century would be the 'New American Century'. As he put it: 'The days of the Cold War, when we sometimes looked the other way when our trading partners failed to live up to their obligations, are over. National security and our national economic security cannot be separated . . . No more something for nothing, no more free riders.'[24]

Kantor's linkage of external economic objectives and US National Security was reflected in Clinton's remoulding of institutions in the core executive. As we have seen, just after his inauguration Clinton created a National Economic Council within the White House, alongside the National Security Council. The choice of name was designed to indicate that the new body would acquire the kind of nodal role in US global strategy that the NSC had played during the Cold War. At the same time, Congress instructed the Commerce Department to set up the Trade Promotion Coordinating Committee (TPCC) to co-ordinate nineteen US government agencies in the area of commercial policy. Instructive also was the fact that the head of the National Economic Council was to be a very experienced hedge fund speculator: Robert Rubin, former senior partner in Goldman Sachs, the hedge fund masquerading as an investment bank.[25] This gave the Clinton team prime links with Wall Street.

The Clinton administration's new international strategy has been characterised by someone who was initially part of it, David Rothkopf, 'Manic Mercantilism'.[26] Stanley Hoffman makes a similar point, noting the new US activism in world economic affairs under the Clinton administration and its drive to open borders to US goods, capital and services.[27]

This essay will not track the US strategy at the level of the European political economy, nor examine US economic statecraft, but will concentrate on the political-military side of US strategy in Europe. With the collapse of the Soviet bloc, the Bush administration had still hoped that the United States' role as controller of security zones and wielder of enormous military resources could remain a potent instrument for strengthening the position of

American capitalism vis-à-vis its economic rivals. Bush's great efforts to ensure that a united Germany remained in NATO were followed by his war against Iraq, one of the main goals of which was to show the rest of the capital world that it had to treat the interests of US capitalism with respect. But this was a false dawn. With the collapse of the Soviet Union itself, the US's ability to make political use of its extraordinary military superiority was bound to diminish.

This was not Washington's only problem with Western Europe, even if it was an urgent one in the 1990s. There was a more long-term and deeply worrying problem, both geopolitical and linked to the global pattern of future capital accumulation: the possibility of a West European–Russian link up. 'One Europe' political ideas precisely expressed such a link up, and ideas of a West European–Russian balance could be a prelude to it. The geopolitical and accumulation consequences of this for US global dominance could be awesome: in the colourful language of geopoliticians, nothing less than the American loss of the planet's Eurasian heartland; and think of the potential for capital accumulation created by yoking together the gigantic human and material resources of Western Europe and the former Soviet Union!

We will not survey here the debates within the US policy community on how to tackle these problems[28] but two central conclusions were drawn for US strategic goals in Europe. The first was that the US had to find a way of regaining its role as gate-keeper between Western Europe and Russia, able to control the flow of relations through the gate between Berlin and Moscow. And the second was that the US should not allow the emergence of a unified West European political will to emerge, autonomous from Washington. Instead, it had to find a way to rebuild US political leadership *above* whatever integration went on in Western Europe. US tactics in Europe had to be geared to these two political goals.

The Bush administration quickly realised that an entirely new NATO was the key to tackling both these basic challenges. NATO needed an entirely new role, new members, new military instruments. The only things that should not be new in NATO was US leadership, and the subordination of West European policy-making, command structures and military-political initiatives to the US. But how to attain this? What mix of tactics could achieve this strategic goal? That was the policy problem.

For Germany, the collapse of the Soviet bloc brought an embarrassment of riches. For as long as the USSR survived, there had seemed to German leaders the real possibility of moving straight to 'One Europe', on one condition:

that France and Germany worked together for that goal and the US did not get too much in the way. But if 'One Europe' was an optimal solution it was not necessarily a bottom line for Germany in the early 1990s. The base of German capitalism was Western Europe. The security of that base depended upon the Franco-German partnership, anchored institutionally in the European Union. In the general expansion of German capitalism, that base and its security anchorage must not be sacrificed: it must be strengthened. This was the cornerstone for Chancellor Kohl.

The second element of Kohl's policy was to secure Germany's new Eastern flank states: above all Poland, what became the Czech Republic and Hungary. Germany's security and her most vital interests required that they were anchored firmly. That meant both fitting their emerging capitalisms into the pattern of Germany's own economic expansion, and being ready to make a commitment to the external as well as the internal security of these states. There were lots of different frameworks for doing this: the Eastern states' eventual entry into the EU, plus bilateral guarantees from Germany, or guarantees from the WEU, or guarantees from NATO, or co-operative guarantees involving both Russia and Germany. Nevertheless, their friendly anchorage was a bottom-line issue for Germany.

A third element for the new Germany was to ensure adequate security frameworks for expanded capital accumulation, both Eastwards and into the US-led global sphere. How this expansion of accumulation was articulated geographically would depend upon both political and economic developments. It would certainly proceed across the whole of East Central and Eastern Europe, but the relationship with the USSR/Russia would depend on unforeseeable developments. Germany had every reason to keep the USA calm and contented while building up its strength by working its way through the huge meal offered to German capitals by the Soviet Collapse. On the other hand, precisely because all could see what potentially colossal gains Germany had made, there were risks of Germany facing a rough ride from the USA and even from some of its West European partners. Thus no German government would wish to fall back under US dominance; rather it would wish to develop a strong, homogeneous West European political force and will, centred on Germany with France as its 'strong partner'.

France was placed in a very difficult situation in terms of its own power strategy by the Soviet bloc collapse. Its accumulation strategy had been entirely centred in the EU, with France as a junior capitalism to Germany but still able to be a political equal and to pretend to political leadership, owing to its possession of nuclear weapons during the Cold War. On these bases, its whole tactical structure was that of France as the 'Europeanist' alternative to Yankee-led Atlanticism: hence its hostility to US neo-liberal civilisational models, to US hegemonism, to the NATO integrated command, to US imperialistic wars in the South and so forth. With the Soviet bloc collapse, all this still suited Germany fine; but did it still suit France? Under Mitterrand, France's orientation concentrated upon locking Germany into its West Europeanist partnership, and sought also a joint Franco-German international political will and line. But Chirac would search for other ways out of a posture which now, with Germany's new strength, made French claims on West European leadership look less like a stance than a piece of posturing.

The Three Competing Programmes for Europe

Against this background we can examine the three programmatic projects for Europe that have been promoted during the 1990s.

1. 'One Europe'

This option has been consistently advocated by the USSR, from 1986, and by Russia throughout the 1990s (insofar as its leaders were not busy with other things). It was, however, only very briefly entertained by the two key West European powers, Germany and France, between 1989 and 1991. The United States has been resolutely hostile to it.

The basic concept involves a pan-European political/security system that includes Russia, as well as all the other East European states; and a pan-European economic system that involves replacing the EU division of labour with a new pan-European one, offering the ex-Soviet bloc states an effective developmental framework. Since the EU was constructed from the start on the principle of breaking West Germany from economic linkages with the East and on excluding the East European economies, it would eventually have to be reorganised to make 'One Europe' work economically. Mitterrand and the Deutsche Bank had two different ways of solving that problem but both basically involved keeping the Comecon region together as a regional economic unit for a whole transition period as its redevelopment took place. (For Mitterrand this also had the key advantages of ending pressure for an overhaul of the EU regime.) Eventually, though, the two regional economies of Europe would grow together into one.

The big loser from 'One Europe' would be the United States: it would lose both political hegemony over Western Europe and control of the new – and potentially very dynamic – capital accumulation process of harmonising the West European and the Russian economies – a frightening prospect for American capitalism, should it develop in the longer term.

In 1989–90 the German government was very interested in this 'One Europe' project; so was the Mitterrand administration in France. The plan of Herrhausen, Chair of the Deutsche Bank and very close to Kohl in the autumn of 1989, embodied the concept: he argued for a collaborative effort between the EC and the USSR to revive the economies of East Central Europe. The initial concept of Jacques Attali and Mitterrand for the European Bank for Reconstruction and Development, along with the concept of a European Confederation from the Atlantic to the Urals, outlined on 31 December 1989, embodied the same idea. The difference was that Herrhausen's plan implied leadership on the economic front by the three big German private banks (Deutsche, Dresdner and Commerz) while Attali's public bank, the EBRD, could be under his (French) leadership. Another aspect of the 'One Europe' project was demonstrated in the support in Germany in 1990 for making the CSCE the central collective security framework for the whole of Europe. Both Kohl and Mitterrand were interested in Gorbachev's proposals for a unified Germany to be neutral and outside NATO and even to a revamping of the entire European security apparatus once the Cold War was over.[29] This Kohl–Mitterrand approach towards building a 'One Europe' project with Russia – at least on the economic front – was still evident at the end of 1990, in their joint support for a free trade agreement between the EC and the USSR which they persuaded the European Council to adopt in December 1990.

The 'One Europe' project failed for a number of reasons: first, because of adamant and vigorous US hostility; secondly, because of the lack of strong unity between France and Germany in advancing the project; and, thirdly, because the Gorbachev leadership was, despite its rhetoric of a Single European Home, unclear itself as to whether it feared a united Germany to the point of preferring a strong US role in Europe. The Soviet leadership also made serious blunders in its external economic policies towards the Comecon region at the time, while the vigorous US efforts (via the IMF) to break up Comecon won support in Czechoslovakia and elsewhere in East Central

Europe. The Bush administration persuaded these states that it would ensure their quick entrance to the EU if they broke up Comecon and took the IMF's Shock Therapy treatment instead.

When the USSR itself collapsed, an effective Eastern partner for France and Germany in this project disappeared as well.

There were two other very important reasons for the failure of the 'One Europe' programme in the early 1990s. First, its economic programme implied a social-democratic-style development strategy for the East which clashed with the whole American paradigm of neo-liberalism and globalisation, a paradigm which was attracting great support amongst the leaders of big capital in Western Europe. The Bush administration, desperate to impose US capitalism-friendly political economies everywhere in the East, moved successfully to impose its regime goals on the Eastern economies. To counter that would have needed a big German push using large German credit capacity and that was not forthcoming. The US ideas quickly gained influence amongst all the West European governments under American and British influence – not least because they were the cheapest way (for the West) of getting capitalism 'over there' as quickly as could be.

The second basic reason for the programme's failure was the lack of a strong political energy linking institution-building with the capacity to generate strong popular support. Only this could effectively resist US hostility. The energy was initially offered by Mitterrand's grand vision of a pan-European Confederation. This did inspire some support from Vaclav Havel, but not from Bonn or Moscow – so it collapsed. Genscher offered a strong peace-making rhetoric, echoing Gorbachev's stirring vision, but neither of them could concretise their visions in a definite institutional form *that they could jointly achieve*. The one they attempted, a qualitatively strengthened CSCE which could marginalise NATO, required too much co-operation from the rest of the European states and hence was an easy target for American diplomacy. As the Soviet Union reeled into terminal crisis in the summer of 1991, Genscher veered off into championing Croatia, a move that looked like a message to the whole of Central and Eastern Europe to turn to Germany alone if they wanted a helping hand with any problems.

At the start of the new millennium, a 'One Europe' project could still be revived; but it lacks support from any of the major powers apart from a much-weakened Russia.

2. EU–Russian balance with Western Europe expanding into East Central Europe

The second option has been that of turning the EC into a fully-fledged political entity which expands its influence over East Central Europe while giving Russia its own sphere of influence in the CIS. The central idea here is that American hegemony in the West is replaced by a solid West European political entity, under whose influence East Central Europe falls. The West European entity would be led by France and Germany. Russia would be acknowledged as having its sphere of influence and leadership over the CIS, if necessary including an independent Ukraine, and Russia would not find a West European entity's expanding influence a threat to Russian security.

This project has had two variants of end-state and two paths to victory. The two end-states have been either the German conception of turning the EU into a more or less fully fledged state or the French conception of turning the EU into a solid political bloc or alliance of states. In either case, NATO would eventually fade into the background, as would US hegemonic ambitions. The project has also involved two different paths to the end-state, paths that are not mutually exclusive. The first path is via the establishment of a Common Foreign and Security Policy for the EU which would eventually include a common defence policy and a common defence force. The second path is via European monetary union and the subsequent necessity of a solid political entity to buttress the euro. Both the CFS path and the europath could produce either the German Federal Europe or the French political bloc.

Without going into the whole very complex story of the pursuit of this broad option, we can briefly mention the main aspects of it for the three zones of EU Europe, Eastern Europe and the West European–US Partnership. As far as EU Europe is concerned, both the euro path and the CFS path were put forward by Kohl and Mitterrand from the spring of 1990 onwards. The euro was the key price that Mitterrand demanded from Kohl in exchange for French support for German unification. Kohl agreed and fought the opponents of monetary union in Germany successfully. Everybody understood that this was not simply an economic project but a political project as well; the euro can only be sustained economically if it is built on solidly united political foundations. Money is a politically created and sustained phenomenon.

The battle for a political entity, linked to the monetary union project of

Maastricht, had to take the path of a genuinely united foreign policy; and there is no such foreign policy unity without a military unity to match it. Therefore, in April 1990, Kohl and Mitterrand agreed to combine the EC's Inter-Governmental Conference (IGC) on Economic and Monetary Union with a second IGC on Political Union which would put a common foreign and defence policy at its core.

They already had a basis of Franco-German co-operation to build on. The Elysée Treaty of 1963 had made provision for defence co-operation between France and Germany and in January 1988 the two countries had established a Joint Defence and Security Council and created a 4,000 strong Franco-German brigade. In the early 1990s, ministerial, military and defence-industrial relations were strengthened.

At the same time, they had a useful wider instrument for building up a political bloc which excluded the Americans: the Western European Union. France had taken the initiative to revive the WEU in 1984, persuading its members to support the so-called Rome Declaration of 27 October of that year. Alarm on the part of the West European states – including the UK – over the Reagan–Gorbachev summit in Reykjavik in 1987 had led to a WEU platform of European security interests being issued by the Hague WEU summit in October 1987. The Hague Platform declared: 'We are convinced that the construction of an integrated Europe will remain incomplete as long as it does not include security and defence.' And it set the goal of a 'more cohesive European defence identity'.[30]

In December 1990, Kohl and Mitterrand wrote to their European Council colleagues suggesting that the WEU be placed at the centre of the debate on European security institutions. This letter was met with a 'stern démarche' from Washington, resulting in a statement from the German and French Foreign Ministers to the effect that the WEU should be subordinated to NATO.[31] But this did not halt Franco-German efforts. In February 1991 Franco-German proposals for the IGC on Political Union again called for the elevation of the WEU at the expense of NATO. Then, in October 1991, the French and German governments shocked the British and Americans with their announcement of a plan to create a Eurocorps. As Paul Cornish explains, this was 'widely seen as an unabashed attempt to undermine NATO'.[32] The Maastricht Treaty followed through with successful Franco-German insistence that there would be a Common Foreign Security policy for the EU, which would eventually lead to a common defence policy and a common defence.

Here, then, were the elements of a full-scale challenge to US hegemony in Western Europe. The West European states were to have an autonomous set of foreign, security and defence policy-making institutions which could take authoritative decisions quite independently of the US. Secondly, with the creation of the Eurocorps, this autonomous West European bloc or state would have its own autonomous military instrument: the Eurocorps, to which Belgium and Spain were soon also to contribute as well as the French and Germans. And the whole operation would be geared to projecting military power outside the EU and NATO areas, engaging in the so called Petersburg tasks (as laid down at the WEU meeting at the St Petersburg hotel outside Bonn in June 1992). These power-projection roles included crisis management, peacekeeping, peace enforcement and humanitarian interventions. And to cap it all, the WEU could itself expand Eastwards, absorbing new associate members as it spread its political influences in ways that would not be perceived by Russian leaders as a threat to their authority. Here was a full-scale alternative organisation of political power in Western Europe, vying with the concept of US hegemony.

This second option actually implied a very different project for East Central Europe from that of 'One Europe'. In practice it involved EU mercantilism, plus 'insulationism'. The EU would use its trade regime as a lever for gaining the economic expansionist interests of Western big capital in the economies of the East. This lever consisted, essentially, of making access to the EU markets for Eastern countries – something they all desperately needed – dependent upon their opening their political economies to entry by Western capital, with the ultimate aim of harmonising their market rules with those of the EU. The Eastern countries' own economic development needs were to be subordinated to these mercantilist goals. In addition, they were offered a vague promise that a few of them might eventually be incorporated within the EU if, over decades, they successfully competed to see who could do most in demonstrating 100% compliance with every possible EU desire. This political-economy strategy was combined with political 'insulationism'. This concept means a rejection of active political intervention to solve the problems of the East. Instead, political policy towards the East would be confined to ensuring that Western Europe was insulated from the consequences of state instability, state failure, civil war or inter-state conflict in the East. A central problem requiring Western insulation in this context was the threat of great movements of refugees, as well as economic migrants, from the East. Anglo-French military involvement in Yugoslavia through UNPROFOR was essentially about that: 'humanitarian aid' in the war zone to ensure that the civilian population did not leave the war theatre. Italian military intervention in Albania in 1997 was about the same thing: staunching the flood of humanity out of Albania Westwards, by rebuilding an Albanian state. Within this general framework, a partial exception to insulationism has been Germany's concern to build a protective buffer on its Eastern flank by drawing Poland, the Czech Republic and Hungary (as well as Slovenia, eventually) under its wing and ensuring that these states were stable, viable entities anchored to the West. But this differentiation was essentially a concomitant of the insulationist policy, rather than a promise that lots of other countries in the region would also be drawn into the Western sphere (although West European propaganda suggested that all would eventually make it to safety on the Western shore). The wider security balance would be assured by a co-operative, spheres-of-influence approach, giving Russia great scope in the East.

As far as the West European–US partnership was concerned, the Franco-German project implied a replacement of US hegemony with a 'two pillar alliance' which would be a partnership of equals. The politics and economics of Western Europe and East Central Europe would be under German–French-led, West European control. Western Europe would have the capacity for autonomous policy making and for autonomous action in the political and military fields, and would shape its own economic relationship with the East. And the US would have to accept Western Europe as a large, international player in world politics and economics.

This was not, of course, remotely acceptable to either the Bush or the Clinton administrations. From the very beginning, they had sought to reorganise post-Cold War Europe in order to maintain albeit in new ways – the political hegemony that they had enjoyed in Western Europe during the Cold War.

3. The new programme for US hegemony

The third option – US hegemony – has been centred on one single clearly defined goal: to bring Europe back under US leadership through the transformation and new ascendancy of NATO in the whole of Europe. To understand this programme, we must start by recognising that, apart from the name and the leadership, the new NATO was to be radically different from the Cold War NATO. The programme for the new NATO contained the following main planks:

Table 1.1 Programmes for Europe

dimension	**'One Europe'**	**European bipolarity**	**US hegemony**	**Renationalisation**
Military-political structure	Collective security including Russia, building of pan-European framework centred on strong OSCE under UN	2 balanced centres: the EU/WEU and Russia in rough harmony; EU sphere of influence in East Central Europe, Russian sphere in the CIS; US playing a distanced role	A split Europe with West and Centre under US-led NATO which is supreme in pan-European high politics and which excludes Russia	Shifting coalitions of increasingly nationalist states with the US and Russia seeking bilateral allies; OSCE, NATO, WEU, CFSP all become shells
Economic structure	A new, Europe-wide division of labour geared to development in the East for catch-up	Subordinating the East European economies to the economic interests of the EU through denying/granting access to the EU market	Globalisation of economies and neo-liberalism in both halves of Europe	EU a la carte/ variable geometry with tendency for EMU not to last
Lead powers	Germany leading; France, Russia supporting	France and Germany leading the EU in combination with Russian leadership in the former USSR	The US as hegemony with Germany and France bandwaggoning	Unstable coalitions with US having the largest weight
East Central and Eastern Europe	Democratic and rapid economic development in a permissive environment; delayed entry into EU; norm-based security and crisis management	East Central Europe fend for itself, but offered the prospect of trying, in very tough conditions, to make its societies acceptable for eventual EU membership; Germany assuring some stability in the Visegrad states	They support US strategic and regime interests and strengthen internal disciplines within their states; or they make links with an excluded and resentful Russia	The region divides as each state seeks external protectors; more nationalist economic strategies

Table 1.1 continued

dimension	**'One Europe'**	**European bipolarity**	**US hegemony**	**Renationalisation**
The United States	Loss of US dominance: threatened by growing Russo-German(EU) axis in economics and politics; likely strong US resistance	Loss of US dominance, but leadership over Western Europe in global field could be maintained; risk of a resentful US seeking to divide the West European states	Restoration of US political dominance, giving stronger leverage to the US over political-economy issues	US could hope to manoeuvre for restored dominance through bilateral coalition-building
Western Europe	Deepen EU, reduced pressure for enlargement, less US tutelage	Deepening EU, esp. in CFSP and EMU, plus small enlargement	Widening rather than deepening of EU, which becomes more a transatlantic system under US leadership	Tendency towards fragmentation of EU and undermining of West European integration

1. NATO as gate-keeper for the US between Russia and Western Europe (especially Germany)

This is the fundamental meaning of the NATO enlargement into Poland, the Czech Republic and Hungary. It is important to see why. In the first place, it blocks the possibility of a unilateral German influence stretching across Poland and the rest of Germany's Eastern flank because the USA is in Poland, and Poland becomes a political base of the US via NATO. But secondly, the form of Poland's integration into NATO serves another crucial purpose. Poland could have joined without integration into the NATO integrated command: joining would just have involved Poland getting the NATO security guarantee. But the USA insisted on its right to have bases in Poland and to station nuclear weapons there if needed. This was a bottom-line issue for the Clinton government. It also deeply angered Russian elites because it drove a US armoured division through the spirit of the Treaty of Paris of 1990 which had settled the external aspects of German unification, specifying that there should be no foreign bases or nuclear weapons in the former GDR territory. Now the US was reserving the right to bring its missiles right up to the Soviet border. Why? Why should the US risk such Russian wrath for this goal?

There are two answers, one political and one military. The political one is that this provides the USA with its role as political Gate-keeper between Russia and Germany. Above all it enables the US to make moves to freeze Russian–German relations if they get too friendly. All that needs to be done is to pick a quarrel with Russia, say over its internal treatment of some group or other or over its operations in the Near Abroad. Then the US can move forces into Poland, polarising West European opinion behind it and that should be enough to put a stop to any hopes of a new Rapallo.

But there is a military purpose in this aspect of Poland's accession as well, and that is to be able to threaten to project power Eastwards to ensure that Ukraine does not fall back under Russian sway, through, for example, entering a security pact with Russia which results in Russian troops on Ukraine's Western borders, changing the entire strategic balance in Central Europe. The Brzezinski circle which has been so central an influence on the US thinking on NATO enlargement (along with Rand specialists like Larrabee) is deeply committed to pulling Ukraine under NATO's wing. This would provide a solid US-led corridor of Poland and Ukraine between Germany and Russia, while transforming the strategic situation in the Black Sea and thus the Caucasus and the Caspian.

There is also the question whether NATO should enlarge further into Central and South East Europe, corralling Slovenia, Slovakia, Romania and even Bulgaria along, eventually with Albania, Croatia and part of Bosnia, too. Such matters are, of course, high on the agenda after NATO's 1999 Yugoslav war.

Thus, NATO enlargement is about Russian exclusion from the institutions of European politics. This is not because the US wants a confrontation with Russia now, or even Russian hostility. Why should it? It just wants to be gate-keeper and Russian hostility was the price that might have to be paid. But the question was whether the West European states, above all Germany, would also consider that Russian exclusion and hostility was a price worth paying in order to insure that the US could play gate-keeper across a new European divide.

2. NATO must be refashioned to play an entirely new aggressive military role 'out of area'

The US slogan for NATO as a military organisation in the 1990s has been 'out of area or out of business'. In the elegant words of François Heisbourg back in 1992: 'In a world without the canonical Soviet menace ambitions, rather than threats, may well have become of overriding importance in determining the future of the Atlantic relationship.'[33] This drawing of NATO into ambitious external military action is a vital goal for the US in its *political drive to regain political leadership of Western Europe.* To understand why we must remember how the US gained hegemony in Western Europe after the war. It did so by helping to create circumstances facing Western Europe which would make West European states demand something that only the US had: the services of its strategic war machine. But when the Soviet bloc collapsed, the US nuclear assets became redundant because NATO's West European territory faced no strategic threat. This then created the problem that 'out of area' could solve. The US had to find a way of persuading Western Europe once again that it needed military services that only the USA could offer, because it needed to do some aggressive 'out of area' jobs. As it happened, the US was rapidly coming up with some new military services: the US Air Force tomahawks, smart weapons and a whole assortment of other goods. These services are not for sale: on the contrary, they are to remain exclusive US property. If the West Europeans had them, no US political leadership. We can sum up the US offer by paraphrasing Kipling: you (West Europeans) need casualty-free weapons:

But we have got
The Tomahawk
And you have not![34]

The US has had lots of other things apart from Tomahawks: it has got its own (not NATO's) huge logistical base in Western Europe; it has got the vital battle-field intelligence systems; and it has got the vital heavy lift capacity (the West Europeans have no heavy military transport planes of their own).

Here, then were the services on offer for a new 'Strong Partnership' going 'out of area'. The idea was immediately enough to gain an extremely sympathetic ear in certain elite constituencies in Western Europe. First there were the military establishments of the main West European states. In the early 1990s they had their backs against the wall as they stood eyeball to eyeball facing finance ministries slashing at their budgetary underbellies with lethal knives. Washington gave them a weapon to fight back with – the slogan, 'We must be protected and revived because you need us to go "out of area".' There was one ally for the NATO bureaucracy.

Washington then found another ally in the form of none other than the West European finance ministries. It could say to them: 'Frankly, we do have to go "out of area". Your military brass are not just greedy, they are right. But we understand that you have a big problem. You have your European Monetary System to protect (against Wall Street) and then your Convergence Criteria to fulfil, by slashing budgets and cutting borrowing. Building up your own West European out-of-area strike force will cost you a budgetary fortune. So maybe we can help. Drop this extravagant notion of your own autonomous West European (WEU or EU or whatever) strike force, and use the USAF instead. All you need to do is stick with US leadership in NATO. We'll supply the Tomahawks, logistics, battle field intelligence, bombers, whatever.'

The third and fourth potential allies came in the form of the two West European states already predisposed to use militarism for political advantage within the Western alliance: France and the UK. The fact that both these states were long geared to military adventure for political gain gave them a great lead on Germany in this field, saturated as it was by pacifism. So they would be predisposed towards a few 'out of area' projects.

There was only one problem: how to convince the West Europeans of the vital necessity to strike aggressively 'out of area', in the first instance, in the eastern hinterland of the EU? This was the great problem with the strategy.

It was a twofold problem: how to find convincing arguments for the two tiers of West European citizens; the elite audiences centred in the core executives had to be convinced; and the mass audience also had to be given a line that could rouse their support.

Convincing the elite audience was the big problem for advancing the US strategy for its revived hegemony. The problem can be simply put: for Germany, going back to US hegemony was not acceptable. Neither was it acceptable for France. They wanted their autonomous capacity to act as a West European political bloc, without invigilation by the USA. And at the same time, they wanted the capacity to decouple their West European political base from Anglo-American adventures all over the world.

But for US strategists there were ways around this elite problem. One key resource was the fact that the West European elites were not unified at all as a single, institutionalised political will. So one could strike bargains with key elite groups in key states for joint political-military démarches under US leadership. This could present the other elite groups in the other main West European states with a big dilemma: join the US-led thrust even though it was potentially dangerous for your own interests, or stay neutral, or even oppose? Then there was a second key resource: the West European mass audience, the children. If the US and its elite partners in Europe could use their political-media power to rouse the children on a fundamentalist basis, that could create major difficulties for the key elite groups in the key state(s) trying to steer clear of the thrust. Threaten that elite with a media-political mass pressure from below and you could drag them into line. Once that was done the other recalcitrant West European states lower down the hierarchy could be dragged, kicking and screaming perhaps, into the common thrust. As indeed they were, when NATO went to war.

Notes

1. Charles Babington and Helen Dewar, 'Clinton Pleads for Support,' *Washington Post*, Wednesday, 24 March 1999, p. A1.
2. For this part of his 23 March speech see Andrew Sullivan, 'Clinton's War Strategy is Hit and Hope', *The Sunday Times*, 28 March 1999, p. 18.
3. Bradley Graham, 'Joint Chiefs Doubted Air Strategy', *Washington Post*, Monday, 5 April 1999, p. A1. The *Post* reported that 'the views of the Joint Chiefs were gleaned from conversations with several officers who know their thinking but declined to be named.'

4. Bradley Graham, 'Cohen Wrestles With Mission Risks', *Washington Post*, Sunday, 11 April 1999, p. A24.
5. Barton Gellman, 'Allies See No Credible Alternative', *Washington Post*, Tuesday, 23 March 1999, p. A12.
6. Ibid.
7. Ibid.
8. Ibid.
9. Ibid.
10. We have examined this in some detail elsewhere. See Peter Gowan, *The Global Gamble* (Verso, 1999).
11. Unless one thinks that NATO is fighting the war either for or against the KLA, both of which seem to be untenable propositions.
12. Carl Schmitt, who died in 1982, was the leading Nazi jurist in the period from 1933–36 and thereafter played a central intellectual role in theorising German hegemony in wartime Europe. The cognitive use of some of his analytical concepts does not, of course, make one a Nazi. For a survey of Schmitt's thought, see Peter Gowan, 'The Return of Carl Schmitt', *Debatte, Review of Contemporary German Affairs*, vol. 2, no.1, 1994.
13. On bandwaggoning, see S.M.Walt, *The Origins of Alliances* (Cornell University Press, 1987).
14. The campaign for this, evidently designed to put a brake upon the very dynamic German–Soviet detente, was at first waged by Bush and Thatcher. But Bush retreated at the NAC that spring. The German government wouldn't budge, so Thatcher was defeated.
15. Samuel P. Huntington, 'Transnational Organisations in World Politics', World Politics, vol. 25, no. 3 (1973), p. 344.
16. David J. Rothkopf, 'Beyond Manic Mercantilism', Council on Foreign Relations.
17. Will Marshall, head of the Progressive Policy Institute, *Washington Post*, 21 December 1992.
18. Roger Morris, 'A New Foreign Policy for a New Era', *New York Times*, 9 December 1992.
19. Aspen, in Defence, had a more activist, radical agenda.
20. See, for example, Anthony Hartley, 'The Clinton Approach: Idealism and Prudence', *The World Today*, February 1993.
21. Of this list, one partial dissident was Robert Reich: he shared a belief in state action in international economics and his concern for labour standards and protection could be usefully instrumentalised in economic diplomacy over trade issues. But he lacked some of the America-First-in-Everything zeal of the others and dropped out of the administration eventually.
22. Gioia Marini and Jan Rood, 'Maintaining Global Dominance: the United States as a European and Asian Power', in Marianne van Leeuwen and Auke Venema (eds.),

Selective Engagement: American Foreign Policy at the Turn of the Century (Netherlands Atlantic Commission, The Hague, 1996).

23. See Laura D'Andrea Tyson, *Who's Bashing Whom: Trade Conflict in High-Technology Industries* (Institute for International Economics, Washington DC 1992); Ira Magaziner and Mark Patinkin, *The Silent War: Inside the Global Business Battles Shaping America's Future* (Vintage Books, 1990); Jeffrey E. Garten, *A Cold Peace: America, Japan, Germany and the Struggle for Supremacy* (New York Times Books, 1992).
24. 'Kantor says US to Fight Farm Trade Barriers', USIS, 23 February 1996.
25. Rubin later was to become Treasury Secretary.
26. David J. Rothkopf, 'Beyond Manic Mercantilism', Council on Foreign Relations, 1998.
27. Stanley Hoffman, Martin Wight Memorial Lecture, LSE, June 1998.
28. For a survey of the debates see the following important article: James Petras and Steve Vieux, 'Bosnia and the revival of US Hegemony', *New Left Review*, no. 218, July–August 1996.
29. See S. Brown, *The Faces of Power: United States Foreign Policy From Truman to Clinton* (Columbia University Press, 1994).
30. See Western European Union, *The Reactivation of WEU: Statements and Communiques, 1984-1987* (London, WEU, 1988).
31. See H. De Santis, 'The Graying of NATO', in B. Roberts (ed.), *US Security in an Uncertain Era* (MIT Press, 1993).
32. Paul Cornish, *Partnership in Crisis* (RIIA, 1997), p. 49.
33. François Heisbourg, 'The European–US Alliance: Valedictory Reflections on Continental Drift in the Post Cold War Era', *International Affairs* (London), vol. 68, 4, 1992.
34. Kipling quipped of the British victory in the Zulu war: 'We had got the Gatling Gun and they had not.'

2

THE BALKAN WAR AND US GLOBAL POWER

Giovanni Arrighi

It will take time before anyone will be in a position to draw a minimally reliable balance sheet of the 1999 Balkan War. From the point of view of the humanitarian objectives for which it was ostensibly fought, all we can do for now is to join Pope John Paul II in declaring its outcome an unmitigated 'defeat of humanity'. Beyond that, any kind of balance sheet requires a preliminary identification of the real objectives of the war.

Noam Chomsky and many others have already shown much better than I ever could how suspect were the proclaimed humanitarian motivations of the war. On this, I will limit myself to pointing out that, throughout the conflict, the humanitarian issue was bound up in the declarations of the US and British instigators of the war with what they referred to as a 'credibility' issue. The United States and its NATO allies had to demonstrate that their threat to use force was credible in the sense that it would actually be carried out if NATO did not get its way and that, if carried out, it would result in NATO getting its way. If the war made one thing absolutely clear, it is that this issue of credibility (which is nothing but a straightforward issue of power) had absolute precedence over whatever humanitarian objectives, if any, were actually pursued by NATO. The most striking thing about the war was indeed the callousness, and the self-righteous determination, with which the NATO command threatened to continue indefinitely an ever-more-destructive air campaign unless Milošević (or better still anyone who might have succeeded in ousting him from power) bowed to NATO power and acceded to its dictates unconditionally.

If additional proof was needed of the absolute priority of US and NATO credibility over humanitarian objectives, it came with President Clinton's 'victory' speech on 10 June 1999. To him, victory meant first and foremost that Yugoslavia had more or less unconditionally capitulated to NATO demands. The human sufferings inflicted on the Yugoslav population, both Serbian and ethnic-Albanian, in the pursuit of unconditional capitulation were hardly mentioned, except for a new intimation to the Serbs that they would not get any help in reconstructing their devastated country unless they got rid of Milošević. As it should have been clear from the start, the demonstration of US and NATO power was the true objective of the war. Appeals to human sentiments were mere means, camouflaged as ends, to mobilize support at home and abroad for a disproportionate use of violence in a patent breach of international law.

But why, we may well ask at this point, was it so important for the United States and NATO to demonstrate their credibility? Was credibility important in the pursuit of some broader objective? And if this was the case, how successful has the war been in attaining that broader objective? In seeking answers to these questions, it is helpful to see this latest US military exploit, not as an isolated event, but as a link in a chain of events capable of telling us something about the trajectory of US global power. Our questions can then be reformulated as follows: Is the need to demonstrate the credibility of the US–NATO military apparatus the sign of a long-term decline in the global power of the United States and the instrument of a US attempt to slow down that decline? Or is it the sign and the instrument of a new great leap forward of that global power? Can the Balkan war be expected to have been successful in slowing down the decline of US global power, or in propelling it to new heights, as the case might be?

The Trajectory of US Global Power since 1968

Let me begin with a sketch of the most basic facts of US global power over the past thirty years. Broadly speaking, over this period US global power seems to have followed a U-shaped trajectory, with each decade showing a different tendency: a precipitous decline in the 1970s, a bottoming-out in the 1980s, a spectacular come-back in the 1990s. Let us briefly look at the forces that shaped this trajectory in each decade.

The precipitous decline of US global power in the 1970s was thoroughly shaped by the two key, world-historical events of 1968–73: the defeat of the United States in Vietnam and the simultaneous collapse of the Bretton Woods system through which the United States had governed world monetary relations. Although in these same years the successful manned moon-landing showed that the United States could easily catch up with and surpass its Soviet rival in the technological developments of the armament race, the US defeat in Vietnam revealed how powerless the high-tech and highly capital-intensive US military apparatus was in enforcing US commands against the determined resistance of one of the poorest peoples on earth. Massive US spending at home and abroad had thus resulted in a major fiscal crisis of the US warfare–welfare state. Equally devastating was the loss of credibility in the capacity of the US military apparatus to do anything other than reproduce – at ever more costly and risky levels – the balance of terror with the USSR. US global power fell precipitously, reaching its nadir at the end of the 1970s with the Iranian Revolution, a new hike in oil prices, the Soviet invasion of Afghanistan, and a serious new crisis of confidence in the US dollar.

It was in this context that in the closing year of the Carter Administration, and then with greater determination under Reagan, a drastic change of US policies laid the ground for the subsequent recovery of US global power. Militarily, the US government began avoiding carefully (as witnessed by the flight from Lebanon) the kind of confrontation on the ground that had led to defeat in Vietnam, in favour either of war by proxy (as in Nicaragua and Afghanistan), or of confrontations of merely symbolic value against insignificant enemies (as in Grenada and Panama), or of confrontations from the air, where the US high-tech apparatus had an absolute advantage (as with Libya). At the same time, the US initiated an escalation of the armament race with the USSR – primarily, though not exclusively, through the Strategic Defense Initiative – pushing its costs well beyond what the USSR could afford economically. The USSR thus found itself caught into a double confrontation, neither side of which it could win: the one in Afghanistan, where its high-tech military apparatus found itself in the same difficulties that had led to the defeat of the United States in Vietnam, and the one in the armament race, where the United States could mobilize financial resources that were wholly beyond the Soviet reach.

This change of US military policies eventually resulted in the collapse of the USSR and the beginning of the great comeback of US global power of the 1990s. Nevertheless, it cannot be emphasized strongly enough that the change in US policies that was most decisive in bringing about the great turnaround in US global power occurred in the financial rather than in the military sphere. Indeed, without this other change in US policies, it would have been impossible to escalate the armament race beyond the financial reach of the USSR.

The policy changes – a drastic contraction in money supply, higher interest rates, lower taxes for the wealthy, and virtually unrestricted freedom of action for capitalist enterprise – constituted the liquidation of the legacy of the New Deal. Through these policies the United States began to compete aggressively for capital worldwide, provoking a major reversal in the direction of its global flow. From being the main source of world liquidity and of direct investment in the 1950s and 1960s, by the 1980s the United States had become the main debtor nation and a major recipient of direct investment. The other side of the coin was the debt crisis that ravaged poor and middle income countries, most of which did not have a chance of successfully competing with the US giant in world financial markets. Latin America and, above all, African economies were devastated. But the crisis made itself felt in Eastern Europe as well, further reducing the capacity of the USSR to compete in the armament race with the United States, and contributing decisively to the tensions that eventually led to the break-up of Yugoslavia and the escalation of ethnic conflicts. Thus, while the United States came to enjoy practically unlimited credit in world financial markets, the Second and Third Worlds were brought to their knees by a sudden exhaustion of their credit in those same markets. What US military might could not achieve, US power in world financial markets did.

There was nonetheless a problem with this victory. Japan and the overseas Chinese operating out of Taiwan, Hong Kong, Singapore and the main commercial centres of Southeast Asia, emerged as the world's leading creditor nations and the organizers and financiers of a region-wide industrial expansion that, for speed and extent, had few parallels in capitalist history. Indeed throughout the 1980s, the East Asian region seemed to be the main beneficiary of the intensifying interstate competition for mobile capital and the new escalation of the Cold War. While world trade and production stagnated, the economic expansion of the East Asian region gained momentum, capturing a growing share of world liquidity. Japanese banks came to dominate international asset rankings and Japanese institutional investors set the pace in the US treasuries market. Earlier prognostications of an 'emerging Japanese superstate' or of 'Japan as number one' seemed to be right on mark. The United States might have recovered from the depth of the crisis of the 1970s by putting its great military rival and the entire Third World on the defensive; but if money rather than guns had become the primary source of world power – as the very recovery of US fortunes seemed to indicate – did not Japanese economic power constitute a new and more insidious challenge to US global supremacy?

These fears were put to rest at the very beginning of the 1990s by the collapse of the USSR and the almost simultaneous crash of the Tokyo stock exchange in 1990–92 – two events that sent the trajectory of US global power soaring. The United States was left as the one and only military superpower with no prospect in the foreseeable future of any power to rival it. Moreover, the taming of the USSR cleared the ground for the US mobilization of the United Nations Security Council to endorse and legitimate its police actions throughout the world. Saddam Hussein's invasion of Kuwait immediately created an ideal opportunity for such a mobilization, which the US promptly seized, putting up a televised show of its high-tech firepower. Attempts to carry the experience one step further through the 'humanitarian' mission in Somalia failed, because an ambush led to one televised snippet of a dead American pulled through the streets of Mogadishu. This revived the Vietnam syndrome at home and led to the immediate withdrawal of US troops. But subsequent safer 'humanitarian' missions in Haiti and especially Bosnia were more successful. By and large, since the collapse of the USSR and the Gulf War, US military power has continued to remain unchallenged and, on its own terrain, unchallengeable.

The Gulf War also demonstrated that Japan, for all its financial and economic power, was wholly incapable of taking an independent stand in world politics, once again falling in behind the United States. But soon even its financial and economic power were to be questioned, as the Japanese economy proved incapable of recovering fully from the crash of 1990–92 – a situation exacerbated by the region-wide financial crisis of 1997–98, which turned the near-stagnation of the Japanese economy into contraction. In the meantime capital from all over the world, and especially from East Asia, continued to flow to the United States, sustaining a long speculative boom on Wall Street and enabling the US economy to expand considerably faster than in the preceding twenty years, in spite of a large and growing trade deficit. As the new millennium approached, not only the US military but also the US economy seemed to be unchallenged and unchallengeable.

In the light of this trajectory, it might seem that the most plausible answer to our questions is that the need to demonstrate the credibility of the US–NATO military apparatus in the Balkan War is more likely to be a sign of an ongoing great leap forward of US global power than of a decline. And since the United States and NATO have demonstrated in the Balkans that their threats to use force until they get their way are not empty or ineffectual, the war can be expected to add new momentum to that great leap forward. It is possible, even likely, that this is the way in which the US and British instigators of the war see the situation. But it is just as possible and likely that the situation is not at all what it appears from the perspective of the 1990s – that is, from the perspective of the rising portion of the U-shaped trajectory of US global power sketched earlier. It is also possible in my view that the Anglo-American misreading of the situation, far from adding new momentum to an imaginary great leap forward in US global power, may precipitate a complete breakdown of what is left of the US world order.

US Global Power in World Historical Perspective

This assessment is based on two studies that have sought clues to an understanding of present tendencies in earlier periods of capitalist history that in key respects resemble the present. The first study, *The Long Twentieth Century*,[1] focuses on the financial expansions that have characterized the closing phases of each and every stage of development of world capitalism, from early modern times to the present. The second study, *Chaos and Governance in the Modern World System*,[2] focuses instead on the analogies and differences between the present hegemonic transition (to a yet unknown destination) with two earlier transitions of world capitalism: from Dutch to British hegemony in the eighteenth century and from British to US hegemony in the late nineteenth and early twentieth centuries. Taken jointly, these two studies provide the following insights into the present dynamic of US global power.

First, to different degrees and in different ways, the U-shaped trajectory that has characterized US global power over the last thirty years has been typical also of the power of all previous leaders of world-scale processes of capital accumulation in the closing phases of their hegemony. In the past, as in the present, the recovery of the fortunes of the declining hegemonic state after an initial crisis was based on a capacity to turn to its own advantage the intense interstate competition for mobile capital that ensued from all major expansions of world trade and production. This capacity was and is based on the fact that the declining hegemonic state still occupies the centre of the world economic system. Although its capacity to compete in the commodity markets is declining, its capacity to act as the central clearing house of the international financial system is greater than that of any other centre, including the centres that are emerging as the most competitive in the commodity markets.

Second, in past hegemonic transitions, though not yet in the present, the resurgence of the power of the declining hegemonic state was the prelude to increasing world disorder and the eventual breakdown of the old hegemonic order. Three tendencies seem to have been particularly important in provoking this increasing disorder. One was the emergence of new military powers which the declining hegemonic state was incapable of keeping under control. Another was the emergence of states and social groups who demanded a share of the system's resources that surpassed what could be accommodated under the existing hegemonic order. And yet another was the tendency of the declining hegemonic state to use its residual (and resurgent) power to transform its hegemony (based on some measure of consent) into an exploitative domination (based primarily on coercion).

Third, in the present transition, in comparison with previous ones, there is virtually no sign of any power emerging that can even remotely challenge militarily the declining hegemonic state. Instead of observing the emergence of new military challengers, we have observed the collapse of the only credible challenger – the USSR. But if there are no signs of the emergence of new powers capable of challenging the United States militarily, there is plenty of evidence that the other two tendencies are stronger than they were in past transitions. Thus, the decline of US global power in the 1970s was due primarily to US difficulties in accommodating Third World demands for a greater share of the world's resources. And the subsequent resurgence of US global power was due primarily to the success of the Reagan global counterrevolution, not just in containing, but in rolling back those demands. The essence of this counterrevolution was precisely the transformation of US hegemony into an increasingly exploitative domination. US hegemony in the 1950s and 1960s rested not just on coercion but also on the consent elicited from Third World countries through the promise of a global New Deal, that is, wealth for all nations through 'development'. In the 1980s and 1990s, in contrast, Third and former Second World countries were asked rather unceremoniously to subordinate 'development' to the imperatives of world financial markets that relentlessly redistributed wealth to the United States and other wealthy countries.

In spite of its apparent success, this transformation can be expected to be as unstable as analogous transformations have been in the past. Two contradictions seem particularly difficult to resolve. One is the continuing shift of the epicentre of global processes of capital accumulation to East Asia. Contrary to widespread opinion, the persistence of the economic crisis in Japan after the crash of 1990–92, and its transformation into a region-wide (East Asian) crisis in 1997–98, do not in themselves support the contention that the shift has been reversed. As my co-authors and I show in *Chaos and Governance in the Modern World System,* in past transitions newly emerging centres of world-scale processes of capital accumulation became the epicentres of turbulence rather than expansion, before they acquired the capabilities to lead the world toward a new order. This was true of London and England in the late eighteenth century and even more of New York and the United States in the 1930s. To say that the Japanese and East Asian financial crises of the 1990s demonstrate that the epicentre of global processes of capital accumulation has not been shifting from the United States to East Asia makes as little sense as saying that the Wall Street crash of 1929–31 and subsequent US economic crisis demonstrated that the epicentre of global processes of capital accumulation had not been shifting from the United Kingdom to the United States.

Moreover, the Japanese and East Asian crises have so far been associated with continuing economic expansion in greater China (that is, in the People's Republic of China, Hong Kong, Taiwan and Singapore). Given the demographic size and historical centrality of China in the region, this continuing expansion is far more significant for the East Asian economic renaissance than the slowdowns and contractions experienced elsewhere in the region. To be sure, in spite of its great advances, China is still a low-income country. Nor is there any guarantee that China's economic expansion will not itself be punctuated by crises. Indeed, the chances are that it will because, as just noted, crises are an integral aspect of emerging economic centres. Nevertheless, the fact that China with its huge population has managed to escape the financial strangulation that brought the Second and Third Worlds to their knees is in itself an achievement of historic proportions. If the inevitable future crises can be managed with a minimum of political intelligence, there is no reason why they cannot be turned into moments of emancipation from US domination, not just for China, but for East Asia and the world at large.

But whether they are or not, the continuing shift of the epicentre of world-scale processes of capital accumulation to East Asia undermines the capacity of the United States to hold the centre of the global economy. Already in the 1990s, the apparently strong performance of the US economy and the underlying speculative boom on Wall Street have been thoroughly dependent on East Asian money and cheap commodities. While the money, in the form of investments and lending, has enabled the US economy to keep expanding in spite of a large and growing trade deficit, the cheap commodities have contributed to keeping inflationary pressures down in spite of economic expansion. It is not clear for how long a situation like this can be sustained, or how it can be remedied by the United States without bringing its own economic expansion to an end. What is clear is that, the longer it lasts, the more the present economic dependence of East Asia on the United States will be turned upside down.

The second contradiction of the resurgence of US power in the 1990s concerns its growing dependence on military means, not just politically, but economically as well. The US military-industrial complex has always been a major (if not the major) source of the US leadership and eventual undisputed supremacy in high-tech production and activities – from the small arms production in the nineteenth century that gave rise to the American system of mass production, to the space programme launched in response to the Soviet Sputnik that gave rise to today's satellite-linked and computerized communication systems. This undisputed supremacy is today the one and only decisive advantage of US industry in global markets. More important, the interpenetration of US high-technology and US military production and activities has provided the US government with a powerful instrument with which to bend the rules of an allegedly 'free' global market in favour of US business. The more competition at home and abroad has intensified, the more essential this not-so-invisible instrument of commercial advantage and self-protection has become.

But while the importance of the US military-industrial complex as an instrument of advancement of US economic interests has increased, its usefulness on strictly military grounds has fallen off dramatically with the collapse of the USSR and the end of the Cold War. As previously noted, the main usefulness of the US military-industrial complex lay in its capacity to reproduce a balance of terror with the USSR at ever more costly and risky levels. But as the US experience in Vietnam showed, and that of the USSR in Afghanistan confirmed, these high-tech military-industrial apparatuses were rather ineffectual instruments with which to police the world on the ground, which required risking one's own citizens' lives in activities that made little sense to the citizens themselves. As a result, as soon as the escalation of the Cold War in the 1980s overshot its mark and brought about the collapse of the USSR, the high-tech, highly capital intensive US military apparatus lost most of its military value. With the loss of its one and only credible military rival, the US military-industrial complex lost its own credibility as a war-making apparatus.

This contradiction between the increasing importance of the US military-industrial complex as the primary source of US economic advantage on the one side, and its decreasing value on strictly military grounds on the other, has never been resolved. The latent, increasingly important economic function of the US military-industrial complex cannot be openly admitted without undermining completely the credibility of its ostensible function. Worse still, such an open admission would also disclose the fact that the US military-industrial complex has probably become the most important instrument for bending and breaking the rules of 'free markets' that the US is so fervently preaching to the world. Therefore a strictly military function for the US military-industrial complex has to be found.

This has been the main purpose of the half a dozen hot 'wars' – in fact, more military exercises than wars proper – fought by the United States since the end of the Cold War. In some instances, especially in the Gulf War and to a lesser extent in the Balkan War, these military exercises were also useful as highly publicized shows of US high-tech merchandise. But the overriding objective has been to find an alternative to the credible military function that the US military-industrial complex had lost with the collapse of the USSR. How successful has this series of wars been in attaining this objective?

It seems to me that they have not been very successful. What they have demonstrated above all is what everybody knew from the start: that the United States has the technological capabilities to bomb out of existence any country it chooses to. Indeed, if it chooses to, it has the technological means it needs to blow up the entire world. But in Somalia, Haiti, Bosnia and Kosovo, they have demonstrated also that the new ostensible function of US wars – the pursuit of carefully selected and highly discriminatory humanitarian objectives – is not worth a single American life. When all is said and done, it would seem that the Vietnam syndrome is alive and well, leaving the US military-industrial complex without a credible function.

In conclusion, the foundations of the present resurgence of US global power are not as solid as they seem. Attempts to use that power to consolidate the exploitative domination of a handful of wealthy countries over the rest of the world are the surest recipe for global disaster. Hopefully, the ruling groups of these wealthy countries will be wise enough to use their still-considerable power to solve rather than aggravate the problems that plague the world. Unfortunately, as Abba Eban once said, 'History teaches us that men and nations behave wisely once they have exhausted all other alternatives.'

Notes

1. Giovanni Arrighi, *The Long Twentieth Century*, Verso, London, 1994.
2. Giovanni Arrighi and Beverly Silver *et al.*, *Chaos and Governance in the Modern World System*, University of Minnesota Press, Minneapolis and London, 1999.

3

RASPUTIN PLAYS AT CHESS: HOW THE WEST BLUNDERED INTO A NEW COLD WAR

Gilbert Achcar

> 'At the end of the twentieth century, after two world wars and a Cold War, we and our allies have a chance to leave our children a Europe that is free, peaceful and stable. But we must – we must – act now to do that.'
>
> Statement by President William J. Clinton
> on Kosovo, 24 March 1999

With the last year of the millennium only half gone, the tensions that have appeared so far in relations between the three pillars of the strategic triad – the United States on the one hand and Russia and China on the other – seem to bode ill for the twenty-first century.

Early in July 1999, not long before these lines were written, two Russian Il-76 giant cargo aircraft loaded with military hardware were prevented from taking off for Priština airport in Kosovo where Russian troops are positioned. To achieve this NATO had asked its new recruit, Hungary, and two countries keen to join the Atlantic Alliance, Bulgaria and Rumania, to deny their airspace to Russian aviation. These moves caused a sharp increase in tension between Moscow and NATO: so brutal a reminder to Russia that its former satellite zones of Central and Eastern Europe have changed sides and are now aligned with the West – even militarily, even at the risk of enraging their great neighbour and being drawn into conflict – understandably exasperated Russians of all political colours.

Moscow seems to have explored the possibility of breaking the interdiction, first securing the cooperation of the Ukraine at a meeting between Boris Yeltsin and the Ukrainian president Leonid Kuchma. (Kuchma is under strong pressure, both from the Russians and internally, to join the union currently being formed between Russia and Belarus. The Serbian parliament also expressed a wish to join during the NATO bombing.) At the same time, Moscow expelled Lieutenant Colonel Peter Hoffman, a member of the American delegation which had negotiated with the Russians in Helsinki on the conditions for a preliminary agreement to end the bombing of Yugoslavia by NATO.[1]

A few days earlier the Russian armed forces had carried out their biggest manoeuvres since the end of the Cold War, involving five military regions and three fleets: a total of fifty thousand troops, more than thirty surface vessels, four submarines (one nuclear-powered) and an air armada carrying ground attack and air-to-air cruise missiles. In the course of these manoeuvres, two Russian Tu-95 turboprop bombers – code named 'Bears' by NATO! – approached within 100 kilometres of the coast of Iceland, a NATO member, in the small hours of 25 June. According to American sources these bombers, carrying long-range missiles, were thus within striking distance of the United States. They were immediately intercepted by Louisiana Air National Guard F-15s based in Keflavik, Iceland, which escorted them on their passage round the island. It was the first incursion into NATO airspace by Russian bombers since 1989.[2]

While all this was taking place, military relations between Russia and China were being strengthened in spectacular fashion, with meetings on the highest political and military levels and in particular the sale of seventy-two Sukhoi Su-30 fighter-bombers, the latest thing in Russian military technology, to Beijing. Negotiations were under way on the production of two hundred and fifty further aircraft under licence in China.[3] Moreover, the Chinese armaments effort has been intensified in recent months, leading one specialist in the military and nuclear potential of the region to comment that 'China and others in Asia will soon have arsenals that will make any outside country think twice about moving forces there in a crisis, or for any political purpose that crosses their interests.'[4]

These signs that Sino-Russian strategic cooperation is being strengthened, along with the increasing tensions on a world scale in general and in the Asia-Pacific region in particular, elicited this anxious comment from a professor of international relations at the Yokosuka National Defence Academy in Japan: 'This climate of tension and mutual suspicion in the Asia-Pacific region has produced something similar to the two opposing sides – the US-led anti-communist camp and the Chinese-Soviet camp – that existed during the early Cold War period.'[5]

Just so: the world seems to be sliding inexorably into a new version of the strategic configuration of the initial phase of the Cold War, with an apparently all-powerful America facing a Soviet-Chinese bloc, arguably in a balance of forces every bit as unequal and unfavourable as the balance of forces between Washington and the Moscow-Beijing axis today. In the definition of this renewed configuration and in the reciprocal 'marking' of the forces at work, the war in Kosovo has played – obviously on a smaller scale and *mutatis mutandis* – a role comparable to that of the Korean war of 1950–53. The most alarmist predictions of my previous essay ('The Strategic Triad: the United States, Russia and China'), finished at the end of 1997 and published in the spring of 1998, have been broadly confirmed.[6]

In under a decade, the last of the present century, the pacifist hopes raised by the end of the Cold War have been cruelly dashed. After the fall of the Berlin wall, the collapse of the system of communist states, the unification of Germany along Federal Republic lines, the collapse of communist rule in the Soviet Union followed by the dissolution of the USSR itself, many were ready to believe, on both sides of the former Iron Curtain, in a prompt exploitation of the 'peace dividend' to devise an East European version of the Marshall Plan aimed at reconstructing the countries ravaged by the dotage of Stalinism. Military budgets were going to be reduced (and they really were, quite substantially, but much less all the same than the gentle dreamers expected). It would be possible at last to give priority to social budgets and the struggle against unemployment: the best antidote to wars, in Keynes's view.

What had been forgotten was that during the current great worldwide neo-liberal offensive, in which the dominant mode of regulation is deregulation – in other words a return to unbridled and pitiless capitalism – Keynes has receded to the utopian skyline of the most radical fraction of social democracy. The capitalism that actually exists today is having increasing difficulty, like its socialist rival in the old days, in giving itself a human face. So that really, between a liberal-pacifist option pivoted on the social and ecological development of the planet and a neo-liberal-militarist option in which 'the icy water of egoistic calculation' (Marx) flows between the dykes provided by the forces maintaining social order and the 'new world order', the choice seemed broadly determined in advance.

The Mutation of NATO

The NATO question perfectly illustrates the nature of the historical options confronting the West's leaders. The death agonies of the USSR faced the members of the Atlantic Alliance with the same type of choice that always confronts a power that has vanquished an enemy power without either annexing or exterminating it: magnanimity or *vae victis* (woe to the vanquished)? A celebrated Cold War historian, Professor John Lewis Gaddis of Yale University, admirably summarized the nature of the basic options confronting the West in an article whose first version was given as a lecture in a seminar at the National Defense University in Washington in October 1997:

> There are three points of reference here – 1815–18, 1918–19 and 1945–48 – and historians are in general accord as to the lessons to be drawn from each. They applaud the settlements of the Napoleonic Wars and of the Second World War because the victorious allies moved as quickly as possible to bring their vanquished adversaries – France in the first case, Germany and Japan in the second – back into the international system as full participants in post-war security structures. Historians tend to criticize (if not condemn) the First World War settlement precisely because it failed to do that for two of the most powerful states in Europe – Germany and Soviet Russia. The resulting instability, they argue, paved the way for yet another conflagration.[7]

The foundering, without direct major conflict, of the Russo-Soviet empire represented a historical turning point at least equivalent in magnitude, in strategic terms, to any of these three references. Even before the final collapse of the Soviet Union and the dissolution of the Warsaw Pact, the July 1990 NATO summit in London stated modestly in an official declaration: 'The North Atlantic Alliance has been the most successful defensive alliance in history.'[8]

This emphatic triumphalism was nevertheless accompanied by benevolent clauses favouring consolidation of the peace: the statement that security does not depend solely on the military dimension but also on the political dimension, which the Alliance vowed to accentuate in future; the statement that the unification of Germany had ended the division of Europe and should be accompanied by a 'European identity in the domain of security'; NATO committed itself to shaking hands with all its Cold War adversaries and emphasized its purely defensive character. 'We have no aggressive intentions and we commit ourselves to the peaceful resolution of all disputes. We will never in any circumstances be the first to use force.'[9] Lastly, the Alliance pronounced itself in favour of the institutionalization of the Conference on Security and Cooperation in Europe (CSCE, which in December 1994 became the OSCE after acquiring the status of an inter-governmental Organization): formed in the 1973–75 period, this grouped the members of NATO and the Warsaw Pact together with the other European states in an entity consecrated to pan-European collective security along lines greatly favoured by Moscow.[10]

What this seemed to mean was that NATO, while maintaining its traditional structures as an elementary precaution ('No one, however, can be certain of the future', the London Declaration cautioned on the heels of its triumphalist proclamation), was giving the impression that it wanted to explore the possibility of strengthening two other elements of collective security: the strictly West European dimension linked to the European Economic Community (EEC) and the extended Euro-Atlantic dimension, with the third dimension – the narrow Euro-Atlantic one represented by NATO – in position to play a pivotal role in the construction of the other two. The question of NATO's 'raison d'être' in the medium or long term was thus being raised, since the statement formulated in London only applied to the short term.

German unification, achieved during the Gulf crisis, followed by the attack on Iraq – which the coalition led by the United States celebrated with enormously triumphant swank, although it had prevailed without the slightest risk of failure – carried out with the assent of a dying Soviet Union and, finally, the crumbling of the last supports of the Stalinist state edifice in Eastern Europe, changed the situation radically. Soothing declarations aimed at 'Moscow the Dotard' (Aragon) were no longer appropriate. Saddam Hussein who, if he did not exist, would certainly have been invented, had conveniently demonstrated that the end of the 'Soviet menace' did not mean that all potential bad guys capable of threatening the West's vital interests, and whom only the American sheriff had enough clout to repress, had been eliminated. It was during the Gulf crisis that George Bush proclaimed the advent of a 'new world order' maintained and controlled by Washington.

The final declaration of the Rome Atlantic summit, in November 1991, was therefore in sharp contrast to the sugary ideas of the previous year: 'The military dimension of our Alliance remains an essential factor; but what is new is that, more than ever, it will serve a broad concept of security.'[11] There was a significant phrase at the heart of the 'new strategic concept' adopted by the summit: a broad concept of security. In other words, NATO had decided to stop restricting itself to the defensive posture laid out in Article 5 of the Washington Treaty (1949), and now envisaged intervening outside its own zone of influence as defined by Article 6. In consequence, the Rome declaration announced that the conventional armed forces of NATO member countries were going to 'be given increased mobility to enable them to react to a wide range of contingencies, and will be organized for flexible build-up, when necessary, for crisis management as well as defence'.[12]

As from 1991, NATO had responded to the existential dilemma posed by the end of the Cold War, tendentiously summarized in the phrase 'out of area or out of business', by extending its jurisdiction. The 'new strategic concept' proposed to set up 'rapid reaction forces' modelled on the US Rapid Deployment Force, formed under the Carter administration with a view to American intervention in the Gulf region following the Iranian Islamic revolution.[13] NATO was proposing to devote itself henceforth to the delights of 'crisis management', dealing with all situations presenting a 'risk' to the security of its members, according to a very extensive definition of possible 'risks':

> Risks to Allied security are less likely to result from calculated aggression against the territory of the Allies, but rather from the adverse consequences of instabilities that may arise from the serious economic, social and political difficulties, including ethnic rivalries and territorial disputes, which are faced by many countries in Central and Eastern Europe . . . The stability and peace of the countries on the southern periphery of Europe are important for the security of the Alliance, as the 1991 Gulf war has shown.[14]

At the very moment when the Yugoslav crisis was taking shape just over the horizon, therefore, NATO was undergoing a radical mutation. A year later, with civil war and 'ethnic cleansing' already ravaging former Yugoslavia, the Alliance's ministerial council was in a position to boast about NATO participation in operations carried out under the aegis of the UN:

> For the first time in its history, the Alliance is taking part in UN peacekeeping and sanctions enforcement operations. The Alliance, together

> with the WEU, is supporting with its ships in the Adriatic the enforcement of the UN economic sanctions against Serbia and Montenegro and of the arms embargo against all republics of former Yugoslavia. UNPROFOR is using elements from the Alliance's NORTHAG command for its operational headquarters. NATO airborne early-warning aircraft – AWACS – are monitoring daily the UN-mandated no-fly zone over Bosnia-Hercegovina.[15]

In the same month of December 1992 George Bush, on the point of yielding the White House to his victorious Democrat rival Bill Clinton, also made him a present of two of his mandate's main achievements: the revival of American military interventionism, after the long paralysis that followed Vietnam, and its European corollary, the metamorphosis of NATO. As a bonus he gave him yet another present, one that would turn out fundamental to the deployment of American hegemony: the humanitarian argument, a media trick enabling the image of the US armed forces to be conflated with that of the Salvation Army.[16] This is what legitimized, in American and world public opinion, the deployment of 28,000 American soldiers in Somalia, a country whose strategic situation on the horn of Africa, facing the Middle Eastern 'crescent of crisis', had made America for many years covet facilities for establishing a military base there.

The Clintonian Dilemma

However, the end of the USSR was too recent for George Bush – who also had the prospect of presidential elections to worry about during the last year of his mandate – to be able to determine all the US's fundamental choices in dealing with the new Russia clambering out of the rubble of Stalinism. This heavy task was to devolve on Bill Clinton. And a man whose best-known campaign slogan had been 'The economy, stupid!', and the bulk of whose political experience had been gained in his home State, Arkansas, was not ideally prepared to confront an international problem of such scale and complexity. In effect this was the third occasion since the beginning of the twentieth century that an American president has assumed the heavy responsibility of making a decisive contribution to the definition of a new international security system (the first two being Wilson and Truman, after each of the two World Wars).

For the first time since Truman, but on an even higher, historically unequalled level, a single world power – America – was sole holder of most of the cards needed to shape the world (or 'shape the international security environment', in the recurrent phrase from recent American strategic documents). Madeleine Albright's taste for grandiloquent phrases ('the indispensable nation' is one of hers) led her to subtitle a recent article in *Foreign Affairs*, adapting from her predecessor as Secretary of State under Truman, the no less emphatic Dean Acheson, the title of his memoirs: 'Present, Again, at the Creation'.[17]

Through elementary prudence, given the scale of the task, Clinton, a relative novice in these matters, began by surrounding himself with representatives of the main tendencies within the Democrat establishment on questions of international relations and strategic options. The result was that the Clinton administration itself became deeply divided on these matters.

The international affairs officials of the new administration very soon found themselves at odds over a key question central to the structure of American 'grand strategy': what attitude to adopt towards Russia, the most formidable of what current Washington vocabulary, also used by the Pentagon and World Bank group, calls 'transitional' countries. (This term can be seen as an indirect tribute to the Trotskyists who used it to describe the same countries when the 'transition' was supposed to be in the other direction.) The quarrel reached dramatic levels of intensity on the issue of NATO enlargement, which was to be the Clinton era's principal achievement in the domain of global policy.

Of course the new team was unanimous in its adherence to the mutation of NATO's function undertaken by the outgoing administration. However, this mutation could be understood either within the limits of an Alliance stuck in the same configuration as at the end of the Cold War, or in the context of a NATO open to ex-members of the Warsaw Pact: former satellites of the Soviet Union and even some former Soviet republics, like the Baltic states and Ukraine. This issue was at the centre of the split in the first Clinton administration; it was arbitrated by an apprentice President who hesitated for several months before deciding in favour of expansion.

The discussion and decision-making process leading to this option is quite well documented thanks to an investigation carried out by Michael Dobbs of the *Washington Post*, later confirmed by another study by a political analyst at George Washington University.[18] It emerges from these essays that two camps were at odds within the Clinton administration in 1993–94 on the future of NATO: on one side what might be called the 'doves' (in traditional American foreign policy terminology), whose main concern was to avoid new tensions in relations between Moscow and the West, the better to ease the integration of the new Russia into the concert of world powers; on the other the 'hawks', whose priority was to annex the countries freed from Moscow's tutelage to the Atlantic Alliance, out of distrust of Russia seen as a potentially hostile major power.

As always in controversies of this kind, each camp paid attention to the main arguments of the other. The 'doves' underlined the need to avoid weakening NATO by dilution, by constructing a sort of outer circle connected with it: the Partnership for Peace, open to all countries emerging from the dissolution of the Stalinist system, Russia included. The second circle would be a military structure that was less restrictive than the Atlantic Alliance proper, but would enable common practices to be established through regular joint manoeuvres, with a view to later adoption of one of two choices: integrating the ex-Moscow satellites if Russia evolved in a dangerous direction, or moving towards full integration of the two structures if Moscow continued with its pro-Western liberal democratic development. The countries of the former Soviet rampart would first be initiated into the Western system by the politico-economic means of recruitment into the European Union (EU), rather than into NATO itself.

The 'hawks' on the other hand preached the immediate expansion of the Alliance to take advantage of the current sclerotic condition of Russia. Since joining the EU would not be possible in the short term, owing to new membership criteria much stricter than those which had admitted Ireland, Greece and Portugal, the integration of countries from the former Soviet rampart into the Western system should proceed rapidly in the politico-military context of the Alliance, before some hostile development in the Russian government made everything much more complicated. To obviate this last development, the (inevitably inflammatory) effects of an expansion of NATO into Moscow's former private domain should be attenuated by a special arrangement between the Alliance and the destitute superpower. This was called the 'parallel track' formula, with the accent on the rapid expansion of NATO ('fast-track').

The main author of this formula was Zbigniew Brzezinski, former National Security Adviser of the last Democrat president, Jimmy Carter, and one of the two most celebrated US foreign policy gurus (the other being his Republican rival Henry Kissinger). The latter also pronounced in favour of

NATO expansion, while criticizing any tendency to soften its military profile that might result from a wish to reassure Russia. Against these two leading tenors, a number of big names from the US defence and foreign policy establishments and think-tanks came out in favour of the doves' option. They included George Kennan, who tried unsuccessfully to sway the President's entourage, as well as David Calleo, Edward Luttwak, Michael Mandelbaum, Robert McNamara, Paul Nitze, Sam Nunn, Richard Pipes, Stansfield Turner and others.

It was Brzezinski, however, who became the main mentor of the new Democrat administration. The natural spokesman for his point of view inside the first Clinton administration was Anthony Lake, appointed to Brzezinski's old job of National Security Adviser. Lake had once worked with Henry Kissinger during the Nixon presidency, but resigned from the Republican administration in 1970 in protest against the bombing of Cambodia. A few years later he returned to work in the State Department under Zbigniew Brzezinski in Jimmy Carter's Democrat administration.

> The Polish-born Brzezinski . . . discussed his ideas in detail with Lake and other administration officials in late 1993 and early 1994. 'From the very beginning, Lake was more sympathetic than other members of the administration,' Brzezinski recalled. 'I did not have to do any proselytizing with Tony.'[19]

As an adviser Lake was an effective advocate of his predecessor's views. In autumn 1993, when the argument inside the administration became heated, he found himself up against heavyweights. As is often the case (contrary to received opinion) the 'dove' camp was strongly represented in Defence circles: in this case it included Defense Secretary Les Aspin and Chairman of the Joint Chiefs of Staff General John Shalikashvili, former Supreme Allied Commander in Europe and also Polish-born. The State Department was split between 'doves' and 'hawks'. The adversaries of rapid NATO expansion tellingly included experts on Russian affairs like Strobe Talbott, one of the prominent 'Friends of Bill'. Secretary of State Warren Christopher (former Deputy Secretary in the Carter administration) was dithering between the two camps.

In the end Lake carried the day against this powerful coalition, as Brzezinski had prevailed over Secretary of State Cyrus Vance in the Carter administration. He persuaded Clinton to come out publicly in favour of

NATO expansion in January 1994, at a meeting in Prague with Central European heads of state. During a speech on this occasion the US president made a remark that caused much comment: 'The question is no longer whether NATO will take on new members, but when and how.'

It should not be thought, however, that this result was due solely to the persuasive talents of Anthony Lake and his guru. A number of other pressures had also contributed: those, for example, brought to bear by the two most admired leaders of ex-Moscow satellites, Lech Walesa and Vaclav Havel; the encouragement of Helmut Kohl, eager to push the frontier of NATO outside German territory, hitherto always in the front line; and also the pressure of vulgar electoral calculation, basic to a president whose eye is always on the poll figures.

> 'The NATO expansion issue has galvanized the ethnic groups into action,' noted the Polish-born Zbigniew Brzezinski, President Jimmy Carter's national security adviser, and a strong supporter of enlargement. 'If Clinton is going to win the next election, he will have to win in the old industrial belt, which begins in Connecticut and ends in Illinois, where the ethnic groups are very strong.'
>
> In late 1993, when the administration appeared to be dragging its feet on NATO expansion, Polish lobbying groups flooded the White House with telegrams and telephone calls. The Polish-American Congress put out a 'legislative alert' to its 34 divisions around the country to prevent a 'new Yalta', political shorthand for the 'betrayal' of Poland by the Western allies that occurred after the end of World War II. A few weeks later, President Clinton announced in Prague that NATO expansion was no longer 'a question of whether . . . but when and how.'[20]

Clinton however was still somewhat unsure of himself, and had also just given the go-ahead for the creation in January 1994 of the 'Partnership for Peace' (PfP) being promoted by the Pentagon. This institution was in no way contradictory with the 'parallel track' system proposed by Brzezinski. But the Prague speech caused Russia to cold-shoulder the PfP for several months, before reluctantly joining the following year. A few weeks after this speech, which marked a turning point in Clinton's options, Defense Secretary Les Aspin resigned, and was succeeded by his Deputy William Perry. Perry shared his predecessor's opinions, and his appointment suggested that Clinton wanted to give the impression that he had not yet made a final commitment.

The second phase of the struggle between the 'doves' and 'hawks', over consolidation of the presidential option, lasted through 1994. There followed a third phase during the launch of the concrete process of NATO enlargement, the 'when and how' phase, lasting until the end of the president's first mandate. Strobe Talbott, appointed Deputy Secretary of State in February 1994, made a U-turn on the enlargement question to keep station with his friend the President, who sidled a step closer to the 'hawks' during a trip to Warsaw in July 1994.[21] Talbott took the initiative of recalling Richard Holbrooke from his post as Ambassador to Germany and appointing him Assistant Secretary of State for European Affairs, where he played a decisive role in preparing for the active phase of NATO enlargement. He won over to the cause another 'Friend of Bill', General Wesley Clark, whom he took as military adviser on his missions to former Yugoslavia in the run-up to the Dayton accords in 1995.

When setting up his second administration, Clinton replaced William Perry with the hawkish Republican William Cohen. He tried to appoint Anthony Lake to the supremely sensitive job of Director of the CIA, but the nomination was turned down by the Senate. To replace him as National Security Adviser, he had designated Lake's deputy for the whole of the first mandate, Samuel Berger (yet another 'Friend of Bill', responsible for introducing both Lake and Madeleine Albright into the administration).[22] A person of somewhat limited outlook, of whom Henry Kissinger once remarked: 'You can't blame a trade lawyer for not being a global strategist',[23] Berger was incapable of playing his predecessor's role of chief strategist (by proxy) to the administration.

This role therefore devolved, in the second Clinton administration, on Madeleine Albright, the replacement of another uninspired character, ex-Secretary of State Warren Christopher. Madeleine Albright had obtained her doctorate at Columbia University with Zbigniew Brzezinski as a thesis adviser, and had worked for him in the Carter administration from 1978 onward. She took over from Lake as representative of her teacher and patron's views. And with the nomination of Wesley Clark to the post of Supreme Allied Commander in Europe – commander-in-chief of NATO's armed forces, in other words – the triumph of what might be called the 'Brzezinski doctrine' was complete.

The new administration was able to move forward on 'parallel track': at the end of May 1997 the NATO–Russia Founding Act was signed in Paris. A few weeks later in July, the Madrid NATO summit officially admitted

Poland, Hungary and the Czech Republic into NATO. All that remained was to have this decision ratified by the member states before sanctioning these admissions during the fiftieth anniversary of the Atlantic Alliance, in April 1999.

Wisdom and Extravaganza in International Policy

Throughout the first Clinton mandate, then, a struggle of crucial importance to the future of humanity was being waged in the corridors of power in Washington (and attracting a great deal less media attention than the president's erotic cavortings in the Oval Office with a White House intern).

Two basic options were vying for control over a decisive issue: the configuration of world security. They required radically different preparations, to be made on the eve of the twenty-first century, and would broadly determine whether the world 'we leave our children' would be 'free, peaceful, and stable' or dangerous, unstable and worrying. The overall concepts behind these two options are explained in two books by the two strategists who confronted each other directly during the first years of the Clinton presidency: Brzezinski, the guru of the Clinton administration, and former Defense Secretary William Perry.

The book describing the 'new security strategy' proposed for the US by Perry was written in collaboration with his faithful friend and assistant Ashton Carter, Assistant Secretary of Defense in the first Clinton mandate. The 'new strategy' is called 'preventive defense'.[24] According to its authors, this concept is 'fundamentally different from deterrence: it is a broad politico-military strategy, and therefore it draws on all the instruments of foreign policy: political, economic and military'.[25] During the Cold War, containment and deterrence inevitably counted for more than prevention in American strategy. In the post-Cold War period it seemed appropriate to bring prevention to the fore once again: in other words, first and foremost, to prevent a new A-level threat from appearing and menacing the very survival of the US (along with the rest of humanity, one might add).[26] To this end, persuasion is more effective than deterrence or coercion; the strategy of preventive defence aims at 'influencing the rest of the world, not compelling it'.[27]

The book's first chapter, on Russia and NATO, has a title – 'Pursuing Marshall's Vision' – that speaks volumes on the two authors' orientation: George Marshall, Secretary of State from 1947 to 1949 after being the US

Army's Chief of Staff during the Second World War, had given his name to the famous Marshall Plan, an aid programme for European reconstruction applied from 1947. In this connection, the authors express regret that the aid allocated for the reconstruction and democratization of Russia should have been so limited, 'certainly nothing close to the Marshall Plan, which sought to prevent a replay after World War II of the tragic collapse of democratic Weimar Germany'.[28] In similar vein, they criticize the limited vision of European governments apparently incapable of the generosity needed for the admission of post-Stalinist states from Eastern and Central Europe into the EU (which would have been an alternative to NATO enlargement).

In pages as explicit as possible given their duty of reserve,[29] Carter and Perry show how strongly they disapprove of enlargement, judging it precipitate and ill-considered at the very least. They suggest a policy pivoted on keeping NATO going and approve the broadening of its scope suggested in 1991, but want it to be a NATO working in close collaboration with Russia and its ex-satellites within a 'reinvented' Partnership for Peace. They regard it as fundamental to do everything possible, politically as well as financially (under the Nunn-Lugar Cooperative Threat Reduction Program), to hasten the reduction of strategic nuclear weapons in both the former Cold War superpowers, thus reducing the risks inherent in having so many nuclear bombs in a country as chaotic as 1990s Russia. In particular, they think it most regrettable that the course of Russo-American relations since the decision to enlarge NATO should have had the effect of making the Russian Duma refuse to ratify the START II accord, thus blocking all progress on START III.

Carter and Perry emphasize the importance of good relations with Russia and China in limiting the risk of worldwide proliferation of weapons of mass destruction. On Beijing, the authors shrewdly judged the Sino-American rapprochement reported while they were writing their book 'highly contingent and fragile'.[30] They favour an open, coherent policy of partnership with China and repudiate any leaning towards containment, while clearly designating the Japan–US alliance as the linchpin of security in the Asia-Pacific region, like the Atlantic Alliance in Europe. As a consequence of this, the policy of 'engagement' with Beijing should be conducted jointly by Washington and Tokyo, just as Moscow policy should be conducted jointly by Washington and its European allies.

They seem to have understood with unusual clarity that any attempt to 'divide and rule' in an acutely delicate world situation could have unintended side-effects altogether harmful to world security and stability. Their book is distinguished by its sobriety and the great perspicacity of its authors, experts by training and experience in the psychological background of the political behaviour of the Moscow and Beijing governments. It was obviously written partly to challenge Brzezinski's ideas, but also and primarily because they refused to wash their hands of the matter and were still trying to steer the Clinton administration – and American politics in general – in another direction, before it was too late.

They therefore proposed to stop for the time being at the three countries newly admitted to NATO, and not to consider any further admissions for a long period. During their time at the Department of Defense, even after losing the enlargement battle, Carter and Perry put themselves out to restore Russo-American relations, notably from the low point they reached after the air strikes in Bosnia in 1995. Insisting that Russian susceptibilities should be considered, and that everything possible should be done to have Russia treated as a fully-fledged partner, Perry played a determining role in preventing Moscow from being left out of the solution to the Bosnian problem in the form of the Dayton accords.

> We believed that the reason to include Russia in the Bosnian peace force was bigger than the Bosnian operation and had to do with Russia itself . . . few others in the U.S. government had much patience for seeking an honorable role for the Russians. To most U.S. and NATO officials caught up in the Bosnia drama, Russia seemed like an unnecessary complication. We believed that they were not seeing the forest for the trees; they failed to recognize that Russia was an indispensable part of the larger European security order of which the Bosnian peace was supposed to be a part.[31]

Unlike those who cannot see the Russian wood for the trees of former Yugoslavia, Perry and Carter were well aware that what was really at stake was the whole of European and world security.[32] After once more evoking the historical precedent of Weimar Germany, the authors came up with the following warning: 'The historical parallels give us, this time, the necessary foresight *if we are wise enough to heed it.*'[33] This last clause seems to merit underlining.

As the ideas advanced by Perry and Carter were sober and pragmatic, so Zbigniew Brzezinski's were immoderate or even extravagant: his tendency to excess was as marked as his undeniable brio. The Clinton administration's guru hinted broadly at the nature of his thought by choosing for his book the title: *The Grand Chessboard*.[34] Seized with the sort of megalomania that quite often overtakes adepts in grand geopolitical designs, the author envisages the world – or more precisely Eurasia – as a big chessboard on which he explains how to 'outplay' the opposition, confident of his own mastery of the game and what he believes to be his genius.[35] The very form of this vision of the world is inherently detrimental to the moderate objective of a truly stable international system of collective security, like that proposed by the first two authors. From the start of play, Brzezinski's game plan (*Game Plan*, incidentally, was the title of one of his earlier books, retailing substantially similar views) is no more nor less than to preserve 'America's capacity to exercise global primacy' and build 'a stable continental equilibrium, with the United States as the political arbiter'.[36]

'For America, the chief geopolitical prize is Eurasia',[37] writes Brzezinski, who places his own thought as a sort of updated extension of the fairly crazed views propagated by Harold Mackinder and Karl Haushofer, the latter an influence on Adolf Hitler.[38] Hardly bothering to apologize for resorting to the terminology of another era, Brzezinski goes on to list 'the three grand imperatives of imperial geostrategy' as: 'to prevent collusion and maintain security dependence among the vassals, to keep tributaries pliant and protected, and to keep the barbarians from coming together'.[39] The whole spirit of the book – and the essence of a geopolitical programme – summarized in a sentence!

The immediate task for the US, in our chess-player's opinion, is to '*consolidate and perpetuate the prevailing geopolitical pluralism on the map of Eurasia*'. To this end it must resort to '*maneuver and manipulation in order to prevent the emergence of a hostile coalition that could eventually seek to challenge America's primacy*'.[40] Manoeuvre and manipulation may be recurrent in chess vocabulary but are seldom cited so openly, or with such Machiavellian relish, in politics. The scenarios seen as most dangerous, to be averted at all costs in this titanic programme to divide and rule, are 'a grand coalition of China, Russia, and perhaps Iran', 'a Sino-Japanese axis' and 'either a German–Russian collusion or a Franco-Russian entente'.[41]

The vassals to be kept dependent are of course the European and Japanese allies. Europe is 'America's essential geopolitical bridgehead on the Eurasian continent'; so that 'with the allied European nations still highly dependent on U.S. security protection, any expansion in the scope of Europe becomes automatically an expansion in the scope of direct U.S. influence as well'.[42] The Franco-German axis is given special status, although the author gives France a clip over the ear in passing. Britain is dismissed as 'increasingly irrelevant': 'a very loyal ally, a vital military base . . . its policies do not call for sustained attention'.[43] Japan, lastly, is a 'world-class power being simultaneously a protectorate'.[44] It should not be pressed to assume a larger geopolitical and security role, but confined to the status of 'a much more powerful and globally influential equivalent of Canada'.[45]

The barbarians who have to be prevented from coming together are of course Russia and China. Brzezinski's scheme is spectacularly simplistic: he expects to get away with maintaining the alliance with Beijing against Moscow, inaugurated by Nixon and Kissinger at the height of the hostility between the two communist capitals and later continued by Brzezinski himself as Jimmy Carter's adviser. His hostility to Russia, evidently far deeper than his aversion to communism, has a visceral quality that has often been linked to the fact of his Polish ancestry; whatever the value of this explanation, the fact is plain enough. Brzezinski is brutally frank on the 'dilemma' underlying the restriction of economic aid to Russia: 'To what extent should Russia be helped economically – which inevitably strengthens Russia politically and militarily . . .?'[46]

What Russia needs is to be put down and made to stop thinking of itself as a superpower. In any case, it seems that unlike the US 'an imperial Russia could not be a democratic Russia'.[47] The ideal solution would be a 'loosely confederated Russia – composed of a European Russia, a Siberian Republic, and a Far Eastern Republic'![48] Revealing that 'parallel track' had been more an argument against opponents of NATO enlargement than a basic principle, Brzezinski suggests roundly that the US 'either negotiate effectively some accommodation with Russia, if it is willing to compromise, or act assertively'![49] Russian vetos should be ignored and NATO thrown open to any 'qualified' European candidate, including the ex-Soviet Baltic republics and the Ukraine. 'If a choice has to be made between a larger Euro-Atlantic system and a better relationship with Russia, the former has to rank incomparably higher to America.'[50]

Brzezinski cannot be accused of carrying subtlety to extremes. Wishing to point out that post-Soviet Russia has not broken completely with its past, notably in the continuation in power of some of the former elite, he comes straight out with an analogy worthy of Ernst Nolte: 'as if post-Nazi Germany were governed by former middle-level Nazi "Gauleiters" spouting democratic slogans, with a Hitler mausoleum still standing in the center of Berlin'.[51]

Having also become an advocate for American oil companies wishing to establish themselves in the former Soviet republics of the Caucasus and Central Asia, Brzezinski regards American predominance in this region, which he calls the 'Eurasian Balkans', as a prime objective. With this in mind, apart from alliances with China and Turkey, our champion of democracy takes a positive view both of the strengthening of relations between Pakistan and Afghanistan (with the Taliban acting as cement) and of the Islamic resurgence in Saudi Arabia as well as Iran (with which he favours an alliance).[52]

China is wooed with a seduction declaration so coarsely woven that anyone expecting the Chinese to be taken in by it must have a poor opinion of them indeed. In passing, Brzezinski warns them off any temptation to form a coalition with Moscow by raising the spectre of economic reprisals: '. . . it would be a coalition of the poor, who would then be likely to remain collectively poor for quite some time'.[53] And after the stick, the carrot: 'A regionally preeminent China should become America's Far Eastern anchor . . . helping thereby to foster a Eurasian balance of power, with Greater China in Eurasia's East matching in that respect the role of an enlarging Europe in Eurasia's West'.[54] China, in a word, is being invited to abandon its barbarian status and join the vassals' camp (where it would count more than Japan, Brzezinski promises) to help complete the encirclement of the other barbarian power.

It is truly astonishing, as well as disquieting to put it mildly, that a character with such extravagant views as president Carter's ex-adviser could ever be the leading policy mentor of the most powerful government on earth. In the guru category, Zbigniew Brzezinski comes across more like a Rasputin than a Brahmin sage with real wisdom. The awful thing is that he has found his Nicholas and Alexandra, in the persons of Bill Clinton and Madeleine Albright.

NATO Enlargement

Russia's uncertain future – something that not only is but ought to be genuinely worrying – is the fundamental unknown in the divergent political equations between which the US president has to navigate. It is clear however that each equation rests on a basic postulate, like the anthropological postulates that subtend theories of international relations. For example, the 'doves' think that Russia, like human nature in Catholic and Kantian thought, is perfectible, and accuse the 'hawks' of 'self-fulfilling prophecy' in adopting an attitude calculated to elicit a hostile response from Russia; while the 'hawks' – self-proclaimed 'realists' – display a measure of Russophobic pessimism and reproach their opponents for wishful thinking.[55]

Apart from all the factors mentioned so far, the evolution of the situation in Russia played a determining role in inflecting the options finally chosen by Bill Clinton. For example, his first pro-enlargement public speech, in January 1994, was undoubtedly heavily influenced by Boris Yeltsin's confrontation with the Russian parliament in the autumn of 1993, and the subsequent strong showing by nationalist and communist forces in the December parliamentary elections that followed the president's dissolution of the chamber. The subsequent massive presence in the Russian legislature of nationalists and people nostalgic for the USSR, and the role of these forces in putting off the ratification of the START II accord, certainly counted for a great deal in Clinton's eventual decision in favour of the 'hawks'. And although Clinton assented in public to the Russian intervention in Chechnya at the end of 1994, the brutal campaign waged there by the Russian armed forces can only have confirmed him in the option.

Brzezinski, in one of the quotations given above, mentioned only one aspect of the dilemma over economic aid to Russia. The two real alternatives, as seen from Washington, are these: either non-assistance to Russia would create a risk of dangerous chaos or the rise of 'revanchism'; or the rebuilding of Russian economic power would revive Moscow's regional hegemony and the reappearance of bipolarity.[56] Hovering between these two equally undesirable options, Washington is giving Moscow somewhat parsimonious help, just enough to avoid a total collapse of the Russian economy (with its inevitable ripple effect through the world economy). The result is a vicious circle sustained by the self-fulfilling prophecy that presents Russia as a bottomless sink.

Fundamentally, then, Washington's Russia policy, although still hesitant, is based on distrust of Moscow. Under the guise of political assistance with the transition in Russia the Clinton administration has chosen to bet everything on Boris Yeltsin. This is a notably controversial choice that also makes it crystal clear that the reform being pursued has more to do with the economic transformation of the country on brutal neo-liberal lines than with consolidating democracy. Where this last is concerned, there is little doubt that 'Tsar Boris' is a poor bet. Nevertheless the economic aid supplied by the IMF is doled out according to a political timetable under US government control, rather than in support of an economic programme.

Thus in March 1996, during the run-up to the Russian presidential elections, the Clinton administration arranged for Russia to be granted an international loan of $10 billion. The loan played a decisive part in the re-election of Boris Yeltsin by enabling his government to pay arrears of salaries and pensions. So the shots in the arm parsimoniously granted to Moscow are used politically, either to prop the president in place or to reward him for services rendered. Yeltsin adapts well to this kind of horse-trading at which he is highly skilled, regularly profiting from his political concessions to Washington. But however well they may serve his personal interests, these practices are perceived by domestic critics and adversaries as undignified and damaging to the country's interests. They help to explain the enormous personal unpopularity that makes Yeltsin ever more dependent on American support.

A few months after being re-elected, Yeltsin paid his dues by turning up in Paris for the ceremonial signing of the NATO–Russia Founding Act on 27 May 1997. In the eyes of a large part of the American establishment as well as the European allies, this pact was an indispensable prelude to the formal decision to enlarge NATO to the East. Once that decision had been adopted, the battle over ratification began. Under most democratic constitutions, international treaties and declarations of war have to be ratified by an elected legislative body. The practice is supposed to guarantee democratic control over the decisions of the executive in those areas that affect the destiny of the population concerned to the highest extent. This is largely a mystification: in reality, decisions taken by the handful of people controlling the executive very often commit their state de facto by creating situations that can only be reversed with great difficulty.

When, for example, the American Congress – one of the world's most powerful parliaments – undertook at a time of post-Vietnam trauma to impose constitutional rule on the executive in this area, by adopting the War Powers Act in 1973, the effect was to authorize the administration to decide on its own, constitutionally, to conduct war operations for a period of sixty days, extendable by another thirty. In these times of lightning wars, in which the Pentagon expects to crush the enemy with massive air strikes within a few weeks, these arrangements in practice authorize the executive to undertake the vast majority of foreseeable wars – everything short of a clash with a great power – and bring them to a conclusion without the need for Congressional blessing. The Kosovo war is a perfect case in point:[57] it certainly exceeded the allotted 60 days, but it was hardly likely that Congress would decide to cut it short when it was obviously close to ending anyway. The European allies for their part resorted to the extraordinary hypocrisy of referring systematically to an indubitable war as an 'intervention' or 'air strikes', so that war would not have to be declared in a constitutional manner. The logic was worthy of Lewis Carroll, but the outcome for many was no joke at all.

Nor does the conclusion of international agreements on military alliances, which commit states even more deeply and durably than a war, escape the arbitrary unilateral decision-making power of executive government. The best illustration here is the enlargement of NATO, a measure whose importance to the future security of Europe and the world in general is incalculable. Before this decision was adopted at the Madrid NATO summit in July 1997, it had not been debated publicly by the legislature of a single one of the countries represented there. The only discussion of any note before the summit was conducted within the US foreign policy and defence establishments, and in a few publications. It goes without saying that when the Clinton administration made up its mind on this subject and announced the decision publicly, back in 1994, the public debate had been even more limited.

With greater or lesser enthusiasm depending on the individual case, the heads of state and government of the European 'vassals' assembled in Madrid rubber-stamped the decision of their American suzerain. And once this had been proclaimed with great pomp by the sixteen, the very terms of the debate were altered at a stroke. It was no longer a matter of deciding whether to enlarge NATO or not, but of deciding whether to disown the sixteen governments which had just voted for the enlargement and officially invited Poland, Hungary and the Czech Republic to make their arrangements for joining the Alliance: a somewhat different ballgame! Under these conditions ratification seems to be what its name suggests: the granting of approval *post factum*, in practice a democratic expedient.

> When the U.S. Senate ratified the addition of Poland, Hungary, and the Czech Republic to NATO, it recognized that to do otherwise would have been a major setback to U.S. credibility and to the U.S. position in Europe. Even the most pessimistic estimates of the risks and costs of expansion portrayed in the vigorous Senate debate preceding enlargement could not justify such a setback.[58]

The debate in the US Senate preceding enlargement had indeed been vigorous, with the administration forced to resort to all sorts of shifts to secure the required two-thirds majority. As the debate raged in the establishment and surfaced in the broadsheet press, itself divided on the issue, the administration brought in all the lobbies with an interest in enlargement. Apart from the military and the State Department, now run by a Madeleine Albright making much of her Czech descent, the leading role was played by the 'ethnic' lobbies of Americans of Central and Eastern European extraction and, of course, the defence industries, well placed to get the lion's share of the military reconversion market in the former Moscow satellites resulting from the principle of 'interoperability' needed for NATO to work properly.[59]

Under the neo-liberal creed that prevails today, with a balanced budget having become a sacred principle, the US Senate paradoxically showed a lot more interest in the costs of this operation than did the Europe of monetary union. With the complicity of the Atlantic Alliance bureaucracy, therefore, the administration strove to reduce the estimated cost of enlargement, in a way that strayed well into the zone of the grotesque. Thus in 1996, after the Congressional Budget Office had estimated the cost of integrating the four Visegrad countries (the three listed above, plus Slovakia) to be, depending on the options chosen, between \$61 billion and \$125 billion over fifteen years, the Department of Defense cut the estimates to a maximum of \$35 billion over thirteen years, with the share of this – still considerable – sum falling to the US not to exceed \$2 billion over ten years! The NATO Military Committee then came to the rescue, estimating in autumn 1997 that the additional cost of enlargement to the organization's budget (of which Washington is responsible for a quarter) should not exceed \$1.5 billion over ten years, a ridiculously low estimate which the Department of Defense quickly approved despite the enormous unexplained drop from its own earlier figures![60]

Ratification was finally voted, on the night of 30 April 1998, by a comfortable majority (80 votes out of the 100 in the Senate), after four days of lively argument. The opponents of enlargement, fighting a disillusioned rearguard action, were broadly defeated, and the Brzezinski doctrine carried the Senate after establishing itself in the administration.[61] The ratification was accompanied by an extremely long (over 7,000 words) resolution containing very detailed and restrictive instructions on the immediate future of NATO and its new strategic doctrine. This document predetermined in effect what the Alliance's fiftieth anniversary summit was going to decide a year later in Washington, and generally corroborated the 'hawkish' line.

The salient points of this important resolution are the following: the main justification put forward for NATO enlargement is 'the potential for the re-emergence of a hegemonic power confronting Europe' and being tempted to invade Poland, Hungary or the Czech Republic; NATO decisions and actions are independent of all other inter-governmental bodies (the UN, the OSCE, the Euro-Atlantic Partnership, etc.); Russia has no right of veto over Alliance decisions, not even in the NATO–Russia Permanent Joint Council set up under the Founding Act; the Alliance may undertake operations outside its own territory, if there is consensus among its members that a threat exists to their interests; US 'leadership' of NATO is reaffirmed, as is the presence of US officers in the main command posts; military and financial 'burden sharing' is to be spread more 'equitably', with enlargement not increasing the US share of the organization's budget; this US share should even diminish, and in any case never exceed the 1998 level; the US president is to consult the Senate in future before any new admissions to NATO.[62]

One might have expected the ratification of enlargement to generate this much debate, perhaps even more, in the parliaments of the European members of the Alliance, even more directly concerned than the United States in a decision whose main import is to determine the security future of Europe. It didn't. Indeed the contrast between the intensity of debate in the US (albeit restricted to high establishment circles) and the way ratification was passed, often with furtive haste, by the European legislatures, was quite striking. Only tiny minorities opposed this extremely weighty decision in Europe: outside a few eccentric right-wing parties like the Italian Lombard League, speaking in the name of an independent 'Padania', the main opposition came from the communists including the French Communist Party, the German PDS and the Italian PRC, along with Green groups some of which, like the parliamentary fraction of the German Greens, were divided on the issue.[63]

Collision Course

The American Senate's resolution, written in a spirit reminiscent of the Cold War, could not fail to exacerbate the irritation felt on the Russian side, by Boris Yeltsin among many others. This annoyance peaked in June 1998 when the IMF, at the risk of aggravating the worldwide effects of the Asian economic crisis, granted Russia – itself hard hit by the crisis – a support package of only $22.6 billion. This sum should be set against the $57 billion granted to South Korea, the $50 billion to Mexico, and the $40 billion each to Indonesia and Brazil. It is clear that the cause of this parsimony involves more than distrust of the chaotic and gangster-ridden state of the Russian economy, for not all the other countries named are paragons of social and economic 'good governance'.

Following the financial crisis in the summer of 1998, the aid obtained by Yeltsin having hardly sufficed to keep the Russian economy afloat let alone relaunch the president politically, he found himself compelled by opposition pressure to appoint Yevgeni Primakov to the post of prime minister, after vainly trying to reappoint Viktor Chernomyrdin. This designation of an old KGB hand who had been the last vice-Foreign Minister of the USSR, a man seen as symbolizing a time when Russian diplomacy still aspired to compete with the US on a global scale, was not well received in Washington. Relations between the two capitals became so strained that a period of dangerous escalation set in.[64]

Pressure from the 'hawks' increased noticeably. Following their exactions in the Drenica area in February 1998, the Serbian forces in Kosovo were conducting brutal reprisals against attacks mounted by the Kosovo Liberation Army (KLA). Bill Clinton in Washington, floundering neck-deep in the Monica Lewinsky scandal, was certainly more concerned with the manoeuvres of special prosecutor Kenneth Starr than those of Slobodan Milošević.[65] Zbigniew Brzezinski and Madeleine Albright, supported by General Wesley Clark, started campaigning for air strikes against the Serbian forces. They found an ally in Bob Dole, Clinton's Republican rival in the 1996 elections, whose help the President sought in the impeachment struggle so as to have his own hands free to act against Milošević. However, Samuel Berger and the Pentagon were dragging their feet. Given the scale of what was at stake, and Russia's opposition, unilateral action by the United States was excluded: NATO had to be involved.

Early in the summer the KLA launched a large-scale offensive, answered by a Serb counter-offensive accompanied by massacres and the movement of Albanian populations. The worsening situation incited Washington to threaten military intervention directly, by authorizing NATO headquarters to make operational plans for it. At this point Alexander Vershbow, the US ambassador to NATO who had been involved in American diplomatic action in Bosnia, sent a confidential dispatch to Washington entitled 'Kosovo: Time for Another Endgame Strategy'.

> The cable spelled out a plan to impose a political settlement in Kosovo with the cooperation of the Russians, longtime allies of the Serbs. Moscow and Washington would then go together to the Security Council. 'Kosovo endgame initiative could become a model of NATO-Russian cooperation,' Vershbow wrote. 'No kidding.'
>
> The proposed deal called for creation of an international protectorate in Kosovo. The settlement would be policed by an international military presence, or ground force. If a peace settlement was negotiated in advance, as many as 30,000 troops might be required to enforce it.[66]

Vershbow's idea was guaranteed a cold reception from the 'hawks', and his dispatch was ignored. The day it reached Washington, 7 August 1998, there occurred the bomb attacks on the US embassies in Kenya and Tanzania, causing great damage and loss of life. It was an opportunity to embrace the opposite line, promoted by Brzezinski: American military action free from all consultation with the Russians (and therefore with the UN Security Council in which Moscow wields a veto). On 21 August American cruise missiles were launched against targets in Sudan and Afghanistan, a strictly unilateral act unconnected with international legality, therefore a pure and simple act of aggression against two countries not themselves guilty of any aggression.

These missile attacks exasperated Moscow, at the same time as highlighting the lack of seriousness with which its views were treated in Washington. However, they did not prevent Russia from voting, a month later, in favour of a Security Council resolution requiring the withdrawal of Serbian forces from Kosovo and negotiations between Serbs and Albanians. Backed by this international unanimity, Richard Holbrooke in October managed to get Milošević to agree to the withdrawal of 10,000 members of the Serb security forces from Kosovo and the deployment of 2,000 members of a Kosovo Verification Mission (KVM) provided by the OSCE. (This agreement was rejected by the KLA, however.)

In December the US, with its 'very loyal' vassal Britain, launched 'Operation Desert Fox': four days of air strikes and cruise missile attacks on Iraq, inaugurating an ongoing practice of military action without UN endorsement, like the missile strikes in August, although Iraq is supposed to be the direct responsibility of the Security Council.[67] This body's three other permanent members, which include the recalcitrant 'vassal' France, were blithely ignored.

What followed in Yugoslavia is well known: although much reduced in intensity, clashes between the KLA and Serb forces continued in Kosovo, culminating in the 'Račak massacre' of January 1999. The Rambouillet negotiations came up short against Belgrade's rejection, with Russian backing, of the US diktat aimed at deploying a military force in Kosovo entirely controlled by NATO.[68] Perhaps the most appropriate commentator on the Rambouillet process is Henry Kissinger, who can hardly be suspected of anti-American attitudes:

> Several fateful decisions were taken in those now seemingly far-off days in February, when other options were still open. The first was the demand that 30,000 NATO troops enter Yugoslavia, a country with which NATO was not at war . . . The second was to use the foreseeable Serb refusal as justification for starting the bombing. Rambouillet was not a negotiation – as is often claimed – but an ultimatum. This marked an astounding departure for an administration that had entered office proclaiming its devotion to the U.N. Charter and multilateral procedures.[69]

At the same time, the US entertained second thoughts on one of the most important achievements in slowing down the arms race, a measure dating back to the Nixon-Brezhnev period of 'détente': the anti-ballistic missile (ABM) treaty of 1972. This treaty, setting a limit to the coverage of each nuclear superpower's territory by anti-missile defence systems, had been put in doubt once before by Ronald Reagan's 'Strategic Defense Initiative' (SDI), perhaps better known by its nickname 'Star Wars'. The SDI was eventually abandoned with the ending of the Cold War. Now, following a report submitted to Congress in July 1998, the US embarked on a process leading towards the installation of a National Missile Defense (NMD) network, on the not very convincing pretext that it needed protection against possible attack by 'rogue states': Iraq, Iran and North Korea![70]

In February 1999 the Defense Secretary, William Cohen, declared that to accommodate the new system the US was going to require the ABM treaty to be amended; failing that, the US would abrogate it unilaterally! In March, the Senate made is own contribution by adopting a National Missile Defense Act (S257).[71] One does not have to be a Russian expert to imagine that such declarations and measures are widely perceived, in Moscow, as unquestionable signs of US arrogance and hegemonic designs on Russia. All the more so as the Clinton administration had announced on 1 February its decision to add an extra $112 billion to projected military expenditure under the six-year Future Years Defense Plan 2000–05, bringing the total to nearly $2,000 billion.[72]

In parallel with this general application of the Brzezinski doctrine to Russia, the Chinese wing of the same doctrine, applied by the Clinton administration with equal zeal, was foundering in lamentable fiasco. The American government's seductive approaches to the Asian giant were so lumbering and ill-conceived that they aroused adverse reactions from the other regional powers. The 'constructive strategic partnership' between Washington and Beijing, proclaimed during the visit by Chinese President Jiang Zemin to the US in October 1997 and enthusiastically confirmed by Clinton on his visit to China in June 1998, caused irritation and anxiety among China's regional rivals: India, whose decision to start nuclear tests in May 1998 was made against this background; Taiwan of course; and Japan at which, despite its very considerable efforts, Washington had pointed the finger as a major causative factor in the Asian crisis, while Beijing got a pat on the back for refusing to devalue the yuan at the height of the same crisis.[73]

It was not long, however, before the Sino-American honeymoon soured in its turn. The contemptuous way Washington had brushed the UN aside, first in August and then in December, was very poorly regarded in Beijing, whose attachment to that essential attribute of its power, its veto in the Security Council, is even stronger than Russia's. Apart from this factor, whose importance to Beijing cannot be too strongly emphasized, there was the unbearable crazed Cold War-style delirium unleashed in the US by the Chinese nuclear 'espionage' affair. But the factor that once again aroused the greatest anger in Beijing was that old bone of contention between the two countries, Taiwan.

The American charm offensive had not stopped China from continuing to work on the acquisition of satellite-guided short- and medium-range ballistic missiles, as well as cruise missiles, with technological help from Russia. The Chinese armaments effort is described in a Pentagon report on security in the Taiwan Strait requested by Congress in the context of the appropriations budget for the 1999 fiscal year. This report, destined to be published and therefore written with evident care for diplomatic niceties, is nevertheless essentially intolerable to China which is jealous of its sovereignty and its right to acquire the military means appropriate to a great power, as well as of Taiwan's status as part of Chinese territory, recognized in principle even by the US.

The report is especially emphatic on Sino-Russian cooperation on sophisticated weapons, bringing into relief Beijing's other 'partnership' – and one that more truly merits the epithet 'strategic' – with Russia. China, the report reveals, is acquiring from Russia technology and sub-systems for land-attack cruise missiles (LACMs); anti-ship cruise missiles (ASCMs) to be mounted on the Sovremennyy-class destroyers already ordered; sophisticated air-to-air missiles to be mounted on the Su-27 aircraft being built under licence in China with the help of Russian technicians; Il-76 transport aircraft; Kilo-class submarines; and satellite images.

The report ends, in a highly maladroit manner which could only provoke Beijing, with a call to equip Taipei with symmetrical means: '[Taiwan's] success in deterring potential Chinese aggression will be dependent on its continued acquisition of modern arms, technology and equipment and its ability to deal with a number of systemic problems – primarily the recruitment and retention of technically-qualified personnel and the maintenance of an effective logistics system – lest Taipei once again risk losing its qualitative edge.'[74]

To all this should be added the Pentagon's own plans, in the context of a regional arms race, to include Taiwan and Japan in a theatre anti-missile defence system (TMD), threatening to neutralize a good proportion of China's efforts to assemble a convincingly deterrent level of conventional weaponry against the much better armed US–Japan–Taiwan alliance (the Pentagon however balancing China's forces against those of Taiwan alone!). Against this background it is not difficult to see the bombing of the Chinese embassy in Belgrade on 6 May 1999 as the last straw that broke the camel's back, nor that the Chinese response was far from being the crazed overreaction, attributable to some peculiarity of oriental culture, that the Western media claimed to have discerned.

The Kosovo War

The war waged by NATO against Serbia was integral to the process described above and the options which determined it.[75] One would have had to be singularly myopic to consider this war in the limited context of the Balkan situation, as just another upheaval in the civil wars that had been tearing Yugoslavia to shreds since the beginning of the decade. Ignorance of what was really at stake and an inability to see the wood for the trees induced very large numbers of well-meaning people, understandably horrified by the crimes committed by Serbian armed forces, to confuse the war in Kosovo with a humanitarian relief operation. Those who spoke of a 'just war' were failing to consider a fundamental aspect of this concept: adequacy of means to ends. Henry Kissinger, never more lucid than when judging the actions of his rivals, had this to say:

> At every stage of the Kosovo tragedy, other mixes of diplomacy and force were available, though it is not clear they were ever seriously considered. A strategy that vindicates its moral convictions only from altitudes above 15,000 feet – and in the process devastates Serbia and makes Kosovo unlivable – has already produced more refugees and casualties than any conceivable alternative mix of force and diplomacy would have. It deserves to be questioned on both political and moral grounds.[76]

The blatant inappropriateness of the means employed to the declared humanitarian ends is more than sufficient to raise questions about the concealed motives, the hidden agenda, behind this war. The alternative choice was not, of course, the famous ground offensive, which would have involved a dangerous lurch much closer to a risk of world conflagration. Those who preached this solution were guilty of military naivety as well as irresponsibility: certain individuals seemed to be using a declared love of humanity as an excuse for playing the lead in *Dr Strangelove*. Zbigniew Brzezinski was outstandingly successful in this role.

Only a few days after the start of the NATO bombing, when it had become manifest that Milošević – contrary to the assurances of US intelligence services[77] – was not going to bow easily to the Alliance's injunctions, Brzezinski wrote an excited exhortation for the *Washington Post*. The article suggested a tactical air campaign in addition to strategic bombing; arming the KLA; committing ground troops if these measures still seemed insufficient; and finally, supporting independence for Kosovo unless Milošević was overthrown.[78]

Not a single allusion, needless to say, to any possibility of a negotiated solution in collaboration with Russia. Nearly two weeks later Brzezinski wrote for the consumption of leaders of the NATO countries, on the eve of their Washington summit, an even more rabid piece that revealed the basis of his thought more clearly than ever:

> The stakes now involve far more than the fate of Kosovo. They were altered dramatically the day the bombing began. It is no exaggeration to say that NATO's failure to prevail would mean both the end of NATO as a credible alliance and the undermining of America's global leadership. And the consequences of either would be devastating to global stability.[79]

Those opposed to the NATO bombing were 'the erratic admirer of Hitler in Belarus and the current Russian regime, which failed in Chechnya in what Milošević is attempting to do in Kosovo'. After criticizing the Pentagon for preventing Wesley Clark from using Apache helicopters, and scolding NATO for wanting to minimize loss of human life,[80] the 'humanitarian hawk' went on to belabour Clinton for putting off the terrestrial option (also rejected by the Pentagon): 'One cannot avoid the suspicion that political expediency was at work here, at a time when genuine leadership was needed . . . The American leadership must project principled courage and not be guided by a political compass.'

The author's own prescriptions followed: make Kosovo a NATO protectorate, instead of giving it the autonomy decided at Rambouillet; intensify the bombing and get rid of current restrictions in the choice of targets; concentrate forces for a large-scale ground offensive or for a 'mopping-up operation' (a civilized version, perhaps, of 'ethnic cleansing'), and so on. But the key point was this warning:

> The alliance should reject the temptation to accept any deal contrived by Russia that would grant Milošević an easing of NATO's original terms. To do so would mark the bombing as a tragically pointless failure, would reward Milošević for his ethnic cleansing, and would represent a great political success for the Kremlin's anti-NATO posture. That has to be made crystal clear.

NATO's failure to bend Serbia to its will, made worse by deepening divisions within the Alliance, provided Boris Yeltsin with an excellent opportunity to sell his services to the West once again. There follows a raw but accurate description of what occurred:

> Yeltsin brilliantly allowed Primakov to position Russia in complete and hostile opposition to NATO. He then brought Chernomyrdin out of

> retirement. Chernomyrdin, an old stalwart of the reform days, appeared to be a dinosaur out of the past. Chernomyrdin delivered two messages. The first was that there was still a chance at reform in Russia. The second was that Russia would help NATO in Kosovo in return for financial aid. Suddenly, $4.5 billion was shaken loose; not enough to bring Milošević to the peace table, but enough to cause Yeltsin to dump Primakov and appoint a new Prime Minister of ambiguous ideology. Outmaneuvering the communists in the Duma by getting Zhironovsky to double cross them (the price for that is not yet clear), Yeltsin is now in a position to bargain with the West. Indeed, Michel Camdessus, head of the IMF, said on Sunday that the IMF was now ready to work with Russia on additional funding.[81]

Unlike some other gurus, Zbigniew Brzezinski possesses no supernatural powers. His advice, having carried the United States and NATO to the brink of catastrophe, was now being increasingly ignored. At a somewhat more morose fiftieth anniversary summit than had originally been anticipated, the NATO heads of state and government voted a resolution that declared them ready to accept the jurisdiction of the UN Security Council, and that stated in passing: 'Russia has a particular responsibility in the United Nations and an important role to play in the search for a solution to the conflict in Kosovo.'[82]

The summit adopted a 'strategic concept', but one that was no longer called 'new' like its 1991 predecessor, and for good reason. The mountain had given birth to a mouse. In fact this text, announced with great fanfare long in advance, contained no striking innovation on changes to NATO, but simply confirmed the mutation inaugurated under George Bush. Worse still, the European members of the Alliance, noticing (not before time) that they had been drawn into a situation fraught with dangers for European security, imposed amendments on their American guest that altered the sense of the document in a direction wholly opposed to the Brzezinski doctrine and the spirit of the US Senate resolution. France in particular insisted that the document should mention the key role of the United Nations. Anxious to preserve the Alliance's unity, under serious threat in its first involvement in a real war, Clinton was forced to acquiesce, and compromise formulae were adopted. The result was a toned-down text, paradoxically more conciliatory to Russia, and more conscientious about the UN and 'international legality', than its 1991 predecessor:[83]

> The United Nations Security Council has the primary responsibility for the maintenance of international peace and security and, as such, plays a crucial role in contributing to security and stability in the Euro-Atlantic area.[84]

> NATO remains the essential forum for consultation among the Allies and the forum for agreement on policies bearing on the security and defence commitments of its members under the Washington Treaty.[85]

> NATO will seek, in cooperation with other organisations, to prevent conflict, or, should a crisis arise, to contribute to its effective management, consistent with international law, including through the possibility of conducting non-Article 5 crisis response operations.[86]

> Russia plays a unique role in Euro-Atlantic security . . . A strong, stable and enduring partnership between NATO and Russia is essential to achieve lasting stability in the Euro-Atlantic area.[87]

Brzezinski had exhorted NATO to maintain the impetus of its eastward enlargement by deciding at the Washington summit to integrate Slovenia, Lithuania (a former Soviet republic whose admission to NATO Moscow would regard as a *casus belli*) and, if possible, Rumania.[88] The summit did none of these things. It did proclaim that the Alliance was still open to new members, but their admission was put off indefinitely, perhaps until the Greek Kalends. By way of a consolation prize for disappointed candidates a 'membership action plan' was established, sarcastically described by *Le Monde* as 'virtual membership'. There can be no doubt that if the Washington summit had taken place in the circumstances that prevailed before the bombing of Yugoslavia its outcome would have been different. It represented an undeniable setback for the policy followed by the Clinton administration since 1994.

As did the result of the Kosovo war. Kissinger's assessment implicitly emphasized the extent to which the result differed from his rival Brzezinski's prescriptions:

> The NATO forces are entering Kosovo on the basis of a U.N. mandate rather than an agreement between Belgrade and the Atlantic Alliance. Kosovo is explicitly described as a part of Yugoslavia, albeit an

> autonomous one (Point 5); the territorial integrity and sovereignty of Yugoslavia are affirmed (Point 8). The provision for a referendum at the end of the three years has been abandoned, and the initial insistence on complete NATO control has been watered down to some extent by a series of U.N. mandates and the presence of Russian forces.[89]

In fact the Security Council resolution which was the basis for the ending of NATO's war in Kosovo was diplomatically ambiguous on the main stumbling block, control of the international forces.[90] As a result this issue, left hanging in mid-air, was settled on the ground after a brisk bout of arm-wrestling between Russia and NATO. At first apparently passive and conciliatory, the Russian position hardened in spectacular fashion with the seizure of Priština airport by Russian troops to plant their flag in Kosovo before NATO. These troops had come from Bosnia without contacting the local NATO command, which they were supposed to keep informed on their movements. This 'stroke of daring', and some of the events that followed, incidentally revealed a growing ascendancy of the Russian military in the Kremlin.

The Alliance forces ended by finding a compromise with Moscow reflecting their advantage in the balance of power, but not without passing through moments of acute tension like those described at the beginning of this work. China abstained in the Security Council, finding that the resolution did not sufficiently emphasize the international legal framework provided by the United Nations.[91] As if to confirm Beijing's worst nightmares, on 12 July 1999 the Taiwanese president Lee Teng-hui for the first time publicly dissented from the official principle of 'one China', starting a downward slide in relations between Beijing and Taipei . . .[92]

The Kosovo war may have marked a decisive turning, in the post-Cold War world, towards a new era of tension and confrontation between two great international coalitions: a new Cold War, in a word. The transition from one to the other will have lasted less than ten years, and this great opportunity to fashion for the twenty-first century a world more peaceful than that of the tragic century now ending will have been lost, largely through the bad decisions of a particularly incompetent man, a man unable to benefit from the main reference of every great maker of history: the lessons of history.

John Lewis Gaddis, quoted at the beginning of this text, noted that American historians, normally a very divided community, were virtually unanimous in condemning the decision to enlarge NATO. For they were in a position to deduce what had to happen as a result.

> If the US could afford to be *inclusive* in dealing with its *actual* enemies Germany and Japan after 1945 – just as Napoleon's conquerors were in dealing with France after 1815 – then why is it now *excluding* a country that, throughout the Cold War, remained only a potential adversary?
>
> The answer most often given is that the Russians have no choice but to accept what NATO has decided to do . . . Not only is that view arrogant; it is also short-sighted, for it assumes that defeated adversaries have no choices . . .
>
> For Russia does indeed have a choice: it is in the interesting position of being able to lean one way or another in a strategic triangle that is likely to define the geopolitics of the early twenty-first century. It can continue to align itself, as it has patiently done so far, with the United States and Western Europe. Or it can do what the US itself did a quarter century ago under the guidance of Richard Nixon and Henry Kissinger: it can tilt towards China.[93]

One man alone, the president, elected to command of the greatest power in history by a system which accepts the saxophone as an electoral argument and whose media are more interested in the sexual cavortings of politicians than the great issues of world politics, has had the main hand in determining the course of human history at the dawn of the twenty-first century, unwatched by a deeply indifferent electorate.

> National scandals about the private morality of public men have not done much to heighten the level of public sensibility or deepen the image of political life to make it central, urgent, and worth while . . .[94]
>
> By virtue of their increased and centralized power, political institutions become more objectively important to the course of American history, but because of mass alienation, less and less of subjective interest to the population at large. On the one hand, politics is bureaucratized, and on the other, there is mass indifference. These are the decisive aspects of U.S. politics today.[95]

These strikingly apposite words were written in the middle of the century by C. Wright Mills, one of the most clear-sighted analysts of American society: a society which has shown the other industrial societies a glimpse of their own future, to which they are all in the process of adjusting as the century draws to a close. Mills fought passionately, throughout his regrettably short life, to change the state of things by alerting his fellow-citizens to the activities of the ruling elite.

> In those societies in which the means of power are rudimentary and decentralized, history is fate . . . But in those societies in which the means of power are enormous in scope and centralized in form a few men may be so placed within the historical structure that by their decisions about the use of these means they modify the structural conditions under which most men live . . .[96]
>
> Given these means of administration, production, violence, it seems clear that more and more events are due less to any uncontrollable fate than to the decisions, the defaults, the ignorance – as the case may be – of the higher circles of the superstates. To reflect upon the present as history is to understand that history may now be made by default. Understanding that, we no longer need to accept historical fate, for fate is a feature of specific kinds of social structure, of irresponsible systems of power.
>
> These systems can be changed. Fate can be transcended. We must come to understand that while the domain of fate is diminishing and in fact becoming organized as irresponsibility. We must hold men of power variously responsible for pivotal events, we must unmask their pretensions – and often their own mistaken convictions – that they are not responsible. Our politics, in short, must be the politics of responsibility.[97]

These lines are quoted from a book whose title, *The Causes of World War Three*, used to seem out of date but has now, like the book itself, acquired an unhappy new relevance.

Notes

1. Michael Gordon, 'Russia Ousts U.S. Officer as Ties Sour Over Kosovo', *New York Times*, 4 July 1999.
2. Dana Priest, 'Russian Flight Shocks West', *Washington Post*, 1 July 1999. The day after this report appeared in the *Post*, the editorial in the *Moscow Times* (2 July 1999) stated,

under the headline 'Fly-Bys Just A Little Bit Of Payback', that 'this was an intentional, political message, and those in Washington who claim to be puzzled by Russia's growing truculence have their heads in the sand. The bombers that appeared near Iceland were simply the fruits of misguided NATO and U.S. policy toward Russia.'

3. According to the strategic analysis agency STRATFOR in 'Kosovo Conflict Accelerates Formation of Russia-China Strategic Alliance', 25 June 1999, published on the World Wide Web (www).
4. Paul Bracken, 'How the West Was One-Upped', *Washington Post,* 3 June 1999.
5. Masahi Nisihara, 'A Climate of Suspicion Threatens Asia-Pacific Stability', *International Herald Tribune,* 29 June 1999.
6. *New Left Review* 228, March/April 1998, pp. 91–126 (reproduced hereafter in this volume).
7. John Lewis Gaddis, 'History, Grand Strategy and Nato Enlargement', *Survival,* IISS, London, vol. 40, no. 1, Spring 1998, pp. 145–46.
8. North Atlantic Council, *London Declaration,* 'On A Transformed North Atlantic Alliance', London, 6 July 1990 (www), point 2.
9. Ibid., point 5.
10. Ibid. In Michael Brown's view, the London Declaration was part of a 'campaign to soften the alliance's image in order to get Moscow to go along with German unification on the West's terms – as a member of NATO'. ('Minimalist NATO' in *Foreign Affairs,* New York, vol. 78, no. 3, May–June 1999, p. 205.) In their jointly written book, George Bush and Brent Scowcroft give full credence to this interpretation (*A World Transformed,* Alfred Knopf, New York 1998, pp. 292–95). According to Scowcroft, 'the declaration was primarily meant to help Moscow save face' (p. 293).
11. North Atlantic Council, *Rome Declaration on Peace and Cooperation,* Rome, 8 November 1991 (www), point 5.
12. Ibid.
13. North Atlantic Council, *The Alliance's New Strategic Concept,* Rome, 8 November 1991 (www). It was the command structure of the Rapid Deployment Force, Central Command (CENTCOM) responsible for South-West Asia, that directed the operations against Iraq in 1990–91, during the Gulf war.
14. Ibid., points 9 and 11.
15. *Final Communiqué of the Ministerial Meeting of the North Atlantic Council,* NATO HQ, Brussels, 17 December 1992 (www), point 5.
16. See Alain Joxe, 'L'ère des expéditions humanitaires', in *La Nouvelle guerre des Balkans, Manière de voir* No. 45, *Le Monde Diplomatique,* Paris, May–June 1999, pp. 10–13. We might add that the Second World War veteran George Bush can also be credited with inventing, for his war against Saddam Hussein, another media trick: resorting to historical analogy with the World War, without fear of excess. The fears expressed by interventionists in the United States on the accession of William Clinton to the presidency, in view of his past as an opponent of the Vietnam war, quickly turned out to be ground-

less. Clinton in fact was the most eminent representative of that part of the generation politicized in opposition to the Vietnam war which, after the Gulf war, was converted to the virtues of imperial war waged for noble pretexts. It is too often forgotten that Clinton, as Governor of Arkansas before his elevation to supreme office, was chairman of the Democratic Leadership Council which, in 1990, pronounced in favour of military action against Iraq. (Founded in 1985, the DLC included Democratic Representatives wishing to compete with Ronald Reagan for an electorate moving steadily to the right. The DLC is behind the 'New Democrats' movement and regarded as one of the three pillars of the 'third way', along with Tony Blair's New Labour and Gerhard Schröder's Neue Mitte.)

17. Madeleine Albright, 'The Testing of American Foreign Policy', in *Foreign Affairs*, vol. 77, no. 6, November–December 1998, p. 62.
18. Michael Dobbs, 'Wider Alliance Would Increase US Commitments', *Washington Post*, 5 July 1995, followed by 'Enthusiasm for Wider Alliance Is Marked by Contradictions', 7 July 1995; James Goldgeier, 'NATO expansion: The Anatomy of a Decision', *The Washington Quarterly*, vol. 21, no. 1, Winter 1998.
19. Dobbs, 'Wider Alliance . . .'. Goldgeier, op. cit., p. 92: 'Brzezinski had been meeting with Lake to share ideas about his two-track approach to expansion, and he also invited Lake to his home to meet a number of Central and Eastern European leaders. . . . These meetings with Brzezinski helped Lake to clarify his own thinking and emphasized to him the importance of keeping the process moving forward.'
20. Dobbs, 'Enthusiasm for Wider Alliance . . .'. This prosaic account contrasts strongly with the romanticized version of the conversion of Clinton given later by Zbigniew Brzezinski and Anthony Lake, 'The Moral and Strategic Imperatives of NATO Enlargement', *International Herald Tribune*, 1 July 1997.
21. 1994 was the year of the mid-term elections in the US.
22. James Bennet, 'Samuel Berger: A Trusted Adviser, and a Friend', *New York Times*, 6 December 1996. Madeleine Albright was US Ambassador to the United Nations during the first Clinton mandate.
23. Quoted by Elaine Sciolino, 'Berger Is Manager of Crises, Not Global Strategy', *New York Times*, 18 May 1998.
24. Ashton Carter and William Perry, *Preventive Defense: a New Security Strategy for America*, Brookings Institution Press, Washington 1999.
25. Ibid., p. 18.
26. The two authors classify B-level threats as touching on the interests of the US but not threatening its survival; level C touches indirectly on the security of the US, but does not threaten its interests. Ibid., p. 11.
27. Ibid., p. 19.
28. Ibid., p. 49.
29. Perry and Carter returned to serving the Clinton administration in November 1998, the first as special adviser and policy coordinator for North Korea, the second as special adviser to the special adviser.

30. Carter and Perry, *Preventive Defense*, p. 105.
31. Ibid., pp. 33, 36–7.
32. This attitude recalls the perspicacity of Friedrich Engels, warning against bellicose posturing over the same Bosnia a century earlier: 'For the sake of a handful of Hercegovinians, to ignite a world war which will cost a thousand times more people than all those living in Hercegovina – that is not my view of the politics of the proletariat.' Letter to Eduard Bernstein, 22–25 February 1882 (*Marx-Engels Werke*, B. 35, Berlin 1967, p. 280). Prophetically, Engels's letter went on: 'Serbs are divided into three religions (. . .). But for these people, religion comes before nationality and each community *wants* to dominate. As long as there is no cultural progress there that makes tolerance at least possible, Grand Serbia will only mean civil war.' (p. 281).
33. Carter and Perry, op. cit., p. 64 (emphasis added).
34. Brzezinski, *The Grand Chessboard*, Basic Books, New York 1997.
35. In reality Brzezinski is a pretty poor player of geopolitical chess: if the essence of a grand master is the ability to anticipate adverse moves, the least that can be said about the way Brzezinski predicts the reactions of other 'players' is that it is highly unrealistic, not to say totally deluded.
36. Ibid., p. xiv.
37. Ibid., p. 30.
38. Ibid., pp. 38–39.
39. Ibid., p. 40.
40. Ibid., p. 198 (emphasized in the original).
41. Ibid., p. 55.
42. Ibid., p. 59.
43. Ibid., pp. 42–43. Tony Blair has incarnated this to perfection.
44. Ibid., p. 152.
45. Ibid., p. 185.
46. Ibid., p. 52.
47. Ibid., p. 104.
48. Ibid., p. 202. Russia may be in an advanced state of disintegration (see David Hoffman, 'Russia Is Sinking Into the Void of a "Failed State"', *International Herald Tribune* [WP service], 27 February 1999), but there is little chance that Brzezinski's vision will come to pass. There is instead every reason to fear a Russia foundering in chaos.
49. Brzezinski, *The Grand Chessboard*, op. cit., p. 79.
50. Ibid., p. 201.
51. Ibid., p. 104.
52. Ibid., pp. 123–50, esp. pp. 133, 149. 'A strong, even religiously motivated but not fanatically anti-Western Iran is in the US interest . . .' (p. 204).
53. Ibid., p. 186.
54. Ibid., p. 193.

55. For a representation of the various imaginary scenarios on the future of Russia, see Daniel Yergin and Thane Gustafson, *Russia 2010 and What it Means for the World*, Nicholas Brealey, London 1994.
56. Hall Gardner, *Dangerous Crossroads: Europe, Russia and the Future of NATO*, Praeger, Westport 1997, p.104.
57. See Robert Borosage, 'A "Splendid Little War" Collides With the War Powers Act', *Los Angeles Times*, 23 May 1999.
58. Carter and Perry, op. cit., p. 55.
59. See Jeff Gerth and Tim Weiner, 'US Arms Makers Lobby for NATO Expansion', *International Herald Tribune*, 30 June 1997, as well as William Hartung's edifying report, *Welfare for Weapons Dealers 1998: The Hidden Costs of NATO Expansion*, published by the Arms Trade Resource Center of the World Policy Institute, New School for Social Research, New York, March 1998. See also William Greider's remarkable investigation *Fortress America: The American Military and the Consequences of Peace*, Public Affairs, New York 1998, pp. 97–101.
60. The last figure was the one presented to Congress by the administration. See, for example, the State Department brochure *The Enlargement of NATO*, PIS, US Department of State, Bureau of Public Affairs, Washington, February 1998. On the cost of enlargement, apart from the study by William Hartung quoted earlier, see Harry Cohen's report for the Economic Committee of the North Atlantic Assembly, 'The Costs of NATO Enlargement', November 1998 (www).
61. The arguments put to the Senators by Zbigniew Brzezinski are deserving of mention. The administration's guru explained that NATO enlargement 'helps a democratizing Russia by foreclosing the revival of any self-destructive imperial temptations regarding Central Europe' and 'will bring into NATO counsels new, solidly democratic and very pro-American nations' (*Introductory Statement On Nato Enlargement*, text dated 9 October 1997 and submitted to the Senate Foreign Relations Committee, www).
62. US Senate, *Resolution of Ratification to the Protocols to the North Atlantic Treaty of 1949 on the Accession of Poland, Hungary and the Czech Republic*, Washington, 30 November 1998, www. By requiring to be consulted in advance next time, the Senate was expressing its reluctance to be presented with another fait accompli. An amendment submitted by Sen. John Warner (Rep., Virginia), fixing a minimum delay of three years before any further admission to NATO, obtained 41 votes: less than it needed to be adopted, but more than enough to block a new admission to NATO if necessary.
63. Left-wing opponents of NATO held other bodies – the OSCE and the UN – to be better able to manage crises in the post-Cold War world.
64. The IMF abruptly suspended its line of credit after a first payment of $4.8 billion in July.
65. On the Washington decision process leading to the war against Serbia, see Elaine

Sciolino and Ethan Bronner, 'How a President, Distracted by Scandal, Entered Balkan War', *New York Times*, 18 April 1999.

66. Ibid.
67. This practice has since become routine, without much attention from the media. Attacks on Iraqi targets by American and British aircraft have become uncountable. They continued as usual during the bombing of Yugoslavia.
68. 'NATO will establish and deploy a force (hereinafter KFOR) which may be composed of ground, air, and maritime units from NATO and non-NATO nations, operating under the authority and subject to the direction and the political control of the North Atlantic Council (NAC) through the NATO chain of command.' *Interim Agreement for Peace and Self-Government in Kosovo* (23 February 1999), Ch. 7, 'Implementation II', art. I, 1, b.
69. Henry Kissinger, 'New World Disorder', *Newsweek*, 31 May 1999.
70. This pretext is wholly false. American retaliatory strike capacity is more than sufficient to deter frontal attack by any state. Any 'rogue' wanting to take reprisals against the US would be much more likely to resort to 'asymmetric' – i.e. 'terrorist' – methods, against which NMD provides no defence. Moreover systems of this sort are of limited effectiveness even against ballistic missiles.
71. On this matter see Rachel Dubin, 'National Missile Defense and the Anti-Ballistic Missile Treaty: Risks and Strategies', *National Defense Monitor* (CDI, Washington), vol. 3, no. 13, 1 April 1999.
72. According to the official news release from the Pentagon, this is 'the first sustained long-term increase in defense funding since the end of the Cold War'.
73. See Ted Galen Carpenter, 'Roiling Asia: U.S. Coziness with China Upsets the Neighbours', in *Foreign Affairs*, vol. 77, no. 6, November–December 1998.
74. Department of Defense, *Report to Congress Pursuant to the FY99 Appropriations Bill on the Security Situation in the Taiwan Strait*, Washington, 26 February 1999 (www). See also report by Tony Walker, Stephen Fidler and Mure Dickie, 'Missile developments shift balance of power over the Taiwan Strait', *Financial Times*, 12 March 1999.
75. This includes, of course, the decision to start the bombing on the same day that the Russian prime minister, Yevgeni Primakov, was expected in Washington. According to Jane Perlez of the *New York Times*, this decision was taken under pressure from Madeleine Albright, 'the most hawkish member of the foreign policy team', and with the support of Vice-President Albert Gore who is said to have 'argued forcefully that the credibility of NATO was more important than paying attention to the sensitivities of the Russians' ('Step by Step: How the U.S. Decided to Attack, and Why So Fast', *New York Times*, 26 March 1999).
76. Kissinger, op. cit.
77. 'One interagency intelligence report coordinated by the C.I.A. in January 1999, for example, concluded that "Milošević doesn't want a war he can't win." "After enough of a defense to sustain his honor and assuage his backers he will quickly sue for

peace," the assessment went on.' Sciolino and Bronner, op. cit.

78. Brzezinski, 'To Stop the Serbs', *Washington Post,* 30 March 1999. The article ended on a characteristic use of the civilization/barbarity opposition: 'A civilized Euro-Atlantic community cannot tolerate genocidal barbarity in its own midst.' An indirect response came from James Schlesinger, former CIA Director and Defense Secretary under Richard Nixon, 'Idealism Won't End It', published the following day in the same journal, and from Edward Luttwak's critique of the simplistic view of the ground offensive, 'NATO Has Power, Milošević Calls Shots', *Los Angeles Times,* 31 March 1999.
79. Published under the title 'Get Serious' in the *National Review* (distributed by CSIS, www), Brzezinski's article was to be republished under the much more explicit headline 'Guerre totale contre Milošević!' in *Le Monde,* 17 April 1999. The quotations that follow are from the same article.
80. 'Instead of shocking and intimidating the opponent, the air campaign has striven to avoid casualties not only to allied airmen but even to Milošević's officials . . .'
81. STRATFOR, *Global Intelligence Update,* 'China, Russia, and the Politics of Manic-Depression', 17 May 1999 (www). In fact the $4.5 billion is simply going to be transferred from one account to another inside the IMF, preventing Russia from defaulting on repayments of its existing debt.
82. *Statement on Kosovo Issued by the Heads of State and Government participating in the meeting of the North Atlantic Council in Washington, D.C. on 23rd and 24th April 1999* (www).
83. On the other hand the much-remarked presence at the NATO summit of the GUUAM countries (Georgia, Ukraine, Uzbekistan, Azerbaijan and Moldova) was a serious blow to Moscow and another indication, in Russian eyes, of America's designs on Russia's traditional marchlands.
84. North Atlantic Council, *The Alliance's Strategic Concept,* Washington, 24 April 1999 (www), point 15. 'On the most controversial point, whether or not NATO always needs a UN Security Council mandate to take military action or can decide on intervention alone, as the member countries did on Kosovo, the United States accepted compromise language that U.S. officials said preserved the essentials of NATO's freedom of action. The document did not stipulate that NATO would operate "under the authority of the Security Council". That phrase, they said, had been pushed by France but rejected by allies who feared that it would give Russia a veto over NATO actions.' Joseph Fitchett, 'Leaders Agree to Protect Frontline States', *International Herald Tribune,* 26 April 1999.
85. North Atlantic Council, *The Alliance's Strategic Concept,* op. cit., point 25.
86. Ibid., point 31.
87. Ibid., point 36.
88. Brzezinski, 'NATO: the Dilemmas of Expansion', *The National Interest* (Washington), no. 53, Fall 1998.
89. Kissinger, 'As the Cheers Fade', *Newsweek,* 21 June 1999 (the article is illustrated

with a photograph of a jubilant Madeleine Albright).

90. 'Deployment in Kosovo under United Nations auspices of effective international civil and security presences, acting as may be decided under Chapter VII of the Charter, capable of guaranteeing the achievement of common objectives. The international security presence with substantial North Atlantic Treaty Organization participation must be deployed under unified command and control . . .' United Nations Security Council, *Resolution 1244 (1999)*, 10 June 1999, Annex 2, points 3, 4 (www).
91. Under pressure from China, the first phrase of the preamble to Resolution 1244 was reformulated to read: 'The Security Council, Bearing in mind the purposes and principles of the Charter of the United Nations, and the primary responsibility of the Security Council for the maintenance of international peace and security . . .'
92. Seth Faison, 'Taiwan President Implies His Island Is Sovereign State', *New York Times*, 13 July 1999.
93. Gaddis, op. cit., pp. 146–47. Concerning the argument that an 'emotional obligation' helped persuade Clinton to opt for the integration of East European countries into NATO, according to the fanciful official version, Gaddis answers with a blindingly apposite argument: 'What we are seeing, then, is a kind of selective sentimentalism. The historic plight of some peoples moves us more than does that of others, despite the fact that they all have compelling claims as victims. Emotionalism, but of a surprisingly elitist character, appears to be at work here' (p. 149). No further comment seems necessary!
94. C. Wright Mills, *White Collar*, Oxford University Press, New York 1951, p. 343.
95. Ibid., p. 350.
96. Mills, *The Causes of World War Three*, Ballantine Books, New York 1960, p. 28.
97. Ibid., p. 184.

4

THE STRATEGIC TRIAD: USA, CHINA, RUSSIA

Gilbert Achcar

The official end of the Cold War, marked by the growing incapacity and then the collapse of the Soviet Union, inevitably meant a reduction of US military expenditure. This had long been regarded as essential from a strictly economic point of view: the extraordinary prodigality of the Reagan years, with a military budget that at its peak in 1985 – after adjustment for inflation – beat all post-1945 records, including those during the Korean and Vietnam wars, had been a major contributing factor to an enormous budget deficit, inflating an astronomical and ever-increasing public debt.[1]

The return of the US to the status of debtor nation in 1985 – for the first time since the First World War – was one major result of this out-and-out *fuite en avant*, whose apparent economic irrationality was explained by a political objective that looked more like an adventurous gamble than a rational calculation. Against all expectations, however, the bet was won: with hindsight, the expenditure of the Reagan era resembles a final sprint in the arms race, one that brought about the collapse of an exhausted competitor.

Since 1990–91, despite the recession and the Gulf War – the latter, it is true, providing a profitable way of liquidating some of the surplus or obsolescent Cold War weaponry – the Bush administration announced the objective for 1995 of a Base Force reduced by 25 per cent from the level of the late 1980s. This first downward revision was accentuated under the Clinton presidency by a further reduction of forces and expenditure following the Bottom-Up Review (BUR) carried out in 1993 by Defense Secretary Les Aspin, aided by his deputy and future successor William Perry. The BUR – conceived, as its name suggests, as a top-to-bottom revision of US military strategy and programming at the 'unipolar moment' that succeeded the defunct 'bipolarity' – was based on a theoretically radical renewal of American grand strategy.[2]

I. Official and Implicit Postulates of the American Defence Budget

The ultimate scenario of the Cold War implied a state of preparedness enabling the US to wage simultaneously a limited regional war and two-wars-in-one against the USSR (a major conventional war and a nuclear war); this would supposedly dissuade Moscow from trying to profit from US involvement in a regional war (like Korea or Vietnam), or even a bigger conflict with China. For this idea of a 'major (world) war and a half', the BUR substituted the scenario of two simultaneous 'major regional conflicts' or MRCs (limited wars or 'half-wars' in Cold War terminology), supposedly taking account of the new element introduced by the absence of a 'global peer competitor' (or rival power of equivalent military weight) and at the same time dissuading any potential regional adversary from trying to take advantage of an American conflict with another, similar-sized regional enemy. The two sample adversaries named in the BUR, like cut-out figures on a shooting range, were Iraq and North Korea. The American armed forces were supposed to hold themselves in readiness to fight these two states at the same time. In addition, to allow for the rapidly changing nature of international relations, the principle of a quadrennial review of military programming – corresponding, in fact, with each new presidential mandate – was adopted by Congress.

The new arrangement envisaged a Target Force for 1997 that would be smaller than the 1995 Base Force. The objective was broadly achieved with a 1997 Department of Defense (DoD) budget of $250 billion, plus the defence expenditure undertaken by other agencies – for example, the Department of Energy's contribution to nuclear armament – amounting at present to about $10 billion. The (five-yearly) Future Years' Defense Program covering 1998–2002 envisages keeping defence spending at this level in terms of constant value until the year 2000, after which there should be a very slight real annual increase of about 0.5 per cent until 2002 – when it should reach $288 billion at current values.

This budgetary programming was not questioned by the Quadrennial Defense Review (QDR) announced by the Secretary of Defense, William Cohen, in May 1997. The QDR continues subscribing to the BUR scenario of two MRCs (renamed Major Theater Wars), while 'placing greater emphasis on the continuing need to maintain continuous overseas presence to shape the international environment and to be better able to respond to a variety of smaller-scale contingencies and asymmetric threats'.[3]

Otherwise the QDR is based on the modernization plan for the armed forces, *Joint Vision 2010*, centred on the use of new technologies whose implications have given birth to the somewhat pompous title *Revolution in Military Affairs* (RMA).[4] As the administration has chosen to subject military spending to the constraints of the total reabsorption of the American budget deficit – contrary to the wishes of many Republicans in Congress, who would like a smaller reduction in military spending at the cost of social spending – the QDR envisages a major redefinition of priorities accompanied by a redirecting of military expenditure, to achieve the supreme objective of modernization.

Against this background, the choice of a Republican for the post of Defense Secretary in 1997 was a skilful move by the Clinton administration. William Cohen was given the difficult task of making Congress swallow the bitter pill of new base closures in the US along with other reductions and cancellations of orders, deemed necessary to find the extra $15 billion that the DoD proposes to spend annually on the modernization of the armed forces. That expenditure should bring the armed forces procurement budget to $60 billion a year after the year 2000. The contradictory requirements posed by a strictly limited budgetary envelope combined with the techno-strategic 'revolution' imply some difficult choices, with the qualitative needing to be strongly favoured over the quantitative while still coming under the heading of 'grand strategy' in the order of the day.[5]

Options for modernization

The basic options allowing for both the indicated parameters have been well summarized in the *1997 Strategic Assessment*, a particularly enlightening document from the Institute for National Strategic Studies (INSS) that predates the publication of the QDR.[6] It identifies three possible 'Force Structure Options':

1. The 'Recapitalization Force Model'; modernization of the existing armed forces by slow degrees. This conservative option is easy to manage but could 'miss the opportunity provided by the present lack of a global peer to experiment with information technologies'.
2. The 'Accelerated RMA Force Model', aiming to 'accelerate the integration of system-of-systems technologies' while adapting to steep quantitative reductions in the armed forces. This 'revolutionary' option has the advantages of being cheaper and more futurist, but the implied

violent break of continuity produces an area of vulnerability, being just as liable to disorient friends as enemies.

3. The 'Full Spectrum Force Model', combining the maintenance of all existing effective forces with the slow and prudent integration of the RMA in such a way as to avoid all disorganizing side-effects. It is the costliest model but also the 'most consistent with the challenge of the emerging strategic environment'.

The last of these options is the one favoured by the QDR, which also refers several times to the formula of a range of forces designed to deal with the full range of possible problems ('Full Spectrum of Crises, Full Spectrum Force'). Under the heading 'Where we are going' in his preface to the report, William Cohen defines three possible options, identical to those in the 1997 *Strategic Assessment*, then rejects the conservative and futurist options to settle on the middle way, the one that 'retains sufficient force structure to sustain American global leadership' while also moving towards the RMA at a reasonable speed.[7]

As the report is meant to be 'fiscally responsible', it announces that the inevitable cuts in the armed forces will affect the 'tail' (logistics and support) rather than the 'tooth' (fighting force), and promises to make the best possible use of the reduction in the cost of military equipment brought about by another 'revolution', the 'Revolution in Business Affairs' (RBA), which includes measures to rationalize procurement procedures, restructure military industries, bring competitive liberalization to the defence market and import more technologies from the civil sector.[8]

This military option, whose financial limits have been determined by budgetary constraint and which is officially based on the BUR scenario of two simultaneous MRCs, is expressed by the Clinton administration – hardly suspected a priori of having militaristic leanings – in an annual national defence budget totalling approximately $260 billion (at 1997 value) from now until the beginning of the next century.

However, to indicate that America really has 'responded to the vast global changes' – the end of the Cold War and the 'peace dividend' it was supposed to produce – William Cohen's preface to the report on the QDR explains that the DoD budget has decreased from $400 million (at 1997 values) and 7 per cent of GDP in 1985, to $250 million and 3.2 per cent of GDP in 1997. This radical drop suggests that the US has really turned the page of the Cold War. But the reality is that the choice of annual figures which support this deduction is of somewhat tendentious nature.

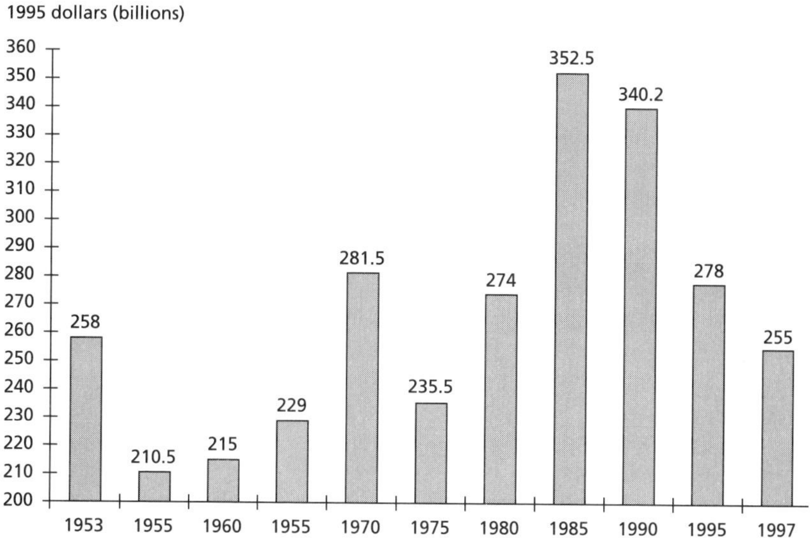

Figure 4.1 US defence spending, 1953–1997

Source: Calculated from figures given in The Military Balance, *IISS, London, 1987–88, 1991–92, 1997–98 and also in* SIPRI Yearbook 1968/69 *(Stockholm 1969) for 1953 and 1960*

The Defense Secretary refers specifically to 1985 which, far from being a year typical of the period 1950–91 (from the Korean rearmament, already announced in NSC-68, to the disintegration of the USSR), actually came at the peak of the extraordinary expenditure of the Reagan era. If we compare the 1997 figure with those for the whole period (see Figure 4.1), a very different conclusion emerges: defence spending for 1997, which the administration wants to maintain at the same level in terms of constant value until the end of its mandate in the year 2000, is higher than in most of the Cold War years before 1980 – the year in which it rose steeply in reaction to the Soviet invasion of Afghanistan – presaging the runaway growth under Reagan. Over the previous three decades this level had only been exceeded at the height of the Korean and Vietnam wars, when the costs of a large-scale regional war were added to those of maintaining a posture of global deterrence against the Warsaw Pact and China.

The $260 billion of current military spending represents more than 85 per cent of the average annual military expenditure of $304 billion (at 1997 values) for the 1948–91 period.[9] So President Clinton's 'centrist' administration[10] is really seeking to stabilize military expenditure until the beginning of the next century at what amounts to a Cold War level. Running adjustments to defence spending since 1991 have been much more like internal adjustments during the Cold War period (in moments of 'détente' following phases of high tension) than the steep fall that immediately followed the Second World War. It is true that American defence spending fell by 27.6 per cent between 1985 and 1996, compared to 18.4 per cent between 1953 and 1955, and 16.3 per cent between 1970 and 1975. But, as we have seen, 1985 spending had reached an altogether extraordinary level, 25.2 per cent higher than in 1970 and 36.6 per cent higher than in 1953.

It is also true that comparisons at constant values do not integrally allow for what Adelman and Augustine call 'techflation'.[11] The growing technological sophistication of military equipment means that its unit costs increase more rapidly than the general level of inflation. The difference, according to the two authors, ranges from about 2.5 per cent for tanks and ships to about 10.5 per cent for planes. They calculate that the average difference for the whole defence sector is of the order of 3.4 per cent. 'Techflation' explains the established fact that a zero-growth defence budget in real dollars does not correspond to a static level of armed readiness, but implies an annual quantitative reduction so long as the equipment is kept up to date.

It is no less true, however, that the quantitative reduction due to 'techflation' is largely counterbalanced by the formidable qualitative leap in the destructiveness (the term 'productivity' being grotesque in this context) of modern weapons in the information-technology era, a leap that Adelman and Augustine also describe very well.[12] To illustrate it, they relate one of the earliest uses of 'smart' bombs, during the Vietnam War. American aviation had flown 873 sorties, dropped 2,000 tons of conventional bombs and lost eleven aircraft in the attempt to destroy the Thanh Hoa bridge in North Vietnam, without hitting a single span. When laser-guided bombs were used, the bridge was demolished in a single raid by eight aircraft, without losses.

The authors add, however, that the first 'smart bombs' were not all that smart and prohibitively expensive, unlike the true 'fire and forget' target-seeking weapons now available. This hardware, the so-called 'second generation' – as opposed to the first generation used in Iraq in 1991 – combined with stealth technology for air dominance, satellite battlefield surveillance and computerized logistics organization, are the key elements in the predominance of American forces ('Force Dominance') according to the chief overseer of the QDR, William Perry, writing in 1996 as Defense Secretary.[13] These elements, along with the professionalization of the army, form the kernel of the 'offset strategy' with which the United States sought to 'compensate' for the greater numbers of the Soviet forces.

Perry added: 'Precision-guided munitions will also indirectly affect logistics because ratios of one or two shots per kill (instead of dozens or hundreds) mean that old estimates of weapons supplies go out of the window. If a target can be hit on the first few shots, the military can achieve huge savings in costs and manpower, since there is little need to build, store, transport and guard massive supplies of weapons.'[14]

A poor peace dividend

So why is the 'peace dividend' so meagre? And in what respect does the American military budget take account of the end of the Cold War? Only one of the arguments seems incontestable: reference to the size of military expenditure in relation to the rest of the national economy. The military share is considerably smaller in percentage terms in 1997 than the proportion it represented in the Cold War years, when it almost never fell below 5 per cent of GDP; according to the administration's forecasts it should fall to the equivalent of 2.8 per cent of GDP in 2001–02 (less than the present shares of GDP of French and British military spending), with the United States drawing further and further away from the 'permanent war economy' that characterized it during the Cold War.[15]

But if the destructiveness of the weapons largely compensates for 'techflation', and since the American GDP is by far the biggest in the world, then it follows that there is no point in measuring the strategic significance of the American defence budget in terms of the proportion of GDP it represents. The only valid criterion, in all logic, is the size of the budget in comparison with the military spending of states that are actually or potentially competitors or adversaries of the US.[16] And the conclusions that emerge from this comparison are more edifying than those emerging from the absolute scale of the spending and its qualitative content.

Even if we go along with William Cohen this time and take 1985 as the year of reference, it is to be noted that according to IISS figures US defence expenditure in that year was only 7 per cent more than Soviet expenditure.[17] Since

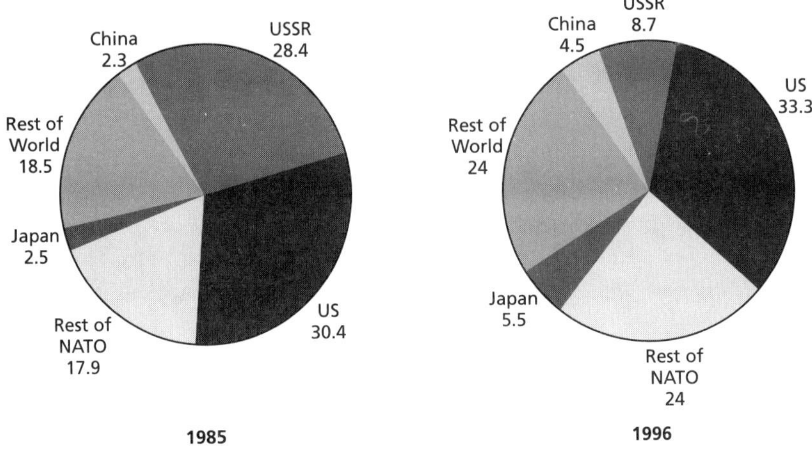

Figure 4.2 World defence spending by proportion (per cent)

Source: Percentages calculated from figures in The Military Balance 1997/98, *IISS, London 1997*

the collapse of the Soviet empire, American defence spending is equal – even slightly superior since 1996 – to the combined spending of the six other countries with the biggest military budgets in the world: Russia, Japan, France, Germany, the United Kingdom and China! American expenditure in 1996 reached $265,823 million (at 1995 values) against $265,260 million for the other six countries in the same year, according to the IISS.[18] So America's share of world military spending is larger now than it was in 1985, at the peak of American Cold War spending. (See Figure 4.2)

Under these circumstances, the claim that the US military budget is tailored to the BUR scenario of two simultaneous MRCs – with prototype enemies like Iraq (or Iran) and North Korea, two debilitated countries with backward military capacities – looks very like a mystification.[19] In any case, even before Iraq was destroyed in 1991, the myth of the 'fourth biggest army in the world' already seemed as exaggerated as George Bush's pompous comparisons with the Second World War. The American deployment against the Iraqi army in 1990–91 was in fact very disproportionate, even in terms of the requirements of Colin Powell's and Dick Cheney's doctrine which posited crushing superiority and minimal risk as essential preconditions for any military intervention.[20]

US critics of the high level of American defence budgets never fail to reproach the Pentagon, with good reason, for leaving allied forces out of its military calculations. Of course this is a deliberate and explicit political choice, and one that speaks volumes about the nature of the American government's hegemonic ambitions. But discounting the allies also gives useful help in camouflaging the disproportion between available means and declared ends. Thus, for the two official prototype enemies under the BUR scenario, the picture of the balance of forces is greatly modified if the ally most directly involved – far more directly, in fact, than the US itself – is considered: the defence spending of the US military protectorate Saudi Arabia alone is currently about four times that of Iraq and Iran combined, while the spending of the Republic of Korea, another US protégé and firm ally, is nearly triple that of its neighbour to the north.

As for NATO, the main military alliance in which the US participates, and which it controls, its military spending is greater than that of the rest of the world – a majority of which also consists of allies and protégés of the Western countries. America alone spends nearly 60 per cent of the total spent by the Atlantic Alliance, and a third of the entire world's defence spending (see Figure 4.2). Contrary to a widespread superstition, however, the US has absolutely no intention – if only for internal political reasons – of playing the world policeman (or 'globocop') by intervening in every crisis all over the world. In the deployment of its forces overseas its policy is essentially conservative, with troops being kept notably in the European and East Asian theatres. Its 'national security strategy of engagement' only envisages limited and selective participation in 'operations other than war' (OOTW: peace-keeping, enforcement, and so forth). Although American participation in OOTW has increased noticeably since the end of the Cold War nobody, even in the Pentagon, tries to claim that the one is somehow a substitute for the other.

Who is the real enemy?

With these considerations in mind, one does not have to be particularly suspicious to imagine that the scenario of two MRCs of an Iraq/Korea type may be an artifice meant to conceal the strategic postulate that really dominates America's military options. In any case, suspicions of this sort were inevitably going to arise in the US itself, in the circles in which international relations and strategy are discussed. There are two recent examples published at the same time but in two journals of widely differing political sensibility, the *World Policy Journal* and *The National Interest*.

Ronald Steel, writing in the *World Policy Journal*, notes that US military expenditure goes far beyond the country's real defence needs, and traces American prodigality in this area back half a century to the National Security Act promulgated in 1947 by Harry Truman. This document, which ended by setting up the strategic institutions of the Cold War, conceived 'national security in terms of global security'. The author adds that from then on it would have been more accurate to call the Department of Defense the 'Department of National Security'. He vigorously rejects such implicit attitudes, favouring a moderate form of isolationism – pursuing global balance rather than worldwide military control – as more appropriate to the prevailing socio-economic priorities of the country.[21]

In the other journal A.J. Bacevitch, in a striking coincidence, also feels that the DoD is a misnomer since in reality 'the Pentagon is in the business of projecting American power in order to undergird American influence around the world'.[22] The author deplores the recent deterioration in civilian-military relations in the United States, judging it damaging to the interests of the grand strategy which, for his part, he supports. In his opinion the problem lies in 'the unwillingness to acknowledge openly the strategic enterprise to which the United States has tacitly committed itself. American leaders will not say out loud what they know American purposes to be.'[23]

Steel and Bacevitch both correctly underline the manifest discord between the avowed ends of American strategy and the means the US maintains. But they define what they believe to be the real objectives of Washington's grand strategy in rather vague terms. The fact is that 'world domination' as a concept, although obviously inherent in American strategy, is too general to inform a military strategy that needs to be translated into techno-strategic, logistical and tactical options, as well as budgetary choices. The more so as the US has no wish, still less the means, to intervene militarily in all zones of conflict worldwide.

'All horizons' is a possible option in the area of deterrent nuclear strategy, the nature of nuclear weapons even making deterrence 'of the strong by the weak' possible – two concepts which were closely connected in the French strategy adopted by de Gaulle. But it would not be feasible to establish an active strategy of world domination, subject to the imperatives of economizing on means, on an 'all horizons' basis: 'one against all' is an impossible military choice in either rational or practical terms. To dominate the world, it is essential to pursue a strategy of alliances and to manoeuvre politically to separate potential competitors and rivals, winning the allegiance of some in order to make the balance of forces work effectively on others. Military strategy for global hegemony has to be adapted to the strongest possible or imaginable hostile military alliance under existing or foreseeable political conditions. It has to establish a firm distinction between strategic allies and the powers it wishes to keep in line – while at the same time the political executive seeks to persuade them to collaborate by economic means.

Planning for the worst case scenario

The options of the DoD are based on scenarios that identify the actual adversaries to whose capabilities its military strategy has to be adjusted, and on the minimum military capability that has to be maintained to deal with the maximum possible risk, in the American tradition of 'worst case analysis'. These extreme hypotheses fix the objective to which the configuration of the armed forces is tailored. Hence the ultimate Cold War scenario of a double war, a major war against the USSR waged simultaneously with a limited war of East Asian type (China, Korea or Vietnam). Hence, too, the official BUR scenario of two limited wars or MRCs waged simultaneously against Iraq/Iran and North Korea. It is the case, however, that the military capability currently maintained by the United States seems altogether out of proportion with this latter scenario.

What then is the scenario that really underlies Washington's military options? Some American critics think to answer this question by referring to a representation of the world currently in fashion, the one centred on the economic triad of the US, Germany and Japan. The two Axis powers conquered in 1945 are held to be the central obsession of Washington, which is thought to fear that their present status as economic competitors of the US could find a military expression. Versions of this theory generally refer back to the Pentagon's famous draft policy text from George Bush's time, *Defense Planning Guidance*, parts of which were 'leaked' to the press in 1992. It will be recalled that this text called for 'the industrially advanced countries' to be discouraged not just from trying to put the US in the shade, but even from 'aspiring to a wider global or regional role'.

This formulation – which scandalized America's allies – is too clumsy and irrational to be wholly credible as a Pentagon draft for a document intended to be made public. The dominant ideology in Washington, as in all the advanced countries, views the natural combination of neo-liberal economics and representative liberal democracy as a solid and durable basis for political collaboration, which can only be strengthened by the increasing liberalization of trade. Nothing has occurred in the development of relations between the US, Japan and Germany (or the European Union for that matter) to confirm Washington's alleged fear of any increase in their military role. Indeed, given the repeated American refrain on 'burden sharing', it seems clear that such an increase is actually favoured – always on condition, of course, that it remains under American supervision.

There is good cause, therefore, to ponder the status of this draft document, and also to wonder whether – as has so often been the case – the 'leak' might have emanated intentionally from the Pentagon or the President's office. What was its real context? The Pentagon had been working on quantifying the 'Base Force' defined by President Bush as the 'minimum essential military force' just after the signing of START I, in its National Security Strategy document of August 1991, the month in which the communist regime collapsed in Russia. At the time of the 'leak' in 1992, the START II treaty was being negotiated – it was to become the object of an agreement between presidents Bush and Yeltsin in June 1992, before being signed officially in January 1993. The military scenario to which the Base Force had to be adequate, and which inspired the document on National Military Strategy published by the Pentagon in January 1992, included the capability to 'deal with regional contingencies – including possibly a limited, conventional threat to Europe'.

In this context, the 'leak', which caused an outcry among the traditional allies of the US, had the effect of reassuring Moscow by suggesting that American armed force was not specifically directed against Russia, contrary to the apparent meaning of the earlier formulation. The leaked draft text planted the idea that the American military posture as envisaged in Base Force – in reality not very different from the Cold War posture – was part of a new American 'all horizons' strategy, not very rational to be sure, but comforting to the Russians. It made America seem to be the guarantor of an interdict on all regional ambitions for the newly reunified Germany and for Japan, the two neighbours Russia fears the most. So the 'leak', whether intentional or not, made it much easier to persuade Moscow to accept the maintenance of American military power, at the cost of a temporary ruffling of allied feathers – soon allayed by energetic denials that the leaked draft really represented official opinion.[24]

The real opponents

In the context of a rational formulation of US strategy, there are only two declared opponents of American hegemony whose behaviour is unpredictable in the middle and long term and whose physical scale places them on comparable footing with the US; only two 'competitors' against which a military confrontation would definitely be more than a live-ammo 'war game' like the Gulf War. These are, of course, Russia and China, each a formidable power on its own, all the more so together or simultaneously. Only these two potential adversaries can justify a hypothesis that explains the level of military readiness maintained by the United States.

This gives some cause for believing that under the current BUR scenario Iraq is in some sense a codename for Russia, and North Korea a codename for China. From this angle, the hybrid category of MRC, a conflict both 'regional' and 'major', designating in nominal terms a limited regional war, would take on the real value of a major (unlimited) war with a power like today's China or Russia, unable to project its forces worldwide but already (or still) capable of projecting them regionally. The overall level of the American armed forces corresponds much better with two simultaneous wars of this type than with two limited regional wars. Of course, the reasoning behind this codification is not difficult to understand.

> A final factor constraining the scenario space examined by the DoD is the desire to avoid embarrassing the governments of so-called 'enemy' countries. For now, Iraq and North Korea are well-suited to playing the role of aggressor in the DoD's scenarios because of their acknowledged status as hostile states. Iran, Libya and Cuba could also be used as scenario adversaries. But the big questions regarding the future geopolitical landscape concern China and Russia. For obvious reasons, the administration would like to avoid having to explain why it regards these countries as potential adversaries in its defence analyses, even if it is quite likely that the Chinese military is doing the same in reverse. Scenarios involving these powers have therefore been ruled out of bounds.[25]

II. The United States versus Russia and China

William Cohen's report on the QDR only raises 'the possibility that a regional great power or global peer competitor may emerge' for the period after 2015, adding in somewhat euphemistic fashion: 'Russia and China are seen by some as having the potential to be such competitors, though their respective futures are quite uncertain'.[26]

More explicit texts on current strategic thinking in American defence circles have to be sought among parallel, semi-official documents. The INSS's *1997 Strategic Assessment*, quoted earlier, has the great advantages of frankness and clarity, authorized by its status as unofficial discourse. It is worth quoting again at some length:

> The short period of great-power cooperation may be coming to an end. While ties among the United Stares, Europe and Japan are growing stronger, despite some strains, the other great powers, Russia and China, are increasingly suspicious of longer-term US intentions. They also feel they are not being treated as great powers, and both are concerned about their peripheries:
>
> - Russia – about the near abroad, populated by 25 million ethnic Russians.
> - China – about areas it regards as part of its sovereign territory: Taiwan, Hong Kong, and the Spratly Archipelago in the South China Sea.
>
> Both are well aware of residual military deficiencies; both are focused on domestic priorities; both wish to avoid conflict for fear of jeopardizing economic development. Therefore, rather than opposing the United States directly during the next decade, China and Russia are more likely to mount a low-intensity strategic competition with the United States designed to reduce or offset US influence in the regions they regard as their special spheres of influence.
>
> Each, however, has nationalist movements, so the possibility of conflict, however unlikely, cannot be discounted. If conflict erupts, it is likely to involve specific issues related to sovereignty and to be limited in scope, scale, and duration.
>
> For the next decade at least, neither China nor Russia will be a global-peer competitor of the United States capable of mounting broad strategic challenges. However, either one could become a theater peer with the US, possibly presenting graver problems than could a regional power. Both China and Russia are: nuclear powers with ICBMs, space powers

> with access to overhead imagery and global communications, nations of enormous size with considerable strategic depth, and important leaders of international institutions, well positioned to block UN actions against their interests.[27]

In consequence, the document continues, the United States should use persuasion with these countries, but also 'Dissuade China and Russia from settling disputes by force by maintaining a US military capability that will discourage them from investing the resources to become future opponents, a force that is at once highly capable but not threatening.'

Later it adds:

> To deal militarily with a theater peer, the US would have to thwart its ambition by deterrence, both nuclear and conventional – that is, by maintaining an adequate forward presence in concert with regional allies. The US would also have to prepare to conduct limited operations on the periphery of the theater peer. Those operations would be:
>
> - Designed to raise the political and economic costs of military operations to an unacceptably high level, not to achieve total victory.
> - Carefully controlled to avoid escalation to nuclear warfare.
> - Managed to maintain superiority in information warfare capabilities.
>
> The key is to prepare for such an eventuality without creating a self-fulfilling prophecy. This will require skilful diplomacy as well as a degree of strategic restraint.[28]

This unvarnished version explains – far more convincingly than the BUR scenario of the two MRCs with Iraq and North Korea – the Full Spectrum Force Model option advocated in the same document, and adopted by the QDR. For there is a real proportion between the ends described in the *1997 Strategic Assessment* scenario and the means kept ready by the Pentagon.[29] And it is not at all difficult to understand how this grand strategy scenario articulates with the American will to power; how it corresponds to the imperial imperative of world domination, to that 'essence of the de facto US grand strategy' which consists, in A.J. Bacevitch's careful phrase, of 'establishing a benign imperium conducive to American interests and values'.[30]

President Clinton's report on national security strategy – which complements the report on the QDR and was published at the same time, in May 1997 – starts its introduction by defining the 'strategic priorities': 'a peaceful, undivided, democratic Europe' including an enlarged NATO and dependent on NATO–Russia relations; and 'a stable, prosperous Asia Pacific community', depending on relations between the United States and China.[31] It so happens that the two traditional wings of American 'national security', the Atlantic and the Pacific, have Russia at one extremity and China at the other. Towards one and the other the United States deploys both deterrence and persuasion, Theodore Roosevelt's 'big stick' along with William Taft's 'dollar diplomacy', embellishing the combination with a few tasteful Wilsonian grace-notes.[32]

Mother Russia – old and new

In the case of Russia, 'dollar diplomacy' comes up against limits of two types: firstly, America cannot afford to run a Marshall Plan for Russia – along with central and eastern Europe – and at the same time sustain a $260 billion defence budget. Of its two richest allies one, Germany, is struggling with the costs of reunification and has still not emerged from its economic recession; and the other, Japan, apart from having economic problems of its own, has little inclination to invest massively in Russia. This reluctance affects both the public and the private sectors: the Japanese government has politico-military reasons for restraint, centred on the territorial dispute over the four islands between the Sea of Okhotsk and the North Pacific, while the private sector is influenced by Russia's history of dishonoured debts and the chaotic state of its national market.[33]

Secondly, and by contrast, all three countries – the US, Germany and Japan – are confronted with the same dilemma: they all fear a strong Russia for obvious historical and geopolitical reasons, and they all know perfectly well that the economic reconstruction of Russia can only help to make it strong. This is recognized openly in the QDR report:

> Russia is also expected to continue to emphasize its research and development program, with modernization of its strategic nuclear capabilities and their continuous operational effectiveness a top priority. However, bringing a significant number of conventional weapons systems into production will depend on the success of its economic recovery.[34]

The *1997 Strategic Assessment*'s observation on the growing distrust affecting relations between the US on one side, and Russia and China on the other, is one that strikes all observers. In Russia's case, the honeymoon of the immediate post-communist period swiftly declined into a bitter-sweet relationship. Russia's dreams of Western economic aid dissipated very quickly: Boris Yeltsin's proposed alliances with the US, Europe and Japan were received loftily, and only yielded a tiny part of the billions of dollars he had hoped to obtain for the gravely damaged Russian economy. Since 1992, under pressure from an increasingly disappointed and embittered population, Yeltsin has simultaneously played on two registers in his dealings with the West: that of alliance and that of hostility, with frequent and systematic recourse to political and military blackmail.

The milestones in this intractable deterioration of relations with the West included the new turn in Moscow's relations with Peking since 1992; the Russian Security Council document of April 1993 underlining clear differences with the US, and demanding that Russia be treated appropriately to its rank as a great power; and the replacement of Andrei Kozyrev by Evgeny Primakov as foreign minister in January 1996 after the strong Communist showing in elections to the Duma the previous month. On the American side, the major turning point was the Clinton administration's decision in 1993, at the behest of Henry Kissinger, Zbigniew Brzezinski and Helmut Kohl, to go ahead with the enlargement of NATO into East Europe.[35]

Humiliated at seeing itself demoted to the rank of a second- or even third-class power on account of its economic weakness, Russia has naturally sought to make the most of its two main strengths, both linked to factors of power in the most classical sense: its armed force and military-industrial complex, the only major sector of Russian manufacturing industry which is still competitive in world market terms; and its internal energy resources, along with those on its marches in the Caucasus and Central Asia. It is quite naturally at the intersections of these two categories, at the points where strategic interests concerning energy and security are interwoven, that the main thrust of Russian policy has taken shape in recent years.

The most obvious example is the Russian activity in the Caspian Sea region, where Moscow has resorted to the most bare-faced expedients of imperial policy – from Machiavellian techniques to 'divide and rule' to the brutal exercise of armed force, via every form of blackmail and arm-twisting and the inevitable switches of alliance – in an effort to re-establish or tighten its grip on the sprawl of former Soviet republics (including the so-called 'autonomous' republics) across the Caucasus and Central Asia. The scope of this article does not extend to a detailed account of these activities. Their transparent purpose, however, is a combination of economic strategy, to establish direct or indirect control (through supply routes) of the Caspian Sea hydrocarbons resources, and military strategy, to dominate the imperial marchlands that command Russian access to the vital Middle East zone.[36]

The grossly imperial policy of the new Russia has evoked, more justifiably than at any time since 1917, numerous analogies with Tsarist policy – most strikingly the revival of the old refrain about access to the 'warm seas', much repeated during the Soviet invasion of Afghanistan. And the very fact that people continue to insist on the continuity of Russia's imperial policy through radical changes in its socio-economic structure and ideological options, clearly shows how this argument from the Cold War has helped establish a perception of Russia as an atavistic enemy of the West.

The rush for oil

Of course, such views are only the ideological justification, in historical terms, of a rivalry which is dictated wholly by current interests. For the last four years or so, the zone around the Caspian Sea has been the setting for an out-and-out 'black gold-rush' by the American oil companies. The companies have chosen to deal with Russia by setting themselves up as champions of the independence of the republics concerned, and are striving to create conditions for breaking their effective encirclement by Russia, notably by trying to establish oil export routes outside Russian control.[37]

They have, however, come up against two major obstacles. First, Armenian-inspired restrictions imposed by Congress on government aid to Azerbaijan have prevented the American oil companies from obtaining loans guaranteed by Washington. It is thus not surprising that in the front line of those calling for the removal of these restrictions are eminent members of the Bush administration, by far the most oil-business-infested government team of recent decades.[38] They are supported by the administration of President Clinton who has personally striven, along with Vice-President Al Gore, to form close links with his Azerbaijani opposite number, Gueidar Aliev, and the President of Kazakhstan, Nursultan Nazarbayev.[39]

The other obstacle concerns Iran. The same circles that are working in the US for the lifting of obstacles to relations with Azerbaijan have been campaigning for months to restore American links with Iran and abandon the policies of 'containing' and isolating that country. This policy has rebounded against the US and is increasingly damaging to its interests. This is not just in the matter of exploiting Iranian hydrocarbons – as the replacement of the American company Conoco, compelled by its government to withdraw, by the French company Total for the exploitation of the Iranian Sirri oil-field, had already shown in July 1995 – but also because Iran, as a stage on the route to the Mediterranean via Turkey, is essential if hydrocarbons are to move from Central Asia to the West without passing through zones under Russian control.[40]

Russia for its part has not been standing still but, profiting from the American 'dual containment' of Iraq and Iran, has been striving to restore its ties with both countries. While Moscow concluded a treaty of peace and friendship for ten years with Teheran – the two countries having common interests concerning the exploitation of Caspian Sea oil, and in the juridical quarrel over the status of the Caspian – and signed (in January 1995) a contract for the reconstruction of the nuclear reactors at Bushehr in southern Iran, on the Gulf, the Russian oil giant Lukoil in March 1997 concluded a contract giving it a 51 per cent share of production from the Iraqi Qurna oil-field, which could eventually amount to a million barrels per day.

The well-known concordance of the Russian and French positions on the United Nations embargo against Iraq is based on the concordance of interests between these two countries, with which Baghdad maintains privileged relations. There are now common interests in Iran, too: the contract signed in Teheran on 28 September 1997 concerning exploitation of the giant offshore gas deposit South Pars Field, in Iranian territorial waters, by Total in association with the giant Russian company Gazprom and the Malaysian firm Petronas – in defiance of American extra-territorial legislation in the form of the D'Amato law, passed by Congress in 1996 in reaction to the Conoco/Total incident – confirmed in striking fashion that the American oil lobby's warnings to its government had been well founded.

So there is an increasing contradiction between American political rulings hostile to Iran and Azerbaijan – rulings many believe to be dictated by internal electoral considerations (the Armenian lobby for Azerbaijan, the pro-Israeli lobby for Iran) rather than rational foreign policy – and US economic and strategic interests in the region.[41] But contrary to its flexibility on Azerbaijani matters, the Clinton administration has so far remained intransigent where Iran is concerned, spurred on by Israel which is worried by

Iranian efforts to achieve strategic parity by acquiring long-range missiles and nuclear weapons.[42]

The NATO vice and nuclear blackmail

Nevertheless the American armed forces are covering this eastern extremity of the southern flank of Europe more and more closely, in the Russian sector as much as the Iranian. When Russia pulled its squadron out of the Mediterranean, it probably hoped the US would do the same, but to Moscow's great disappointment the Sixth Fleet is still there in force. Worse still, the US and its NATO allies, after ignoring Russian warnings in carrying out air strikes on Bosnian Serb forces, then deploying their troops in Bosnia, since 1995 have clearly indicated that 'NATO's southern flank' – from 1990, extended de facto south-eastwards as far as the Gulf – now stretches north-eastwards to the Caspian Sea, taking in the Black Sea.

The fleets of the Atlantic Alliance are more present than ever before in the Black Sea, that vital Russian maritime outlet. As a sign of protest, the Russian fleet has boycotted the naval exercises organized there since 1995 under the Partnership for Peace, all the more irritating to Russia because they followed the decision to associate Bulgaria and Romania, both ex-communist countries bordering the Black Sea, with the Western European Union, closely linked to NATO. Under the circumstances, it is not all that astonishing to learn that Russian military men have been known to call this rampant eastward lunge by NATO a *Drang nach Osten*.[43]

The inevitable upsurge of exasperation in Russia as the NATO vice tightens has been redoubled by the accompanying feeling of impotence. For the fact is that the lamentable failure of the Russian troops in Chechnya – so complete that Moscow had to back off in 1996, and negotiate a modus vivendi to prevent further damage to its imperialist oil policy in the Caucasus – cruelly confirmed the advanced state of decay of the conventional forces of what is officially the world's second most powerful army. Another illustration of this decay is the condition of the Russian Black Sea fleet, which cuts a deplorable figure in comparison with the splendour of the US Sixth Fleet.

This generally degraded state also explains more than any other reason why the Russian Duma, with the tacit complicity of the executive, has still not ratified the START II accords of January 1993. In effect, the greatly weakened state of the conventional parts of its armed forces can only give

Russia cause to retain its nuclear capability, to maintain Russia's credibility as a great military power.[44] So the ratification of START II has become a means of blackmail, a factor rendered all the more precious by the virtual absence of others. This emerges clearly from a warning delivered by one of the originators of Russian foreign policy, Alexei Pushkov, who outlined Moscow's conditions and limitations on the expansion of NATO and added that 'Russia's present conventional military disadvantage would incline it to rely more heavily on nuclear weapons in planning its defenses – just as NATO did in similar circumstances starting in the late 1950s'.[45]

Thus the conventional disadvantage of today's Russia induces it to feature nuclear force more prominently in its deterrent posture and to make the same strategic choices as NATO did in the past when it believed, or claimed to believe, that it was at a conventional disadvantage. This is the context in which the Russian Staff in 1993 abandoned the pledge made in 1982 by Brezhnev's USSR to make no first use of nuclear weapons adopting instead the doctrine of graduated response. Inversely, it is now the United States that wants to reduce the importance of the nuclear factor in the strategic balance, owing to the fact that it now enjoys massive conventional superiority. Now it is the American turn to be resolutely in favour of reducing nuclear arsenals.[46]

According to Alexei Pushkov, if NATO were enlarged, the Duma would not ratify START II, and any prospect of concluding START III would vanish. The result would be a situation which this member of the Russian Council on Foreign and Defence Policies describes in terms that confirm the analysis and forecast of the QDR quoted above: 'As long as Russia's economy remains weak, no extensive new arms race will resume, but by conserving their huge nuclear arsenals Russia and the United States will enter into a grey zone of heightened strategic insecurity.'[47]

With friends like that . . .

The fact that Yeltsin's Russia has been so swift to resume its ancestral imperial practices, along with manoeuvres against Washington worthy of the 'zero-sum game' of the bipolar era, and the fact that it has not given up its great power ambitions and refuses to lower its nuclear guard, make it clear to American strategists that there is no point in counting on the idealistic conviction that the end of ideological confrontation means the 'end of history' and the advent of a liberal-pacifist Adam Smith-style utopia. Realists know very well that between states – as the well-known saying goes – there are no friends, only interests. And the interests of a pretender to a share of world hegemony must sooner or later inevitably come up against the interests of the supreme *hegemon.*

This collision of interests, both actual and anticipated, has led to a clear change of tone in American analyses of Russia.[48] While some commentators try to comfort themselves by pointing to the weakness of the ex-superpower's present forces, a consensus emerges that Russia is still dangerous.[49] In the internal US debate on the expansion of NATO, those who are trying to persuade President Clinton to give up the idea argue that one should not provoke the Russian bear without good reason, not that it has turned into a lamb. Richard Pipes, one of 46 signatories of an open letter to President Clinton against the expansion of NATO that was published on the eve of the July 1997 Madrid Atlantic summit, was asked by *Foreign Affairs* to write an analysis of Russia for its 75th anniversary special issue on 'The World Ahead'. His article was eloquently entitled 'Is Russia Still an Enemy?'[50]

The author's central thesis is that, owing to the widespread decomposition of the structures of Russian state and society, the army is now the vector for the 'reintegration' of society and the reconstruction of the empire. Pipes draws an imposing picture of this army and its imperial activities, giving the impression that its present state of dilapidation is only temporary. The Russian army, he claims, is as independent of the political executive as the military were in Weimar Germany, and has adopted the RMA in imitation of its American rival, following the demonstration of its efficacy in the Gulf War. A reorganization of the Russian armed forces is therefore under way, one that privileges the qualitative over the quantitative. A high level of budgetary priority is being given to high-technology research and development, exploiting the substantial knowledge the country has accumulated in this area. Given Russia's considerable economic backwardness, the military route is the only one open to it if it wants to regain its standing as a superpower – and no one doubts that it does.

Contrary to the author's conciliatory position on the NATO question, this thesis supports the idea of a 'window of opportunity' provided by the temporary incapacity of Russian military power; a window which has to be exploited before it is too late to achieve irreversible gains on the ground. The very fact that – as everyone agrees – the political future of Russia is highly unpredictable makes it rational to guard against the worst. This thinking is reinforced by a negative 'culturalist' vision of the future of Russia.[51] To all appearances, it underlies the American government's decision to ignore the near-unanimous opposition of Russians of all political colours and start the process of NATO expansion.[52]

Encouraging Russian hostility

Zbigniew Brzezinski and Anthony Lake, two of the principal ideologues of this expansion, advanced three arguments in the *New York Times* to justify President Clinton's position on the eve of the Madrid NATO summit. The first is somewhat perplexing: it suggests that expansion is 'a necessary step for keeping the trans-Atlantic link strong'.[53] How exactly would the expansion of NATO into East Europe help strengthen Euro-American ties? The argument would seem purely rhetorical if it were not clarified by the one that follows: the two former national security advisers assert without shilly-shallying that 'an expanded alliance provides a hedge against the unlikely but real possibility that Russia will revert to past behaviour. It must also contribute to the goal of preventing that from happening.'[54]

These two arguments should in fact be in the reverse order: if Russia is thought of as threatening, then the expansion of NATO strengthens the Atlantic Alliance, whose purpose has always been containment of Russia. In any case, the Clinton administration, taken aback by the very animated American debate on its decision, no longer hides its underlying postulate: 'The alliance must be prepared for other contingencies, including the possibility that Russia could abandon democracy and return to the threatening behaviour of the Soviet period . . . '[55]

This postulate really is a typical example of a self-fulfilling prophecy, since the behaviour resulting from it helps strengthen Russian hostility to the Atlantic Alliance. Richard Pipes's fellow-signatories of the open letter to President Clinton are not mistaken about this: 'In Russia, NATO expansion which continues to be opposed across the entire political spectrum will strengthen the non-democratic opposition, undercut those who favour reform and cooperation with the West, bring the Russians to question the entire post-Cold War settlement, and galvanise resistance in the Duma to the START II and III treaties.'[56] This is yet another illustration of the famous 'security dilemma', that measures to improve security may have the perverse effect of increasing insecurity.

Moreover, the Clinton administration's decision has created a situation which is difficult to reverse without harming America's strategic interests.

Since the best way to encourage blackmail is to give into it, it is obvious that if Washington were now to back down on the NATO question to avoid compromising the ratification of START II, as the critics of expansion recommend, Moscow would happily attempt to extract endless further concessions by the same means.

The Clinton administration can claim in all honesty that it was simply unwilling to drop the substance for the shadow. In going ahead, though, it offered various consolation prizes to take the sting out of Russia's acquiescence, and to limit the negative effects on its former rival: a jump-seat on G-7 and the Paris Club, economic concessions, the promise to strengthen the Organization for Security and Cooperation in Europe, to revise the CFE treaty and above all the NATO-Russia Founding Act.[57]

This last document, signed in Paris on 27 May 1997, starts by affirming in clause 2 that NATO and Russia do not see themselves as enemies – indicating, if nothing else, that this is not something that goes without saying. It outlines a consultation and cooperation mechanism whose real value will depend on the state of global relations between Russia and the NATO countries, something that is certainly not dictated by SHAPE, at Mons in Belgium.[58] It affirms that NATO has 'no intention' of deploying nuclear weapons on the territory of its new member-states, which is not at all the same thing as undertaking never to do it. Lastly, the Founding Act affirms that NATO 'in the present and foreseeable security context' will not resort to 'further permanent stationing of substantial combat forces', a phrase that leaves the maximum scale of permanent deployment vague and authorizes temporary deployments of unlimited size.[59]

For good reasons, the Founding Act does not contain the basic clause that might have calmed Russian anxieties: an undertaking to refrain from integrating former Soviet republics into NATO. Russia is in a position where it has to try to halt its loss of territory and strategic depth due to the collapse of the Soviet Union and the satellite regimes of its European security buffer. The Russian leadership knows there is nothing much it can do to arrest the emancipation of states in central and eastern Europe, or discourage their choice of Western-style trim. But it would like at least to preserve an informal or semi-formal empire in the formal Soviet imperial domain, among the former Soviet republics.

Where the Baltic states are concerned, Moscow is resigned to accepting a Finlandized outcome, seeing it as the lesser evil, given the manifest anti-Russian feeling in these countries and their proclaimed wish to join Western organizations, NATO in particular. For the other republics, Russian leaders see the CIS as a sort of surrogate USSR, perhaps less centralized but still constricting and incompatible with NATO membership.[60] But at no point has the Atlantic Alliance, let alone the dominant American power, agreed to exclude from NATO expansion any former Soviet republics manifesting a wish to join. Quite the contrary.

So close examination of the Founding Act, far from proving that NATO-Russian relations are in a good state, shows that they are in the 'grey zone of heightened strategic insecurity' evoked by Alexei Pushkov. One has only to look at what happened to the Ukraine on the day the Founding Act was signed and the two days that followed. On 27 May 1997 the Ukrainian president Leonid Kuchma and his Polish colleague Alexander Kwasniewski, speaking in Tallinn, Estonia, supported the request by the Baltic states to join NATO.[61] The very next day, taking the Atlantic Alliance (whose foreign ministers, meeting in Cintra, Portugal, on 29 May, were due to approve a security charter with the Ukraine, to be signed at the Madrid Atlantic summit in early July 1997) by surprise, the Russian Prime Minister Victor Chernomyrdin arrived in Kiev to sign three agreements on the Black Sea Fleet, creating a political sensation.

Broadly, these agreements are based on an extensive and sudden relaxation of the Russian positions – most notably the recognition of Ukrainian sovereignty over the Crimea – and are accompanied by other economic cooperation agreements favourable to the Ukraine. But they also contain 'provisions which, if implemented, could move Ukraine's economy – and its substantial defence industry – towards Russia, rather than towards the West's market economies, and which might complicate closer integration with the European security structures, not to say NATO. Moreover, the mere fact that the Black Sea Fleet . . . will be present for twenty, if not twenty-five years, raises the question whether Ukraine will find itself hostage to the vagaries of Russian politics – for the next quarter century.'[62]

During the same month Russia also signed agreements with Moldova, and a peace treaty with Chechnya which resulted in the agreement of September 1997 on the transit of Baku petroleum through Chechen territory to the Russian Black Sea port of Novorossiysk. It is clear enough that Russia is reacting to the strategic and economic 'eastward thrust' of NATO and the US by trying to reorganize its traditional imperial domain.[63] Moscow is well aware that it does not have a free hand, that it is less and less able to afford the brazen imperial practices of recent years without driving one or other of its dominions irreversibly into the arms of the US. Thus superpower rivalry remains intense, although altered in nature, as both states now officially speak the same market-economy language.

The new face of the new China

In Beijing a month earlier, Boris Yeltsin and his Chinese hosts had been protesting in barely veiled terms against American hegemony. 1997, marked by large-scale opposing manoeuvres between Russia and NATO, with the corollary of an upsurge of hostility to Moscow in the US, also saw a vast debate on China taking shape in the American publications that cover foreign policy and grand strategy: the eloquent title *The China Threat* appeared on the front cover of the March/April issue of *Foreign Affairs*, while the Autumn number of *The National Interest* used – also on the front cover – the more neutral headline *The China Question*. The debate was first stirred up by the publication at the beginning of the year of a book with the alarmist and attention-grabbing title, *The Coming Conflict with China*, by Richard Bernstein and Ross Munro.[64] It spawned numerous articles in these journals and a number of others.

The heightened tone of this debate was a direct consequence of the great tension that accompanied the Sino-American tussle over Taiwan in March 1996: China had chosen to assert its claims on the island, on the eve of the presidential elections due to take place there, by firing missiles in the strait separating the two, quite close to the Taiwan coast. The US reacted to this dangerous gesture by sending two battle carrier groups to patrol the Taiwanese coastline.

Washington had no other choice, as anything less might have tempted Beijing to go even further. Taiwan is at least as important to the US as the state of Kuwait: not just because of the island's economic importance and its considerable monetary reserves, but because if it allowed Beijing to seize it by force the US would 'lose forever its claim to be the great-power guarantor in the Asia-Pacific region', as Bernstein and Munro rightly put it.[65]

The role of Japan

In April, the month following this Sino-American arm-wrestling bout, President Clinton and Japanese Prime Minister Hashimoto agreed in Tokyo to strengthen the military alliance between their countries, to increase the

Japanese defence effort and maintain American forces in Japan at the existing level, but with partial redeployment. In consequence, Japanese participation in the joint naval exercises in Asia-Pacific regional waters increased. Then, in June 1997, a few days before the retrocession of Hong Kong to China – itself due to take place under inauspicious circumstances, owing to the diplomatic tension provoked by Beijing and the military exercises being carried out by Taiwan – a US State Department report lifted the veil on changes to the framework and modalities of the Japan-US strategic alliance, under revision since the April 1996 summit. It emerged that the governing theme of this revision is a larger role for Japan in the event of US involvement in a regional military conflict.

This was confirmed in an agreement on 23 September 1997 – but still to be ratified by their respective parliaments. Under the new agreement, Japan would lend support to the US in the event of conflict in the Asia-Pacific region by allowing it to use its ports, air bases and hospitals – a sort of official rear base role; by cooperating with it in the area of communications and aerial and maritime surveillance; by taking part in minesweeping and rescue missions in international waters; and by making a naval contribution to inspection tasks aimed at enforcing any embargo decreed by the UN. Japanese support is supposed to be limited to areas outside the zone of conflict, but the Japanese defence perimeter is defined in such imprecise terms ('border area') that it has been possible to interpret the agreement as an extension of the zone of Japanese-American military cooperation to take in not only the Korean peninsula, but Taiwan and perhaps even the straits of Taiwan.

The Chinese island can be considered part of Japan's 'border area', being separated by a scant hundred kilometres from the south-western tip of the Japanese archipelago of Okinawa; current practice is to proclaim exclusive economic zones 200 sea miles wide in the China Sea. As for the strait separating Taiwan from mainland China, it was annexed into the zone of Japanese-US military cooperation by an unfortunate if revealing statement by a Japanese government spokesman. The remarks caused a diplomatic incident between Beijing and Tokyo, and elicited a public apology from the Japanese Prime Minister, but their basic import has never been formally denied.

To understand how these developments are seen by the two great powers of East Asia, one must bear in mind that Japan invaded the island of Taiwan in 1895, on its way to the invasion of the Chinese mainland, and occupied it until the end of the Second World War. Only American protection, officially proclaimed in 1955, enabled the Kuomintang government to survive there after 1949. It is thus not difficult to see that any manifestation of the Japan-US alliance touching on Taiwan is perceived in China as an aggressive imperialist act, contrary to the way the Chinese attitude is seen in the West and even, increasingly, in Japan itself, which these days is tending to get over its 'guilty conscience' for past behaviour, and to view China as a menacing power.[66]

The strategic tension between the two Asian powers is aggravated by the fact that they both depend on energy imports. Behind the quarrel that divides them (along with Taiwan and South Korea) over ownership of the Senkaku/Diaoyu islands, five coral atolls in the eastern China Sea, lies the issue of possible oil deposits in the economic zones around these islands. Similarly, Japan – although not directly involved in the complicated, apparently endless squabble over the Spratly islands, involving several ASEAN countries as well as China and Taiwan – does have an interest in ensuring that the islands do not fall into Beijing's hands. This is because, owing to the Spratlys' strategic position, China would then be in a position to control sea routes vital for Japanese hydrocarbons imports, along with much other regional, inter-regional and intercontinental maritime traffic and the circulation of warships, with US warships heading the list.

Adding these two disputes to all the others involving China in the seas of East Asia, from the one with South Korea in the Yellow Sea to the ones with Indonesia, Malaysia and Vietnam over the Natuna islands zone, via the Gulf of Tonkin (Vietnam again);[67] and also bearing in mind China's armament efforts, especially in the domain of naval equipment and other means of projecting armed force, at a time when America's long-term military commitment to the region is perceived as uncertain, it becomes clear why the arms trade and industry are more flourishing than ever in East Asia, unlike most other parts of the world.[68]

It is not difficult to grasp the key to the apparent paradox that in this part of the world, the end of the Cold War, far from reducing tension, seems to have increased it. The collapse of the Soviet Union caused East Asia to shift from a polarization against Moscow and its Indochinese allies by most of the forces allied to the US, jointly with China, to the release of latent tensions between a fast-growing China and the rest of the region, backed by the United States. This reality, which Bernstein and Munro do not fail to mention, counts for a lot more than the anxieties – marginal for the time being in any case – that might be aroused by the other regional power, Japan.[69]

The modernization of China's forces

The removal of the previous cause of tension has had its corollary in Chinese military doctrine, pointed out in an interesting article by an Australian intelligence official, A.D. McLennan: 'The collapse of the Soviet Union . . . liberated the PLA from the Maoist "people's war" doctrine – defence by depth and density of population in lieu of firepower. China is developing smaller, more professional forces with greater mobility and striking power, both typical goals of force modernization generally.'[70] McLennan also points out that China's minimal nuclear deterrence posture corresponds both to its means and its strategic interests; general nuclear disarmament would suit it even better, given its nuclear inferiority to Russia and the US, and the fact that in conventional terms it has the advantage of numbers and of greater willingness to expose itself to human losses.

China's demographic mass and density mean that its pledge to make no first use of nuclear weapons conforms to its strategic interests, rather than revealing any pacifist tendency. And even if such a tendency existed, it would not apply to Taiwan, as the no-first-use pledge does not apply to Chinese territory, according to a senior Chinese official quoted by McLennan.[71] This shows that the tension between China and the American-protected zone of Asia-Pacific, of which the Taiwan question is the sorest point, is real and dangerous; far more so than the oft-mentioned prospect of a new conflict in the Korean peninsula.

Korea

On this last eventuality, Leon Sigal has re-established a number of truths, obscured by media propaganda amounting to caricature against the North Korean regime – which, it is true, lends itself to this distortion as much as the Iraqi dictatorship does. 'Ever since the 1970s, some US intelligence assessments have concluded that South Korea has the military edge, especially in the air, and could repulse a North Korean attack even without throwing US forces into the balance.'[72] This advantage has grown continuously, to such a point that it is now reasonable to wonder which of the two Koreas most fears the departure of Uncle Sam's troops. The fact is that it is the growing conventional superiority of the South, combined with the American nuclear threat and the disappearance of the Soviet nuclear umbrella, that has driven the North to try to obtain atomic weapons.[73]

So it is on the opposition between China and the US, and certainly not on the conflict with North Korea, that the new regional strategic setup, including the revised terms of the Japanese-US alliance, is arranged. The image of China current in the US has evolved in parallel. The view of Bernstein and Munro is that since the disintegration of the Soviet empire at the end of the 1980s 'China is seeking to replace the United States as the dominant power in Asia'.[74] In somewhat more measured style than the title of their book would suggest, the two authors insist on the possibility – rather than the probability – of a conflict with China provoked by an invasion of Taiwan or a regional conflict in the South China Sea. These allegations – leading to the triple conclusion that the US presence and supremacy in Asia should be maintained and Taiwan and Japan reinforced – are based on an analysis of the Chinese state hinged on the country's armament effort, whose considerable real scale, they believe, is hidden behind misleading official figures.

Similarities and differences in US attitudes to China and Russia

There is an altogether remarkable similarity between American analyses hostile to China and those hostile to Russia, not only because both analyses see the mote in China's or Russia's eye while remaining oblivious to the beam in America's, but because they both place the emphasis on the army which they believe, along with the related military-industrial complex, to be the all-powerful central institution of the country concerned.[75] Richard Pipes, quoted earlier, analyses the position and role of the Russian army in terms virtually identical to Bernstein's and Munro's. And while Pipes draws a parallel between Russia and Weimar Germany, Bernstein and Munro consider the most likely outcome of present Chinese political evolution to be 'a kind of corporatist, militarized, nationalist state, one with some similarity to the fascist states of Mussolini or Francisco Franco'.[76]

However, unlike Russia which has few defenders in the United States, China has considerable numbers. The difference is not simply due to the legacy of hostility accumulated against Russia in the Cold War years and cooperation established during the Sino-American alliance over the last two decades of that period. Even more important is the fact that the economic interests that currently bind the US to China have no common measure with those that have been established with Russia. So that the distrust of China maintained in American defence circles, out of conviction as well as self-interest, is balanced by the favourable attitudes cultivated in the trade and business communities, with foreign policy makers split between the two attitudes. The traditional divisions between hawks and doves, realists and idealists, are every bit as muddled here as they are in the debate over the expansion of NATO.

The role of China advocate in American foreign policy journals has fallen on Robert Ross, a Harvard academic.[77] He does not have much trouble dealing with alarmist exaggerations of Chinese military potential put about by China-detractors: Japan alone is greatly superior to China in both air and naval terms, and will retain this superiority for the foreseeable future, owing to its much more advanced technology and much higher defence budget. The underlying idea is that China could regard the US as a guarantee against any resurgence of Japanese military imperialism, placing the US in the ideal position – according to Kissinger doctrine – of guarantor of the balance of forces. Nevertheless, China could go against American policy in the domain of weapons proliferation. The US should therefore seek Chinese assurances in this area, as well as those of economic liberalization and human rights. In so doing, Ross insists, it is important to avoid souring relations with China and to pursue a policy of 'engagement' with it instead of putting it in quarantine.

The visit to the US of the Chinese president, Jiang Zemin, at the end of October 1997, was a vivid moment and a good illustration of this last policy. In exchange for Chinese assurances on ending deliveries of nuclear materials and missiles to Iran, Washington unblocked the supply of power stations to China, to the great profit of the American nuclear industry. Beijing also undertook to buy fifty Boeing aircraft for a total of $3 billion, and agreed to reduce customs tariffs on American products so as to reduce the large US commercial deficit with China, now nearly $40 billion.

But the visit also showed the limits of the policy of engagement when, during a joint press conference with his American opposite number, the Chinese President suddenly adopted a menacing tone on Taiwan: 'We do not pledge to renounce the use of force, which is not directed against our compatriots in Taiwan but rather against external forces trying to interfere in Chinese internal affairs, as well as those who try to bring about Taiwan's independence or separation from the rest of the country.'[78] If there were any dreamy idealists among those responsible for US foreign policy, the Chinese President meant to bring them down to earth.

Behind the façade for public consumption, in any case, there are very few who nourish illusions. Robert Ross's declared concern, like that of the American campaigners against NATO expansion, is to avoid the creation of a self-fulfilling prophecy: to avoid setting China against the United States by treating it openly as an enemy. Looking closely at Ross's views on the American strategic and military presence in Asia, however, it becomes apparent that he hardly differs from Bernstein and Munro, for the good reason that engagement is an uncertain gamble, like the political future of China itself.

> There is no guarantee that engagement will work . . . At times, Washington will have to protect its interests unilaterally. It will also have to maintain its current military deployments in Asia. US strategic retrenchment would do far more to alter the Sino-American bilateral balance of power and the regional balance of power than any combination of Chinese military and economic policies.[79]

The main strategic difference that might arise between the two sides of the American debate on China is more concerned with the Japanese-American alliance. Where Bernstein and Munro argue vigorously for an enlarged Japanese military role, a warm supporter of closer ties between Beijing and Washington like Zbigniew Brzezinski is to be heard warning against any strengthening of Japan-US cooperation.[80] This view is far from unanimous among supporters of an appeasement policy towards Beijing. But what they all fear is that a souring of US relations with both Russia and China at the same time might result in a strengthening of the sketchy alliance which has taken shape between those two countries.

The Sino-Russian 'strategic partnership'

Comment on the possibility of a Russo-Chinese alliance is difficult, if not impossible, to find in American official or even semi-official strategic literature. Despite the very real progress of strategic and military cooperation between the two countries, the taboo against raising this question seems even stronger than the one against naming Russia and China as potential enemies in war scenarios.

The collapse of the Soviet Union effectively opened the way for a new era in relations between Moscow and Beijing, the two governments driven by common and reciprocal interests. Their economies are potentially complementary: China can benefit from transfers of Russian technology, especially in the energy sector, including nuclear energy, and in the arms sector. In the latter sector, where Russian technology is at its most advanced, Chinese demand is heavy while Russia has a vital need to export, to help cover the costs of an industry whose losses it cannot afford to subsidize as heavily as it once did. Moreover, China will soon be a net hydrocarbons importer and seems destined, with Japan, to be a natural customer for the petroleum and enormous natural gas reserves of Siberia and the Russian Far East – fields at Sakha/Yakutsk, Irkutsk and the offshore field near the island of Sakhalin.[81] In exchange, Russia could import great quantities of Chinese consumer goods, whose prices are more in line with its internal market than Western products.

For the time being, however, these exchanges remain potential rather than real. China continues to favour Western technology whenever it has the choice. Meanwhile Western countries are locked in cut-throat competition for access to the Chinese market with, in the US's case, Russia-related strategic considerations also in mind. For example, one of the reasons persuading Washington to lift the ban on supplying power plants to China is undoubtedly to keep Moscow out of that market, which has direct strategic implications.[82]

The one domain in which the Western countries, led by the US, cannot displace Russia is that of exports of military material and technology, partly because of politico-strategic self-restraint, and partly for reasons related to the quality/price ratio of advanced equipment. Very soon after the collapse of the Soviet Union, China became Russia's biggest military customer, alone absorbing 26 per cent of Russian arms exports, worth a total of around $1.7 billion, in the 1992–94 period. As early as 1992 China acquired twenty-four Sukhoi Su-27 fighter-bombers, and in 1995 ordered another seventy-two Su-27s costing $2.8 billion, around fifty of which have already been delivered by Moscow. Bigger still is the contract concluded at the same time, in 1995, under which China is to make up to two hundred Su-27s under Russian licence, starting production in 1999.

Beijing has also purchased S-300 air defence missile systems from Moscow, along with four Kilo-class submarines, of which two have already been delivered. After the March 1996 face-off in the Taiwan straits, China ordered two Russian Sovremennyy destroyers equipped with cruise missiles. It is also interested in constructing or acquiring an aircraft carrier – Russia recently finished building its first – and acquiring in-flight refuelling tankers.

These Russian military deliveries to China establish strategic links which are more important and durable than the ties resulting from Beijing's acquisition of fifty Boeing civil aircraft. Beijing now depends on Moscow for the maintenance and repair of the most sophisticated submarines and fighter-bombers it possesses, in other words two of the mainstays of its regional military power. That is why the quality of relations between the two countries should not be measured solely by the yardstick of the overall volume of their trade, which remains relatively small. It also explains why their political relations are so much more advanced than their non-military or overall trade relations.

After the first Yeltsin-Jiang summit in December 1992, the two governments began a procedure to settle their frontier disputes, which the Russian President is now trying to conclude in a way that favours Chinese requests. They also agreed on the principle of limiting the forces deployed on either side of their common frontier. At the second summit, in September 1994, the two countries declared themselves tied by a 'constructive partnership', decided on new reductions of their frontier forces, undertook not to use nuclear weapons against each other, and pronounced themselves in favour of a 'multipolar world system'.

Then, at the third summit in April 1996, the two countries declared themselves henceforth linked in a 'strategic partnership'. The Chinese President proclaimed his support for the Russian positions against NATO expansion and on Chechnya, while his Russian colleague supported the Chinese positions on Taiwan and Tibet. Further measures showing reciprocal trust along the common borders of China with CIS member states were instituted and formalized by treaty. There was of course nothing fortuitous in the timing of this new 'strategic partnership's' proclamation, just a month after the Sino-American confrontation off Taiwan and in the same month that the Clinton-Hashimoto summit decided on the upward revision of the Japan-US military alliance.

In December 1996, the Chinese Prime Minister Li Peng joined Boris Yeltsin in Moscow to reject any prospect of a 'unipolar world' and defend the principle of a 'multipolar international order'. Then, in April 1997, the fourth Sino-Russian summit, held in Moscow, adopted a 'Joint Statement on Global Multipolarization and the Establishment of a New World Order'. This document, clearly aimed at the US without naming it directly, affirms that no country should seek to impose its hegemony on others or assume that it has a monopoly of international relations. The statement also condemned all consolidation of military blocs which, in the political context, could only be taken to refer to NATO expansion and the revision of the Japan-US alliance.[83]

Needless to say, the Sino-Russian communiqués are not without elements of feint, blackmail and bluff. But the irritation expressed by the two governments is not assumed for the occasion: there is no shortage of reasons for their rancour against the US, as has been shown. And these protests against a 'unipolar world' are taken a lot more seriously in Washington when they come from a Yeltsin-Jiang summit than when they come (for example) from a Chirac-Yeltsin summit.

However, something that is a lot less believable, at least so far, is the so-called Sino-Russian 'strategic partnership', which in fact is not really based on firm and solid foundations of mutual trust. For the time being, both countries are using this partnership, each in its own way, as a threat or means of exchange, either to obtain concessions or shifts of position from the American government, or to persuade it to attenuate or desist from its encroachments on their own respective positions.[84] American official strategic documents affect to ignore any possible alliance between Russia and China precisely for this reason: to minimize the weight of blackmail to which the US can be subjected.

The hub and its spokes

For the time being, certainly, neither of the two 'partners' can afford the luxury of an open break with the US: the fact is that they both need the US more than they need each other. From the economic point of view above all, Josef Joffe is not mistaken in thinking the Sino-Russian 'strategic partnership' anachronistic, and affirming that Boris Yeltsin is not going to look for computers in Beijing and that China will not risk the loss of its main export market.[85] In any case, the 1997 visit by the Chinese President to the US showed that China knew how to be cooperative, when necessary, to obtain economic advantages. Current American strategy really does seem to contain the Bismarckian dimension that Joffe describes: it corresponds closely to the image of hub and spokes, with the US as the hub and Europe, Japan, Russia and China as the spokes of the wheel, all needing the US more than they need each other.[86]

Even so, the author is being too hasty when he suggests that the US, simply because of its nuclear weaponry, has nothing to fear from any military alliance against it, even a coalition of Russia and China.[87] No one has forgotten that once nuclear deterrence has become mutual it can no longer be used, or that the deterrent effect is greatly reduced when used against enemies whose nuclear destructiveness potential is qualitatively equivalent. As Edward Luttwak so aptly points out, nuclear weapons are 'too effective to be effective'.[88]

It is difficult enough to believe that the US would really be willing to use nuclear weapons against China, which has a real – if quantitatively limited – capacity for nuclear retaliation, if Beijing were to try to seize Taiwan by force (and even less so if the invasion followed a unilateral declaration of independence by Taiwan).[89] So it is even more difficult to accept that the US would take the initiative in resorting to nuclear weapons against a China-Russia coalition in a dispute over a third country. The deterrent credibility of American nuclear capacity against nuclear peers of the US is restricted to the protection of American territory against direct aggression. And of course there is no state that aspires to such an act of folly.

Furthermore – in a 'post-heroic' era in which the US armed forces, not to mention American public opinion, are not very eager to take risks, even the minimal risks of an intervention somewhere like Somalia or Haiti – it is far from certain that the US would even risk a major conventional war in defence of Taiwan, especially as Washington subscribes officially to the principle of Chinese territorial unity.[90] Would not direct US military involvement be even more risky with the American nuclear deterrent neutralized by a coalition of China and Russia, and with Russian military technology available to a Chinese army – still fully manned at present – that remains far more willing to risk human losses than the US army? And might not a military confrontation between the US and China in East Asia lead to the risk of Russia opening a second front, directly or through proxies, in (say) the Ukraine or the Persian Gulf?

Is this really an unbelievable scenario? Certainly unlikely but nevertheless not impossible, in Raymond Aron's celebrated phrase, it is a scenario well in the tradition of 'worst case analysis'.[91] The preceding pages have sought to demonstrate that it is this scenario – and not the scenario of two simultaneous wars against adversaries like Iraq and North Korea – that corresponds most convincingly to the global military posture of the United States. A close reading of the QDR report does reveal something rather like an admission: after judging it likely that there will be no 'global peer competitor' until 2015, and before proceeding to separate examinations of Russia and China, treated as regional powers for the time being, the report affirms that 'it is likely that *no regional power or coalition* will amass sufficient conventional military strength in the next ten to fifteen years to defeat our armed forces, once the full military potential of the United States is mobilized and deployed to the region of conflict'.[92]

Conclusion

Starting from the observation of a manifest disproportion between the American defence budget and the official war scenario to which it is supposed to correspond, this article has deduced that the implicit scenario to which US defence expenditure really conforms, but which cannot be made too explicit for political, strategic and tactical reasons, is that of two simultaneous wars against Russia and China, disguised by the official hypothesis of two 'major regional conflicts' against Iraq and North Korea. The image of these two wars should be understood as coming from a school of deterrence through escalation that still persists in the Pentagon and the US administration.

To check the plausibility of this reading, relations between the United States, Russia and China have been reviewed. Examination of the Russian and Chinese cases shows that the hypothesis of this implicit scenario in American strategy is in keeping with the concrete development of these relations. In reality, the doctrine and practice of 'engagement' are still accompanied by a clear American effort at containment of Russia and China, in the strict sense of the term. In the case of Russia, which unlike China is in a state of institutional and imperial deliquescence, it is even possible to talk about an American practice of post-ideological 'roll back', no longer directed against 'communism' but simply against Russian imperial hegemony. In seizing the historic opportunity provided by Russia's present dilapidation, from which there is no guarantee that it will not recover in the medium or long term, the United States is encroaching much more today on the zones of Europe and Asia under Russian influence than it ever did in the days of the USSR, after the Second World War.

The current level of the US defence budget corresponds rationally to the US aspiration to imperial expansion and exclusive global hegemony. In full strategic coherence, the United States is prepared for the worst case scenario: in other words, it has taken the appropriate measures against its two main potential military rivals, the two main candidates for the position of 'global peer competitor', Russia and China. It is all the more plausible to consider them jointly in that they are naturally tempted to form an alliance against the sole superpower of the moment.

These strategic choices keep up a level of tension with these two powers that justifies the US suzerainty over their neighbours, Germany, Europe and Japan, and blocks any move towards possible regional alliances – Euro-Russian or Sino-Japanese – which might be able to challenge American hegemony. Yet the expanded military role of Germany and Japan, in the context of an American alliance directed against Russia and China, should have the effect of heightening the anxieties of these two countries and leading them to try, each on its own behalf, to get into the good graces of the United States. For the time being this seems to be working better with Beijing than with Moscow. But, when all is said and done, this is no more than an ancient and well-tried imperial recipe.

Notes

1. This essay has benefited from criticism and comments from members of the CIRPES (EHESS, Paris), especially its director Alain Joxe, and Maurice Ronai, and I extend my gratitude to all of them. It goes without saying however that the views expressed herein are entirely my own responsibility. The essay was first published in *New Left Review* 228, March/April 1998, pp. 91–126.
2. The expression comes from Charles Krauthammer, 'The Unipolar Moment', in G. Allison and G.F. Treverton, eds., *Rethinking America's Security: Beyond Cold War to New World Order*, NewYork 1992.
3. Department of Defense, *Report on the Quadrennial Defense Review*, Washington 1997, published on the World Wide Web (www).
4. See *Le débat stratégique américain 1995–96, Cahier d'Etudes Stratégiques*, 20, CIRPES (GSD, EHESS) Paris 1997.
5. For the technical arguments inevitably raised by the administration's choices, see (among others): Zalmay Khalilzad and David Ochmanek, 'Rethinking US Defence Planning', *Survival* (IISS, London), vol. 39, no. 1, Spring 1997; D.S. Zakheim, 'Tough Choices: Toward a True Strategic Review', *The National Interest* (Washington), no. 47, Spring 1997; W.E. Odom, 'Transforming the Military', *Foreign Affairs*, vol. 76, no. 4, July–August 1997, and replies to this article in the November–December issue (vol. 76, no. 6) of the same journal.
6. National Defense University (NDU), *1997 Strategic Assessment: Flashpoints and Force Structure*, INSS, Washington 1997 (www).
7. William Cohen, *The Secretary's Message*, in Department of Defense, *Report on the QDR*.
8. The last few years have seen the Pentagon more 'revolutionary' than ever before.

One reason for this inflation of the word 'revolution' is the book by Kenneth Adelman (former director of the ACDA in the Reagan era) and Norman Augustine (then CEO of Martin Marietta, later CEO of Lockheed Martin), *The Defense Revolution: Strategy for the Brave New World*, San Francisco 1990.

9. See '1998 Military Spending: Behind the Numbers', *The Defense Monitor* (Washington), vol. xxvi, no. 3, June 1997.
10. See J.G. Mason, 'La République du centre: intérêts extérieurs et coalitions intérieures', in *Le débat stratégique américain 1995–96*.
11. Adelman and Augustine, *The Defense Revolution*, pp. 90–99.
12. Ibid., pp. 45–76.
13. William Perry, 'Defense in an Age of Hope', *Foreign Affairs*, vol. 75, no. 6, November–December 1996.
14. Ibid., p. 78. Khalilzad and Ochmanek go even further than the ex-Defense Secretary. Giving the example of target-seeking anti-tank weapons – so-called 'brilliant' weapons . . . no doubt 'genius' ones are on the way – that hit several targets with one firing, they assert that it is now possible to think in terms of 'kills per sortie' rather than 'sorties per kill'. 'Rethinking US Defence Planning', p. 60.
15. As a *New York Times* editorial, reprinted in the *International Herald Tribune* of 2 May 1997, put it: 'Pentagon spending is not the flywheel of prosperity in a $7 trillion national economy'.
16. This common-sense reasoning appears in Thomas Hobbes's *Leviathan*: 'The Multitude sufficient to confide in for our Security, is not determined by any certain number, but by comparison with the Enemy we feare . . .' London 1985, p. 224.
17. See IISS, *The Military Balance 1997/98*, London 1997.
18. This figure is calculated by adding the figures published in *The Military Balance 1997/98*. The criteria for evaluating and comparing military spending in different countries are always open to doubt, but the evolution of figures over time retains an indicative value. The general trend in relations between American military expenditure and that of the rest of the world, in the direction of increasing American preponderance, cannot be doubted.
19. For a good critique of the QDR, examining the total disproportion between the military means wielded by the US and the danger represented by declining 'rogue states', see Carl Conetta, 'Backwards Into the Future: How the QDR Prepares America for the Wrong Century', *Project on Defense Alternatives*, Commonwealth Institute, Cambridge, Mass., June 1997 (www).
20. In reality, the superabundant means brought into play were motivated not by any fantasized fear of Iraqi strength, but by the enormous importance to US supremacy of getting over the 'Vietnam syndrome'. The challenge had to be met without the slightest slip. What was at stake was the very credibility of US power.
21. Ronald Steel, 'A New Realism', *World Policy Journal*, vol. xiv, no. 2, Summer 1997, p. 8.
22. A.J. Bacevitch, 'Tradition Abandoned: America's Military in a New Era', *The National Interest*, no. 48, Summer 1997, p. 20.

23. Ibid.
24. It is difficult to know for certain what impression this text made on the Russians when it was first made public. What is known is that it became a favoured reference for many Western opponents of Pentagon and American supremacy, because it fitted so well with their own representation of US policy. And in fact the text made its most lasting impact on American critics, being (for example) a principal source for two recent articles in successive issues of the *World Policy Journal*, one on Europe and the other on Asia: Benjamin Schwarz, 'Permanent Interests, Endless Threats: Cold War continuities and NATO Enlargement', *WPJ*, Fall 1997, pp. 24–30; and T.G. Carpenter, 'Washington's Smothering Strategy: American Interests in East Asia', *WPJ*, Winter 1997–98, pp. 20–31.
25. Khalilzad and Ochmanek, 'Rethinking US Defence Planning', p. 49. The authors both know what they are talking about: Zalmay Khalilzad was Assistant Deputy Under-Secretary of Defense for Policy Planning in Washington between 1991 and 1993, and David Ochmanek Deputy Assistant Secretary of Defense for Strategy between 1993 and 1995.
26. Department of Defence, *Report on the QDR*, section II.
27. NDU, *1997 Strategic Assessment*. This document makes the distinction between 'theater' (reserved for Russia and China) and 'regional' (for states such as Iran, Iraq and North Korea) in a manner which clarifies the substitution of 'Major Theater Wars' for 'Major Regional Conflicts' in the QDR. This change is in conformity with the hypothesis of this essay.
28. Ibid.
29. This essay, written for the annual conference on US strategy (CIRPES, EHESS) held on 20 October 1997, was largely completed when Michael Klare's article 'La nouvelle stratégie militaire des États-Unis' appeared in the November 1997 issue of *Le Monde diplomatique*. Our two analyses concur in emphasizing the importance given to Russia and China in American strategic thought, and we both refer to the NDU/INSS *1997 Strategic Assessment* among other sources. They diverge, though, when Michael Klare views the scenario of two MRCs as matching current military capability of the US, and the Russian or Chinese threat as something brandished by people who 'think the armed forces budget should greatly increase'.
30. Bacevitch, 'Tradition Abandoned', p. 20.
31. William Clinton, A *National Security Strategy for a New Century*, The White House, Washington 1997. This document is based on the report presented in March by the President's Adviser on national security, Samuel Berger, *A Foreign Policy Agenda for the Second Term*, CSIS, Washington 1997 (www).
32. There is nothing new about this combination, picked up by Bacevitch. It has been recurrent since the Second World War.
33. See Chikahito Harada, *Russia and North-East Asia*, Adelphi Paper 210, IISS, Oxford 1997, pp. 49–60.

34. Department of Defense, *Report on the QDR*, Section II.
35. On the circumstances surrounding this decision, see the romanticized account by Zbigniew Brzezinski and Anthony Lake, 'The Moral and Strategic Imperatives of NATO Enlargement', *International Herald Tribune*, 1 July 1997; and Mark Danner's analysis 'Marooned in the Cold War: America, the Alliance, and the Quest for a Vanished World', *World Policy Journal*, vol. xiv, no. 3, Fall 1997.
36. On Russian policy in the Caucasus and Central Asia, see S. Frederick Starr, 'Power Failure: American Policy in the Caspian', *The National Interest*, no. 47, Spring 1997; Thomas Goltz, 'Catch-907 in the Caucasus, *The National Interest*, no 48, Summer 1997; Vicken Cheterian, 'Grand jeu pétrolier en Transcaucasie', *Le Monde diplomatique*, October 1997, and from the same author an excellent account of the development of Russian policy in the Caucasus over the last ten years, *Dialectics of Ethnic Conflicts and Oil Projects in the Caucasus*, PSIS, Geneva 1997; see also the supplement published in *Le Monde*, 12 November 1997, as well as the news item by Sophie Shihab, 'Russes et Américains s'opposent sur le tracé du grand oléoduc de la Caspienne', *Le Monde*, 15 November 1997.
37. On the recent history of Russo-American rivalries in this part of the world, see Cheterian, 'Grand jeu pétrolier en Transcaucasie', as well as *Newsweek*, 12 May 1997.
38. See 'Azerbaijani Oil Gathers Clout in U.S.', *International Herald Tribune*, 7 July 1997.
39. On the signature in Washington of two important oil contracts by the Kazakh President on 19 November, see *Le Monde*, 21 November 1997.
40. See Zbigniew Brzezinski, Brent Scowcroft and Richard Murphy, 'Differentiated Containment', and Graham Fuller and Ian Lesser, 'Persian Gulf Myths', in *Foreign Affairs*, vol. 76, no. 3, May–June 1997. The first article affirms: 'One negative consequence of current policy is the damage inflicted on America's interest in gaining greater access to the energy sources of Central Asia' (p. 28), adding that American government opposition to American oil company activity in Iran helped nobody but Total. The second article says in a similar vein: 'Flat rejection of pipelines through Iranian territory – which, for practical reasons, most of the region's states and many oil companies would prefer – opens the way to Russian monopoly' (p. 48). See also S. Frederick Starr, who says that the American policy of isolating Iran 'is having a disastrous impact on Central Asia and Azerbaijan by denying to them the obvious outlet for their oil and gas and forcing them into Russia's arms' ('Power Failure', p. 29).
41. See James Schlesinger, 'Fragmentation and Hubris: A Shaky Basis for American Leadership', in *The National Interest*, no. 49, Fall 1997. This vigorous protest points out, among other things, that President Clinton chose, unusually, to announce the strengthening of American sanctions against Iran in a speech delivered before the World Jewish Congress in New York (p. 5).
42. See Éric Leser, 'Les manoeuvres de Téhéran pour acquérir l'arme nucléaire', *Le Monde*, 1 October 1997.

43. For a frank expression of Russian irritation over what Moscow perceives as an attack on its vital interests and its security, see Nicolai A. Kovalsky, 'Russia and Mediterranean Security', in *Mediterranean Security at the Crossroads*, special issue of *Mediterranean Quarterly* (Washington), vol. 8. no. 2, Spring 1997. For a clear exposé of American policy on the southern flank of NATO and its eastward extension, see in the same collection W. Bruce Weinrod, 'The US, NATO, and the Mediterranean Region in the Twenty-First Century'. See also remarks by Admiral Joseph Lopez, American commander of allied forces in southern Europe, in 'Is NATO's Southern Flank Exposed?', *International Herald Tribune*, 20 May 1997. The arguments presented by Weinrod, who was vice-deputy to the Secretary of Defense for Europe and NATO under George Bush's presidency, and by Admiral Lopez, explain the American intransigence in the face of the French demand to have the NATO southern command entrusted to a European.
44. It is also the case that START II would be very costly to Russia if it had to replace its multi-warhead ICBMs with single-warhead missiles – this is why the Clinton administration proposed START III to Moscow before START II had even been ratified.
45. Alexei K. Pushkov, 'Don't Isolate Us: A Russian View of NATO Expansion', *The National Interest*, no. 47, Spring 1997, p. 62.
46. After these lines were written, the *International Herald Tribune* of 8 December 1997 published two articles from the *Washington Post* confirming these tendencies. One concerns a CIA report to the American Senate revealing the pressure being exerted in Moscow to give a larger role to nuclear weapons in Russian strategy, and even to develop options for first-strike and 'limited' use. The other reports on a secret directive from President Clinton (Presidential Decision Directive, PDD) containing a major revision of US nuclear doctrine, abandoning the insensate objective of 'victory' in a prolonged nuclear war (contained in the previous PDD signed by President Reagan in 1981) and falling back on a strictly deterrent posture, better adapted to the nuclear weapons reduction objectives advanced during the negotiations for START III.
47. Pushkov, 'Don't Isolate Us', p. 62.
48. Boris Yeltsin himself is a good deal less appreciated, paradoxically, than Gorbachev used to be. See Peter Rutland, 'Yeltsin: The Problem, Not the Solution', which dubs him a 'Potemkin President', *The National Interest*, no. 49, Fall 1997, p. 38.
49. For an analysis of that weakness, see Sherman Garnett, 'Russia's Illusory Ambitions', *Foreign Affairs*, vol. 76, no. 2, March–April 1997.
50. Richard Pipes, *Foreign Affairs*, vol. 76, no. 5, September–October 1997.
51. The Washington oracle Henry Kissinger, asked by *Newsweek* to describe the future, said, 'Early in the new century, after many ups and downs, Russia is likely to have restored its central authority. It may well be closer to the political structures favoured by Pinochet or Salazar than to a Western pluralistic system – though it will be freer than Communism.' 'A World We Have Not Known', *Newsweek*, 27 January 1997.

52. To see the decision to expand NATO as having been dictated by the arms lobby is clearly too reductionist, even though arms industry interests are real enough and have played a part in the process. See 'US Arms Makers Lobby For NATO Expansion', *International Herald Tribune*, 30 June 1997.
53. Brzezinski and Lake, 'NATO Enlargement'.
54. The security-based argument directed against Russian ambitions in Europe explains, in particular, the strong German support for the principle of NATO expansion, so strong that it is backed by an overwhelming majority in the Bundestag, Greens included. The third argument of Brzezinski and Lake addresses the democratization of the countries concerned. It will only convince those who really want to believe that belonging to NATO is a measure of democracy in itself.
55. Written responses from the administration to questions from Senator Hutchinson and nineteen other senators, in 'The Debate Over NATO Expansion', *Arms Control Today* (Washington), vol. 27, no. 6, September 1997, p. 3.
56. George Bunn, Robert Bowie, David Calleo et al., *An Open Letter to President Bill Clinton.*
57. Two days after the announcement on 14 May that an agreement between the Boris Yeltsin administration and NATO was about to be signed, the IMF unblocked a tranche of nearly $700 million, held back for some time out of a total credit to Russia of $10 billion over three years. At the same time the Russian government started to negotiate a steep increase in its EU borrowings over the 1996 level. These economic accompaniments to the expansion of NATO have generated the view in the US that the Yeltsin administration's conciliatory attitude resulted from the need to finance economic interests – energy interests for the most part – which predominate in Moscow (see 'NATO and Russia: The Gazprom Factor', *International Herald Tribune*, 27 May 1997). It is an irony of history that this is an exact reflection of the explanation that used to be given for US foreign policy choices in the Soviet Union. The fact is however that hydrocarbons-sector interests weigh even more heavily on Russia than they ever did (or do) on the US.
58. A lucid Boris Yeltsin said of the accords with NATO that 'their success will depend on their application'.
59. Extracts from 'The NATO-Russia Founding Act' published in *Le Monde*, 28 May 1997.
60. Russia wants the frontiers between member states of CIS to remain unmarked, as they were in the Soviet Union, and for its own troops to be directly involved in the defence of all the Community's external frontiers.
61. The request was repeated at Vilnius (Lithuania) on 5 September 1997.
62. James Sherr, 'Russia-Ukraine *Rapprochement?*: The Black Sea Fleet Accords', *Survival*, vol. 39, no. 3, Autumn 1997. The author gives a detailed analysis of the content of the Russia-Ukraine accords.
63. Within the limits of the divide-and-rule principle. Thus, for example, Russia has no interest in a peaceful settlement of the conflict between Armenia and Azerbaijan over

Nagorno-Karabakh, since this would raise the possibility of Baku oil reaching the Black Sea through Armenian and Turkish territory, thus escaping Russian control.

64. Richard Bernstein and Ross H. Munro, *The Coming Conflict with China*, New York 1997. See also, by the same authors, 'The Coming Conflict with America', *Foreign Affairs*, vol. 76, no. 2, March–April 1997, in which they expose their main theories in the framework of the China debate.
65. Bernstein and Munro, 'The Coming Conflict with America', p. 30.
66. See the news story by Philippe Pons, *Le Monde* of 4 September 1997, as well as the article by the Singapore official Kishore Mahbubani, 'An Asia-Pacific Consensus', *Foreign Affairs*, vol. 76, no. 5, September–October 1997. On the Japanese debate over China and the treaty with the US, see Selig S. Harrison, 'L'alliance américano-japonaise cimentée', *Le Monde diplomatique*, November 1997. On the worried reaction of the Chinese to the revision of the Japan-US treaty, see James Chace, 'Taming the Tiger: Report from the Middle Kingdom', *World Policy Journal*, vol. xiv, no. 4, Winter 1997–98.
67. For an overall view of these disputes and their links with energy and military questions, see Mark J. Valencia, 'Energy and Insecurity in Asia', *Survival*, vol. 39, no. 3, Autumn 1997.
68. See Susan Willett, 'East Asia's Changing Defence Industry', *Survival*, vol. 39, no. 3, Autumn 1997.
69. 'The collapse of the Soviet Union removed China's main regional security threat and increased, virtually overnight, China's comparative power in Asia.' Bernstein and Munro, 'The Coming Conflict with America', p. 23.
70. A.D. McLennan, 'Balance, Not Containment: A Geopolitical Take from Canberra', *The National Interest*, no. 49, Fall 1997, p. 54.
71. Ibid., p. 56.
72. Leon V. Sigal, 'Who Is Fighting Peace in Korea? An Undiplomatic History', *World Policy Journal*, vol. xiv, no. 2, Summer 1997, p. 45.
73. On the North Korean menace seen from Japan, see Harrison, 'L'alliance américano-japonaise cimentée'.
74. Bernstein and Munro, 'The Coming Conflict with America', p. 19.
75. For a contrary view about China see Lu Ning, *The Dynamics of Foreign-Policy Decision-making in China*, Boulder 1997, which says that the Chinese army is subordinate to the civilian political leadership in foreign policy matters.
76. Bernstein and Munro, 'The Coming Conflict with America', p. 29. Compare Henry Kissinger's forecast on Russia cited above in footnote 51.
77. Robert S. Ross has defended friendly relations with China in the above-mentioned special issues: 'Beijing as a Conservative Power', *Foreign Affairs*, vol. 76, no. 2, March–April 1997, and 'Why Our Hardliners Are Wrong', *The National Interest*, no. 49, Fall 1997. See also, from the same author in collaboration with Andrew J. Nathan, *The Great Wall and the Empty Fortress: China's Search for Security*, New York 1997. See also, in the same vein, Ezra F. Vogel, ed., *Living with China: US-China Relations in the Twenty-First*

Century, New York 1997. And in an even more apologetic register, see Thomas A. Metzger and Ramon H. Myers, *Greater China and US Foreign Policy: The Choice between Confrontation and Mutual Respect*, Stanford 1996.

78. See the news story by Laurent Zecchini, *Le Monde*, 31 October 1997 .
79. Ross, 'Beijing as a Conservative Power', p. 44. Ross's line on Beijing is basically identical to the one traditionally defended by Henry Kissinger. For a summary of the former Secretary of State's arguments on this subject, see his article, 'Outrage Is Not a Policy', *Newsweek*, 10 November 1997.
80. Zbigniew Brzezinski, 'A Geostrategy for Eurasia, *Foreign Affairs*. vol. 76. no. 5, September–October 1997, p. 62, summarizing the main themes of his last book *The Grand Chessboard: American Primacy and its Geostrategic Imperatives*, New York 1997.
81. See Valencia, 'Energy and Insecurity in Asia'. Development of these fields requires big financial and technological means which only Japan has in the region. Hence Boris Yeltsin's charm offensive in Tokyo, with a promise made at the Yeltsin-Hashimoto summit on 1 and 2 November 1997 to settle the dispute over the Kuril islands before 2000 with a decision favouring the Japanese claims. In the same area, Russia is very anxious to restore and stiffen its dominance in central Asia, exploitation of its eastern oil and gas fields being in competition with the project for transporting gas from Turkmenistan into East Asia (the Energy Silk Route).
82. The Russian atomic energy minister, Viktor Mikhailov, declared in Beijing that 'the United States is doing all it can in China to marginalize Russia'. See Sophie Shihab, *Le Monde*, 31 October 1997.
83. For a description of these meetings see Harada, *Russia and North-East Asia*, pp. 37–48 .
84. Incidentally, the Chinese President concluded a 'constructive strategic partnership' with his American opposite number during his visit to the US in October 1997, reducing the relative importance of the Sino-Russian accords in the context of the transactions concluded with Washington. The fact remains however that only the first 'partnership' contains a genuine military dimension.
85. Josef Joffe, 'How America Does It', *Foreign Affairs*, vol. 76, no. 5, September–October 1997, p. 25.
86. Ibid., pp. 19ff. Josef Joffe had already developed the same theory in '"Bismarck" or "Britain"? Toward an American Grand Strategy After Bipolarity', *International Security*, Spring 1995.
87. Joffe, 'How America Does It', pp. 20–21.
88. Edward N. Luttwak, 'Strategy', in Robert Cowley and Geoffrey Parker, eds, *The Reader's Companion to Military History*, New York 1996, p. 451.
89. The 1979 American commitment on Taiwan holds that any non-peaceful pressure to change the status of Taiwan would constitute a threat to peace in the region, and would involve the US.
90. Edward N. Luttwak, 'A Post-Heroic Military Policy', *Foreign Affairs*, vol. 75, no. 4, July–August 1996.

91. The Taiwan Strait and the Russo-Ukraine border are the most dangerous spots on the planet, the two places where wars between and among great powers could erupt in the post-Cold War period, Michael Mandelbaum affirms in 'Westernizing Russia and China', *Foreign Affairs*, vol. 76, no. 3, May–June 1997, p. 89. We might add what Fred Coleman calls the 'Kaliningrad scenario', an invasion of Lithuania by Russian tanks to ensure the corridor between Russia and the Russian military base at Kaliningrad on the Baltic Sea, in response to a decision to incorporate the Baltic countries into NATO. See 'The Kaliningrad Scenario: Expanding NATO to the Baltics', *World Policy Journal*, vol. xiv, no. 3, Fall 1997.
92. Department of Defense, *Report on the QDR*, section II (emphasis added).

PART II

On 'Humanitarian Warfare'

5

HUMANITARIAN WAR: MAKING THE CRIME FIT THE PUNISHMENT

Diana Johnstone

The order of events is strange. On March 24, 1999, NATO forces led by the United States began an eleven-week-long punishment of Yugoslavia's President, Slobodan Milošević, which amounted to capital punishment for an undetermined number of citizens of that unfortunate country. Two months later, on May 27, the US-backed International Criminal Tribunal for former Yugoslavia issued an indictment of Milošević for 'crimes against humanity' that had occurred after the punishment began. Then, in late June, the Clinton administration dispatched 56 forensic experts from the Federal Bureau of Investigation to Kosovo to gather material evidence of the crimes for which Milošević and five of his colleagues had already been indicted and for which his country had already been severely and durably punished.

The FBI had no instructions to search for evidence of crimes as such, including those that might have been committed by, say, armed rebels fighting against the established government of Yugoslavia. The only crimes of interest were those for which Milošević had previously been accused, and all evidence was assumed in advance to point to his guilt.

Thus the world entered the new age of humanitarian vigilante power.

At the end of World War II, a world political system was put in place to outlaw war. In its triumph as sole superpower destined to govern the world, the United States is currently striving to replace the system that outlaws war by a system that uses war to punish outlaws. Who the outlaws are is decided by the United States. Alongside economic globalization, this vigilante system corresponds to a dominant American world view of a capitalist system inherently capable of meeting all human needs, marred only by the wrongdoings of evil outcasts.

At home and abroad, the social effort to bring everybody into a community of equal rights and obligations is abandoned in favour of universal competition in which the rich winners exclude the losers from society itself. On the domestic scene, as the rich get richer, the well-to-do escape from the very sight of the poor by moving into gated communities, social programs are cut, while prisons and execution chambers fill up. Punishment, and even vengeance, have become popular values.

Twenty years ago, the United Nations and its agencies provided a political forum for discussions of such matters as a 'new economic order' or a 'new information order' that might seek to narrow the enormous gap between the rich Atlantic world and most of the rest of the planet. All that is past, and today, the United Nations is instrumentalized by the United States to pursue dissident states which it has chosen to brand as rogues, terrorists or criminals. Capitalist competition is being forced onto the entire world as the supreme law by bodies such as the World Trade Organization. NATOland is a gated community whose armed forces are being prepared to intervene worldwide, at the bidding of Washington, to defend members' interests, in the name of the war against crimes against humanity.

The Clinton Doctrine

The NATO war against Yugoslavia marks a great leap forward toward the depoliticization and criminalization of international relations. In the case of the similar war against Iraq, the regime of Saddam Hussein was in fact a military dictatorship, which did in fact violate international law by invading Kuwait (leaving aside eventual extenuating circumstances), and the United States did obtain a mandate from the United Nations Security Council for at least some (but not all) of its military operations. In the case of Yugoslavia, the military operations were carried out without UN mandate against a state with an elected civilian government, which had not violated international law.

NATO's war, directed from Washington, was intended as a pure demonstration that the United States could make or break the law. For it was Yugoslavia, which had not violated international law, that was branded a criminal state. Already on November 5, 1998, the American presiding judge at the International Criminal Tribunal for former Yugoslavia, Gabrielle Kirk McDonald, described Yugoslavia as 'a rogue state, one that holds the international rule of law in contempt'. During the bombing, US and British leaders regularly compared Milošević to Hitler. And afterwards, the US Senate on June 30 adopted a bill describing Yugoslavia as 'a terrorist state', in the total absence of any of the usual criteria for such a designation. The United States is free both to commit crimes, and to criminalize its adversaries. Might is sure of being right.

'A Clinton Doctrine of humanitarian warfare is taking place', rejoiced columnist Jim Hoagland,[1] a leading voice in the chorus of syndicated columnists who have nagged away at the President to get up the gumption to lead NATO through the Balkans into a brave new millennium. This 'doctrine' is not quite as spontaneous as it is made to seem by the media chorus which portrays Uncle Sam as a reluctant Hamlet generously stumbling into greatness.

Since the end of the Cold War, United States leaders have been searching for a grand new design to replace the containment doctrine developed after World War II. To this end, the oligarchy that formulates American foreign policy has been hard at work in its various exclusive venues such as the Council on Foreign Relations, private clubs, larger assemblages such as the Trilateral Commission (which specializes in the great American ruling class art of selective cooptation and conversion of potential critics), and a myriad of institutes, foundations and 'think tanks', overlapping with a half dozen of the most prestigious universities and, of course, the boards of directors of major corporations and financial institutions. All are united by an unshakeable conviction that what is good for the United States (and the business of the United States is business) is good for the world. American policy-makers may be more or less generous or cynical, crafty or forthright, but all necessarily share the conviction that the system which has made America great and powerful should be bestowed on the rest of an often undeserving and recalcitrant world. There is no conflict between this conviction and ruthless pursuit of economic self-interest; they are part of the same mindset.

None better epitomizes the combined power and good conscience of American capitalism than the Carnegie Endowment for International Peace, founded in 1910 by the Scottish-American steel king Andrew Carnegie (1835–1919) who recycled part of his vast rags-to-riches fortune into philanthropic enterprises. It is fitting that in formulating the Doctrine of Humanitarian Warfare now attributed to Clinton, a major ideological role appears to have been played by the Carnegie Endowment under the presidency of Morton I. Abramowitz.[2]

The Importance of War Crimes

In May 1997, three months after taking office as US Secretary of State, Madeleine Korbel Albright created a new post, ambassador-at-large for war crimes issues. The creation of the post indicated the crucial importance of 'war crimes' in Albright's foreign policy. Two days later, crime was linked to punishment as she delivered her first policy speech on Bosnia to senior military officers aboard an aircraft carrier in the Hudson River. These gestures showed that the first woman Secretary of State was out to demonstrate the serious meaning of her famous remark, 'What's the use of having the world's greatest military force if you don't use it?'

Albright and the man named to the new 'war crimes' post, David Scheffer, were putting into practice new policy concepts they had helped develop before Clinton was elected President, and before the war in Bosnia-Herzegovina, when they had been part of what a privileged observer[3] recently described as 'a small foreign policy elite convened by the Carnegie Endowment for International Peace to change US foreign policy after the Cold War.'

During the last years of the Bush administration, the Carnegie Endowment for Peace was confronting the major question raised by the collapse of the Soviet bloc: what new mission could save NATO, the necessary instrument for US leadership in Europe? And it found an answer: humanitarian intervention. Reports by group members Albright, Richard Holbrooke and Leon Fuerth 'recommended a dramatic escalation of the use of military force to settle other countries' domestic conflicts.'[4]

The Carnegie Endowment's 1992 report entitled 'Changing Our Ways: America's Role in the New World' called for 'a new principle of international relations: the destruction or displacement of groups of people within states can justify international intervention'. The US was advised to 'realign' NATO and the OSCE to deal with these new security problems in Europe. Release of this report, accompanied by policy briefings of key Democrats and media big shots, was timed to influence the Democratic presidential campaign. Candidate Bill Clinton quickly took up the rhetoric, calling for Milošević to be tried for 'crimes against humanity' and advocating military intervention against the Serbs. However, it took several years to put this into practice.

At the Carnegie Endowment, as member of a study group including Al Gore's foreign policy advisor Leon Fuerth, David Scheffer had co-authored (with Morton Halperin) a book-length report on 'Self-Determination in the New World Order' which proposed military intervention as one of the ways of 'responding to international hot spots'. A major question raised was when and to what end the United States should become involved in a conflict between an established state and a 'self-determination' – i.e. a secessionist – movement. Clearly, the question was not to be submitted to the United Nations. 'The United States should seek to build a consensus within regional and international organizations for its position, but should not sacrifice its own judgment and principles if such a consensus fails to materialize.'[5]

In general, the authors concluded, 'the world community needs to act more quickly and with more determination to employ military force when it proves necessary and feasible'.[6] But when is this? 'When a self-determination claim triggers an armed conflict that becomes a humanitarian crisis, getting food, medicine, and shelter to thousands or millions of civilians becomes an inescapable imperative. A new intolerance for such human tragedies is becoming evident in the post-Cold War world and is redefining the principle of non-interference in the internal affairs of states.'[7]

Now, in theory, this sounds almost indisputable. However, in practice the question becomes one not of theory but of facts. When does a crisis in fact correspond to this description, and when, on the contrary, can it simply be made to seem to correspond to this description?

In the official NATO version, vigorously endorsed by mainstream media, the Kosovo war was precisely an instance when 'a self-determination claim triggers an armed conflict that becomes a humanitarian crisis . . .' However, there is considerable, indeed overwhelming evidence that the 'self-determination claim' quite deliberately provoked both the 'armed conflict' and the 'humanitarian crisis' precisely in order to bring in, not humanitarian aid, but military intervention from NATO on the pretext of humanitarian aid. For there was never any need of NATO intervention in order to provide food, medicine and shelter to civilians within Kosovo before the NATO bombing. The 'humanitarian crisis' was a mirage until NATO triggered it by the bombing.

But in the culture of images, temporal relationships are easily obscured. What came before or after what is forgotten. And with temporal relationship, cause and effect are lost, along with responsibility.

Can Kosovo be detached from Serbia? 'The use of military force to create a new state would require conduct by the parent government so egregious that it has forfeited any right to govern the minority claiming self-determination'.[8] But who decides that conduct is sufficiently 'egregious'?

Clearly, Madeleine Albright was so eager to put these bold new theories into practice that she worked mightily to make the crime fit the punishment.

Morton Abramowitz himself, who as Carnegie Endowment President nurtured Albright, Holbrooke, Fuerth, Scheffer and the others as they jointly developed Clinton's future doctrine of 'humanitarian warfare', has also played an active role. In 1997, he passed through the elite revolving door from the Carnegie Endowment to the Council on Foreign Relations. He has contributed his wisdom to a new, high-level think tank, the International Crisis Group, whose sponsors include governments and omnipresent financier George Soros. The ICG has been a leading designer of policy toward Kosovo.

Putting into practice the hypothesis of 'a self-determination claim triggering an armed conflict', Abramowitz became an early advocate of arming the 'Kosovo Liberation Army' (UÇK). At Rambouillet, Abramowitz discreetly coached the ethnic-Albanian Kosovar delegation headed by UÇK leader Hashim Thaqi.[9]

Back in February 1992, before civil war broke out in Bosnia-Herzegovina, television producer John B. Roberts II was asked to design a publicity campaign to gain public support for the soon-to-be-published Carnegie Endowment recommendations. When he saw that 'Changing Our Ways' proposed 'the revolutionary idea that a US-led military first strike was justified, not to defend the United States, but to impose highly subjective political settlements on other countries', that it 'discarded national sovereignty in favour of international intervention', Roberts 'began to regret [his] efforts to build publicity for the report'.[10]

One way or another, the 'revolutionary idea' has been widely propagated during the 1990s. Humanitarian intervention was an idea whose time had come because it met a certain number of perceived needs. It provided a solution to the problem formulated by Senator Richard Lugar, that once the Cold War ended, NATO must be 'either out of area or out of business'. A new missionary mission not only kept NATO alive, thereby nourishing a vast array of vested industrial and financial interests, primarily but not solely in the United States; it also could be seen as a potential instrument to defend less broadly perceived geostrategic interests without submitting them to public controversy.

Humanitarian Realpolitik

When Madeleine Albright took over the State Department from Warren Christopher in early 1997, her promotion was presented to the public more as a personal success for a woman than as a corporate success for a policy design. At its most informative, *The New York Times*[11] mentioned influential policy-makers as if they were benevolent uncles ready to give encouragement to a lady. Three months after she took office, it was reported: 'Ms. Albright has reached out for advice. She has talked with Zbigniew Brzezinski; the departing president of the Carnegie Endowment, Morton Abramowitz; the philanthropist George Soros; and Leslie Gelb, president of the Council on Foreign Relations.'

If Abramowitz may be considered the éminence grise behind the whole 'humanitarian intervention' policy, Brzezinski provided a geostrategic rationale. Brzezinski has no inhibitions about using high principles in the power game. In Paris in January 1998 to promote the French edition of his book, *The Grand Chessboard,* he was asked about the apparent 'paradox' that his book was steeped in Realpolitik, whereas, in his days as National Security Adviser to President Jimmy Carter, Brzezinski had been the 'defender of human rights'.

Brzezinski waved the paradox aside. There is none, he replied. 'I elaborated that doctrine in agreement with President Carter, as it was the best way to destabilize the Soviet Union. And it worked.'[12]

Of course, it took more than nice words about human rights to destabilize the Soviet Union. It took war. And Brzezinski was very active on that front. As he told a second French weekly[13] during his book promotion tour, the CIA had begun bank-rolling counter-revolutionary Afghan forces in mid-1979, half a year before the Soviet Union moved into Afghanistan on a 'stabilizing' mission around New Year's Day 1980. 'We did not push the Russians into intervening, but we knowingly increased the possibility that they would. That secret operation was an excellent idea. The effect was to draw the Russians into the Afghan trap.'

Brzezinski rightly felt he could be forthright about such matters as humanitarian entrapment in Paris, where the policy elite admires nothing so much in American leaders as unabashed cynical power politics. This admiration is most acute when the French are offered a share in it, as was the case with Brzezinski and his book. France, wrote Brzezinski, 'is an essential partner in the important task of permanently locking a democratic Germany into

Europe', which means preventing Germany from building its own separate sphere of influence to the east, possibly including Russia – a connection that Brzezinski's policy recommendations are designed to forestall at all costs. 'This is the historic role of the Franco-German relationship, and the expansion of both the EU and NATO eastward should enhance the importance of that relationship as Europe's inner core. Finally, France is not strong enough either to obstruct America on the geostrategic fundamentals of America's European policy or to become by itself a leader of Europe as such. Hence, its peculiarities and even its tantrums can be tolerated.'[14]

These assurances may contribute to explaining the mystery – as it was widely perceived in other countries – of France's strong support to NATO's Kosovo war, second only to Britain and in disharmony with reactions in Germany and Italy. That is, the French elite had been given to understand this war as part of the Brzezinski design for a transatlantic Europe giving France a politico-military leadership role offsetting Germany's economic predominance.

Brzezinski frankly sets the goal for US policy: 'to perpetuate America's own dominant position for at least a generation and preferably longer still'. This involves creating a 'geopolitical framework' around NATO that will initially include Ukraine and exclude Russia. This will establish the geostrategic basis for controlling conflict in what Brzezinski calls 'the Eurasian Balkans', the huge area between the Eastern shore of the Black Sea to China, which includes the Caspian Sea and its petroleum resources, a top priority for US foreign policy. In the policy elites of both Britain and France, perpetuation of trans-Atlantic domination could be understood as a way of preventing a Russo-German rapprochement able to dominate the continent.

Along with Jeane Kirkpatrick, Frank Carlucci, William Odom and Stephan Solarz, Brzezinski has joined the anti-Serb crusade in yet another new Washington policy shop, the 'Balkan Action Council', calling for all-out war against Yugoslavia over Kosovo.

In the Brzezinski scheme of things, Yugoslavia is a testing ground and a metaphor for the Soviet Union. In this metaphor, 'Serbia' is Russia, and Croatia, Bosnia, Kosovo, etc., are Ukraine, the Baltic States, Georgia and the former Soviet Republics of 'the Eurasian Balkans'. This being the case, the successful secession of Croatia and company from Yugoslavia sets a positive precedent for maintaining the independence of Ukraine and its progressive inclusion in the European Union and NATO, which Brzezinski sets for the decade 2005–15 as a 'reasonable time frame'.

The little Balkan 'Balkans' appear on a map on page 22 of *The Grand Chessboard* interestingly shaded in three gradations representing US geopolitical preponderance (dark), US political influence (medium) and the apparent absence of either (white). Darkly shaded (like the US, Canada and Western Europe) are Hungary, Rumania, Bulgaria and Turkey. Medium shading covers Slovakia, Moldavia and Ukraine as well as Georgia and most of the 'Eurasian Balkans'. Glaringly white, like Russia, are Yugoslavia and Greece. For Brzezinski, Belgrade was a potential relay for Moscow. Serbs might be unaware of this, but in the geostrategic view, they were only so many surrogate Russians.

Cultural Divides and Caspian Oil

Samuel Huntington's notion of 'conflict of civilizations', by identifying Orthodox Christianity as a civilization in conflict with the West and its famous 'values', has offered an ideological cover for the 'divide and conquer' strategy, which has less appeal, but is not incompatible with, the 'humanitarian' justification. It has been taken up by influential writer Robert D. Kaplan,[15] who sees a 'real battle' that is 'drawn along historical-civilizational lines. On the one side are the Turks, their fellow Azeri Turks in Azerbaijan, the Israelis and the Jordanians . . . On the other side are those who suffered the most historically from Turkish rule: the Syrian and Iraqi Arabs, the Armenians, the Greeks and the Kurds'.[16] It is not hard to see whose side the United States must be on in this battle, or which must be the winning side.

Kaplan places Kosovo 'smack in the middle of a very unstable and important region where Europe joins the Middle East' while 'Europe is redividing along historic and cultural lines'.[17] 'There is a Western, Catholic, Protestant Europe and an Eastern Orthodox Europe, which is poorer, more politically unsettled and more ridden with organized crime. That Orthodox realm has been shut out of NATO and is angrier by the day, and it is fiercely anti-Moslem', Kaplan declares.

An oddity of these 'cultural divide' projections is that they find the abyss between Eastern and Western Christianity far deeper and more unbridgeable than the difference between Christianity and Islam. The obvious short, three-letter explanation is 'oil'. But there is a complementary explanation that is more truly cultural, relating to the transnational nature of Islam and to the importance of its charitable organizations. Steve Niva[18] has noted a split within the US foreign policy establishment between conservatives (clearly absent from the Clinton administration) who see Islam as a threat, and 'neo-liberals' for whom the primary enemy is 'any barrier to free trade and unfettered markets'. These include European leaders, oil companies and Zbigniew Brzezinski. 'Incorporating Islamists into existing political systems would disperse responsibility for the state's difficulties while defusing popular opposition to severe economic 'reforms' mandated by the IMF. Islamist organizations could also help fill the gap caused by the rollback of welfare states and social services . . .', Niva observed.

In any case, all roads lead to the Caspian, and through Kosovo. Kaplan publicly advises the nation's leaders that an 'amoral reason of self-interest' is needed to persuade the country to keep troops in the Balkans for years to come. The reason is clear. 'With the Middle East increasingly fragile, we will need bases and fly-over rights in the Balkans to protect Caspian Sea oil. But we will not have those bases in the future if the Russians reconquer southeast Europe by criminal stealth. Finally, if we tell our European allies to go it alone in Kosovo, we can kiss the Western Alliance goodbye.'[19]

Looking at a map, one may wonder why it is necessary to go through Kosovo to obtain Caspian oil. This is a good question. However, US strategists don't simply want to obtain oil, which is a simple matter if one has money. They want to control its flow to the big European market. The simple way to get Caspian oil is via pipeline southward through Iran. But that would evade US control. Or through Russia; just as bad. The preferred US route, a pipeline from Azerbaijan to the Turkish Mediterranean port of Ceyhan has been rejected as too costly. Turkey has vetoed massive oil-tanker traffic through the Bosporus on ecological grounds. That leaves the Balkans. It seems the US would like to build a pipeline across the Balkans, no doubt with Bechtel getting the building contract – former Bechtel executive and Reagan administration Defense Secretary Caspar Weinberger is a leading Kosovo warhawk. Bechtel has already obtained major contracts in Tudjman's Croatia. It is interesting that the Danube, likely to fall under German control, has been blocked for serious transport by NATO's bombing of Serbia's bridges.

On the way to the Caspian, the next stop after Yugoslavia could be the big prize: Ukraine, which like the other former Soviet Republics is already under US influence through NATO's 'Partnership For Peace'. Early this year, asked by a German magazine whether NATO should be the world policeman, NATO commander Wesley Clark observed that the 'countries on the Caspian Sea are members of the "Partnership for Peace". They have the right to consult NATO in case of threat.' Clark 'didn't want to speculate on what NATO might then do . . .'[20]

Scenarios Reach the TV Screen

As television producer Roberts recalls, it was a Ukrainian friend who, seeing the implications for his own country of the Abramowitz humanitarian war plans, set him to worrying. 'If the US endorsed this new foreign policy principle the potential for international chaos was immense. Real or trumped up incidents of destruction or displacement would be grounds for Russian or American military intervention in dozens of countries where nothing like a melting pot has ever existed.'

'Real or trumped up' – that is the question. For once so much is at stake – nothing less than the future of the greatest power the world has ever seen – events are all too likely to follow the imaginary scenario laid out by the policy planners.

This can happen in at least three ways.

1. Reality imitates fiction. It is a common human psychological phenomenon that people see what they are looking for, or have been led to expect to see, often when it is not there. This happens in countless ways. It may account for desert mirages, or apparitions of the Virgin, or simple errors of recognition that occur all the time. When reporters unfamiliar with the country are sent into Bosnia or Kosovo to look for evidence of 'Serbian war crimes', and only evidence of Serbian war crimes, that is what they will find. And if Croats, Muslims and Albanians who are fighting against the Serbs know that that is what they are looking for, it will be even easier. If they are expecting, say, Serbs to be criminals, everything Serbs say or do will be interpreted in that light, with greater or less sincerity. Every ambiguous detail will find its meaning.
2. Evidence will be trumped up. This is an age-old practice in war.
3. Circumstances can be arranged to incite the very crimes that the power wants to be able to punish. In police language, this is called entrapment, or a 'sting' operation, and is illegal in many countries, although not in the United States.

The Kosovo scenario has been advanced in all three ways.

Military intervention may be justified 'when a self-determination claim triggers an armed conflict that becomes a humanitarian crisis', wrote Scheffer and Halperin.

The much-praised non-violent movement of Ibrahim Rugova could not meet this criterion. It failed precisely because it was not a movement for political equality but a movement for secession. A non-violent movement for political equality can find many active ways to illustrate its exclusion and press its demands for inclusion. But the goals of the Albanian movement were not inclusion but complete independence from the existing state. To show their rejection of Serbia, Kosovar Albanians in the Rugova period refused to use the democratic rights they had, boycotted elections, refused to pay taxes, and even set up their own parallel schools and public health service. The odd thing is that this movement of passive resistance was met for the most part by passive resistance on the part of the Serbian state, which allowed Dr Rugova to go about his business (obviously in defiance of Serbian laws) as 'President of the Republic of Kosova', let people get away with not paying taxes and did not force children to attend Serbian schools. Certainly, there were numerous instances of police brutality, although their extent is hard to judge, inasmuch as Kosovar Albanian Human Rights Groups notoriously exaggerated such incidents in order to claim that their people were being brutally oppressed – a claim which was not accepted by the German government,[21] incidentally, despite its support to the separatist movement. But in reality, internal separatism was too easy. The two communities grew ever farther apart, but peacefully. There was an impasse.

That impasse was broken by the UÇK/KLA, acting with the backing of the United States. The strategy was summed up by Richard Cohen:

> The KLA had a simple but effective plan. It would kill Serbian policemen. The Serbs would retaliate, Balkan style, with widespread reprisals and the occasional massacre. The West would get more and more appalled, until finally it would, as it did in Bosnia, take action. In effect, the United States and much of Europe would go to war on the side of the KLA.[22]

It worked.

This version perhaps gives the KLA/UÇK a little too much credit. The United States has been watching Kosovo closely for years, and there are strong indications that it both passively and actively assisted the armed rebels in their humanitarian sting operation. The KLA did indeed kill Serbian policemen, as well as a number of civilians, including ethnic Albanians who failed to boycott the Serbian state. But in between these killings and the Serb retaliation, 'Balkan style', there was a very significant encouragement from Robert Gelbard, acting as US proconsul for former Yugoslavia. Normally, Gelbard's visits to Belgrade were marked by utterances berating Serbian authorities for not doing Washington's bidding in one respect or another. But on February 23, 1998, Gelbard visited Priština and declared publicly that the KLA/UÇK was indeed 'unquestionably a terrorist organization'.

To the Serbs, this simply seemed to be recognition of what to them was an obvious fact. Naively believing that the United States was, as it continued to declare, sincerely opposed to 'international terrorism', Serbian authorities took this remark as a green light to do what any government normally does in such circumstances: send in armed police to repress the terrorists. After all, they were not hard to find. Unlike guerrillas in most conflicts, they made no effort to conceal their whereabouts but openly proclaimed that they were hanging out in a number of villages in the Drenica hill region. Far from heading for the hills when the police approached, the UÇK let civilians who didn't want to get shot head for the hills while they themselves hunkered down at home, sometimes with a few remaining family members, and shot it out with police. This suicidal tactic may have stemmed from the fact that Albanian homes often double as fortresses in the traditional blood feuds, but could not withstand Serbian government fire power. In any case, the results were enough dead Albanians in their villages to enable Madeleine Albright and her chorus of media commentators to cry 'ethnic cleansing'. It was not 'ethnic cleansing', it was a classic anti-insurgency operation. But that was enough for the trap to start closing.

It is easy to imagine how the same scenario could enfold again in some remote area of the 'Eurasian Balkans', where folk customs are not frightfully different from those of the Albanians.

How to Get the Job of UN Secretary General

The Abramowitz–Albright policy for Yugoslavia has been used as the event, the fait accompli, to complete a major institutional shift of power. Institutions based on the principle of decision-making equality between nations (the

United Nations, its agencies, and the OSCE) have been drastically weakened. Others, effectively under US control (NATO, the International Criminal Tribunal), have enlarged their scope, under the heading of a vague new entity, the 'international community'.

The first target of this shift has of course been the United Nations. Already weakened by the successful US undermining of UN agencies such as UNESCO and UNCTAD which threatened to promote alternative and more egalitarian concepts of 'globalization', the United Nations has been reduced by the conflict in Yugoslavia to a rubber stamp to be used or ignored by the United States as it chooses.

Certainly, responsibility for weakening the United Nations is widely shared among world powers, but the United States' role in this demolition enterprise has nevertheless been outstanding. Far from trying to help the United Nations seek an even-handed solution to the Yugoslav crisis, the Clinton administration used its influence to secure decisions of benefit to its own chosen clients, the Bosnian Muslims and the Albanian secessionists. In Bosnia, United Nations forces were given impossible missions: hanging around deceptively declared – deceptively because never demilitarized – 'safe areas', as fighting continued. Their inevitable, not to say programmed, failure could be, and has been, trumpeted as 'proof' that only NATO can carry out a proper peacekeeping mission.

A significant high point in the United States' reduction of the United Nations to a pliant tool came on August 30, 1995, when the United Nations momentarily relinquished its control over Bosnian peace-keeping to NATO, aka the Pentagon, in order to let the United States bomb the Bosnian Serbs.

For Washington, the primary significance of this bombing had less to do with the people of Bosnia than with US power. According to Richard Holbrooke, this was correctly grasped by columnist William Pfaff who wrote the next day: 'The United States today is again Europe's leader; there is no other.'

In his memoir *To End a War,* Richard Holbrooke recounted this proud achievement and lavishly praised the United Nations official who made it possible: the Ghanaian diplomat Kofi Annan, then in charge of peacekeeping operations.

Madeleine Albright, at the time the US ambassador to the United Nations, was carrying on a 'vigorous campaign' in favour of bombing the Serbs. Luck smiled:

> fortunately, Secretary-General Boutros-Ghali was unreachable . . . so she dealt instead with his best deputy, Kofi Annan, who was in charge of peacekeeping operations. At 11:45 a.m., New York time, came a big break: Annan informed Talbott and Albright that he had instructed the UN's civilian officials and military commanders to relinquish for a limited period of time their authority to veto air strikes in Bosnia. For the first time in the war, the decision on the air strikes was solely in the hands of NATO – primarily two American officers . . .
>
> Annan's gutsy performance in those twenty-four hours was to play a central role in Washington's strong support for him a year later as the successor to Boutros Boutros-Ghali as Secretary General of the United Nations. Indeed, in a sense Annan won the job on that day.[23]

Bosnia was the main reason for getting rid of Boutros-Ghali. 'More than any other issue, it was his performance on Bosnia that made us feel he did not deserve a second term – just as Kofi Annan's strength on the bombing in August had already made him the private favorite of many American officials', Holbrooke explained. 'Although the American campaign against Boutros-Ghali, in which all our key allies opposed us, was long and difficult . . . the decision was correct, and may well have saved America's role in the United Nations.'

How to Sabotage the OSCE

With the collapse of the Soviet bloc, the Organization for Security and Cooperation in Europe (OSCE) was widely favoured to succeed both the dismantled Warsaw Pact and NATO as an all-inclusive institution to ensure security, resolve conflicts and defend human rights in Europe. This naturally encountered opposition from all those who wanted to preserve and expand NATO, and with it, the leading US role in Europe – that is, from many important officials in many NATO countries, especially Britain and the Netherlands, as well as the United States itself.

On the eve of the Kosovo war, the tandem of Richard Holbrooke and Madeleine Albright once again moved to cripple a rival to NATO and clear the way for NATO bombing.

On October 13, 1998, under threat of NATO bombing, US envoy Richard Holbrooke got Yugoslav President Slobodan Milošević to sign a unilateral deal to end security operations against armed rebels. The agreement was to be monitored by 2,000 foreign 'verifiers' provided under the auspices of the OSCE. From the start, opinions in Europe were divided as to whether this Kosovo Verification Mission (KVM) marked an advance for the OSCE or a kiss of death, designed to prove the organization's impotence and leave NATO as the uncontested arbiter of conflicts in Europe.

The mission's fate was sealed in favour of the second alternative when the European majority in the OSCE was somehow persuaded to accept US diplomat William Walker to head the KVM. Walker was a veteran of Central American 'banana republic' management, who had collaborated with Oliver North in illegally arming the 'Contras' and had covered up murderous state security operations in El Salvador as US ambassador there during the Reagan administration.

Walker brought in 150 professional mercenaries from the Arlington, Virginia-based DynCorp which had already worked in Bosnia, drove around in a vehicle flying the American flag, and did everything to confirm what his French deputy, Ambassador Gabriel Keller, described as the 'widespread conviction in Serbian public opinion that the OSCE was working under cover for NATO, . . . that we acted with a hidden agenda'.[24]

That impression was shared by many members of the KVM. A number of Italians, whose comments were published anonymously in the geostrategic review *LiMes*, accused the Americans of 'sabotaging the OSCE mission'. Said one: 'The mission in my view had two primary aims. One was to infiltrate personnel into the theatre with intelligence tasks and for special forces activities (preparatory work for a predetermined war). The other was to give the world the impression that everything had been tried and thus create grounds for public consent to the aggression we perpetrated.'[25]

According to Swiss verifier Pascal Neuffer: 'We understood from the start that the information gathered by OSCE patrols during our mission were destined to complete the information that NATO had gathered by satellite. We had the very sharp impression of doing espionage work for the Atlantic Alliance.'[26]

KVM members have criticized Walker and his British chief of operations, Karol (John) Drewienkiewicz, for rejecting any cooperation with Serb authorities, for blocking diplomatic means to ensure human rights, for controlling the mission's information flow, and most serious of all, for using the mission to make contact with UÇK rebels and train them to guide NATO to targets in the subsequent bombing.[27] Since the Serbs were quite aware of this activity, as soon as the bombing began on March 24, Serb security forces set out to root out all suspected UÇK indicators. These operations are very probably at the heart of what NATO has described as ethnic cleansing.

However, prior to the bombing, KVM members testify to a low level of violence, as well as a pattern of UÇK provocations. According to Keller, 'every pullback by the Yugoslav army or the Serbian police was followed by a movement forward by [UÇK] forces . . . OSCE's presence compelled Serbian government forces to a certain restraint . . . and UÇK took advantage of this to consolidate its positions everywhere, continuing to smuggle arms from Albania, abducting and killing both civilians and military personnel, Albanians and Serbs alike.'

By the end of 1998 and the beginning of 1999, an increasingly audible split was taking place within the KVM between Walker and most of the Europeans. Every incident was an occasion for Walker and the US State Department to denounce the Serbs for breaking the truce, and to accuse Milošević of violating his commitment. The Europeans saw things differently: the Albanian rebels, with US encouragement, were systematically provoking Serb attacks in order to justify NATO coming in on their side of the conflict.

In mid-January, Walker settled the score with his European critics by bringing the world media over to his side. This was the political significance of the famous 'Račak massacre'. On January 15, 1999, Serb police had carried out a pre-announced operation, accompanied by observers and television cameras, against the UÇK believed to be hiding out in the village of Račak. As the Serbs swept into the village, the UÇK gunmen took refuge on surrounding high ground and began to fire on the police, as TV footage showed. But the Serbs had sent forces around behind them, and many UÇK fighters were trapped and shot. After the Serb forces withdrew that afternoon, the UÇK again took control of the village, and it was they who led Walker into the village the next day to see what they described as victims of a massacre. It may be, as Serb authorities claimed and many Europeans tended to believe, that the victims were in fact killed in the shootout reported by the police, and then aligned to give the appearance of a mass execution, or 'massacre'.

In any case, the extremely emotional public reaction by the high-profile head of the KVM, condemning the Serbs for 'a crime against humanity', 'an unspeakable atrocity' committed by Serbs 'with no value for human life', ended any possible pretence of neutrality of the OSCE mission.

Walker's accusations were quickly taken up by NATO politicians and editorialists. A complex conflict was reduced to a simple opposition between Serbian perpetrators of massacres and innocent Albanian civilian victims. The UÇK and its provocative murders of policemen and civilians were to all intents and purposes invisible. Presented as a gratuitous atrocity, 'Račak' became the immediate justification for NATO war against Yugoslavia.

In Kosovo itself, KVM members have testified, after Račak the Serbs were totally convinced that the OSCE was working for NATO and began to prepare for war, while the UÇK became still more aggressive. KVM members have also complained of the fact that Walker evacuated the mission to Macedonia on March 20, 1999, five days before the bombing began. This way, no outside observers were there to see exactly what did happen when the bombing began, much less try to prevent it. Walker's leadership had effectively removed all pressure or incentive for either side to show restraint.

'In the history of international missions it would be hard to find such a chaotic and tragically ambiguous enterprise', concluded an Italian participant.

How to Obtain Justice

The importance of crimes in this new world order was highlighted by the establishment in May 1993 of the International Criminal Tribunal for the former Yugoslavia (ICTY). This tribunal was established by Security Council resolution 827 under its Article 29, which allows it to set up 'subsidiary bodies' necessary to fulfil its peacekeeping tasks. It is more than doubtful that the framers of the United Nations statutes had a criminal tribunal in mind, and many jurists consider resolution 827 to be a usurpation of legislative and judicial powers by the Security Council. In fact, this act went contrary to over forty years of study, within the framework of the United Nations, of the possibilities for setting up an international penal tribunal, whose jurisdiction would be established by international treaty allowing states to transfer part of their sovereign rights to the tribunal. The Security Council's ICTY went over the heads of the states concerned and simply imposed its authority on them, without their consent.

On April 5, 1999, as NATO was bombing Yugoslavia, the ICTY's presiding judge Gabrielle Kirk McDonald (a former US federal judge in Texas) told the Supreme Court that the Tribunal 'benefited from the strong support of concerned governments and dedicated individuals such as Secretary

Albright. As the permanent representative to the United Nations, she had worked with unceasing resolve to establish the Tribunal. Indeed, we often refer to her as the "mother of the Tribunal".'

Because it is also located in The Hague, very many well-informed people confuse the Tribunal with the International Court of Justice, or at least believe that, like the ICJ, the ICT is a truly independent and impartial judicial body. Its many supporters in the media say so, and so do its statutes. Article 32 of its governing statute says the Tribunal's expenses shall be borne by the regular budget of the United Nations, but this has been persistently violated. As Toronto lawyer Christopher Black points out, 'the tribunal has received substantial funds from individual states, private foundations and corporations'. The United States has provided personnel (23 officials lent by the Departments of State, Defense and Justice as of May 1996), equipment and cash contributions. More money has been granted the Tribunal by financier George Soros' Open Society Foundation, the Rockefeller Foundation and the United States Institute for Peace, set up in 1984 under the Reagan administration and funded by Congressional appropriations, with its board of directors appointed by the US President.

The Tribunal is vigorously supported by the Coalition for International Justice (CIJ), based in Washington and The Hague, founded and funded by George Soros' Open Society Foundation and a semi-official US lawyers' group called CEELI, the Central and East European Law Institute, set up to promote the replacement of socialist legal systems with free market ones, according to Christopher Black.

On May 12, 1999, ICTY president Gabrielle Kirk McDonald, in a speech to the Council on Foreign Relations, said that: 'The US government has very generously agreed to provide $500,000 and to help to encourage other states to contribute. However, the moral imperative to end the violence in the region is shared by all, including the corporate sector. I am pleased, therefore, that a major corporation has recently donated computer equipment worth three million dollars, which will substantially enhance our operating capacity.'

Moreover, during the bombing, Clinton obtained a special $27 million appropriation to help the Tribunal, especially in collecting anti-Serb testimony from Albanian refugees along the borders of Kosovo. Finally, Clinton has offered a bounty of $5 million for the arrest of Yugoslav President Slobodan Milošević.

Ethnic Divisions, Unified Empires

An extremely significant feature of the humanitarian intervention policy is its emphasis on collective in contrast to individual rights.

'In the aftermath of the breakup of the Soviet empire,' runs the summary of 'Self-Determination in the New World Order', 'new nations are emerging rapidly, and more and more ethnic groups are pushing for independence or autonomy.' So the question is 'how the United States should respond'. The authors 'propose criteria for decision makers who are weighing whether to support groups seeking self-determination, to offer political recognition, or to intervene with force.'

This approach has practically nothing to do with democracy, and everything to do with empire construction. Although the words 'democracy' and 'democratic' are still used, they tend increasingly to be without meaning other than to designate favoured client leaders or groups in countries of interest to the United States. Certainly, Hashim Thaqi, the UÇK leader who counts Madeleine Albright's spokesman James Rubin (husband of CNN's Christiane Amanpour) among his fans,[28] is scarcely more 'democratic' than Milan Milutinović, elected President of Serbia, indicted with Milošević by Albright's 'International War Crimes Tribunal'. In fact, the selection of particular groups, ethnic or social, as clients, is the traditional way in which a conquering empire can reshape social structures and replace former elites with its own.

The imperial project is becoming increasingly open. Protectorates are being established in Bosnia and Kosovo, President Clinton is vigorously calling for the illegal overthrow of the legally elected Yugoslav president.

Totally disregarding the feelings and wishes of the real, live people who live there, Robert Kaplan announced[29] that 'there are two choices in the Balkans – imperialism or anarchy. To stop the violence, we essentially have to act in the way the great powers in the region have always acted: as pacifying conquerors.' Like the Romans and the Austrian Habsburgs, 'motivated by territorial aggrandizement for their own economic enrichment, strategic positions and glory.'

Merely to suggest that the United States might 'intervene with force' on behalf of an ethnic group seeking self-determination is to cause trouble. There are potentially hundreds of such groups not only in the former Soviet Republics but throughout Africa and Asia. The prospect of US military intervention will, on the one hand, encourage potential secessionist leaders to push their claims to the point of 'humanitarian crisis', in order to bring in the Superpower on their side. By the same token, it will encourage existing states to suppress such movements brutally and decisively in order to prevent precisely that intervention. A vicious cycle will be created, enabling the single Superpower to fish selectively in troubled waters.

The concept of 'ethnic group' rests on the notion of 'identity'. If individual identity is problematic, group identity is even more so. That is, just as individuals may have multiple or changing 'identities', groups may have changing compositions as people come and go from one 'identity' group to another. Especially in the modern mobile world, ethnic identity is therefore a highly questionable basis for claim to political recognition in the form of an independent state. The forceful affirmation of 'ethnic identity' tends to strengthen traditional patriarchal structures in places such as Kosovo, at the expense of individual liberation. Stress on ethnic identity enforces stereotypes, mafioso structures and leadership by 'godfathers'.

Foreign policy based on ethnic identity has notorious antecedents: it was precisely the policy employed by Adolf Hitler to justify his conquest of the same Eastern European territories that Brzezinski now watches so attentively. Both the takeover of Czechoslovakia and the invasion of Poland were officially justified by the need to protect allegedly oppressed German minorities from the cruel Czechs and Poles. The British government's understanding for Herr Hitler's concern about Germans in Czechoslovakia is the real 'Munich'. Before invading Poland, Hitler had the SS manufacture an 'incident' in which wicked Poles stormed an innocent German-language radio station in order to desecrate it with their barbarous Slav language. The dead body left on the scene to authenticate the incident was in fact a prison convict in costume.

In Yugoslavia, Hitler 'liberated' not only Germans but also and especially Croats and (in conjunction with fascist Italy) Albanians, long selected as the proper *Randvölker* to receive German protection, the better to crush the main historic adversary, the Serbs, the people who more than any other had fought for independence from empires. (The Serbs themselves as they became 'Yugoslavs' were less and less unified around Serbian identity, even if they have continued to pay for it.)

Making policy by distinguishing between 'friend' and 'enemy' peoples is pure Hitlerism, and this is what the Anglo-American NATO leaders are now doing, while ironically pretending to reject 'Munich'.

History As Melodrama

The media that recount Balkan ghost stories to the 'children'[30] back in NATOland rarely go into detail about the peculiarities of these various customs and situations. Popular culture has prepared audiences for a simpler version. The pattern is the same as in disaster movies, outer space movies, etc.: there is always the trio of classic melodrama: wicked villain, helpless victim (maiden in distress) and heroic rescuer. Same plot. Over and over. Only in the Abramowitz humanitarian war plan, the trio is composed of ethnic entities or nationalities. There is the 'good' ethnic group, all victims, like the Kosovar Albanians. Then there is the 'bad' ethnic group, all racist hatred, ethnic cleansing and even 'genocide'. And finally, of course, there is Globocop to the rescue: NATO with its stealth bombers, cruise missiles and cluster blade bombs, its depleted uranium and graphite power-plan busters. A bit of fireworks, like the car chase at the end of the movie.

The whole concept of ethnic war as pretext for US military intervention implies this division of humanity between 'good' and 'bad' nationalities, between 'oppressor' and 'victim' peoples. Since this is rarely the case, the story is told by analogy with the famous exceptional cases where the categories fit: Hitler and the Jews being the obvious favourite. Every new villain is a 'Hitler', every new ethnic secessionist group to be used as pretext for new NATO bases is the victim of a potential 'Holocaust'. At this rate, the two terms will cease to be proper nouns and become general terms for the new global Guignol.

Starting with the pretence of militant anti-racism, 'humanitarian intervention' finishes with a new racism. To merit all those bombs, the 'bad' people must be tarnished with collective guilt. At the G8 summit in Cologne in June 1999, Tony Blair clearly adopted the doctrine of collective guilt when he declared that there could be no humanitarian aid for the Serbs because of the dreadful way they had treated the Kosovar Albanians. With their incomparable self-righteousness, the Anglo-American commanders are leading this new humanitarian crusade to extremes of inhumanity.

Notes

1. Jim Hoagland, 'Developing a Doctrine of Humanitarian Warfare', *International Herald Tribune*, June 28, 1999.

2. A former US Ambassador to Thailand, Abramowitz served as Assistant Secretary of State for Intelligence and Research in the Reagan administration. In January 1986, he took part in an interesting mission to Beijing alongside top CIA officials with the purpose of persuading China to support supplying Stinger missiles to Islamic Afghan rebels in order to keep up pressure on the Soviet Union, even as Gorbachev was trying to end the Cold War. In the mid-1990s, he was part of a blue-ribbon panel sponsored by the Council on Foreign Relations which advised the Clinton Administration to loosen restrictions on CIA covert operations such as dealing with criminals, disguising agents as journalists, and targeting unfriendly heads of state.
3. John B. Roberts, 'Roots of Allied Farce', *The American Spectator*, June 1999.
4. Ibid.
5. Morton H. Halperin & David J. Scheffer with Patricia L. Small, *Self-Determination In the New World Order*, Carnegie Endowment, Washington, DC 1992, p. 80.
6. Ibid., p. 105.
7. Ibid., p. 107.
8. Ibid., p. 110.
9. Charles Trueheart, 'Serbs and Kosovars Get Nudge From Their Hosts To Speed Up Peace Talks', *International Herald Tribune/Washington Post*, February 9, 1999: 'On Monday, the Kosovo Albanians won a small tactical victory when their American advisers, initially barred by conference hosts, were allowed to visit them at the chateau. They included two former US diplomats, Morton Abramowitz and Paul Williams.'
10. John B. Roberts, op. cit.
11. Steven Erlanger, 'Winning Friends for Foreign Policy: Albright's First 100 Days', The New York Times, 14 May 1997.
12. 'Il n'y a pas de paradoxe. J'ai mis au point cette doctrine en accord avec le président Carter, car c'était la meilleure façon de déstabiliser l'Urss. Ça a marché.' *L'Evènement du jeudi*, 14 January 1998.
13. *Le Nouvel observateur*, 14 January 1998, reported by AFP.
14. Zbigniew Brzezinski, *The Grand Chessboard*, Basic Books, New York 1997, p. 78.
15. Kaplan's 1993 book *Balkan Ghosts* was notoriously read by President Clinton, who, however, had to be chided later by the author for having drawn the wrong conclusion. That is, Clinton's initial conclusion was to stay out of the Balkans, whereas Kaplan has, he explained, always been an interventionist.
16. *New York Times/International Herald Tribune*, 23 February 1999.
17. Robert D. Kaplan, 'Why the Balkans Demand Amorality', *The Washington Post*, 28 February 1999.
18. Steve Niva, 'Between Clash and Co-Optation: US Foreign Policy and the Specter of Islam', *Middle East Report*, Fall 1998.
19. *The Washington Post*, 28 February 1999.
20. *Stern*, 4 March 1999.

21. In mid-April 1999, the International Association of Lawyers Against Nuclear Arms (IALANA) obtained, and distributed to news media, official documents from the German foreign office showing that in the months leading up to the NATO bombing of Yugoslavia, the foreign office had repeatedly informed administrative courts of the various German Länder that there was no persecution of ethnic Albanians in Kosovo or the rest of Serbia. Example: Intelligence report from the Foreign Office, January 12, 1999, to the administrative Court of Trier, 'Even in Kosovo an explicit political persecution linked to Albanian ethnicity is not verifiable. The East of Kosovo is still not involved in armed conflict. Public life in cities like Priština, Uroševac, Gnjilane, etc. has, in the entire conflict period, continued on a relatively normal basis.' The 'actions of the security forces [were] not directed against the Kosovo-Albanians as an ethnically defined group, but against the military opponent and its actual or alleged supporters.' These reports were published in the German daily *Junge Welt* on 24 April 1999.
22. Richard Cohen, 'The Winner in the Balkans Is the KLA', *Washington Post/International Herald Tribune,* 18 June 1999.
23. Richard Holbrooke, *To End a War,* Random House, New York 1998, p. 103.
24. 'The OSCE KVM: autopsy of a mission', statement delivered by Ambassador Gabriel Keller, principal deputy head of mission, to the watch group on May 25, 1999.
25. Italian military participant 'Romanus', in *LiMes* 2/99, cited by *Il Manifesto,* 19 June 1999.
26. *La Liberté,* Genève, 22 April 1999, and *Balkan-Infos* No. 33, Paris, May 1999.
27. Ulisse, 'Come gli Americani hanno sabotato la missione dell'Osce', *LiMes,* supplemento al n. 1/99, p. 113, L'Espresso, Rome 1999.
28. 'Throughout the Kosovo crisis, Mr. Rubin personally wooed Hashim Thaci, the ambitious leader of the Kosovo Liberation Army', the *Wall Street Journal* reported on June 29, 1999, even going so far as to 'jokingly promise that he would speak to Hollywood friends about getting Mr. Thaci a movie role.'
29. Robert D. Kaplan, 'Why the Balkans Demand Amorality', *The Washington Post,* 28 February 1999.
30. Peter Gowan, in 'The Twisted Road to Kosovo', *Labour Focus on Eastern Europe,* no. 62, Spring 1999, explains (p. 76) that the foreign policy elite discuss the sordid realities of power politics in a closed arena, and 'not in front of the children', that is, the citizenry of the NATOland countries, who are regaled with versions that appeal to their values and ideals.

6

IN PLACE OF POLITICS: HUMANITARIANISM AND WAR

Robert Redeker

Each day the NATO-Serbian conflict has taken on slightly more of the aspect of a new type of war, presaging a twenty-first century that seems more likely to resemble a new age of Mars than the Garden of Eden-like age of Aquarius. This conflict seems in fact to have taken a form which is unprecedented in our history: war is no longer going to be 'the continuation of policy by other means' but will become, on the contrary, the action taken as a substitute for policy which is absent. We would thus have a war which is the direct heir of the 'end of politics' analysed by the Situationists and Jean Baudrillard. Far from signifying the end of war, the end of politics is preparing the ground for war to make an energetic comeback. That is how war, that old, obsolete (but never out of fashion) partner of humanity, has made its return to the heart of Europe: as the executor of the death of politics. Traditionally, war continued policy, accompanied policy, was another form of policy. This year, perhaps for the first time since the appearance of Graeco-Roman western civilization, we have witnessed the spectacle of war in the total absence of policy: a disheartening preamble to the next century.

War already existed before the emergence of politics, in humanity's pre-political age. Pierre Clastres, in his book *La Société contre l'État,*[1] has convincingly shown the function of wars in primitive societies to be a device supposed to prevent the emergence of the State and political institutions. In just the same way after politics, in the post-political age now taking shape, war is getting ready to reign as absolute iron mistress over a humanity threatened by evils that all bear anti-political names: *tribalization, ethnicism, naturalism.* The war without politics (a war that wasn't even declared, that developed in default of policy) that ravaged the Balkans in the spring of 1999 recalls the war against politics that humanity knew in its remote past.

Humanitarian war – this conflict being marked by the alliance, rather strange at first sight, between those two concepts – rests on government by emotion; the two, united like the spiritual and temporal arms of old, base their power on the affective force of images. For how can we resist the emotion that invades us in a tumultuous tide when our televisions regurgitate images of innumerable masses of unfortunates fleeing from the land that was their country, tearful suffering mothers, mutilated children, wounded bodies, bodies in pieces, villages in flames, old men dying of exhaustion in the snow? How can we curb our emotion before these images that suggest to us that the air strikes are necessary, that someone ought to help these peoples that we see suffering on screen, and that the help they need is double: that one of its faces is humanitarianism, and the other is war? This type of emotion, generated by televised images, mechanically makes a double appeal at the very moment that we sit transfixed in front of these images: an appeal for humanitarian action, and an appeal for war. To this infinite misery, exhibited to the entire world, only two answers seem possible: humanitarian action, immediately, and war, immediately.

Politics – policy – makes different and heavier demands on the citizen than war and humanitarianism: it requires for example the difficult deployment of reason, a faculty that has become unbearable to opinion-makers obsessed with audience ratings. It necessitates subtle and carefully-reasoned reflection, conceptual finesse, solid and upright judgement: all things that need emotion to be kept at a distance. War and humanitarianism, two answers made of the same emotional papier-mâché as the televised messages, are the only solutions able to take root in the mind of the television viewer, that wordless citizen. In fact, humanitarianism is an indubitable weapon of war; for the ultra-urgent temporality that always goes with it turns humanitarian action into a deterrent bomb, forbidding the emergence of an exclusively political approach to the issues. Thus humanitarianism is neither a new way of making policy nor an adjunct to politics; humanitarian ideology is a substitute for the evaporated policy but, above all, it sterilizes, by dissuasion, the ground in which politics might germinate.

The coalition of war and humanitarianism, united by the marketing of emotions, has temporarily erased debate in France, gummed up all our arguments. Before March 1999 we were still quarrelling, differing, polemicizing, on the future of the family, the role of women, parity, educational reforms; between March and June, the conjunction of war and humanitarianism gave the government the chance to rush certain reforms through without meeting serious opposition. All through that sour spring humanitarianism was substituted for all arguments, making any concern other than caring for the war victims seem indecent. From supermarkets to schools, via TV and radio stations, town halls, presbyteries, sports clubs, local government offices and so on, the duty of humanitarian aid to the Kosovars was universally proclaimed as a categorical imperative on which reflection was not advised. A double duty: support the war, give humanitarian aid to the Kosovars. Strengthening what had existed since the establishment of Restos du Coeur, humanitarianism swathed the country in its unanimous caring uniform, imposed unanimity and correct sentiments. But the fact is that the proper way of life for a citizen worthy of the name includes confrontation, disagreement, quarrelling and division. In the name of the 'emotion first' principle, humanitarianism silenced critical thought. The consensual moralism imposed by the humanitarian hegemony stifled the differences that make democracy live.

The way this conflict was managed and presented to public opinion ushered in the era of citizenship by proxy. Who now remembers the idea of a 'proxy strike' being touted in France in the winter of 1995? That December, there developed a strike that took place after the time when it had been possible for everyone to strike, a strike reserved for certain professional categories, a strike that happened after the official end of the class struggle; in the spring of 1999 we were in a war that took place after the abolition of compulsory military service for all, a war that happened after the constitutional death of military citizenship. Everyone waged this war by proxy; it couldn't be any different now that armies are professionalized, since the liquidation of the citizen-soldier's revolutionary heritage. Humanitarianism also works on the proxy system, in parallel with war, in the sense that after watching the television we will be invited, gogglebox subscribers that we are, to help some NGO to pack parcels. It is crucially important not to confuse proxies with representatives. The NATO soldiers are proxies who fight in our place, as the crisis workers of humanitarianism are proxies who comfort the sores of war in our place. At the same time the complacent flaunting of images of misery, the spectacularization of victims' flesh, the televisual harping on pain and discomfort, enable us to suffer by proxy. Proxy action is the negation of political citizenship. Under cover of this war a new model of social organization is appearing, one that abolishes the canonical distinction (from Rousseau to Castoriadis) between direct democracy and indirect democracy: what is being substituted for representative democracy is not direct democracy, but democracy by proxy.

And what could that be but something beyond politics? What is it, if not the regime that imposes itself worldwide when the last dreams of a return to politics, a revival of citizenship, the pursuit of voluntarist action aimed at transforming social relations, have all evaporated? What is it, if not a parody of participation fabricated for the consumption of populations (humanitarianism speaks more readily of *populations* than of *peoples*) by that parody of political commitment, humanitarianism? Let us invert Jean Baudrillard's false axiom on the Gulf war (he had been bold enough to write that the war had not taken place): this war, war of this type, along with all the others to come, did take place because politics no longer takes place. The true drama of this conflict, beyond all the woes being inflicted on the Balkan peoples, can be summarized thus: war and humanitarianism, linked together like Siamese twins, are acting in concert against politics.

This has been a strange time, with intellectuals, humanitarians and the military all using the same vocabulary (one shared, moreover, by the most powerful Empire the world has ever seen). One thing it has shown us is an eclipse of intelligence, the rout of intellectuals faced with war. It has confronted us with the *inhuman* face of humanitarianism, along with war, both springing like weeds from the rubble which is all that is left of politics and thought.

Note

1. Pierre Clastres, *La Société contre l'État*, Editions de Minuit, 1974.

7

THE IDEOLOGY OF HUMANITARIAN INTERVENTION

Alex Callinicos

'Good has triumphed over evil, justice has overcome barbarism, and the values of civilization have prevailed.'

Tony Blair[1]

'With phrases which on close examination dissolve into thin air, such as the defence of civilization, nothing tangible can be defined.'

Prince Klemens von Metternich[2]

'The profound hypocrisy and inherent barbarism of bourgeois civilization lies unveiled before our eyes, turning from its home, where it assumes respectable forms, to the colonies, where it goes naked.'

Karl Marx[3]

The Balkan War of 1999 was the moment at which 'humanitarian' imperialism stepped fully clothed onto the historical stage. In earlier conflicts, the West had frequently invoked concepts of democracy and human rights. Thus, during the Gulf crisis of 1990–91, as Peter Gowan puts it, 'the dominant language of public debate was that of rights, justice and law . . . In the perception of millions, international affairs became a depoliticized process of crime and judicial punishment.'[4] In that case, however, the specific justification for the war prosecuted by the United States-led Coalition against Iraq was the violation of Kuwait's sovereignty by the Iraqi invasion of August 1990. NATO's war against Serbia, by contrast, overrode Yugoslavia's territorial sovereignty on humanitarian grounds – namely securing the physical safety and political rights of the Kosovo Albanians. It was thus the first major humanitarian war.

This justification for the war played an important role in securing the support of many on the Western left. Tony Blair, the most bellicose of the NATO leaders, sought to project the assault on Yugoslavia as a social democrats' war, waged by 'a new generation of leaders in the United States and in Europe, who were born after World War II, who hail from the progressive side of politics, but who are prepared to be as firm as any of our predecessors right and left in seeing the thing through'.[5] NATO's was, he insisted, 'a just war, based not on any territorial ambitions but on values'.[6]

Left-liberal commentators were quick to take up the same theme. In Britain, Hugo Young, the *Guardian*'s premier columnist, proclaimed it 'a war for international values'.[7] In Germany, Jürgen Habermas, perhaps the leading philosopher of the Western left, went even further. In a major article entitled 'Bestiality and Humanity', he argued that NATO's 'armed peacekeeping operation, authorized by the international community (even without a UN mandate)', represented 'a step on the path from the classical international law of nations towards the cosmopolitan law of a world civil society'.[8]

Other essays in this collection demonstrate the collective delusion under which Habermas, Young, and many other left liberals laboured. The Balkan war was not a humanitarian war. It precipitated the humanitarian catastrophe – the flight of the Kosovars – that it was supposed to prevent. Moreover, the war that began by failing to prevent the ethnic cleansing of the Kosovo Albanians ended with the ethnic cleansing of the Kosovo Serbs. This topsy-turvy logic concealed the real reasons for the war, namely the strategic and economic interests of the US and the other Western powers. In a rare moment of lucid honesty, Bill Clinton outlined at the beginning of the war the interest of the US in 'a Europe that is safe, secure, free, united, a good partner with us for trading; . . . and someone who will share the burdens of taking care of the problems of the world . . . Now,' he explained, 'that's what this Kosovo thing is all about.'[9]

But, on the whole, the ideological defence of the Balkan war was not conducted in the realist discourse of interests favoured by Henry Kissinger's version of American policymaking, but in the language of democracy and humanitarian concern. In this essay, I wish not so much to expose the interests behind this discourse, as to trace the process through which humanitarian intervention became the ideological rationale for NATO's first war.

The Legacy of Moral Imperialism

As Habermas stresses, a critical feature of the ideology of humanitarian intervention is that it seeks to identify cases in which it is legitimate to override the sovereignty of nation-states. The most basic principle of international law since the 1648 Peace of Westphalia, which is normally regarded as inaugurating the modern state-system, was thereby abrogated. Habermas linked it to the case of Pinochet, held liable in foreign courts for crimes against humanity committed in Chile. Ken Livingstone argued along similar lines that the war and Pinochet's arrest 'could be the first steps in creating a global resolve so that those with power are not allowed to abuse it with impunity within their own borders'.[10]

This suggests that NATO was waging a new kind of war. Others have been more sceptical. In one of the few substantial anti-war pieces to have sneaked past the *Guardian*'s editorial censorship, Richard Gott argued that the project of 'humanitarian interventionism' is 'a throwback to the colonialism of the last century, when the imperial powers intervened at will in the affairs of independent states and peoples'. He compared 'today's phalanx of pro-war columnists and leader-writers in the *Guardian*' to H.H. Asquith and other 'Liberal Imperialist' supporters of the Boer War.[11] (There is a sad contrast here with the performance during that conflict of the *Manchester Guardian*, which, under its great editor C.P. Scott, braved considerable hostility and reduced profits for its opposition to the war.)

In Gott's support one might cite the stance taken by Michael Foot, then Labour Leader of the Opposition, in backing the 1982 Falklands War. Anthony Barnett has argued that Foot displayed a much longer-standing attitude which he calls '*moral imperialism*. For behind the presumption that a British voice must speak out against violations of humanity elsewhere (which is welcome) lies the assertion that the Anglo-Saxon accent can and should arbitrate across all frontiers.' This attitude is well brought out by F.S. Northedge's description of British 'national arrogance', which Barnett cites: 'the idea that the rest of the world is rather like an unruly child which has a divine obligation to defer to its elders and betters like the British . . . but which from time to time may be prevented from doing so by either sheer stupidity, or suppression by some upstart dictator'.[12] (True to form, Michael Foot was one of the more bloodthirsty supporters of the war with Serbia.)

Undoubtedly Northedge here captures very accurately the patronizing attitudes, sometimes verging on the racist, displayed towards the Serbs, and indeed Balkan peoples more generally, by NATO's liberal apologists. The most striking instance of this attitude was provided by Daniel Goldhagen, who used the spurious authority provided by his trash history of the Holocaust to announce: 'The majority of the Serbian people, by supporting or condoning Milošević's eliminationist politics, have rendered themselves legally and morally incompetent to conduct their own affairs and a presumptive ongoing danger to others. Essentially their country must be placed in receivership.'[13]

Imperialist Ideology after the Cold War

But whatever the continuities displayed by such defences of the new Euro-American colonialism in the Balkans, the idea of humanitarian intervention is advanced today in a very different historical context from that of the last *fin de siècle*. Since 1945, with the establishment of the United Nations and the dissolution of the European empires, the nation-state has become the dominant form of political organization in the world. How, in these circumstances, have the leading Western powers come to assert a liberal-democratic version of the Brezhnev Doctrine giving them the right to intervene in the affairs of sovereign states?

Two factors are of critical importance here. The first is the problem of how to justify the existence and the assertion of the military power of the US and its allies after the Cold War. Tony Giddens, New Labour's court philosopher, has proclaimed the contemporary liberal-democratic state 'the state without enemies'.[14] Such notions may provide an interesting theme for discussion at White House seminars on the Third Way. Meanwhile, down in the basement, the officials who meet regularly in the White House Situation Room to direct US international policy preside over a vast military machine whose size and strategy imply the existence of many real or potential enemies, most notably Russia and China.[15]

How to justify this mighty military establishment and its indispensable accompaniment, the new NATO, currently expanding deep into the Eurasian continent?[16] Plainly the old Cold War discourse of freedom versus totalitarianism no longer fits the new situation. There were, however, certain ideological themes that were carried over. In the late 1970s, the Carter administration began to use the language of universal human rights: the Soviet Union's acknowledgement of these rights in the 1975 Helsinki Final Act, though no doubt cynically conceived by policy-makers on both sides such as Kissinger and Gromyko, provided Washington with new ideological leverage as the Second Cold War developed towards the end of that decade. Indeed Kissinger himself was led admiringly to describe how, under Ronald Reagan in the 1980s, '[t]he high-flying Wilsonian language in support of freedom and democracy was leavened by an almost Machiavellian realism.' In its struggle against Moscow-aligned regimes, especially in the Third World, '[t]he Reagan Administration dispensed aid not only to genuine democrats (as in Poland), but also to Islamic fundamentalists . . . in Afghanistan, to rightists in Central America, and to tribal warlords in Africa.'[17]

After the Cold War, human-rights violations could still be used selectively to justify action against disobedient Third World regimes: thus during the 1990–91 Gulf crisis Saddam Hussein's numerous crimes, previously ignored by the Western powers when they regarded him as a bulwark against the Iranian revolution, became part of the ideological campaign for war with Iraq. Even sometime Marxists such as Fred Halliday were persuaded to conceive the conflict as one that pitted democratic imperialism against 'fascism'.[18] More generally, the demand that states outside the Western core of the system should adopt norms of 'democratic governance' became a standard feature of the neo-liberal policy packages imposed by bodies such as the IMF, the World Bank, and the European Bank for Reconstruction and Development.

New concepts were, however, required to identify and characterize those regimes that, ostensibly because of their failure to observe these norms, became the objects of Western action. During the 1980s a new theme began to emerge in Western policy discourse – the threat of Islamic fundamentalism. Its roots lay in the Iranian revolution of 1978–79 and the debacle of US and Israeli intervention in Lebanon in the early 1980s, which together represented the most serious defeat for US foreign policy since Vietnam, but it was further fuelled by other incidents, most notably the Rushdie affair, which made vivid to Western liberal intellectuals the potency of the alleged Islamic threat.

Demonizing Muslims was, however, only of limited and rather problematic use. On the one hand, the US had other actual or potential enemies who had no Muslim associations. On the other hand, among its most important allies were several Islamic regimes, most notably Saudi Arabia, where the ruling family's legitimacy depended crucially on its custody of the Muslim holy places. In the event, NATO's first two military actions – the bombing of

Bosnian Serb positions in 1995, and the 1999 war with Yugoslavia – were conducted purportedly in defence of Muslim peoples, respectively the Bosniaks and the Kosovars.

The veteran Cold War academic Samuel Huntington stepped into the breach. In a notorious article (later developed into a book), he sought to find a new *raison d'être* for the Pentagon by arguing that the main lines of global conflict are becoming cultural rather than economic, political, or ideological. Among the 'clashes of civilizations' he detected was that arising from 'the cultural division of Europe between Western Christianity, on the one hand, and Orthodox Christianity and Islam, on the other'. The historical illiteracy of Huntington's argument is revealed by his presentation of China and Iran as an anti-Western cultural bloc, a 'Confucian-Islamic connection that has emerged to challenge Western interests, values, and power'![19] Nevertheless, it did have the advantage of being much more comprehensive, and more flexible, than other attempts to conceptualize the West's new enemies.

The Huntington thesis was thus put to work during NATO's war with Yugoslavia. One of the most striking examples was provided by an article in the *Financial Times,* a paper which should know better. Citing Huntington, it sought to explain the massive opposition in Greece to the Balkan war by the influence of Orthodox Christianity: 'The key element in defining anti-Western attitudes is not any particular aspect of Orthodoxy, but the relative weakness of Western European cultural values.' The article went on to quote one Greek journalist who complained: 'The Greeks missed out on everything, from the Renaissance to May 1968 . . . Orthodoxy sees the West as a threat, a place where conspiracies are hatched against it.'[20] Such appeals to reified 'cultural values' leave out a rather more obvious explanation for Greek hostility to NATO, namely bitter historical experience of Western intervention – the British occupation of Athens in 1944, Anglo-American support for the monarchist right during the Greek Civil War of 1946–49, Washington's backing for the colonels' putsch in April 1967, and Western acquiescence in the Turkish partition of Cyprus in 1974.

Falsehood is, of course, no objection to ideological beliefs that perform a useful social function. Even from this perspective, however, the Huntington thesis has its limitations. By differentiating humanity into civilizations embodying distinct and potentially antagonistic systems of values, it conflicts with the ideology of multi-culturalism that has become an important part of the theory, if not the practice, of liberal democracy over the past two decades. Moreover, Huntington offers no positive justification for the most ideologically dramatic aspect of the NATO operation, the overriding of Yugoslav sovereignty.

The Rise of Humanitarian Intervention

This second ingredient of the new ideological cocktail emerged independently, through processes initially far removed from Western chancelleries and war-rooms. Alex de Waal chronicles in his important book *Famine Crimes* the development of the idea of humanitarian intervention from the increasing involvement of non-governmental organizations (NGOs) in Third World crises, commencing with the Biafran war of the late 1960s. *Médecins Sans Frontières*, founded in the wake of Biafra, pioneered a more aggressive and politicized style of intervention compared to the practices of Western governmental and international aid agencies. Its founder, Bernard Kouchner, initially a member of the French Communist Party, became in the 1970s a key figure in the group of disillusioned ex-leftists, many of them former Maoists, who animated the daily *Libération*, looked to Foucault for a critique of Marxism, and rallied to the Socialist Party.[21] Kouchner himself served as a minister under both Mitterrand and Jospin, before, appropriately enough, being appointed the West's proconsul in Kosovo after the war – moving, as it were, from doctors without frontiers to bombing without frontiers; while *Médecins Sans Frontières* itself was beatified with the 1999 Nobel Peace Prize.

De Waal describes how, in a context defined by the ideological triumph of neo-liberalism in the 1980s, and the associated privatization of Western aid programmes, NGOs used a succession of disasters, chiefly in Africa, to compete for public support. The NGOs' dependence on media – and especially TV – coverage to secure attention encouraged a depoliticized interpretation of the causes and solutions of humanitarian crises. And the need to show results in order to prove their worth to Western public and private donors led the NGOs to assert what came to be known as the 'Kouchner Doctrine', according to which their right of access to disaster areas overrode the sovereignty of the state in question, and to demand military protection for their activities. In the 1990s, the Western powers began to take up the idea, leading to 'the universal forcible intervention in a state's territory, violating sovereignty under the authority of the UN Security Council, avowedly in pursuit of humanitarian aims', first with the establishment of 'safe havens' for the Kurds of northern Iraq in 1991, and later in Bosnia and Somalia.[22]

Somalia indeed represented the first clear-cut case of what de Waal calls '[p]hilanthropic imperialism, manifest in military intervention' – a UN-sanctioned but US-led operation purportedly to defend relief convoys in a country wracked by civil war. 'Operation Restore Hope', launched during the dying days of the Bush administration in December 1992, rapidly developed into a war with the most popular Somali warlord, General Aidid. In a succession of confrontations, the UN forces fired indiscriminately on crowds of civilians. 'The normal rules of engagement do not apply in this nation,' one UN spokesman explained. Said another after a helicopter gunship opened fire on a crowd, killing sixty: 'There are no sidelines or spectator seats – the people on the ground are considered combatants.'[23]

The Somalian operation was generally considered a disaster in Washington – not, of course, because UN forces killed thousands of Somalis, but because 18 American soldiers died. Nevertheless, the concept of humanitarian intervention was too potent to be abandoned. Pioneered mainly in disintegrating African polities, it was then exported to Europe to legitimize first UN and then NATO military involvement in the wars that accompanied the break-up of Yugoslavia. The Bosnian war indeed provided additional support for unilateral Western interventions. The horrors of that conflict persuaded a section of the Western left-liberal intelligentsia that expansionist Serb nationalism was solely responsible.[24]

Viewing the Milošević regime as fascist also brought into play an older ideological theme that had for much of the post-war period been heard more on the right than on the left, namely that those who opposed military action against such a regime were 'appeasers'. Used in Britain by Tory governments to justify the Suez adventure and the Falklands War, this now activated analogies possessing more progressive connotations, notably with the Spanish Civil War, that did sterling service for social-democratic supporters of the NATO campaign against Yugoslavia.

Saving the World?

The 1999 war involved one extra ingredient. Unlike previous humanitarian interventions, it did not take place under UN auspices. Celebrating NATO's victory, the *Financial Times* commented: 'the alliance has set an important precedent by launching a military operation against a sovereign government in defence of that nation's own citizens. It did so without the authorization of the UN Security Council and thus it greatly extended the legal justification for military action.'[25] Creating this precedent for NATO's acting as a global policeman was arguably one of the main reasons for the war in the first place.

The UN permanent bureaucracy might be relatively compliant. (According to Richard Holbrooke, Kofi Annan's backing for NATO air-strikes against the Bosnian Serbs in August 1995 'was to play a central role in Washington's strong support for him a year later as the successor to Boutros Boutros-Ghali as Secretary-General of the United Nations. Indeed, in a sense, Annan won the job on that day.'[26]) Nevertheless, Russia's and China's vetoes made the Security Council an unreliable instrument of Western policy. Hence the redefinition of NATO as what Madeleine Albright called 'a force for peace from the Middle East to Central Africa'.[27]

Tony Blair offered the most ambitious version of the interventionist ideology in a speech in Chicago just before NATO's fiftieth anniversary summit in April 1999. This 'doctrine of international community' was based on a general analysis of the post-Cold War world that, like Giddens's apologias for the Third Way, sought to derive everything from the remorseless march of globalization. Blair argued that contemporary liberal democracies are ruled, not by national interests, but 'by a more subtle blend of mutual self interest and moral purpose in defending the values we cherish. If we can establish and spread the values of liberty, the rule of law, human rights and an open society then that is in our national interests too.' 'Global interdependence' requires that the Western powers should be prepared to intervene militarily, in certain circumstances, against 'regimes that are undemocratic and engaged in barbarous acts'.[28]

Blair's hawkish pose reflected both the political security provided by his massive parliamentary majority and Britain's relatively marginal position among the Great Powers, still trailing behind the US, and far from the heart of the European Union. Bill Clinton's greater caution did not merely arise from his habitual tendency to calculate every possible angle. *Pace* the over-excited briefings of Downing Street spin-doctors, the American president was the real leader of NATO. He had an empire to run: like British prime ministers when they possessed the reality and not merely the trappings of imperial power, he had carefully to weigh the risks and costs of the various options facing him. Freed from the burdens of empire, Blair could go wherever his belligerent imagination took him.

The diplomatic endgame to the war left him relatively isolated as, between them, Washington, Bonn and Moscow framed a deal that would offer Milošević enough concessions to persuade him to give way, and thereby prevent a ground offensive that might bring down the Red-Green coalition in Germany and further weaken the American public's already shaky support for the war. Russian mediation was critical in securing a compromise settlement on terms significantly more favourable to the Serbian regime than the Rambouillet 'accord' (more accurately ultimatum) whose rejection by Milošević triggered the bombing – though NATO subsequently reneged on the deal, trying to wrest from it an unequivocal victory, and in the process further antagonizing the Russians. The intelligence analysts Stratfor cynically taxed the NATO leaders for failing to understand that 'it's not about Kosovo. It is not about humanitarianism or making ourselves the kind of people we want to be. It's about the Russians, stupid! And about China and the global balance of power.'[29]

Realism and Consistency

NATO's victory over Serbia will nevertheless strengthen the belief that, in the post-Cold War era, the military power of the United States and its European allies can be used for democratic and humanitarian ends. The obvious difficulty with this argument is that there are, to use Blair's own words, plenty of 'undemocratic' regimes 'engaged in barbarous acts' that the US and its allies tolerate or even actively support. Closest to home is, of course, Turkey, a NATO member whose armed forces continued to massacre and expel Kurds in the eastern part of the country while, further west, its airbases were being used to bomb Yugoslavia. There are, however, many other cases where the West cheerfully ignores massacres and indeed often supplies the weapons used in them.

To this objection the pro-war liberals responded, not, as they should, with embarrassment, but with contempt. 'Consistency is the argument of fools,' declared one leading exponent of Western intervention in both Bosnia and Kosovo, Michael Ignatieff.[30] It's OK to be Eurocentric and worry more about Kosovo than about comparable catastrophes in Africa, said another, Susan Sontag.[31] The closest to an argument in support of such assertions involved the claim that the West was turning over a new leaf. Thus Polly Toynbee denounced 'the old British left who took a blood oath to oppose anything American imperialists ever do . . . Something new and better is struggling to be born, messily of necessity, and at risk of stillbirth, but a brave and probably only chance for the West collectively to create a more ethical foreign policy.'[32]

The thought seems to be that, however bad their record, the US and its allies, in doing good in Yugoslavia, have stumbled into a new kind of international policy. As Toynbee put it, 'playing King Arthur in one theatre of war will now require the West to behave as parfait knights elsewhere as well'. To this there are two answers. In the first place, her premiss is false. The West did *not* do good in the Balkans. The NATO assault on Yugoslavia turned a nasty but low-intensity war in Kosovo into a full-blown humanitarian disaster. Indeed, as one leading defender of the war, the veteran left-liberal journalist Jonathan Steele, conceded at the conflict's end: 'NATO has achieved its aims in Yugoslavia, but the war need never have been. The deal it extracted from Slobodan Milošević last week could have been obtained twelve months ago without the horror of bombing at all.'[33] Far from representing, as Habermas claimed, a move towards 'a world civil society', the war was a step back into barbarity – into a condition where the Great Powers use their military might to bully small states into submission.

So the new-leaf argument applies at most to the motives with which the war was conducted. In other words, NATO's intentions were good, even if the consequences of its actions were not. But identifying the reasons for which an action is performed requires more than taking at face value the actor's professed motives. If this principle applies to the appraisal of individual actions, how much more should it do so to that of the behaviour of states? And when trying to elicit the real reasons for an action, is not consistency – for example, setting this particular action in the context of the actor's conduct in other situations – typically a guiding consideration? Far from consistency being the argument of fools, only a fool would fail to give it proper weight.[34]

In demanding that the NATO governments' professed moral and humanitarian motives are taken at face value the liberal apologists were trying, in effect, to short-circuit realistic political analysis. This is very much in the spirit of the Third Way. A major aim of Blair's crusade is to take the politics out of politics. Issues are either technical (included under this heading are most economic and social issues, where neo-liberal nostrums are now treated as self-evidently valid), and therefore raise no matters of principle, or they are moral, in which case only the wicked or the foolish can disagree with the dictates of universal reason as interpreted from Downing Street and Pennsylvania Avenue. As a result, the analysis of interests and the calculation of consequences – as Max Weber pointed out, necessary conditions of responsible political action – vanish from the radar screen.[35] Refusing this false dilemma is essential. The capacity critically to analyse the assertions of rulers is a prerequisite of effective democratic citizenship.

Those who opposed this war should thus remain vigilant; in the event of future 'humanitarian' interventions they should remain ready to expose their roots in Great Power interests and conflicts. This has important theoretical implications. For ideologists of 'globalization' such as Giddens and his willing pupil Blair, inter-state antagonisms represent survivals from a past era. The emergence of 'the state without enemies' reflects both the formation of a world economy that transcends and constrains the activities of nation-states and the inherently pacific tendencies of liberal democracies. The experience of the Balkan war of 1999 indicates something very different – the persistence of inter-state competition rooted in economic conflicts among capitals. As Clinton let slip, 'that's what this Kosovo thing is all about'.

The Marxist theory of imperialism was developed precisely to analyse the interrelations of economic and military competition. Far from having become irrelevant in the era of global capital, it remains indispensable to any understanding of the main lines of conflict and to motivating the forces of resistance. The course of the past decade has seen two ruthless assertions of military power by the leading states in the world – first in the Gulf and now in the Balkans; their roots need to be traced in the shifting relationships of economic and political power.[36]

Such realistic analysis does not rule out appeal to normative considerations, including the discourse of rights to which the pro-war liberals appealed: there is no reason to concede this language to NATO's apologists. But unless ethical concepts are married to the attempt to probe the underlying structures of power, they are likely to serve as mere decoration for policies ruled by very different interests. Indeed, what was striking about the debate on the Balkan war in Britain at least was the way in which high-minded moralism was frequently accompanied by self-abasement before the mighty.

In a very different conjuncture, George Orwell described the way in which power-worship tends to shape the political choices of intellectuals. The same mechanisms are evidently at work in Britain today, as journalists and academics re-align themselves to take full account of New Labour's dominance of the political scene. Sometimes the results are simply comic, as when Jonathan Freedland, perhaps the *Guardian*'s most vehemently pro-war columnist, announced that Tony Blair had just won . . . the Israeli general election![37]

In this case the sycophancy reflected sincere belief in the Third Way *pur et dur*. But in many others it is more a matter of resigned accommodation to realities that are perceived to be unalterable. The end of the Cold War, far from fulfilling the liberating promise of the 1989 revolutions, has led to a narrowing of horizons.[38] Little wonder that many left-of-centre intellectuals have concluded that, since there was no realistic prospect of real social change, they may as well make the best of things by aligning themselves to the reigning Blair-Clinton consensus, in the hope of achieving both a few minor reforms and their own personal advancement. The lamentable intellectual and moral consequences were evident in the debate over the war. It was a time like that during the Boer War, when, as the *Manchester Guardian*'s anti-war leader writer C.E. Montague later recalled, 'the island unsubmerged by meanness seemed deuced small'.[39]

But this debased climate provides good reasons for refusing to go with the stream. By challenging the incoherent and reactionary apologias offered for the war, its opponents helped to keep genuinely critical thinking alive. Such movements of resistance can also prevent the idea of a genuine social transformation – as opposed to the quack remedies of the Third Way – from dropping out of sight.

Notes

1. T. Blair, 'Statement on the Suspension of NATO Air Strikes against Yugoslavia', 10 June 1999, www.fco.gov.uk.
2. Quoted in H. Kissinger, *Diplomacy* (New York, 1994), p. 86.
3. K. Marx and F. Engels, *Collected Works*, XII (London, 1979), p. 221.
4. P. Gowan, *The Global Gamble* (London, 1999), p. 142; see generally ibid., ch. 8.
5. *Newsweek*, 19 April 1999.
6. T. Blair, 'Doctrine of International Community', speech given to the Economic Club of Chicago, 22 April 1999, www.fco.gov.uk.
7. *Guardian*, 27 April 1999.
8. J. Habermas, 'Bestialität und Humanität', *Die Zeit*, 29 April 1999.
9. 'Remarks of the President to AFSCME Biennial Convention', 23 March 1999, p. 3. Peter Gowan deserves much credit for drawing attention to this fascinating speech in 'The Twisted Road to Kosovo', *Labour Focus on Eastern Europe*, 62 (1999).
10. *Independent*, 21 April 1999.

11. *Guardian*, 20 May 1999.
12. A. Barnett, 'Iron Britannia', *New Left Review*, 134 (1982), pp. 20, 21 n. 14.
13. *Guardian*, 29 April 1999.
14. A. Giddens, *The Third Way* (Cambridge, 1998), p. 70.
15. G. Achcar, 'The Strategic Triad: The United States, Russia, and China', *New Left Review*, 228 (1998).
16. J. Rees, 'NATO and the New Imperialism', *Socialist Review*, June 1999.
17. Kissinger, *Diplomacy*, p. 774.
18. F. Halliday, 'The Left and the War', *New Statesman and Society*, 8 March 1991.
19. S. Huntington, 'The Clash of Civilizations?', *Foreign Affairs*, 72:3, Summer 1993, pp. 29–30, 45.
20. S. Wagstyl et al., 'Christendom's Ancient Split Filters Today's View of Kosovo', *Financial Times*, 4 May 1999.
21. The evolution of this group can be traced in D. Eribon, *Michel Foucault* (Cambridge MA, 1991) and D. Macey, *The Lives of Michel Foucault* (London, 1994).
22. A. de Waal, *Famine Crimes* (London, 1997), p. 155.
23. Ibid., pp. 179, 187, 188.
24. For an outstanding analysis of the break-up of Yugoslavia, which highlights its complex causes and the generally negative impact of Western intervention, whether economic, diplomatic, or military, see S. Woodward, *Balkan Tragedy* (Washington, 1995).
25. *Financial Times*, 5 June 1999.
26. R. Holbrooke, *To End a War* (New York, 1999), p. 103.
27. *Financial Times*, 23 April 1999.
28. Blair, 'Doctrine of International Community'.
29. Stratfor's Global Intelligence Update: Weekly Analysis June 14, 1999, www.stratfor.com. Apparently the key role in brokering the deal was played by Peter Castenfeldt, a Swedish financier linked to the Russian government who worked closely with senior German officials: *Financial Times*, 14 June 1999.
30. BBC 2 *Newsnight*, 16 April 1999.
31. *Observer*, 16 May 1999.
32. *Guardian*, 12 April 1999.
33. Ibid., 7 June 1999.
34. Critics of the war were also taxed for concentrating exclusively on the consequences of the bombing campaign as opposed to the motives with which it was conducted. But where – let us concede for the purposes of this argument – someone does the wrong thing for the right reasons (or for what would have been the right reasons had the situation been as she thought it was), it is not the actor's intentions, but the nature of the situation, and the relevant moral principles which make that action right or wrong. My thoughts on this matter have been greatly clarified by hearing a paper by T.M. Scanlon, 'Intentions, Reasons, and Permissibility', at the Political Theory Workshop, University of York, 8 June 1999.

35. M. Weber, 'The Profession and Vocation of Politics', in *Political Writings* (Cambridge, 1994). To insist on analysing the interests shaping the policies of the Great Powers is, of course, not to endorse the realist theory of international relations: for a critique, see J. Rosenberg, *The Empire of Civil Society* (London, 1994).
36. See A. Callinicos et al., *Marxism and the New Imperialism* (London, 1994).
37. *Guardian*, 19 May 1999.
38. For a recent, overly pessimistic diagnosis, see R. Jacoby, *The End of Utopia* (New York, 1999).
39. Quoted in J.L. Hammond, *C.P. Scott of the Manchester Guardian* (London, 1934), p. 185.

8

KOSOVO AND THE NEW IMPERIALISM

Ellen Meiksins Wood

The war in Yugoslavia has taken place at a time when words like 'imperialism' are scarcely uttered any more; but there is no other currently available 'discourse' that can adequately capture what has been going on in the Balkans. At the same time, some old assumptions about imperialism and how it works may need to be revised; and, within the new imperialism, we may need to rethink the role of military force.

War Just for the Hell of It?

What, then, was really going on in the war over Kosovo? We can start by hearing it straight from the horse's mouth. Here is Bill Clinton: 'If we're going to have a strong economic relationship that includes our ability to sell around the world, Europe has got to be a key . . . That's what this Kosovo thing is all about.'[1]

So there it is: forget humanitarian motives, this is about US global hegemony. And more immediately, it is about the role of NATO as the US conduit to Europe, at a time when the European Union is developing as a major pole of global capitalism which the US needs to control. No doubt, as many commentators have pointed out, it is also about Russia and the geo-political containment of what still remains a big player, the one major power that sits athwart Europe and Asia. And for those who wonder what's in it for Clinton's chief henchman, Tony Blair (whose hawkishness has exceeded even that of his mentor), just consider this: the EU is now in the process of constructing common security and defence arrangements. The UK, which under Blair has finally given up its long resistance to such arrangements, is clearly asserting in the military sphere the European leadership that has eluded it in other domains (or, perhaps more precisely, is trying to consolidate its partnership with the US for their mutual benefit in Europe, through both NATO and through these new security arrangements). With all these larger objectives in mind, it is probably unnecessary to invoke oil supplies and pipelines – which are regularly, and often correctly, cited to explain US military adventures, including to some extent this last one.

But even these large objectives have to be seen in the context of a still larger strategy, which can be sketched out only very briefly here. What the Clinton regime has been doing, as wild and unthinking as it seems, is completely consistent with a now well-established pattern in US foreign policy. So well established and habitual has this pattern become that an irresponsible President and his lunatic Secretary of State can follow it blindfolded, without plan or forethought. US wars have long been about one thing above all others: demonstrating that the US can deploy its massive military power any time any place, with or without intelligible reasons, objectives, or strategies. This is a seemingly irrational use of military force which may appear to have no identifiable purpose, certainly nothing so unambiguous as establishing sovereignty over territory or acquiring and dominating colonies.

Maybe we need a whole new vocabulary for this kind of militarism, but so far, we know no other word for it than imperialism. To make sense of it, though, we have to trace the changes in the nature of imperialism. Capitalist imperialism, as Harry Magdoff has often pointed out, is essentially different from earlier forms of imperialism, because its objectives are specifically capitalist. They are not, for instance, the objectives of the slave-holding Roman empire but the objectives of an expanding capital, the search for markets and resources in pursuit of capitalist self-expansion, and so on. But something more needs to be said, about the ways in which capitalist imperialism itself has changed.

In the old days, capitalist imperialism was based on a division between a capitalist and a non-capitalist world. Imperialist powers typically conquered colonial territories or used direct military force to control them. And, of course, imperialist states competed over those territories, typically by military means. So, though its objectives and its basic logic were fundamentally different from pre-capitalist imperialism, capitalist imperialism in its earlier days may not have been quite so different from those older forms in its methods and instruments, the modalities of territorial conquest or control, or in the forms of inter-imperialist rivalry.

But the story today is different. Today, imperialism is not really about the relation between a capitalist and a non-capitalist world. It has more to do with the relations within a global capitalist system. Imperialism today is taking place in the context of what can be called the 'universalization' of capitalism. It is not now primarily a matter of territorial conquest or direct military or colonial control. It is not now a matter of capitalist powers invading non-capitalist territories in order to bleed them dry directly and by brute force. Now, it is more a matter of ensuring that the forces of the capitalist market prevail in every corner of the world (even if this means marginalizing and impoverishing parts of it), and of manipulating those market forces to the advantage of the most powerful capitalist economies and the US in particular. It is not just a matter of controlling particular territories. It is a matter of controlling a whole world economy and global markets, everywhere and all the time.

This happens not only through the direct exploitation of cheap labour by transnationals based in advanced capitalist countries but also, more indirectly, through things like debt, currency manipulation, and so on. And with these changes in the form of imperialism, inter-imperialist rivalries have changed too. They are still there, but in less direct, unambiguous military forms, in the contradictory processes of capitalist accumulation, in which cooperation among capitalists is never far removed from competition and struggles for domination. These changes in the nature of imperialism have, among other things, intensified the contradictions and instabilities of capitalism, and this may open up new possibilities of anti-capitalist and anti-imperialist struggle. But there are also other consequences. If today's imperialism does not typically express itself in the direct military domination of colonies, this does not mean that it is any less militaristic than the old variety. The point is certainly not that the world is more peaceful because the old principles of military conquest have given way to less violent means of commerce and financial domination. On the contrary, military force is still central to the imperialist project, in some ways more than ever. But now it is used – it has to be used – in different ways and with different immediate objectives.

The point can be put very simply: there is a big difference between, on the one hand, establishing sovereignty over territory – a specific, clearly identifiable territory with known boundaries – and, on the other hand, establishing sovereignty over an anarchic global economy. The minute we get that distinction clear in our minds, it starts to make sense out of all kinds of apparently inexplicable things, such as repeated military actions by the US that consistently fail to achieve their stated objectives, and which even worsen the situations they are supposed to correct.

But while we have to recognize that the new imperialism is not about the colonization of one state by another, we also have to keep in mind that the universalization of capitalism which is the context of this kind of imperialism still takes place within a world of nation-states. So the effort to establish sovereignty over global markets, no less than the sovereignty over specific colonial territories in the past, is a project pursued by state powers, and by one state power above all.

The question is how this kind of boundless hegemony, this sovereignty without territory, this imperialism without frontiers, can be achieved. When all is said and done, after we take account of all kinds of specific interests, or apparent interests, it finally comes down to a naked display of force, just for the sake of it, just for the sake of asserting US hegemony. Sabre-rattling has, of course, always been part of imperialist strategies, but massive displays of force have a new importance in the new imperialism. The point is that, in today's conditions, we won't necessarily find any specific and concrete objective to military action. We won't find it, simply because the object of the exercise is not necessarily direct control of territory or even resources.

This is something that even some old-fashioned military men can't quite get their heads around. For instance, a few years ago, General Colin Powell, then chairman of the Joint Chiefs of Staff, enunciated what has been called the 'Powell Doctrine', laying out the basic conditions for the use of military force: there must be some clear and vital national interest, there must be a clear goal, there must be sufficient force to achieve that goal, and there must be a clear exit strategy. When Madeleine Albright was the US ambassador to the UN, she challenged Powell on these principles. 'What's the point of having this superb military that you've always been talking about,' she is reported to have said, 'if we can't use it?'[2] The idea seems to have been that US military might should be used more flexibly, even where none of Powell's conditions are present, even where there is no clear, or clearly attainable, objective and no clear exit. The US, in other words, should use its military power when, and because, it can.

Whatever deliberate strategies were being pursued by Albright and Clinton, then, Albright's irresponsible attitude at least makes some kind of sense in the context of the new imperialism. In fact, it has been a basic theme in US foreign policy for a long time. What it's about is making it clear to the world at large that US power can be deployed anywhere at any time. And, to cite a principle enunciated by Henry Kissinger, part of that strategy is unpredictability – some would say, irrationality.

'A Manifesto for the Fast World'

This thesis would seem to be confirmed by a recent article by Thomas L. Friedman, one of the premier columnists of the *New York Times*, in fact, one of the leading commentators in the US media. In a long piece entitled 'A Manifesto for the Fast World', published in the *New York Times* magazine on March 28, just a few days after the bombing in Yugoslavia began (though the piece was apparently printed a few days before), Friedman gives us what amounts to his own political testament; it turns out to be a manifesto for the new imperialism precisely as just outlined here.

What makes Friedman's manifesto particularly interesting is not simply that he's one of the most prominent columnists in the US (who 'seems to be emerging as the pop theoretician of the era, just as George Gilder was for the 1980s'[3]) but that he's relatively 'liberal' (in the American sense) by the standards of the mainstream US media, and could even be said to represent the more 'liberal' elements in the current administration. In the manifesto itself, in fact, he seems to identify himself as a social democrat, and it's clear that he thinks he's saying something humane and progressive. So the ease and smug assurance with which he very explicitly lays out his imperialist program is especially blood-chilling.

Friedman's conception of imperialism is based on precisely the distinction drawn here between hegemony over specific territories and hegemony over global markets. And he also shows how the new type of imperial hegemony requires displays of military force designed not so much to achieve specific and immediate objectives as to make a general point about US domination.

Since the US is the country that benefits most from globalization, Friedman tells us, it's also the one that has to take the main responsibility for sustaining it. 'Sustaining globalization is our overarching national interest . . . Globalization-is-US.' This, he says, is different from 'old-fashioned imperialism, when one country physically occupies another'. Now, it's a matter of maintaining 'an abstract globalization system'. And this 'requires a stable geopolitical power structure, which simply cannot be maintained without the active involvement of the United States'. The point is then nicely summed up: 'The hidden hand of the market will never work without the hidden fist –

McDonald's cannot flourish without McDonnell Douglas, the designer of the F-15. And the hidden fist that keeps the world safe for Silicon Valley's technologies is called the United States Army, Air Force, Navy and Marine Corps.'

Naturally, the hidden fist has to come out of hiding with some regularity, if it's going to make its point. Friedman goes on to quote approvingly from foreign policy historian Robert Kagan: 'Good ideas and technologies need a strong power that promotes those ideas by example and protects those ideas by winning on the battlefield. If a lesser power were promoting our ideas and technologies, they would not have the global currency that they have.'

So much for those who say that US objectives in the war over Kosovo must be humanitarian because there's no obvious national or strategic interest there for the US. The defence of the 'abstract system of globalization' knows no bounds. It comes as no surprise, then, that Friedman illustrates his point by citing the example of Kosovo as a case for US intervention. Although the bombing campaign had just begun, and, according to the *Times*, the article went to the printer before it actually started, Friedman has since then laid to rest any doubts about just what kind of intervention he had in mind. He has become one of the most avid supporters of the bombing. In an article on April 23, for instance, he calls for a 'merciless air war', to 'pulverize' the Serbian nation, bombing it back to the fourteenth century if necessary. 'You want 1950? We can do 1950. You want 1389? We can do 1389 too,' he tells the Serbs. 'Give war a chance,' he says to Americans. In preference to a ground invasion that might bog the US down as an occupying force for years, 'Let's see what months of bombing does.'

Of course, after more than two months of bombing, we have some idea of what it does; but if its sheer destructiveness, its damage to human beings (never mind its failure to save a single human life), is a funny way to achieve 'humanitarian' objectives, it has certainly worked much better as one of those exemplary displays of the fist.

In his Manifesto, Friedman explains that Americans, who 'were ready to pay any price and bear any burden in the Cold War,' are unwilling to die for that 'abstract globalization system'. That's why 'house-to-house fighting is out; cruise missiles are in'. He could just as easily have said 'that's why ground troops are out and high-tech bombing is in. We don't want to die ourselves for globalization, but we don't mind killing others.'

Humanitarian Imperialism?

Where, then, are the tens, even hundreds, of thousands who used to come out to protest US imperialism, in Vietnam or Central America? Where, in particular, is the left? There has certainly been growing opposition to the war in various NATO countries, but, it must be said, no coherent movement has emerged.

Some of the difficulties are obviously inherent in this specific situation. We're not here dealing with an imperialist attack on heroic freedom fighters, and it's clearly not easy to make people understand how this war can be opposed without condoning atrocities. It's also true, as supporters of the war have gleefully noted, that there have been certain ambiguities in the anti-war position: are opponents against the war because it has been bungled, or are they against it in principle?

No doubt some have opposed the war for the first reason, and others for the second, but, given the nature of the NATO action, it is possible consistently to hold both positions at once. There are many reasons, including purely logistical considerations such as those invoked by military opponents of the war, for believing that the 'bungling' has from the beginning been inherent in the very logic of this war. Some of us see the 'bungling' as inevitable simply because the war is driven by overriding factors quite distinct from, and in opposition to, its stated objectives. So it makes perfect sense to draw attention to the bungling while opposing the war in principle. Here again, the apparent ambiguities in the anti-war position are responses to the real ambiguities in the war itself.

But a larger question arises here. Is it possible that people don't recognize imperialism when they see it? Given the seeming irrationality of the new imperialism, it may be understandable that so many people, even those on the left with strong anti-imperialist commitments, have trouble acknowledging it. The indiscriminate use of military force is certainly harder to understand than the outright capture of territory and the exploitation of colonies; and surely, many people will think, it can't be true that any sane person or government would use military power in this way, killing and destroying without definable objective.

There is, though, another reason for the remarkable weakness of the opposition to this new form of imperialism. The new imperialism, as practised by the US, has adopted a very effective disguise. We now have what some have called 'human rights imperialism', based on a conception of human rights in which the particular interests of the US and its arbitrary actions have effectively displaced the common interests of humanity and the international instruments designed to represent them.[4] The notion of 'human rights imperialism' nicely captures the mystification that seems to have swayed a lot of people on the left in the case of Kosovo.

What, then, can we say about the humanitarian claims being made for this war? Let's be very clear, first, that opposing the war is not the same as condoning atrocities, committed by Serbs or anyone else. It is, to be sure, unlikely that anyone will ever be able to sort out the truth from the lies on all sides. As much evidence as there now is of atrocities in Kosovo, there is growing evidence that NATO went to war with surprisingly little to support its claims of atrocities in any way commensurate with the war it was about to launch.[5] But let's start from the premise that there was indeed a humanitarian disaster which people of good will wanted to see stopped. What do we say to them?

Though supporters of the war like to dismiss as irrelevant the failures of the US and its NATO allies to apply their alleged humanitarian principles in other countries, there is surely something to be learned about their motivations from all the cases of atrocities perpetrated by friends of the US which have elicited no 'humanitarian' response. The most dramatic instance is, of course, the Turkish government's long-standing and systematic oppression of Turkey's Kurdish population, which continued as Turkish planes flew over Belgrade.

We can surely also deduce something from the consequences of the war itself. Professions of moral outrage (and accusations that opponents of the war were morally insensitive appeasers and who would all be ashamed when the mass graves were opened) would be far more persuasive if the war had saved a single human life. But we all know that the opposite is true. Supporters of the war may feel absolutely certain about what would have happened if the bombing hadn't started, but this speculative certainty counts for nothing against the verifiable reality that the ethnic cleansing of Kosovo Albanians was all but completed not before but *during* the war, and that substantially more of it happened after the war began than before, whether because of the war or despite it. No matter what the eventual outcome, it's hard to see how things could have been worse for the Kosovars if NATO hadn't gone to war in March 1999. So where is the proportionality between means and ends?

This disproportion seems to leave us with two choices. On the one hand, if we accept the humanitarian motivations of the war, we can only fear the kind of moral sensibility that is so careless about the discrepancy between means and ends, or, more particularly, between professed objectives and actual consequences. We have to ask whether there is anything these humanitarian hawks wouldn't do in the name of their moral superiority. Is there no amount of destruction and human suffering they could cause that would put them in the wrong?

On the other hand, the discrepancy between means and ends may simply cause us to question the ends. And, on balance, that seems the most reasonable option. If we take Clinton (not to mention Friedman) at his word, we have to accept that the war is really about something else.

What, then, if we accept that the war is not driven by humanitarian motives? What about the fairly common argument that the motives aren't important? If your wife is being raped or your husband beaten to a pulp, the argument goes, you call the cops, even if you know they're rotten and corrupt.

There are some painfully obvious answers. Even if you can't stop to ask who appointed those cops and on what authority, even if you have no time to consider the long-term effects of calling on self-appointed cops, the effects on the rule of law itself, would you really call the cops if you believed that they themselves would rape or beat your partner? Motives do matter, if only because they tell us a lot about what the actor will and will not do, and what the outcome is likely to be.

If we assume that NATO was acting on imperialist motives, we are unlikely to be surprised at the failure of its action to help the victims, whose conditions became palpably worse after the bombing began. We are unlikely to be surprised at the destruction of the country's infrastructure which will, as in Iraq, do far more harm, and for much longer, to innocent civilians than to their oppressors. We are unlikely to be surprised at the destruction perpetrated by the NATO military machine, the immediate killing and maiming of civilians by bombs, and the long-term killing and maiming, of this and future generations, by ecological catastrophe through the bombing of refineries and chemical plants (which is nothing short of biological warfare), and the use by the US of depleted uranium, which is not a million miles away from nuclear war.

For that matter, we are unlikely to be surprised that an action supposedly intended to stabilize the Balkan region has transparently resulted in its destabilization, or that an action supposedly intended to weaken if not destroy

Milošević gave him the strength to continue. We certainly won't be surprised by the consistent use of a military method that has long been the method of choice for the US: high-tech bombing, which has never yet, in any war, achieved the objectives claimed for it but which is guaranteed to cause maximum and indiscriminate destruction, in the short and long term. Everything down to the most basic tactics – such as flying bombers at great heights to avoid any risk to US forces, while absolutely guaranteeing civilian casualties (not least among people who are supposed to be the bombing's beneficiaries) for the simple reason that the targets are hardly discernible – becomes intelligible and predictable once we recognize the underlying motives. Thomas Friedman makes sense of it all.

We could, of course, try to make sense of it simply by saying that the NATO action has been monumentally inept. Inept it certainly has been. There can be no doubt that it was based on gross miscalculations, and that it's likely to prove destabilizing for NATO itself in the long term. But, again, the new imperialism makes sense of the blunders and ineptness, too. In a way, they hardly matter, if the aim is a display of military force and of the naked power to destroy at will. At any rate, it seems reasonable – and in keeping with a long and consistent record of US military actions – to accept what its perpetrators themselves have said about the war: that it's about US global hegemony. We should just acknowledge that in the light of that objective no other consequences count.

Beyond the consequences for Kosovo, for Yugoslavia, for the Balkans, and for Europe, there are the consequences for the world as a whole. Few now have any illusions about the feeble safeguards put in place after two world wars to preserve some semblance of international order, but it can't be a matter of indifference to see them completely dismantled, the UN effectively defunct and every commitment to international law discarded. If there was ever any hope of even the most minimally effective and decent solution to a crisis like the one in Kosovo, surely it was more likely to be found by institutions intended for such purposes than by instruments of war and imperialism.

But maybe the monumental damage done by NATO and the growing unease felt by citizens of NATO countries, not to mention the rest of the world, will mark the beginning of the end for NATO, and one small nail in the coffin of the new imperialism.

Notes

1. Quoted in Benjamin Schwartz and Christopher Lane, 'The Case Against Intervention in Kosovo', *The Nation,* 19 April 1999.
2. Eric Schmitt, 'The Powell Doctrine Is Looking Pretty Good Again', *New York Times,* 4 April 1999, p. 5.
3. Doug Henwood, 'The American Millennium', in *Capitalism at the End of the Millennium,* the special summer issue of *Monthly Review,* July/August 1999.
4. See Uwe-Jens Heuer and Gregor Schirmer, 'Human Rights Imperialism', *Monthly Review,* March 1998, vol. 49, no. 10, pp. 5–16.
5. See, for example, an article, 'Failure of Diplomacy', by Rollie Keith, a Canadian monitor who worked with the OSCE Kosovo Verification Mission near Priština, the capital of Kosovo, till March 20, a few days before the bombing began. The article appeared on 9 May 1999 in *The Democrat,* the newspaper of the New Democratic Party in British Columbia, and challenges in detail NATO's account of the humanitarian disaster in Kosovo on the eve of the bombing. It can also be found on the web site of the British Columbia NDP: www.bc.ndp.ca/welcome-frame.htm. See also extracts from leaked German foreign ministry documents on the web at www.jungewelt.de/1999/04-24/011.shtml. And on more recent evidence, see Audrey Gillan, 'In Search of a Massacre', *London Review of Books,* 27 May 1999.

PART III

Balkan Landscapes: The Sleep of Reason

9

WAR: BUILDING STATES FROM NATIONS

Susan L. Woodward

As a political force, nationalism is an empty vessel to be filled by all those who see their interests in political independence and states' rights. Its key characteristic is its definition of a political community – its principles of membership, its cultural and territorial boundaries, and also, therefore, its enemies. In contrast to communism, nationalism has no intrinsic substantive goals beyond affirmation of a particular collective bond among people and the creation of an independent state around that identity. Exclusion is as important as inclusion. Nationalist expression may be a positive assertion of commonality in culture, political history, and obligations of social reciprocity. But it is at the same time necessarily a negative assertion of who does *not* belong, of mistrust, fear, even hatred of persons seen as 'other,' as 'foreigner,' and of the characteristics of persons who should be excluded.

Nationalism's virulent capacity is not so apparent when it manifests itself as cultural or religious revival and in intellectuals' demands for rights to personal expression, as if to open debate, rather than to draw cultural borders between people. As a vehicle for resolving distributive conflicts by claiming ethnic rights or national ownership over incomes, jobs, economic assets, and tax revenues, it is so familiar to the workings of most societies that it is easily accepted. What society does not seek to defend privilege or wealth as a national right or to organize social roles and patterns of discrimination (positive and negative) in part along cultural lines? When aspiring politicians in countries formerly ruled by communist parties used nationalist symbols and novelties to maximize votes world popular support, to coopt opposition intellectuals, or to neutralize competitors with charges of being unpatriotic, they did not appear threatening to Western governments that heard the anticommunist language in which it was often cloaked. The ease with which aroused passions could substitute in the short run for ideology and organization and avoid representing individual interests also caused little alarm because it was seen as part of a democratic revolution.

Despite the Jekyll and Hyde potential of nationalism, people tend to distinguish among separate nationalisms, calling some 'good' and others 'bad' according to the goal sought or the methods used.[1] But this evaluation is always subjective, and it depends on the institutional context within which it appears. In an atmosphere of tolerance and institutionalized pluralism, nationalism can remain a positive expression of cultural or religious identity – ethnic differences – that does not deny the same freedom to others. Even politicized ethnicity, while discriminating against those who do not belong to or identify with officially recognized groups, can exist peacefully under favourable economic conditions if it provides the same rights to members of different groups and ensures institutionalized channels of appeal. But political nationalism defines rights of membership itself: black and white, in or out; on this one defining trait it cannot compromise.[2] Because the goal of nationalist politicians is to use the coercive instruments of the state to enforce that principle, what one thinks about a particular nationalism depends most on whether one is being included or excluded.

Nationalism is often compared with communism as a collectivist ideology, but in fact it defines the membership characteristics of individuals, not the quality of their social interaction. In contrast to communist parties, moreover, its membership is ascriptive and exclusive rather than open to people regardless of racial, religious, and cultural background. And that membership is not only in a party, with its obligations and privileges, but in society itself – as citizen, and with no recourse against others' decision to exclude. But nationalism is compatible with communist rule, either together or as its successor, because both deny (for very different reasons) the need to provide institutional mechanisms to regulate and protect differences (such as permitting an opposition, critical thought, conflicts of interest, or minority rights).

The label of nationalism is not sufficient to describe a situation or predict behaviour, however, because of its empty-vessel character – its absence of programme outside the insistence on political power for some imagined community. It can therefore ally easily with others, including dispossessed communists who believe in a strong state against international exploitation or who hold bureaucratic positions. Such allies may be ideologically contradictory groups from far left to far right joined only by political expediency.

Nationalist parties most often attract individuals when political organizations representing their specific interests are absent or have not sought their support, when individuals – out of a growing rootlessness or anomie – seek a restored sense of community.[3] Because it is a principle of exclusion, however, it tends to surface in conditions that are not conducive to its more benign expression alone. Its potential for violence is ever more manifest as it moves from intellectual expression and economic discrimination to criteria for citizenship and claims for territorial sovereignty. In multinational states such as Yugoslavia, it must destroy while it builds.

This process can be understood not by the labels of historical ethnic hatred or Balkan culture, but by the clash between nationalist goals and Yugoslav reality and by the consequence of translating socioeconomic and political divisions into contests over territory. The wars to create new national states out of Yugoslavia contained many elements: psychological warfare against multiethnic identities and loyalties; the culture surrounding the defence of rights to land; class warfare; the dissolution of the governmental and economic functions of the former state; and the construction, of borders, foreign relations, economic infrastructure, and armed forces of defensible, viable, new states.

Psychological Warfare: Honi Soit Qui Mal y Pense

Despite the claims made by nationalist leaders, the reality of multinational Yugoslavia still existed in the lives of individual citizens in 1990–91 – in their ethnically mixed neighbourhoods, villages, towns, and cities; in their mixed marriages, family ties across republic boundaries, and second homes in another republic; in their conceptions of ethnic and national coexistence and the compatibility of multiple identities for each citizen; and in the idea of Bosnia-Herzegovina. Because people had not expressed their differences politically under one-party socialism, their loyalties were scattered among many associations. These tended to be highly localized and personal – to one's village or town, to school friends, to neighbours, to the town or region of one's origin and parents, to Yugoslavia as an idea and a stature abroad, to workplace colleagues, or to an occupation or profession. A one-time, multiparty election thus was not sufficient to develop partisan identities. The exception to undeveloped political identities was communists – not individuals who had simply been members of a party that had folded, but those who identified broadly with its ideals, traditions. or wartime struggle. But as it was common to say, 'I come from a communist family,' this had become for most a private identity, however strong it remained.

To legitimize new states on the basis of political loyalty to a nation, nationalist politicians had to draw out the ethnic element in all these social bonds and identities, nationalize it, and win the loyalty of citizens whose allegiances were in doubt. A vote in 1990 for a political party that emphasized ethnonational identity was not the same thing as a vote for a national state, and even a vote for the sovereignty of one's republic was not necessarily a vote for independence, let alone commitment to war, should that be necessary. In Bosnia-Herzegovina, where votes were cast most overwhelmingly for ethnonational parties, public opinion polls in May and June 1990, and again in November 1991, also showed overwhelming majorities (in the range of 70 to 90 percent) against separation from Yugoslavia and against an ethnically divided republic.[4]

To win against public opinion, nationalist leaders had to engage in psychological warfare. They sought to persuade audiences both at home and abroad that the alternative to national states was no longer viable: in other words, to destroy forever the Yugoslav idea that they could live together. The first stage in the wars of 1991–95, therefore, occurred earlier in the mass media and on the political stump.[5] The domestic objective of various nationalists was to persuade citizens of one nationality that they were under threat from other nationals. Accusations of being cheated economically by other nations (in federal taxation or in jobs) or being overcome biologically (by the higher Muslim and Albanian birth rates) and warnings of plots by other groups to create states that would expel citizens from their homes played on a local inclination to conspiracy theories and on growing economic insecurity and rapidly shifting, uncertain political conditions. In a country where everyone was a minority in ethnonational terms, politicians willing to raise consciousness about national survival and the danger of being in a minority had the potential to create a collective paranoia that was self-perpetuating. It was then only a short step to persuade those who accepted this argument that the security of their identity, way of living, and perhaps even person lay with their national group.[6] As terrorists reason, elemental fears were to force people to take sides.

In view of this tactic, the political rhetoric of the 1980s found in debates over the federal budget and constitution from Slovenia to Serbia, and in nationalist themes from anticommunist intellectuals, therefore became, whether intended or not, a long, psychological preparation for war.[7] In Slovenia nationalists claimed that Slovene standards of living were threatened by federal taxes and that their democracy and pluralism were endangered by Serbia. In Serbia nationalists linked the Albanian demand for a republic in Kosovo with Serbia's 500 years of subjugation to Turkish rule after its defeat in 1389; the nationalist programmes of Slovenes, Croats, Muslims, Albanians, and Macedonians in the 1980s, with the progressive splintering of Serbs and Serbia after 1945 and 1974 into ever more separate political units; and the anti-Serb coalition, with a similar alliance of the Vatican, the Comintern, and Germany during World War II.[8]

It was true that in the decade-long struggle over Kosovo between Serbian state power and Albanian demographic power, Albanians had made Serbs and Montenegrins feel unwelcome, persuading them to leave. It was also true that church leaders and intellectuals had given these Serbs and Montenegrins aid in their political campaign with Belgrade to take back political power and property. But the political problem was the hypercharged emotional atmosphere of mutual suspicions within Kosovo in which rumours of Serbs poisoning drinking water and of Albanians raping Serb women suggested the beginnings of mass hysteria.[9] The Serbian political campaign referred to 'genocide' against Serbs and used a 'discourse of violence, rape particularly, aiming to spread the fear of communication over ethnic boundaries.'[10] It was in this context that Serbian president Slobodan Milošević first gave the war cries, which he repeated often, 'No one will be permitted to beat you' and 'They will never humiliate the Serbian people again.' In some villages, local authorities began to issue permits to citizens to draw arms from the local TDF arsenal 'just in case.' Croatian leader Franjo Tudjman's revisionist history about the genocide against Serbs, Jews, and Romany under the Croatian independent state in 1941–45 became politically threatening when Tudjman's election as Croatian president was bankrolled largely by right-wing émigrés from that period and brought back its state symbols and a special tax on Serbs from Serbia who had second homes in Croatia (but not on such persons from any other republic).

By 1991 many who might have been expected to fight these developments also had begun to succumb emotionally. Pro-Yugoslav Slovenes began to 'recall' unpleasant encounters in Belgrade or in the army. Non-nationalist Croatian intellectuals, who had opposed Tudjman's attempt to deny centuries of communal coexistence and intermarriage between Serbs and Croats or the history of competition between Serbs in Habsburg territories and

Serbs in Serbia, began to reassess their own contacts with Serb friends and the stereotypes of ordinary people. Once dismissed by such intellectuals as religious and cultural prejudice, their way of talking about the 'other' ethnic group now seemed to reveal a deeper truth – that there was, after all, an ineradicable cultural difference between the two peoples. The cultural revival initiated by Serb nationalist intellectuals from Belgrade in the 1980s in minority areas of Croatia began to appear to non-Serbs as part of a plot to create a Greater Serbia. The discovery in Croatia and Herzegovina of caves and mass graves revealing victims of World War II massacres heightened fears of impending danger and obligations of revenge.[11]

Operating within stable democratic systems, this emotional momentum might have encountered limits even late in the crisis. Instead, those willing to use the extremist language for political ends sought to increase or consolidate their local power in the republics by gaining control over the mass media. The democratic elections in 1990 provided this opportunity, by giving nationalist politicians access to state resources in a system that was constitutionally still the socialist one-party system, and the incentive, because most of them won office with less than a majority and because more than one party claimed to represent each nation's interests.

Censorship of the press and total control of television were essential to the power and wartime tactics, for example, of both Milošević in Serbia and Tudjman in Croatia.[12] As early as December 1990, Tudjman justified such censorship by a 'state of war,' decreed – as was most other governmental business – by an extraconstitutional security council with emergency powers. When pro-Marković reformers attempted to counteract censorship within the republics with a new all-Yugoslav and antinationalist television channel, YUTEL, Tudjman's government (and the government in Slovenia) gave it an unfavourable slot after midnight. Milošević's strength lay, in particular, in his near total manipulation of television. Without that, it would have been difficult to maintain his portrayal without qualifications of the threats to Serbs in Croatia and Bosnia-Herzegovina and therefore his role as protector and defender of Serb lives and interests, on which so many of his supporters and his leverage with international negotiators came to depend once war had begun.

In Bosnia-Herzegovina the fact that three national parties shared power after the November 1990 election did not prevent all three from collaborating in an attempt to impose state control over the media through legislation whereby each would appoint one-third of the governing boards and editors in TV and newspapers. Although struck down as unconstitutional on appeal, the intention here was the same as in Croatia and Serbia – to hinder rival political parties within the same national community in their access to public opinion, and to appropriate for one political party the right to speak and interpret for its particular nation. This was not a case of interethnic conflict, but of intraethnic competition: of consolidating one-party rule within a nation by eliminating competition for the single constituency each was trying to develop and claim to represent. The Serbian Democratic Party (SDS) sought to eliminate the Serbian Movement for Renewal (SPO), the Muslim Party of Democratic Action (SDA) to squeeze out the Muslim Bosniak Organization (MBO), and the Croatian Democratic Union (HDZ) to undermine pro-Bosnian or anti-Zagreb Croats. Yet the voices in danger from these attempts to divide up turf among the three ruling parties were the nonethnic, multinational alternatives and – because the three parties appealed to national identities and crossed republican borders in their search for supporters and organizing activities – also the Bosnian.[13]

Just as in the conflict within the SDS in Croatia, between moderate parliamentarians oriented to Zagreb and radical militants oriented to Serbia, the links with Zagreb of the Bosnian branch of the HDZ and with Belgrade of the SDS meant that the propaganda of partisan struggle within Bosnia-Herzegovina was not confined to the republic. The most active wing of Tudjman's HDZ, including campaign contributions, was the western Herzegovina branch from Bosnia. By the fall of 1991, this area of Bosnia (which would be proclaimed the state of Herzeg-Bosnia on July 3, 1992) was well integrated into the Croatian state; its Croat citizens had been granted dual citizenship in Croatia in 1990, with the right to vote in Croatian elections, and its local authorities used Croatian educational curricula, currency, state symbols (such as the flag and crest), police uniforms, and car registration plates. As early as 1989–90, Bosnian Serbs in Belgrade (including right-wing radical Vojislav Šešelj, leader of the Radical party) were active participants in the campaign to reshape opinion in Serbia. Given refuge and encouraged by Belgrade publishing houses, they claimed to be in exile from Bosnia after being forced to leave Sarajevo, which they portrayed as a 'world of perpetual darkness' (*tamni vilajet*) where Serbs were endangered.[14] A daily feature section, 'Echoes and Reactions,' running two pages in the main Belgrade newspaper, *Politika* (by then under control of the Serbian Socialist party of Milošević) published carefully selected letters that targeted people who were 'anti-Serb' including many members of the Bosnian political and cultural elite.[15]

The struggles for independence in 1991–92 added another audience to this media war – world opinion – and intensified the need to secure loyalties on ethnonational criteria. As the main architect of Tudjman's foreign propaganda policy explained in mid-July 1991, 'The West can do a lot for us by seeing the difference between "us" and "them," that we are democrats and they are not.' He then specified how the West could help: by 'giving Croatia economic aid and technical help' and 'intervening firmly to give them the time necessary' to wait for the army and federal idea to fall apart.[16] With war, however, the democratic freedom to present an alternative reality and to oppose the nationalization of all identities had itself become an enemy – its very expression both an act of war and an obstacle to the war effort. In Croatia, the president's office issued a series of state directives, such as forbidding the media from using the terms 'Chetniks' and 'extremists,' requiring them to refer to Serbs exclusively as 'Serb terrorists' and to the Yugoslav People's Army (YPA) only as the 'Serbo-Communist occupation army.'[17] Urban intellectuals whose political identities were not ethnic but philosophical, such as liberal or social democratic, were publicly told instead that their identity was Serb or Croat.

Because the cease-fire in January 1992 did not end Croatia's war for territorial control and a secure independence, but rather shifted the battle back to the domestic political front, Tudjman actually intensified the campaign against independent newspapers and weeklies and harassment of journalists and intellectuals suspected of independent views. The process of property privatization through nationalization and state licensing provided a means and a cover for dismissing editorial boards, closing journals and newspapers, and imposing state control, as well as a way – especially after the middle of 1992 – to squelch opposition, ensure Tudjman's reelection, and prevent discussion of policies toward minorities and the UN protected areas (UNPAs) in Croatia.[18] HDZ-nominated administrators at the University of Zagreb began a purge of 'suspicious Croats' from its faculty in the fall of 1992, and Croats who showed any sympathy for multiethnic and pluralistic thinking were labelled *Jugonostalgičar* (Yugo-nostalgic) and *Jugozombi,* 'for dar[ing] to remember what the country used to be.'[19]

Milošević's control over the print media was always less complete than Tudjman's.[20] This control declined when the war in Croatia temporarily energized the opposition in Serbia to try to overthrow him. But the imposition of economic sanctions against Serbia, beginning with the EC and the United States in November 1991 and then the UN (Security Council Resolution

757) on May 30, 1992, worked to restore his control by cutting alternative sources of information and communication with the outside world and making subscriptions to print media prohibitively expensive. The sanctions also prevented his opposition from obtaining the foreign financial support and imported equipment (such as a transmitter with enough power to beam the one truly independent television station, Studio B, beyond Belgrade) that were necessary to compete with Milošević's domestic control through police and customs officials. Thus when Serbia was isolated, it was far easier for Milošević to control information given to the Serbian population about the wars in Croatia and Bosnia-Herzegovina and about world opinion. By late 1994, he was even copying Tudjman, applying the tactics used on *Danas* and *Slobodna Dalmacija* to silence the independent and increasingly critical daily *Borba.*

Nationalists in five of the Yugoslav republics needed only to persuade the majority of their populations and the outside world of the inevitability or desirability of separate national states. The violence of this propaganda war to persuade of the impossibility of nations living together was visible largely where conditions for an alternative view and political opposition existed – in ethnically mixed or ethnic minority areas. But in a sixth republic, Bosnia-Herzegovina, this argument met very different conditions. As a political fact and a cultural ideal, Bosnia-Herzegovina was multiethnic and multinational. The entire territory was ethnically mixed, blatantly defying the argument that national states were inevitable or that people of different national identities could not coexist. Not one of its three constituent nations (Muslims, Serbs, Croats) was a majority, so no one of their separate national projects could dominate the others. In fact, any alliance to create a majority could only be tactical and short-lived, as demonstrated by the SDA-HDZ alliance over sovereignty and national security in the fall of 1991, which placed the Serbs in a minority, or by the many instances of military cooperation between Bosnian Croats and Bosnian Serbs during 1992–94, which squeezed the Muslim party and Bosnian government forces. All the evidence suggested that there was majority support for a Bosnian identity and survival, from public opinion polls on the constitutional debates up to 1990, the civic initiatives, editorial policy in leading mass media, intellectuals' projects for a Bosnia based on individual citizenship and rights, and antiwar rallies in the fall of 1991 and March–April 1992. Because the Yugoslav constitution did not recognize Bosnia as a political nation and because the three ruling political parties represented constituent nations, however, there was no official desire to gather such data, and few political representatives of such a (potential) majority.

Whatever these trends in public opinion and loyalty during 1990–91 were likely to produce in the long run, therefore, they were preempted by the EC decisions on Slovene and Croatian sovereignty as nations and the breakup of Yugoslavia at the end of 1991 (including US insistence on recognizing Bosnian independence in early 1992). Power-sharing arrangements over voters and state offices would not suffice for *territorial* sovereignty. Slovene, Croatian, and Serbian republican leaders had mobilized domestic sentiment along nationalist lines in order to bargain more effectively over reform and national rights at the federal level, and then parlayed their official position as representatives of the so-called national interests of their republics in talks with international bodies – beginning in the spring of 1991 – into national leadership ('fatherhood') of their republics.

In Bosnia-Herzegovina, this same process now played out between its party leaders and international negotiators. These leaders, to retain their position as representatives of their nation, not just in electoral terms but in terms of territorial rights to self-determination, had to go beyond holding a monopoly over an ethnic voting constituency within Bosnia-Herzegovina to destroying the constitutional alternative for an independent Bosnia – the idea of a civic state where ethnic difference was not politically defining and citizens were loyal to ethnic tolerance and multicultural civilization. To secure their monopoly within their national community and also maximize their bargaining position in the EC-sponsored negotiations over a political settlement, they also had to persuade Western negotiators and world opinion that this alternative was no longer viable – that their own citizens believed it was not possible to live together and preferred to live under nationally identified governments. But in contrast to the other republics, Bosnia-Herzegovina had no political force to represent the republic as a whole against outsiders or its idea of multinational identity and civilization, any more than Yugoslavia itself had had. The EC negotiators confirmed this when they began talks in February 1992 with the representatives of the three national parties.

In this new propaganda effort, the HDZ-BH under the Croatian nationalist leadership of Mate Boban (once Tudjman removed the pro-Bosnian Stjepan Kljuić) had an advantage, because the Croat stronghold of western Herzegovina was relatively homogeneous ethnically, with the important exception of the regional capital, Mostar. Moreover, its only political rival was another party in Croatia (the right-wing Croatian Party of Right

[HSP]). The SDA had an initial advantage because the majority of Bosnian citizens who were against ethnic division did not have to be persuaded of its goal to protect an integral Bosnia and because EC and US support for republican boundaries seemed to give it (through its president, Alija Izetbegović) the upper hand with international negotiators and opinion.[21] It did, nonetheless, mount a substantial propaganda campaign at home and abroad, including the creation of new state symbols to demonstrate the venerable historical identity of Bosnia.[22] The SDS had the most difficult task, and was accordingly the most active in its propaganda war, because it was the most actively opposed to Bosnian independence from Yugoslavia and because Serbs lived in communities that were particularly heterogeneous in ethnic composition.

SDS leader Radovan Karadžić was at the forefront of the campaign to persuade all citizens of Bosnia-Herzegovina that it was impossible for Bosnian nations to live together. But it was only when the Bosnian Serbs left the government and prepared for war, setting up headquarters in Pale – a mountain-resort suburb of Sarajevo – that the SDS also created a separate television station, Channel S, and a Bosnian Serb News Agency (SRNA). The difficulty of its task can be measured in the intensity and crudeness of its message. A barrage of commissioned television commercials caricatured Serbian battles against the Ottomans, beginning with Kosovo in 1389, to revive Serbian national myths of heroism and to persuade Bosnian Serbs that it was impossible for them and Muslims to live together. Muslims were frequently referred to as Turks. In an effort to create new national heroes, Channel S televised ceremonies in 1992 in which soldiers were given awards for the number of Muslims they had killed.

The towns and cities of Bosnia-Herzegovina presented a formidable obstacle to the nationalist propaganda aimed at making national states appear the natural condition. With their mixed populations, which were living proof of multiethnic coexistence and multicultural civilization, they could not be taken psychologically. They would also, as a result, put up stronger resistance to military takeover by armies loyal to ethnic parties.[23] Moreover, the rapid urbanization of Bosnia-Herzegovina in the postwar period (from 15 to 36 percent during 1953–81) had loosened ethnic and agrarian identities. Of people choosing Yugoslav nationality in the 1981 census, 83 percent lived in cities, and the majority of them were educated, nonbelieving, often party-member Serbs.[24] As a result, the cities were filled with people who had something to defend, and they were ready to resist an attack on even the idea of mixed communities. Although more villages and towns were ethnically mixed than in Croatia, urban spaces and mixed apartment buildings are far more difficult to identify and separate ethnically than are farmsteads and single-family homes.

The siege of the capital, Sarajevo, drawn out over more than seventeen months – from April 5, 1992, to August 1993, and revived with a vengeance in November 1993 until a cease-fire was negotiated in February 1994 – was the most dramatic example, along with Mostar in Herzegovina, of the campaign to destroy the symbol of Bosnian identity and to weaken the physical resistance of citizens still committed to living together. Far more than a military target, Sarajevo stood as a mockery to national exclusiveness. Serb and Croat self-determination, by cantonizing Bosnia-Herzegovina into three ethnic parts, would at best make Sarajevo into a capital of a Muslim canton. Karadžić's map at Lisbon identified 'Serbian quarters.' By the end of 1993, the Bosnian Serbs' plan for Sarajevo was 'twin cities,' one Muslim, one Serb. To transform it into separate national cities, they could not destroy it but tried instead to force the Bosnian government to negotiate by progressive strangulation, while its symbolic status served the Bosnian Muslims' strategy so well that it had to be kept a hostage with periodic reminders to the world television audience, if necessary by provoking Serb attacks and preventing the restoration of utilities. Bosnian Croat military forces collaborated with Bosnian Serbs by standing aside when the Serbs took suburbs to the north and northwest of Sarajevo, in exchange for territories such as Stup elsewhere (and reciprocal arrangements for Bosnian Croats when they were fighting Bosnian Muslims in Mostar and elsewhere).[25] Natives of Sarajevo, dwindling from half a million to less than 350,000 during the siege, responded to the essence of the assault by building ever greater resistance on cultural terms and a worldwide campaign to save the 'spirit of Sarajevo.' At the same time, the lack of world attention to the nearly incessant bombardment of Mostar, which suffered far greater human and physical damage than Sarajevo and had at least as venerable a multicultural tradition, demonstrates the effect of such a campaign and the capacity to manage the media.

The military siege of the cities also reflected the nature of the war as the work of politicians against public opinion, for their bombardment reflected the fact that the balance of resources lay with equipment and not with infantry sufficient to overcome civilian or guerrilla resistance and the cost in human lives of urban warfare. Military tactics were aimed to isolate rather than to defeat: artillery and mortar shelling, the cutoff of food and fuel, and an early attempt to destroy means of communication both within the city and with the outside. Deliberate sabotage of the telephone lines included disconnecting neighbourhoods selected by ethnicity.[26] Very early targets were pro-Bosnian media – the television and radio stations, aerial transmitters, and offices of the Sarajevo newspaper, *Oslobodjenje*, which was conspicuously multiethnic and pro-Bosnian. When Bosnian Serb army troops agreed with UN forces to withdraw from their murderous perch on Mount Igman above Sarajevo in mid-August 1993, their parting shot was to blow up the television tower on the highest peak, Bjelašnica. Yet because artillery barrages are far more visible and countable than infantry attacks, parties disadvantaged in heavy weapons but not in infantry could turn that disadvantage into a propaganda victory by provoking firepower and keeping cities vulnerable.

The psychological warfare to justify the creation of national states would be to no avail if diplomatic recognition did not follow. Military engagements aimed not merely at physical control of territory but at foreign support. Military strategists and political leaders chose targets and managed media coverage so as to shape international opinion and local sympathies. The Croatian government, for example, placed sharpshooters on the walls of Dubrovnik to draw fire from the federal armed forces, attracting world attention to that internationally protected city that even the total destruction of Vukovar could not obtain. The Croatian and Bosnian governments placed mortars and artillery batteries within the walls of hospitals (such as at Osijek, Sarajevo, and Goražde) for the same purpose, drawing fire from Serb gunners to gain international reaction. To generate war hysteria, both Serbian and Croatian television stations showed footage of war atrocities by the other side that was as likely to have been taken from their own side, even from World War II films. All sides used attacks (and mutual recriminations of blame) on cultural monuments, on civilians in breadlines, on wedding and funeral parties, on busloads of orphans, and on international troops to mobilize sympathies and hostility at home and abroad.

The Right to Land

The source of the conflict raised by the European actions on recognition was the issue of territory. In contrast to ethnic conflict or civil war, national conflict is over rights to land. 'Nationalism always involves a struggle for land, or an assertion about rights to land; and the nation, almost by definition, requires a territorial base in which to take root.'[27] In the multinational environment of the Yugoslav space, the multiple and incompatible claims on territory of its many nations had been accommodated through constitutional rights. The exclusivity of nationalism, once war over territory and borders began, jettisoned that accommodation. Once leaders justified their goals of national states on the claim, 'we can't live together,' they had to open a process of defining *which persons* had a right to live on that land. The nationalist argument led to the *physicalizing* of citizenship rights and democracy. The expulsion of persons according to ethnic background, which came to be labelled *ethnic cleansing*, had nothing to do with ethnicity, but rather with securing national rights to land. And because the resulting war is waged to define who can belong to a particular state and its territory, it makes no distinction between soldiers and civilians, between military and civil targets.

Outsiders explained the character of the fighting in Croatia and Bosnia-Herzegovina, including the ethnic cleansing and brutal violations of humanitarian law, by citing ethnic conflict, historical enmities, and – in the actions of the Serbs – genocide. But, in fact, these were the results of the wars and their particular characteristics, not the causes. The conditions of breakdown of a state and civil order, on the one hand, and the ideologies and goals of nationalist politicians, on the other, came together in alliance only with war to decide national sovereignty over land.

The advent of war also initiated an element of ethnic conflict. The final collapse of all formal institutions for providing security left individuals and households to provide for their own through informal networks and relations they could trust. In defending land, particularly in villages where the fighting first raged and in a war characterized by *local* battles, there was the natural tendency to rely on older (pre-state) mechanisms of solidarity and insurance adapted to survival – family, kinship, ethnicity.[28] Individuals' resort to family and ethnic bonds and the patriarchal culture of social obligations attached to land created a predisposition to support the distinctions – such as the idea that safety and freedom were only secure in a national state – being made by politicians. The localized, predominantly rural character of the war in border areas, where nationalists could compete because populations were ethnically mixed – regardless of the particular ethnic or national identity of those involved – also tended to revive historical memories of earlier wars for land and who could live there and gave some credibility to the fears of genocide raised by nationalist propaganda.

The essential association between national rights and territorial control was already apparent in the political language of cultural nationalism in the 1980s and the electoral campaigns of 1990, in which the most commonly used word politically, from Slovenia to Serbia, was *hearth (ognište/ognjište)*. The focal point of a home or homestead, hearth became a metaphor for property, community, citizenship, and patriotism, all in one. But using the symbols of land, even for those who had been urban dwellers for generations was quite different from fighting for it and for the physical borders of a national community. Once war began, behaviour was increasingly governed by the mores associated with land ownership and the social organization built to protect it.

What had been an urban movement shifted its cultural fulcrum to the countryside and its traditions of self-defence. The rural population, less in touch with the pluralist conditions of urban culture, more likely to rely on state-controlled television or radio for information, and having less formal education, had voted in large numbers for ethnonational parties in the 1990 elections. Where people might have been more receptive to the political language of paranoia and threat from the outside, war brought a very real possibility of loss.

The culture of the village contrasts sharply with that of the city, with its moderating forces of cross-cutting associations built on schooling and occupation, psychological and physical mobility, and tendency toward greater religious and political liberalism as a result of the higher education levels of its population and exposure to foreign ideas. The culture surrounding smallholding villagers remained patriarchal, a culture of the Mediterranean type, not necessarily inclined toward ethnic prejudices or nationalist views.[29] Men defended property through soldiering and household unity, maintained through a family's honour and the sexual shame of women. This rural culture is based on obligations to kin, intergenerational transfer of knowledge, the perpetuation of communal rituals and myths focused on the life cycle (especially death), and the social influence retained by clerics in the villages.[30] It did not help that churches remained more influential in villages, despite high levels of reported atheism in society as a whole (with the exception of Croats), because of the strong, shared patriarchal elements in the dogma of all three. Moreover, the strategy for industrialization in socialist Yugoslavia had reinforced the cultural divide between rural and urban residents. Those who sought economic improvement and social mobility left the villages for cities and towns, leaving the countryside disproportionately populated by the elderly or people with little schooling. Although rural in origin, this patriarchal culture was also largely characteristic of the urban underclass of unskilled workers, day labourers, the unemployed, and criminals who were recruited to do much of the fighting when conscripted young people resisted mobilization or deserted.

The character of the wars, particularly as they began, drew out this particular culture. Sites were local, for control of particular settlements. Armies were not yet fully organized or reorganized, and multiple armies, militia, and armed gangs *within* one national camp extended the political party competition to control over turf and citizens' loyalties (voluntary or forced). Where armies at this time pursued a strategy of territorial gain, they nonetheless relied on untrained irregulars, such as criminals released from jails and the urban unemployed who were free or needed pay, and on the 'shock troops' of radical paramilitaries and volunteers organized by political parties who did the dirty work of creating interethnic suspicions through terrorizing villagers. As outsiders to the villages and towns where they fought and undisciplined by professional army structure, these two groups had no particular obligation to neighbours, an important social bond in the region.[31] Nor did they have any professional honour to limit the inclination to rape, mutilation, burning, looting, and revenge. Individual motivations differed. To the extent that the fighting involved more than individual aggrandizement, and did aim to identify people as outsiders and exclude them from land, women became particularly vulnerable, regardless of age, because the culture of patriarchy viewed their sexual purity and shame as essential to the honour and unity of the family – to violate women is to destroy the family's ability to resist.

The spontaneous role of patriarchal culture in the fighting was reinforced by political rhetoric. To the extent that nationalist leaders played on religious differences in defining the threat to each national community, they were able to tap a reservoir in rural communities of negative memories or stories of historical conflict between churches, intolerance, and even genocide once that population was exposed to war. The reinforcement was particularly evocative on the Serbian side because the rhetoric of Serb nationalism in the 1980s was based on the same patriarchal themes – the obligation to protect family and community against an external threat, and the reassertion of manhood wounded by perceived victimization, genocide, and the rape of their women.[32] The apparent callousness and insensitivity of Serbian leaders to international accusations – that began in the summer of 1992 in hopes of putting a stop to the violence through publicity and threats of criminal prosecution – of genocide and blatant violation of Geneva conventions in the war in eastern and northern Bosnia can be explained in part by this psychology. While it may well have contributed to more systematic violations of international humanitarian law by Serbs than by other groups, it was simultaneously possible for individuals committing such acts to perceive themselves innocent of genocide and for leaders to insist that they had no such policy.

Alongside the culture surrounding the protection of land and family, the transition from constitutional and partisan conflict to military fights over land introduced elements of historical conflict. The political rhetoric of national assertion by intellectuals and politicians during the 1980s, on all sides, had engaged in historical reinterpretation and a culture of revenge for past wrongs. The politics of the democratic elections and sovereignty declarations had revived symbols and alliances of World War II (the Croatian wartime state and its symbols, the Chetnik regalia of Serbian paramilitaries, the Croat-Muslim alliance in Bosnia-Herzegovina). But once fighting began, the memory of World War II became relevant to ordinary citizens. Even where individuals had come to terms with that war trauma, the revival of such memories in the 1970s and 1980s by writers, historians, clerics, and political leaders could reawaken sensitivities and mutual suspicions, and predispose many to expect the worst or to reinterpret behaviour in the light of physical danger.[33]

The historical analyses of intellectuals are a far cry from the moral obligations to avenge the deaths of kin and the tradition of blood revenge *(krvna osveta)* still practised in some regions of the peninsula. It is war over territory that links the two. The previous instance of such life-and-death choices of political loyalty and the rights to land and settlement for villages occurred during World War II and its aftermath. Whole villages had latent political identities associated with that conflict. Regions in Bosnia-Herzegovina, Montenegro, and Serbia were splintered into Partisan (led by the Communist party) and Chetnik (Serbian royal army forces) villages; in Croatia and Bosnia-Herzegovina among Partisan, Chetnik, and Ustasha (Croatian fascists) villages; in Macedonia among Partisan, Chetnik, and pro-Bulgarian villages; and in Kosovo between Partisan and the more common pro-Italian villages. Ethnically mixed villages experienced mass atrocities, particularly at the hands of the German army and of fascist collaborators.[34] A mechanism of revenge also played out in the subsequent revolutionary upheaval of 1945–47 and civil war of 1948–49. The population resettlement programmes of the Yugoslav government during 1945–48 attempted to place Partisan soldiers from poor, food-deficient regions in the Dalmatian hinterland in Croatia and Bosnia-Herzegovina in homesteads in the rich farmlands of Slavonia and Vojvodina of expelled collaborators (Volksdeutsche and Hungarian, Austrian, and Catholic Church landlords) as a reward for soldiering, and a solution to their lack of self-sufficiency in food. This settled a loyal class of veterans in vulnerable borderlands. Such policies created the mixed populations in the border area contested in 1991–93 between Serbia and Croatia.

Thus, for example, the fears on which Serbian nationalist policy towards Serbs in Croatia and Bosnia-Herzegovina fed had a very real grounding in a recent memory of genocidal atrocities against ordinary Serbs during World War II. Many argue that President Tudjman could have undercut the strength of Milošević's appeal to Serbs in Croatia if he had been willing to dissociate his regime from that period in history with a public apology, instead of reviving fears by questioning, as he did, the actual number of Serb victims.[35] Many Serbs felt a moral obligation, at two levels, to prevent a recurrence; the collective obligation of all Serbs to say 'never again,' and the individual, cultural imperative to avenge the deaths of kin. Both of these obligations required loyalty to other Serbs (even among those who vehemently opposed Milošević, nationalists, and war). For some it also obliged rejection of the idea of peaceful coexistence with Croats and Muslims. But such challenges between national groups aroused defensive loyalties on all sides; there were more than enough historical memories or myths to be used as justification, to create fears, and to reshape perceptions by politicians aimed at gaining nationally defined support.

One important factor was not national at all, but the economic and cultural divide already present between city and country, for during World War II cities tended to collaborate with the occupying armies. Urban dwellers who joined the resistance did so by escaping to the forests and mountains, whereas villagers had little choice but to take active sides in the civil war that ran parallel to the anti-Axis war of liberation.[36] The pattern of fighting in Croatia in 1991 and in Bosnia-Herzegovina in 1992 could be seen to repeat this past, beginning in towns infamous for World War II atrocities, and distinguishing house-by-house in Slavonian villages between post-World War II migrants and old residents.[37]

Nonetheless, social change had occurred, and people had lived together for more than forty years in spite of their war experiences. The major political trace during the 1945–90 period was the oft-spoken fear that multiparty democracy would bring back ethnically based political competition. Thus the attempt by nationalists to control the mass media and the ability during wartime in 1991–95 to legitimize such control and censorship, were unusually important. Control of the media gave full reign, without opposing views, to the nationalists' myth of 'we cannot live together.' It made it possible for politicians to connect their message to the world of ordinary people. And it limited the audience of alternative voices – which reminded people that the world had changed, that their history was far more one of coexistence and nonethnic bonds, that their fears were unjustified, and that the moral obligation was not revenge but tolerance– to those who could buy and did read newspapers and journals.

Regardless of the multiple predispositions of culture and memory, the fight to create states out of nations in territories that are ethnically mixed eventually becomes a fight over persons and their rights to live on particular tracts of land. This became known to outsiders during the Serbian onslaught in eastern Bosnia in the spring and summer of 1992 as a policy of 'ethnic cleansing.' Based on racial beliefs (in the physicalizing of ethnic identity and prerogatives), this policy has had many parallels, such as apartheid in South Africa or the massive population exchanges between Greece and Turkey in 1922, or after the division of India and Pakistan in 1947.[38] Its immediate prelude in Yugoslavia was the exodus of Serbs and Montenegrins from Kosovo – the result of a mixture of reciprocal fears and political tactics during the 1980s in which both the Serbian government and Albanian residents played their part.[39] Nationalist Serb extremists referred loosely to Serb victims of ethnic cleansing and genocide.

The next phase, in 1989, used legal instruments. Republican constitutions redefined citizenship in terms that distinguished between the majority nation and others, and effectively created semi-disenfranchised minorities (in relation to previous rights) most explicitly in Croatia and Macedonia.[40] When war came to ethnically mixed areas in Croatia, mutual fears and local harassment, often provoked by outsiders (paramilitary gangs from central Croatia and from Serbia proper; returned Croat émigrés and mercenaries of Serbian origin), turned the language of endangerment and politics of revenge into invitations to expel unwanted persons.[41]

As a war strategy pursued by Croats and Serbs alike in Croatia and in Bosnia-Herzegovina, however, the association between persons and rights to land became a deliberate policy to clear a territory of all those who were considered not to belong in their national territory and who might be suspected of disloyalty. In Bosnia-Herzegovina, 'random and selective killing,' detention camps as way stations with 'inadequate shelter, food, and sanitation,' and even massacres were reportedly used as 'tools' to remove populations.[42]

The basis of this policy of ethnic cleansing lay not with primordial hatreds or local jealousies, but with political goals. According to the German criterion on which the Badinter Commission and the EC decisions were made, international recognition of national sovereignty required a referendum of residents in a territory on their choice of a state; where that choice had been ignored, nationalist leaders found their political prejudices vindicated. Military control of territory was not sufficient to recognition; it had to be supplemented eventually by a vote. Thus cease-fires only led to a change in the methods of ethnic cleansing. After the cease-fire in Croatia and in towns of Bosnia-Herzegovina where fighting had ceased, local authorities continued this process by negotiating population exchanges on an ethnic basis between towns. These exchanges were hardly more voluntary because they were peaceable, but their objective – to consolidate ethnically pure territories that would vote correctly in a referendum on sovereignty and in future elections and to justify government administration by their national group – had not been fully obtained by warfare.[43]

Their methods of population transfers varied. In places like the village of Kozarac in northeastern Bosnia, members of the local Muslim elite who might organize such opposition were first murdered or brutally expelled. Serbs in the Croatian *krajina*, such as the village of Pod Lapača, appealed to the UN forces sent to protect them to help them leave the area instead out of fear after a Croatian army scorch-and-burn attack on three neighbouring villages just outside the UNPA in September 1993. Elsewhere, local rivalries were encouraged to play out, perhaps given a boost by the terrorizing tactics of outside extremists and then fed by a cycle of revenge between neighbouring villages. One measure of the level of resistance by many local leaders and citizens to such cleansing and of the strength of commitment to mixed environments and nonnationalist political preferences is the fact that the process gained momentum in later stages of the war. Official exchanges of minorities between villages of different majority ethnicity to create overwhelming majorities and justify government administration by their national group became systematic after the Washington agreement of March 1, 1994, was signed by Bosnian Croats and Muslims. Local radicalization, as those who opposed ethnic partition of the republic became ever weaker or had left, brought renewed expulsions in the spring and summer of 1994, such as the forced expulsions by Serbs of Muslims from Banja Luka and Bijeljina areas or the voluntary exodus of Croats and Serbs from Tuzla the same year. Whatever the method, however, ethnic cleansing was a particularly extreme reminder of the conflict between the goal of national states and Yugoslav reality.

The victimization of Muslims through ethnic cleansing was also a result of the political contest behind the wars, not ethnic or religious hatreds. Claiming a unified Bosnia as its base instead of a separate national enclave, the SDA could not win with a policy of ethnic cleansing. Its political difficulty in settling on a consistent strategy for national sovereignty – against the two other parties, the SDS and the HDZ – extended to this tactic. A referendum confirming the national sovereignty of Bosnia had to be supported by more voters than those who identified politically with the SDA as Muslims, and depended, therefore, on maintaining mixed communities. When relief agencies of the Office of the UN High Commissioner for Refugees (UNHCR) and the International Committee of the Red Cross (ICRC) chose to help evacuate Muslims from towns in eastern Bosnia, such as Srebrenica and Konjević Polje, in order to save lives in April 1993, they were not only accused of being accomplices to Serbian ethnic cleansing, but were in many towns blocked by local Muslim (SDA) officials and Bosnian government army commanders who knew that once people left, they had lost political control over that territory (whatever military objectives they might accomplish).[44] Similarly, in withholding support from the peace plan drawn up by the Geneva international conference on former Yugoslavia in October 1992–January 1993 based on creating mixed communities and provinces and an integral Bosnia-Herzegovina (the Vance-Owen plan), on the grounds that it did not guarantee enough land to Muslims and rewarded the 'aggression of Serbs,' the Clinton administration in January–February 1993 doomed the Muslims as well to a policy of ethnic cleansing.

Whether the failure of a political agreement on the Vance-Owen plan was a result of military gains and ethnic cleansing on the ground that were impossible to reverse, as some claimed, or a result of US encouragement of Izetbegović to bargain for more Muslim territory, as those seeing the parallels with the failed Lisbon Accord the previous March claimed, the appearance of ethnically based massacres and fighting between Croat and Muslim forces in central Bosnia was not an attempt to realize the Vance-Owen plan. Many observers argued that the plan legitimized the assignment of territories ethnically and that armies were fighting between December 1992 and May 1993 to take those territories militarily, but it in fact only acknowledged national rights to form governments and territorial administrations over provinces that would remain ethnically mixed and a part of a sovereign Bosnia. It was the failure of international support for the plan – in the same manner as the EC decision in December 1991 on recognition was made without first obtaining agreements on borders and principles of national self-determination – that led politicians and armies to settle the question of territorial rights on the ground. In the face of territorial losses and without a political settlement, the Bosnian government in December 1992 had begun a temporarily successful campaign to take back areas of eastern Bosnia and to control central Bosnia. As Bosnian Croats, through ethnic cleansing, extended their territory in the fall of 1992 beyond western Herzegovina into mixed towns in central Bosnia, such as Prozor at the end of October, Muslim militias (not Bosnian government forces) also began to expel Croats.

The move from nationalist psychological warfare to nationalist warfare over land on territory that was multinational had predictable outcomes in the character of that warfare. The political goal of creating national states made little distinction between military and civilians, either as fighters or as targets.[45] What would seem only to be a matter of military doctrine, in which the YPA held preponderant power with artillery designed to delay an attacker and then to hit invaders' supply routes with ambushes, land slides, and artillery, and the TDF in rural villages would swing into guerrilla warfare in a long war of attrition, if necessary, was reinforced by the sharp urban-rural divide within the country's social and political structure. Heavy artillery shelled population settlements and had to make up for the refusal of urban young people to fight. Cities were encircled by artillery, using supply depots intended for repelling invaders. Guerrilla warfare in urban settings comprised snipers from all political sides and commando raids by small groups of disciplined soldiers in the early mornings to demoralize soldiers of the other side. The objective of such tactics and the threat of death by starvation, disease, and cold, however, was to persuade civilians of a different ethnicity to leave without putting up a fight. Psychological and economic pressure to force capitulation of cities to ethnic definition and loyalties included destruction of the physical infrastructure on which urban life depends – electricity, heating plants, kiosks selling newspapers, TV and radio transmitters, the communal bakery – but one of the first objects of attack in cities as well as towns and villages was also the church or mosque of the 'other' group.

The goal of national control of land meant that male civilians of any age but of the 'wrong' nationality were sent to detention camps on the assumption that they were potential soldiers for the enemy or were forcibly conscripted to the front line to dig trenches or initiate assaults on armies of their own ethnicity. Bosnian Serbs in Banja Luka and Bijeljina were accused by the ICRC and UNHCR of forcibly separating non-Serb men from their families during waves of ethnic expulsions to do 'work detail' on the front.[46] Even the Croatian government – in violation of the Geneva conventions – forcibly returned Bosnian men of all ages who had taken refuge from the Bosnian war in camps across the border in Croatia.[47] Women of any age were victims of rape, in part for reasons always associated with warfare and in part to demoralize armies composed not of professionals but of fathers, sons, and brothers from the region. Because the purpose of the warfare was largely defence of village and land, even if a particular military engagement were classified as offensive, the armies were largely composed of people from the region. Except for small elite units, army units were not mobile, were locally recruited among farmers and villagers of all ages, tended to be led by commanders from the area, and were known to be fiercely loyal to that local commander, even if doing so meant that they disobeyed orders given higher up the normal chain of command.

Even if political leaders wish to reverse course and sign cease-fire agreements in good faith and citizens desperately want an end to the fighting, the momentum of such wars becomes increasingly difficult to stop. The limit on ethnic expulsions begun with local quarrels or as a result of political rivalry between radicals and moderates within a political party is only reached when there are no more people of that particular category to be expelled. The political rhetoric that prepared the way for war by emphasizing group danger tended to perpetuate the practice in conditions of anarchy and ever further unravelling of legal and moral standards and stable social organization. Localized fighting for the territory and soul of a village, and then between villages as refugees fled or as fighting fanned out, eventually drew in villagers who had tried to stay out of politics but found they had to fight or be killed or expelled. Those who did not flee sought to ensure their own security by turning on those from the threatening group and torching their homes, cultural monuments, and places of worship to discourage their return.

Among soldiers, the horrors alone and the fact that 'many of them didn't understand what they were fighting for, or didn't approve of a war in which people from two nations with the same language and origin were killing each other' led to the emergence of what was called the 'Vukovar syndrome,' in which psychological breakdown turned them not away from war but into 'uncontrolled killers.' The explanation offered by a clinical psychologist for the 'Bijeljina (Bosnia) case' – a twenty-three-year-old reservist mobilized by the army who 'gunned down three other solders from the Bijeljina barracks and then his girlfriend's family' on February 1, 1992 – was the psychological pressure of this particular type of war: 'it's neither war nor peace, they've been living for months in trenches, their position as well as their mission is unclear, they lose their nerves and they drink heavily.'[48]

On all sides of the war, the expulsion or execution of rival local elites and the exodus as refugees of moderates repelled by the war meant that, as the war went on, an ever larger proportion of those who remained or reappeared ready to fight in other towns were militant radicals most committed or bound to that land. By committing atrocities to clear that land, engendering the likely revenge of the ethnic group of its victims, these radicals had even more reason to continue fighting for fear of retribution and no honourable exit. This was particularly the case for Serbs in eastern Croatia and in Bosnia-Herzegovina, who aroused global condemnation and outrage because they were accused, as a result of reports by human rights organizations and by UN inquiries, of a systematic policy of genocide and mass rape and blamed for the overwhelming portion of the wars' atrocities. In other cases, such as the fratricidal fighting in central Bosnia in the summer of 1993 between Croatian and Muslim forces that had remained at peace or fought side by side during the previous eighteen months, the continuation of war created its own momentum in the rising numbers of displaced persons who had lost everything (often including families) and who had little left to do but to fight for some other land or take revenge.

Civil War

In the course of the constitutional struggle of the 1980s, nationalist politicians at the republic level had channelled social unrest and economic grievances into demands for national rights. This did not, however, remove those grievances. As the above discussion of urban-rural differences implies, the characteristics of these wars for new states owed as much or more to the social and economic divisions that existed within Yugoslav society before the war as to the ethnic conflict proclaimed by nationalist elites and outside powers.

In interrupting the process of democratization begun with the elections in

1990, the Slovene and Croatian declarations of sovereignty and the European response in 1991 taking these declarations at face value prolonged representation throughout the region in terms of national self-determination and ethnic political rights. Instead of a change in the organization of economic life and interests in the socialist period toward organizations like class-based political parties and interest groups more suited to parliamentary democracy and market economies, the political organization of elections by republic and by ethnonational parties therefore reinforced the territorial, vertical, and state-based organization of the socialist regime. The regionalized specializations, relative immobility of labour and capital, and geopolitically influenced economic policy characteristic of all socialist countries created a pattern of economic advantage and disadvantage that was defined by territorial (including urban-rural) lines. Thus national movements were subject to few if any checks and balances that might dampen political escalation once they mobilized grievances and interests in the political and economic transition.

When the European Community and the United States ignored the difference between Slovenia and the rest of the country and the likelihood of conflicts over borders and land, they exposed to territorial dispute those very areas most threatened by the policies of the liberal economic reformers and less privileged in economic development. In the Croatian *krajina*, central Bosnia, the 'Serbian corridor' of northern Bosnia, Kosovo, and Macedonia, deindustrialization and declining demand since the mid-1970s had led to severe economic decline largely as a result of economic policy or global change outside the immediate control of these areas.[49] Dominated by extractive industries (minerals, timber, transport) or military production with uncertain demand in foreign markets and in government contracts, these areas had been hard hit by the reform policies favouring export-orientated manufactures to convertible currency countries. They also tended to have declining per capita income in the 1970s and 1980s, so that local budgets for services and welfare were increasingly dependent on federal subsidies; they were therefore also hurt more by the drastic cuts in government budgets under policies of stabilization and liberalization. Local industries were more dependent on sources of investment capital that were being sharply curtailed – the development funds of their republican budgets and the investment and services of the army and military industries financed by the federal budget. Unemployment in these areas was rising and income falling far faster than in the rest of the country.[50]

These were areas that traded more with the markets that collapsed in the

Council for Mutual Economic Assistance (CMEA) and the Middle East. In the line being drawn through the country's centre between Europe and the Balkans, moreover, there was increasing uncertainty over the fate of the areas of the former military border between Habsburg and Ottoman empires, the Danubian region, and Bosnia-Herzegovina. Were they West or East?[51]

Individual prospects also had a pronounced territorial dimension. Upward social mobility in the socialist period through education eventually required a move to the cities, leaving poorer interior areas with people of lesser prospects, lower status, and a sense of cultural inferiority. Although poverty and open unemployment were increasingly urban phenomena in the 1970s and 1980s, urban areas retained their association with the privileges of public sector employment, social welfare, and opportunities not dependent on the land. Rural communities retained a secondary status, where those who had no opportunities to leave (whether through lack of education, urban relatives or cash incomes) remained tied to the rural or semirural community of their birth. Decentralizing reforms to reduce federal expenditures and favour the TDF in national defence had also had the effect of concentrating security forces and retired soldiers in localities in these areas, for reasons of World War II experience and poverty.

Patterns of migration, because they followed routes laid by family and by schooling, also had an ethnic dimension, particularly in Bosnia-Herzegovina. Overall, studies for the 1960s–80s show that emigration occurred in economically declining villages and regions, and was greatest in ethnically mixed communes.[52] This pattern created more ethnically homogeneous villages within districts *(opština/općine)* that remained heterogeneous (a pattern more common in Croatia). In particular, Serbs left for other republics and cities (primarily in Serbia) and Croats most frequently went abroad. Both poor and elite Muslims, on the other hand, tended to stay 'at home' in Bosnia-Herzegovina. Migration and the relative differences in birth rates between these groups had reversed the numerical preponderance of Serbs over Muslims.[53] Bosnian Serbs and Bosnian Croats were thus more likely to be those left behind by their own ethnic group.

This situation may have made these people receptive to politicians who, in the 1990–93 period, encouraged resentment against new elites of a different ethnicity, particularly Muslims, who were at earlier, more assertive stages of national consciousness. The 1990 elections had not yet replaced at the local level the single-party system of the previous forty years, except for takeover by the ethnonational party corresponding to the local political elite.

Politicians often used the excuse of an anticommunist purge to expel members of other political parties, but because the main electoral victors were identified with the nation, this process had left interethnic emotions occasionally raw.[54]

The actual characteristics of the fighting on the ground, however, reflected the socioeconomic basis of these politics far more than the ethnic coloration and historical revenge that characterized politicians' rhetoric. For many, war became a rare opportunity for enrichment, through theft or smuggling, in a period of serious economic decline. Early pictures in the war in Bosnia-Herzegovina show soldiers looting VCRs and stereos, urban furniture and appliances, and foreign automobiles such as BMWs – most originally bought with the enviable foreign hard currency. Illiteracy and mobilized resentments over who were the 'rightful owners' of land help to explain the destruction of cultural monuments, razing of prosperous farms, and crowds of village women who prevented aid convoys from reaching their destinations.

Although soldiers were frequently paid two to three times more than they were earning in civilian jobs, the actual pay was still meagre and was often given in alcohol and cigarettes instead of cash. The incentive for class-based revenge was high. The recruitment of soldiers when the state collapsed also reinforced this class division, because more urban and better educated youth could escape the draft, often by leaving the country. The unemployed, poorer village youth, and industrial workers, unpaid for months, were more vulnerable to the draft and promises of pay and veterans' benefits. In the first stages of the war in Croatia, the promise in Serbia of significant discounts on the price of electricity and fuel for households was sufficient for many heads of households to enlist.

War closed schools and factories in many areas, either because of the fighting or because of the interruption of transport and supplies in other areas, compounding the number of people left idle. Paramilitary forces, in particular, were filled with teenagers faced with the choice either to leave the country or to join a military organization, but under little organized command or adult standards of behaviour. Evidence also suggests that those who felt excluded in the socialist period, such as unskilled workers or troubled young people, tended to volunteer to fight; war presented an opportunity for them to achieve a certain status and honour unavailable in peace or to get revenge for their previous impotence and discrimination. They were also more inclined to the culture of patriarchy and protection than to the norms defining the Geneva conventions on war.[55] At the same time, like the right-wing teenagers rampaging against foreigners in west European countries, the war attracted 'weekend Chetniks' from a lost generation of educated youth with meagre prospects in Serbia. These unemployed high school or university graduates, living on the outskirts of big cities, went on shooting sprees with Kalashnikov rifles from Friday night to Sunday in villages of little consequence to them over the border in Croatia or Bosnia.[56]

As in the events leading up to war, independent forces became mutually reinforcing in ways that accelerated violence. Class-based resentment and revenge legitimized as national liberation and anticommunism were a potent force. Those who took up arms to defend their land and communities were also incited and led by people who saw themselves as outsiders – dissidents against communism (from Franjo Tudjman to Alija Izetbegović to Vojislav Šešelj), urban migrants from poor regions (such as Radovan Karadžić), in many cases actual criminals (the most infamous was Željko Ražnatović, or Arkan). This self-perception was reinforced by the language of combat, such as the labelling of all Serbs as barbarians and the urban professionals' derision of Bosnian Serb leader Karadžić for his 'village' speech. Given the Western judgement that Slovenes and Croats were democratic and peace-loving whereas Serbs were aggressors in Slovenia, Croatia, Bosnia-Herzegovina, and, potentially, Kosovo and Macedonia, it was doubly unfortunate that the Slovenes had captured the liberal space in the Yugoslav political spectrum and that Serbian nationalism under Milošević had come, accurately or not, to represent the fears or reaction of the less privileged and the political forces under attack.

Dissolution of a State

In recognizing Slovene and Croatian independence, the European Community was not only creating new states but dissolving an existing one – Yugoslavia. It approached this problem ad hoc, with the result that the primary mechanism became an arbitration commission of jurists with advisory authority only, set up at the request of the Slovene government in August – almost two months before the end of the moratorium on moves toward independence – for an independent, European body to deal with the economic questions of succession. Sceptical about their ability to resolve such questions without outside arbitration, the Slovenes also argued that they could not participate in the setting up of some new 'Yugoslav' institutional forum, however temporary it first appeared. The Badinter Commission soon found its effective mandate expanded, under the auspices of the EC peace conference at The Hague, from arbitrating disputes over the allocation of federal economic assets and obligations among the republics to advising on border disputes and the criteria for recognition.

Even this minimal regulation of the process of dissolution fell victim to the diplomatic recognitions in December, January, and April, however, and the deadly pause of ten months before the second peace conference was set up at Geneva in September. The work on economic issues of succession was handed to one of the conference's six standing commissions, which remained in Brussels for continuity. Its authority depended on that of the Geneva conference and its co-chairmen, who rapidly became preoccupied by the work of another of its standing commissions, that on Bosnia-Herzegovina, in its efforts to negotiate a political agreement that would end the Bosnian war. Like the European decision that the republican borders were legitimate international borders, moreover, the issues of dissolution were also coloured by their assumptions regarding economic accounts – that the assets and debts of the former state belonged to the republics and that the only issue was what proportions would govern their distribution among the six.

The question of state succession was, in fact, decided in May 1992 by Western policy aimed at ending the war in Bosnia-Herzegovina. As part of its strategy to hold Serbia and the YPA responsible for the war and to exert pressure on the Serbian leadership to end its military aid and political support to the Bosnian Serbs, the UN Security Council denied successor status to the Federal Republic of Yugoslavia (created between Serbia and Montenegro on April 27, 1992). Declaring that it could not continue 'automatically the membership of the former Socialist Federal Republic of Yugoslavia in the United Nations,' the UN rejected the argument of the new Yugoslav leadership that it bore the right of successor in the way that Russia had since been accredited the UN seat of the Soviet Union, because the other republics had seceded. Thus the Security Council let the question of state succession die on September 19, 1992 (SCR 777), in a way similar to the EC's de facto usurpation of the federal presidency and cabinet during the summer and fall of 1991 by its mediating intercession.

But the reality was that this had been a country, not only a confederation of states – however autonomous the republics had been. There were not only psychological interdependencies that needed to be broken, but also economic interdependencies and an entire structure of security – local police, internal security police, territorial defence forces, federal army, and all-Yugoslav laws and standards – protecting civil order and external defence. In line with its incorrect assumption that there was no conflict between the independence of the republics and the right to national self-determination, the EC in particular paid no attention to the disposition of the armed forces and security apparatus or to the consequences for the security of citizens if it removed the last vestiges of authority from the common procedures and guarantees of the entire structure of civil order.

The disintegration of internal security and civil order

The country's system of territorial defence and security could not be rearranged neatly in accordance with the republics, as if they were already states in which the loyalties and authority of police, TDFs, intelligence agencies, and army were not in doubt and the only issue was to expel aggressors from other states. The federal army was a significant political actor in its own right, which could not succumb to the lack of quorum and simply disperse among republics, as the federal parliament chose to do after months of debate. It was not simply a body representing the republics, but an independent, coequal partner representing Yugoslavia as a whole and its multinational ideal and antifascist origins. In contrast to other federal institutions, such as the central bank, its fate and the distribution of its assets could not wait for decades of diplomatic wrangling. As an integral part of the constitutional and then the political-military contest, the YPA would have to undergo a process of reorientation: from its defence of Yugoslavia, through disorientation as an army without a state, to a state-building project of its own. Moreover, military districts had not coincided with republican borders since the reorganization of the mid-1980s. Just as troops in Croatia were part of the Slovene operation, troops from the Banja Luka (5th) Corps in Bosnia participated in the Croatian conflict over the border in Slavonia and in the Dalmatian hinterland.[57] The war in Bosnia-Herzegovina reflected, in part, the YPA's division between eastern Herzegovina – which fell under the command of the fourth military district headquartered in Podgorica (Montenegro) – and areas of central and eastern Bosnia, which were in the first military district headquartered in Belgrade and encompassing parts of Serbia proper and Vojvodina.[58]

There was no reason, moreover, for the territorial defence forces to become automatically national armies of the separate republics. Although nominally under republican authority in the previous order, the TDFs were simultaneously integrated into the central command and control structure of the federal armed forces and under the administrative jurisdiction of the local governments. Local politics were most decisive, therefore, in the role and loyalties of TDF units. Whereas Slovenia had constructed its national army on the basis of the TDF in the course of its conflict with the federal army over several years, the Croatian army evolved only after the elections held in the spring of 1990 as a result of two conflicts – one with the army over federal or republican rights to TDF assets and the other with local Serbs over 'national' (Croat) control of local police and TDF units. In part because the YPA was quicker than the Croatian government to take control of some TDF assets and in part because Serbs had sought to defend themselves in Baranja-Slavonia and in the Dalmatian hinterland and around Knin with civil defence units (and later paramilitary groups) using local TDF weapons and facilities, Croatia built its national army instead on the basis of internal republic-level security forces called MUP and their counterinsurgency activities during 1990–91. President Tudjman held the first public parade of this National Guard Corps (ZNG), which would later become the core of a standing Croatian army (HV), in March 1991, and it had active and reserve motorized brigades poised in the field against Serb militia by May.[59]

The disposition of the TDF in Bosnia-Herzegovina followed the same, though more complex, political evolution: from interrupted democratization through national self-determination to armed conflict. When power changed hands with the elections of December 1990, most local TDF units became instruments of local political elites, their political ambitions, and the consolidation of power behind their political party. Along these political party (and therefore ethnic) lines, these units began to combine into militia beyond the local level. TDF units in western Herzegovina were active, through HDZ politicians, in helping form the HV, and the HV then sent troops and equipment to organize Croat units in Bosnia (eventually the HVO), for example. Local officials and SDS party leaders in the Bosnian *krajina* lent logistical and economic support to Serbs in the Croatian *krajina* and were aided later in turn. The war in Croatia thus sped up the preparation for war in Bosnia-Herzegovina through these reciprocal networks among political parties in forming armies and also through refugees who poured over the border (both Croats and Serbs) for sanctuary and who kindled tensions along partisan, ethnic, and military lines.[60] This earlier formation of military and partisan paramilitary links between Bosnia-Herzegovina and Croatia, among Croats and among Serbs, meant that the Bosnian government army would be built largely on the basis of internal resources in Bosnia-Herzegovina among local SDA (Muslim party) elites. President Izetbegović created a National Defence Council on June 10, 1991, as an arm of his party, and was illegally purchasing weapons from Slovenia during the fall.[61] Despite the political alliance between Croatian and Muslim parties, in fact, a defence alliance appeared necessary between Bosnia-Herzegovina and Croatia in June 1992 to gain access to arms through HVO-controlled supply routes and Croatian ports on the Adriatic. The Bosnian army was eventually built on the basis of TDF units – in addition to a separate militia called the Patriotic League – largely from areas outside Croatian and Serbian strongholds where the SDA governed or the town was indisputably ethnically mixed. The continuing predominance of the local character of military formations meant that, while armies were primarily organized by ethnonational parties, their soldiers were often of a different ethnicity, such as the thousands of Bosnian Muslims fighting in the HVO, for example, or the Bosnian Croats and Bosnian Serbs who fought in the Bosnian army.[62]

Local leaders who commandeered the Bosnian TDF, with its stockpiles of weapons and civil defence units of all-citizen training, were called warlords after war came officially to the republic in April 1992, but they remained preoccupied largely with local power. The system of civil order at the local level had already begun to disintegrate as a result of the 1990 elections. The shift from Communist party oversight of judgeships and police to that of a nonpartisan, independent branch of government had also been interrupted – no longer communist but still controlled by the local party or preoccupied with an intense battle between types of judicial systems. Police forces tended to take partisan sides, form their own paramilitary groups with criminals released from jails, and often exploit 'business opportunities' in league with mafia trafficking in lucrative contraband in drugs and illegal arms.

At the time of the Slovene and Croatian declarations of independence, the primary source of rising tensions and armed confrontations was not the armies based in the TDF or the YPA but the paramilitary groups formed by political parties. In Serbia the powerful internal security police supported Milošević and the Socialist party.[63] All the major parties and renegades created their own armies: the Chetniks of Serbian Radical party leader Vojislav Šešelj; the Serbian Guard of Vuk Drašković's Serbian Movement for Renewal; and the White Eagles, Dušan Silni, and the Serbian Volunteer

Guard (also known as Arkanovci or Tigers) organized by Željko Ražnatović-Arkan, a criminal wanted in Europe for political assassinations and drug trafficking. In Croatia the interior police (now National Guard) were similarly attached to Tudjman's party, while Ustasha units of the Black Legion, the Zebras, and the 5,000-strong Croatian Defence League (HOS) of the Croatian Party of Right of Dobroslav Paraga all operated in both Croatia and Bosnia-Herzegovina.[64] The SDA organized its Green Berets. Five separate militia were operating in the *krajina* region of Croatia alone by June 1991, and there were twenty such paramilitary groups in Bosnia-Herzegovina.[65]

The military wings and activities of political parties were no more confined within republican borders than were their electoral activities. With the internationalization of the political contest, however, the purpose of these military wings changed as the determinants of interparty competition shifted from the size of voting constituencies and ability to form local alliances to the willingness to use armed force to control persons and territories. It also gave rise to a new struggle within political parties and between political parties claiming to represent the same nation: that between moderates who believed in or counted on international support and peaceful negotiations for their national goals and radicals who believed in the inevitability of an armed contest and prepared for military confrontation – the diplomatic versus the war option. Citizens reoriented their loyalties from political identities and preferences to physical survival and therefore to those parties, leaders, and identities they thought most likely to win in the end. The conditions of anarchy and territorial contest favoured the armed radicals.

Thus by the fall of 1991, paramilitary gangs, foreign mercenaries, and convicted criminals roamed the territory under ever less civil control.[66] Shady deals between the police and black marketeers confirmed that the line between what was legal and what was not had evaporated. Republican intelligence agencies were offering their services to political parties. Engaged in their own fight for political control locally, civil authorities were not inclined to restore order if it required collaboration with political enemies. Rising criminality, local shoot-outs and armed provocations in contested areas, as well as politically aroused fears about the neutrality of the law and police and the untrustworthiness of other national groups, left many citizens with the impression that the only true security was ownership of a firearm. Locals also raided army barracks. In some areas local police and army units have been charged with distributing weapons from official stocks to villagers and militia of the same ethnic group.[67]

The federal army

The federal army was simultaneously engaged in this local process, since its actual command structure was substantially decentralized, and in the high politics of state formation taking place. While the assets of the TDFs and arms purchases from abroad (despite the embargo) were falling into various hands, a complex internal struggle over the YPA's political identity, goals, and appropriate strategy was taking place, paralleling the path of European mediation of the Yugoslav dissolution.

The army's evolution began in the contest with Slovenia. The growing antagonism between the YPA and Slovenia in the 1980s culminated in March 1991, when Slovenia withheld its conscripts and confirmed the impossibility of reconciliation. The Croatian government paraded its new army (still based legally on the rights of the TDF and the MUP) that month as well and, like the Slovenes, rejected any suggestion of negotiation with the YPA. (Some generals, such as Generals Martin Špegelj and later Anton Tus in Croatia, had defected early from the YPA to command national security in their republics.) In the view of the Croatian government's top strategists, the sovereignty of the republics was not achievable until the army, as the last remaining Yugoslav institution and the one most committed to the Yugoslav idea, succumbed to internal disintegration from the contest between what they called Titoist elements still committed to Yugoslavia and Serbian elements which, like the Slovenes and Croats, were nationalists committed to an independent state. The nationalist momentum was such, in their view, that Serb nationalists had to win and the Titoists had to concede defeat. The events of March 1991, when the Serbian bloc in the presidency and the minister of defence pushed for emergency rule and when one section of the army general staff agreed to assist Milošević by sending tanks into the streets of Belgrade against opposition demonstrators, seemed to fit their scenario. The fight between the army and Prime Minister Ante Marković came to a head in July, when Marković turned on Defence Minister Kadijević, accusing the army of illegal action in Slovenia.[68] Then, in early July, with the collective presidency, the prime minister, and the president of Croatia gathered in the presidential palace in Zagreb to attempt negotiation of Croatian independence, someone faked an air attack on the palace and blamed it on Kadijević.[69] The intention apparently was to end any possibility of reconciliation between the military and civilian authorities of the federal government. Moreover, monitoring of the cease-fire negotiated by the federal presidency in Croatia during July and August was assigned not to the army but to representatives of the Federal Secretariat of Internal Affairs (although by August 30, the republican governments of Bosnia-Herzegovina and Macedonia, which had agreed to share this task with federal authorities, decided not to participate, and they withdrew their representatives from the monitoring groups on September 4).[70]

Nonetheless, the army did not dissipate on demand. While the republican declarations of independence in June 1991 forced Slovene and Croatian recruits and officers to choose between competing loyalties, their cohorts from other republics continued to be conscripted and to fight into 1992. The senior officer corps, the composition of which had followed the strict application of the rule of national parity (the *ključ*) did not reflect Croatian propaganda. One of the three generals in the supreme staff at the time of the Slovene war was a Slovene (Admiral Stane Brovet). The army was led by the representative of Croatia on the supreme staff, Veljko Kadijević, a Yugoslav born in Croatia of mixed Croat-Serb parentage, minister of defence, and commander of the army. He resigned in January 1992 when he accepted full responsibility for the air force attack on an EC helicopter monitoring the cease-fire in Croatia that killed its five crewmen (and which appeared to be another stage in the rivalries internal to the armed forces). General Zvonko Jurjević, the chief of the air force, obliged to resign because of the same attack, was also Croatian. At the time of the Bosnian declaration of sovereignty, in October 1991, Kadijević promised President Izetbegović to do everything possible to prevent war from spreading to Bosnia-Herzegovina. This promise was honoured until April 1992, when those working throughout the fall and early winter to keep the peace (such as Generals Nikola Uzelac in Banja Luka and Milutin Kukanjac in Sarajevo – both Serbs) lost to those seeking to escalate fighting (officers of Serbian ethnicity – Ratko Mladić and Momčilo Perišić – and of Muslim ethnicity – Colonel Vehbija Kadić, who then left to command the Bosnian territorial forces).[71] The purge of the Titoists, or Partisan faction, of the YPA began only after Kadijević's resignation: twenty generals in February 1992, thirty-eight in March. It continued over the next eighteen months, even after the army's small residual officer corps and employees originating from Serbia and Montenegro had been renamed the Yugoslav Army and the internal struggle (favouring the air force) interacted with the political struggle in Serbia.[72]

The stages of the YPA's transformation and its reassessment of political goals were driven, however, by international decisions. The army's apparent military strategy in Slovenia, to combine surprise and overwhelming force in a blitzkrieg assault, on the assumption that there would be little local resistance, had no political objective other than its constitutional duty to defend Yugoslav integrity. According to James Gow, a British specialist on the YPA, the YPA's backup strategy to begin a slow, calculated escalation was foiled by the unexpected intervention of EC mediators; 'confused and constrained,' it hesitated.[73] The Brioni Agreement of July 7, 1991, obliging the army to return to barracks and levelling accusations from both the EC and Prime Minister Marković of illegitimate and aggressive use of force, was the first step of a process by which the army was forced to retreat, step by step, from each republic that had declared independence. As the violence increased in Croatia, but long before the army had adjusted politically to events, the EC and the United States began to call it a Serbian army and to view the fight as some old Croat-Serb conflict played out between the Croatian government and the army. The policy question in July and early August 1991 was whether to interpose forces (whether Western European Union [WEU], Eurocorps, or UN) between them or to enable Croatia to build up its army and air force legally by recognizing its sovereignty. In fact, the army had been attempting for some months already, and continuing into September 1991, to provide such a neutral buffer between Serbs and Croats, particularly in eastern Croatia, so as to dampen the fighting and create cease-fires. Like Slovenia and Croatia, the EC monitors (ECMM) refused to speak to the army and by early fall of 1991 had joined Croatia in labelling the YPA an occupation force. Still, UN envoy Cyrus Vance began to have greater negotiating success during November 1991 than his EC counterpart, Lord Carrington, in part because he included the Yugoslav minister of defence. When Kadijević resigned, Vance considered it a serious blow to his efforts.

By the second month of the Croatian war, however, this Western response forced the army leadership to reassess totally its political and strategic position. Critical to this reassessment, according to Gow, was the Persian Gulf war, which YPA analysts saw as a 'true paradigm for the use of modern technology and a credible model for the use of force in a hypothetical war in similar military-political circumstances, something which (with reference to our crisis and its possible internationalisation) cannot leave us indifferent.'[74] That war demonstrated the 'instrumentalisation of the UN, as a system of global security, serving to realise the global strategic interests of the greatest world powers,' and thus the necessity of US leadership and international consensus for any armed intervention in cases such as Yugoslavia. The United

States at the time was preoccupied with Iraq and thus unlikely to back the EC militarily. Consensus in the UN Security Council was also unlikely, particularly if the fear of another Vietnam could be sown. Intervention seemed improbable if the army accepted that Yugoslavia was no longer salvageable and moved to secure the strategic quadrants of a new state – what was being called, by August–September 1991, a rump Yugoslavia (*krnja Jugoslavija*) – without Slovenia and without most (but not all) of Croatia. In Gow's estimation, the consequences of this reassessment could be seen in Croatia by October in the army's participation in the siege taking place for Vukovar, on the Danube, and the campaign in Konavli, south of Dubrovnik, in the Montenegrin military district, to ensure control of the Prevlaka peninsula and therefore its naval base on the Adriatic and the most strategic point on the entire coastline. But Miloš Vasić, the military expert of the independent Belgrade weekly *Vreme*, saw the army floundering, without 'any proper political aim' and a 'resulting strategic confusion,' into the end of December (and long after the 'Pyrrhic victory' of the fall of Vukovar).[75]

Whether a YPA strategy existed at the time, the political path of dissolution continued. The UN-negotiated cease-fire in Croatia required the YPA to withdraw, which it did beginning November 29, and to be replaced by UN troops. The Macedonian government accompanied a request for recognition of its sovereignty to the EC in December 1991 with negotiations for the army to leave (redeployed to Kosovo). UN troops would remain in Croatia, at the behest of the Secretary General and Security Council, until the rebel Serbs disarmed and political negotiations resolved the contest between the two in a political settlement for the country as a whole.[76] This agreement not only met with opposition from the Serbian leader in the *krajina*, Milan Babić – against the public reprimand of his former patron Milošević – but also meant a loss of territories in Slavonia for the faction within the army fighting to create a new, smaller Yugoslavia.[77] Although it still did not include the army in its negotiations, now over Bosnia-Herzegovina, the EC began to demand on April 11, 1992 – only five days after Bosnian sovereignty was recognized – that the army withdraw from the republic. In 'alarm over the rapid deterioration of the situation' in Bosnia-Herzegovina, the UN Security Council declared in its resolution of April 10 that it would demand on April 24 that 'all interference from outside cease.' UNSCR 752 (May 15, 1992) demanded that 'JNA [YPA] or Croatian Army units in Bosnia-Herzegovina be withdrawn or subject to Bosnia-Herzegovina government authority or disarmed and disbanded with weapons under international supervision.' While repeating the same demand in Resolution 757 on May 30, the Security Council also imposed 'wide-ranging sanctions' against the new federal republic of Yugoslavia (Serbia and Montenegro) because of the 'failure of Serbia, Montenegro and JNA [YPA] authorities to meet Resolution 752.'[78]

Despite this foreign view that the army was an external aggressor on Bosnian sovereignty, a primary reason for concern if war erupted in Bosnia was the intimate bond between the Yugoslav People's Army and that republic. The fate of the army would not be determined before the fate of Bosnia-Herzegovina, for the relationship between the two was of a different order altogether than the question of political loyalties or of obtaining diplomatic recognition of sovereignty. For geopolitical, geological, and historical reasons, Bosnia-Herzegovina had been the heart of the country's defence. Located in the interior of Yugoslavia with the natural resources of mountainous terrain, Bosnia-Herzegovina was ideal for the location of military production – coal, iron, timber, metallurgy, steel, hydroelectric power, armaments, and industrial crops. The industrialization of Bosnia-Herzegovina under the Habsburgs after 1878, the removal of strategic industries from borderlands into the interior after 1938 (before World War II) and again in the quarrel with the Cominform in 1948–49 (leading the army to call Bosnia its 'Dinaric Fortress'), and the massive federal investment in Bosnian industry in 1948–52 were all consequences of Bosnia-Herzegovina's military significance. Even in the 1980s, when the army was being substantially downsized, 40 to 55 percent of the Bosnian economy was tied to military industries; 50 to 55 percent of its industry was federally mandated investment for that reason; and 40,000 people were employed directly in military production. Sixty to 80 percent of the army's physical assets (armaments factories, supply routes, airfields, mines and basic raw materials, stockpiles, training schools, oil depots) were located in Bosnia-Herzegovina. On the eve of the war, 68 percent of the federal army's 140,000 troops were stationed in the republic.[79] To the extent that the Yugoslav army was fighting a war for its own integrity and state, it could not easily be a neutral party in Bosnia-Herzegovina or abandon its own economic foundations.

Even if the army's identity is equated with its permanent personnel alone, it was inextricable from Bosnia-Herzegovina. Because the primary site of Partisan fighting against Axis powers in World War II was in Bosnia-Herzegovina, an estimated 80 percent of the officer corps originated there. Early accusations of Serbian aggression in Croatia and Bosnia were commonly supported with the allegation that the army was 70 percent Serbian. It is not fully clear how these data were compiled, since a large portion of the officer corps identified their nationality as Yugoslav, and reliable statistics on the ethnic composition of the army were not publicly available. Moreover, the army experienced substantial turnover for political and natural reasons. To obtain such an estimate, Serbs, Montenegrins, and Yugoslavs would have to be equated as Serbs; the data would have to represent only the professional corps of officers and its civilian employees and not the entire army or armed forces; and the differences between ethnic Serbs from Serbia proper and from outside Serbia would have to be ignored. The full active component, including conscripts, reservists, and reserve officers, was far more representative of the ethnic composition of the population. This was even more true if one assessed the total armed forces, which included the TDFs of each republic. The senior officer corps and assignment of commands strictly followed the legal requirement – the key (*ključ*) – of national proportionality.

More important, the labelling of the YPA as a Serbian army, with all its implications, accepted the nationalist argument that ethnic origin was equivalent to political loyalty and partisanship. In the hands of outsiders who were insisting on borders and sovereignty as defined by the former republics, the label was also confusing, if not hypocritical, for like the nationalists, it seemed to deny the difference between ethnic origin and republic of origin or residence. But the army was ideologically a communist institution, dogmatically antinationalist.[80] To the extent it had a Serbian 'character' in terms of ethnicity, these Serbs came largely from Bosnia-Herzegovina and Croatia as a result of the army's origins during World War II, when ethnic Serbs in the areas of the former military border between Austria and Turkey took sanctuary with Partisan units against the fascist Ustasha campaign of genocide against them. Along with many officers of the royal army from Serbia proper, they chose to join the Partisans under Tito rather than the Serbian Chetniks.[81]

Relations between the army and the Bosnian government nonetheless deteriorated as the country dissolved. At the time of the Slovene and Croatian independence declarations, the Bosnian government and Parliament had made no particular effort to communicate with the army, in part because of internal divisions among the parties. From the beginning, the Croatian party took the position of its Zagreb superiors that the YPA was an army of occupation. Bosnian Serb party leaders issued calls to the YPA as early as mid-July to protect the Serb minority, just as its other SDS branch had done in Croatia. While preparing actively for armed conflict like the others, the SDA leadership under Izetbegović began to talk as a state-building party about transforming the army within Bosnia-Herzegovina into the republic's national army in a future Yugoslav confederation. The declaration of Bosnian sovereignty by the Croat-Muslim alliance on October 15, 1991, however, was a direct reaction to the army decision to mobilize troops in the Bosnian *krajina*, as part of the intensified fighting in Croatia during September. Although President Izetbegović ordered draft boards to ignore the order for mobilization, he was sensitive enough to the Slovene and Croatian precedents and to the YPA's commitment to some form of a Yugoslavia that included Bosnia to issue a warning to all sides not to do anything against the army. Minister of Defence Kadijević promised to do everything necessary to prevent the war's spread to Bosnia.

Such a commitment in the midst of a rapidly deteriorating and shifting political scene depended, however, on the ability of these two men to maintain a consistent position and keep control over their own forces. Izetbegović's mandate as president expired in November 1991 and the means used to extend it a second twelve months were not universally considered legitimate. Kadijević felt obliged to resign in January 1992. Officers loyal to both the YPA and Bosnia who tried to play a neutral and pacifying role faced a rise in incidents requiring damage control during the fall. In September 1991, within days after the Belgrade Initiative issued its proposal for a new Yugoslavia, reservists from Serbia went on a shooting spree in Tuzla, the truly multiethnic city in northern Bosnia, and cross-border raids began to terrorize citizens in eastern Bosnia into ethnic factions. Refugees from the war in Croatia brought with them the polarizing epithets of Chetniks (for all Serbs) and Ustasha (for all Croats) and provoked clashes with local army units. Officers unsure of which way the political wind would blow manoeuvred their own local alliances and provocations to test the waters, which had the effect of exacerbating tensions.[82]

Also during the fall, while the YPA was preparing to leave Croatia, Izetbegović sought to negotiate a political accommodation and partial demobilization, promising that officers and their families could keep their apartments and receive their pensions, and that the government would assist their transition to employment in the civilian sector. Yet it was not at all clear where he would find the funds necessary to make the promise credible. The economy had already begun to collapse as a result of the country's dissolution and of an economic embargo imposed on Bosnia-Herzegovina during the fall by Croatia (on transportation routes) and Serbia (on most trade in food and fuel).

Izetbegović appealed to German foreign minister Genscher in early December to wait to recognize Croatia until Bosnia's political relations were more settled, but he also showed his hand by requesting UN peacekeeping troops to guard the border on December 6. The EC decisions on recognition in December and the decision of the Croat-Muslim faction within the Bosnian government to request recognition and of the Serb party to declare in response that it would create its own republic within Bosnia-Herzegovina appeared to force YPA units and officers toward an alliance with Serbs wishing to remain within Yugoslavia and TDF units in Serb majority localities. All other territorial defence forces began to mobilize on the side of the Croat-Muslim alliance. Yet the period between Kadijević's resignation in January 1992 and the EC demand of April 11, 1992, that the YPA leave Bosnia-Herzegovina still presented opportunities for reversing the polarization and for preventing open war. The confrontation mounted only after April 4, when the Bosnian government, assured that recognition was coming on April 6, called up the national guard to fight Serb insurrection and declared the YPA untrustworthy and on the side of the Bosnian Serbs. Following the tactics chosen earlier by Slovenia and then Croatia, it blockaded YPA barracks and insisted on the army's retreat under UN supervision.[83]

Although President Milošević had been resisting for over a year calls from the Serbian parliament and nationalists for the formation of a Serbian national army, he acknowledged the fait accompli on May 8 when the new Yugoslav army (VJ) retired thirty senior officers known as Titoists. Života Panić, who had been commanding officer at Vukovar, was appointed the new state's minister of defence. Only a week after Panić claimed that the YPA would remain in Bosnia-Herzegovina at least five years, he ordered its withdrawal from the republic.[84]

The YPA project for a rump Yugoslavia disappeared with the YPA. But the retreat of the YPA from Bosnia-Herzegovina May 4–10 meant in fact the departure of the 20 percent of its personnel who originated from Serbia and Montenegro, the two remaining republics of the former federation that joined into a new Yugoslavia on April 27. Left in Bosnia were two-thirds of the YPA's ammunition, much heavy artillery and equipment and 80,000 troops who were Bosnian citizens. These were largely transferred to the territorial defence forces of the 'Serb Republic of Bosnia and Herzegovina,' the core of a new Bosnian Serb army formed on May 13.[85] Bosnian loyalist Milutin Kukanjac was replaced by General Ratko Mladić, the openly pro-Serb militant from Bosnia who had been commander of the Knin corps of the YPA.[86]

Mladić's military campaign to keep eastern and northern Bosnia within Yugoslavia so as to create a corridor between Serbia and the areas claimed by Serbs in the Croatian *krajina* and a strategic buffer along the Drina River had become explicitly Serb nationalist in its motivations, attached to the Bosnian Serb party (SDS) leadership and it political aims. At the same time, the forced retreat of YPA officers from Croatia and Bosnia-Herzegovina had been to Belgrade; the senior ranks of the new Yugoslav army were former colleagues of Mladić, veterans of the campaigns in Croatia and Bosnia, and, in many cases, exiles from their origins in these republics. In contrast to the moderate Panić, for example, was General Nikola Uzelac, responsible for arming Serb irregulars in the Banja Luka region, who was appointed to the general staff and commander of the third army (of three) with jurisdiction over Kosovo.[87] Moreover, on June 16, Bosnian president Izetbegović announced that he had signed a formal military alliance with Croatian president Tudjman.

The proliferation of weapons

In addition to the influence of EC and UN diplomatic negotiations to recognize republican sovereignty and obtain a cease-fire, the UN arms embargo imposed in September 1991 in response to the war in Croatia contributed to further chaos in the system of defence. It gave impetus to political groups throughout the country to seize local stockpiles of weapons and ammunition (such as the move by Croat forces in Herzegovina to secure TDF assets and keep them from the YPA) and to plan the relocation of assets in preparation for war (as appeared to be the motivation of YPA troop movements out of Bosnian cities during the fall of 1991). It made control over Bosnia and sites of domestic defence plants and installations more critical and led governments (especially Croatia and Serbia) to begin war production from the substantial domestic arms industry.[88] Such production, however, did not interrupt co-operation between Croatian and Serbian tank and arms producers even while Croats and ethnic Serbs were at war in Croatia.

The embargo gave an initial advantage to those who had built up armies during 1990–91, those who had taken the early initiative over TDF assets, and those aided by the army from existing stocks. Slovene territorial defence forces used Armbrust rocket launchers and antitank weapons from Germany in the ten-day war; in Croatia and Bosnia, Serb irregulars used new German submachine guns and sniper rifles sold to an arms buyer in Belgrade; and the

Croatian government had little difficulty purchasing west European anti-tank weapons, east German AK–47 and Argentine self-loading rifles, Stinger missiles, and west German light arms and, apparently, even Leopard tanks.[89] The initial disproportions in access to domestic stocks and the uncertainty and higher risks and cost attached to foreign supplies encouraged a local arms race. Croatia captured arms in September 1991 by blockading YPA barracks and by seizing about thirty ships and all bases of the former Yugoslav navy.[90] The YPA supported some Serb groups in Croatia. Slovene war booty was transferred to Croatians, and YPA equipment, including heavy artillery and planes, to Bosnian Serbs. This led to the development of new arms industries, such as Croatia's construction of a fully equipped army, navy, and air force of 110,000 troops by November 1992 from its own plants – the Djuro Djaković tank factory, Zmaj aircraft centre, and shipyards.

The primary source of continuing disadvantage, in fact, was physical location and the dependence of some areas – above all, central Bosnia – on others within the former country for access to supply routes and transport. The UN embargo thus reproduced the effects of economic reform and westernization and the EC decisions on recognition and aid. In its early stages the embargo largely affected the Bosnian army, Muslim paramilitaries, and special forces created by Albanians in Kosovo. Able to purchase or receive from foreign patrons, émigrés, and arms markets abroad substantial imports of light arms and ammunition, they could not overcome their disadvantage in access to heavy weapons (artillery, tanks) and aircraft of the Slovenes, Croats, and Serbs, because supply routes were controlled by their potential or real enemy. Thus President Izetbegović's military alliance with Croatia aimed to gain access to the sea for arms, fuel, and supplies. When Croatian war aims extended beyond their political stronghold in western Herzegovina, during the fall of 1992, Croatian forces that controlled those routes began to insist on a 50 to 70 percent cut of all weapons traffic, if they let any through at all (which they did less and less after September 1992).

The Bosnian government's dependence on Croatian co-operation to allow arms and refugees to flow prevented President Izetbegović, in fact, from calling for international sanctions on Croatia, even when it was clear that the alliance meant little to the fighting on the ground and that the Croatian army (HV) was an active participant against Bosnian forces. Indeed, it led Izetbegović to protect Tudjman by muting international criticism on numerous occasions. At the same time, the borders between Serbia and Montenegro and areas of Bosnia-Herzegovina claimed by Bosnian Serbs were so permeable and its legitimacy as an international border so rejected by locals that Serbian assistance of weapons, fuel, supplies, and 'weekend warriors' were easily provided and difficult to interdict. Landlocked Bosnian forces and Albanians in Serbia thus had to rely more than the others on attracting international sympathy to obtain the foreign military assistance, such as air cover for their ground troops or actual attacks on enemy heavy artillery, that the embargo was designed to make unnecessary.

Economic disintegration and the collapse of trade

Inseparable from the collapse of civil order and the protracted process of transformation from a single Yugoslav to many separate armies and paramilitary groups that characterized the fighting was the dissolution of their common economy. Also not obedient to republican borders, economic relations and the flow of goods and transport necessarily were casualties of the political conflict – in part, a spontaneous breakdown and, in part, deliberate destruction of the economic interdependencies of the former state. But the fact of these interdependencies also provided weapons of war. Thus the Serbian attempt to boycott Slovene goods after December 1990 had little effect on the Slovene economy. But when Serbia and Croatia both imposed an embargo on goods going into Bosnia-Herzegovina during the fall of 1991, in order to sabotage the Bosnian economy and facilitate their respective war aims, the effect was devastating.[91] The economy of Bosnia-Herzegovina not only was fully integrated into the Yugoslav economy, but also particularly depended on the import of food. While Bosnians reeled from the inflationary effects, the areas claimed by militant Bosnian Croats (their state of Herzeg-Bosnia) had an important buffer of stability from their early economic incorporation into Croatia proper, Croatian currency, and Dalmation trade routes. This also helped to facilitate the payment and therefore loyalty of soldiers and local administrations that were critical to the Bosnian Croats' war aims.

The persistent efforts during 1991 and again in mid-1992 by the leadership in Montenegro to distance itself from Serbian policies and be more independent were also futile without international support, because Montenegro's transportation routes, energy grids, and similar lifelines were connected to Serbia and because the republic's dependence on federal budgetary subsidies had been transferred to Serbia after the collapse of

Yugoslavia. The Croatian decision on September 11, 1991, to shut off the Adria oil pipeline feeding Serbia (and central Europe) and the war's disruption of links with Croatia and Slavonia meant that Serbia could not easily afford to lose its access to the sea through Montenegro. Each Montenegrin move, therefore, was met by some form of economic pressure, such as an overnight rise in the cost of electricity or a blockade of fuel oil, from Serbia. Unable to gain even international acknowledgement of its separate interests, the Montenegrin liberals had nowhere to turn, and the Montenegrin government had to find accommodation with Milošević (particularly after December 1992, when its support for the campaign of Yugoslav prime minister Panić to end the war was defeated along with Panić in the Serbian presidential election). The UN economic sanctions on Serbia and Montenegro after May 30, 1992, imposed to stop the war in Bosnia, not only made Serbia's alternative routes in the east more risky, but also caused serious hardship for Macedonia. Macedonia was landlocked and nearly all of its road, railway, energy, power, and telecommunications links went through Serbia. Macedonia sold about two-thirds of its agricultural and manufactured goods to Serbia.[92]

The actual path of the dissolution of the state had a direct consequence on the character of those wars. The first stage of fighting (seen in both the wars in Croatia and Bosnia-Herzegovina, when the world was least attentive or prepared to react) was not a calculated military strategy between contending armies or between the Yugoslav army and republican militias. The situation was, instead, chaotic. Competing militias and gangs marauded, only loosely linked to centres of command and control or fully freewheeling, and paramilitary extremists escalated small confrontations to force political leaders to greater militancy. The declining number of regular troops and difficulty finding conscripts willing to fight led to supplementation with militant extremist volunteers and criminals released from jails, who were more often motivated by the invitation to loot and plunder than nationalist fervour. The worst excesses of reported massacres, rape, and mutilations emerged because of such conditions. Local interests and alliances predominated, giving a very different character to warfare in different regions and municipalities. To the extent that battles had a strategic character, each commanding officer also faced a choice among competing loyalties (based on a calculation of the probable fate of the army itself as well as personal sentiments and bonds of obligation).

The political conflict within national and military organizations over political goals and strategy, the absence of appropriate equipment for communication among local units, and the continuing dominance of local loyalties interfered throughout the period with efforts to impose central control or enforce negotiated agreements. Events such as the shelling of Dubrovnik at the end of October 1991 and the attack on an EC monitoring helicopter that killed five airmen in January 1992 appear to have been the result of policy disagreements within the YPA senior command and the branches of the armed forces. It remains unclear whether there would have been a three-month siege (August 24–November 17, 1991) and destruction of Vukovar, the worst battle of the Croatian war, had renegade forces from the Croatian National Guard (called the Wolves of Vukovar) and neofascist Ustasha bands such as the Zebras, who were loyal to local politicians (particularly the right-wing radical in the HDZ, Tomislav Merčep), not chosen to ignore Zagreb authority and put up a stiff resistance – in order to draw the government into a more aggressive strategy.[93] They succeeded in escalating the war because they were matched on the Serb side by right-wing radicals from Serbia, such as Šešelj, who had attempted to make eastern Slavonia a Chetnik base through radicalizing campaigns during the spring. In similar fashion, these irregulars were also outside much control but had allies within the army among officers who were attempting to drag Belgrade into the war.[94] The army, for its part, faced increasing problems of recruitment and desertion. Two units of the TDF refused to fight; morale was declining and there were insufficient soldiers in a location of major geopolitical significance. The commanding general, Života Panić, assessed that there would be no YPA left within two months unless he turned to artillery. Each fighting their own battles as much as each other, they continued until there was nothing left to destroy.[95]

In Bosnia-Herzegovina, lack of communication affected the command and control of both the Bosnian Serb and Bosnian government armies and emphasized the dominance of local territorial forces in their origins and the psychology of defending home territory. The Bosnian government tended to fight many battles with small units of 1,000 to 2,000. Even after December 1992, by which time the organization of a new army made it possible to launch serious campaigns, they continued to have difficulty concentrating forces and creating mobility. Local alliances and local commanders held sway for the Croatian HVO and even the Bosnian Serb army, despite the Serbs' mobile elite units and slightly higher proportion of former YPA officers.

Moreover, the dissolution of the country erased the security guarantees for most individuals and families. The bases of self-restraint and mutual trust that make civil order possible without massive coercion were already fragile after a decade of economic depression and social disintegration. The tactics of outside terrorists, the mass media propaganda, and the political interests of ethnically pure local administrations or police were additional assaults. The many recorded examples of heroic neighbourliness across ethnic lines and in village solidarity against outside radicals could only provide for many a temporary protection against displacement or voluntary exile once the last vestiges of trust were destroyed by the unexpected hostility of other neighbours.[96]

State-Building

Perhaps the most negligent element of the European policy to recognize the republics of the Yugoslav federation as separate nation-states was its disregard for the characteristics of states, as opposed to nations. States are more than communities of political identity. In addition to legitimacy and citizens, they require strategically defensible borders, economic assets sufficient to survive against external threats, and a monopoly on the use of force over territory claimed. The borders of the republics had never had to satisfy the needs of independent states. Once nationalists turned to state-building, there was an additional reason on many sides for contesting existing republican borders. While political rhetoric and propaganda continued to emphasize ethnic criteria, the actual goals of military activity would be driven by strategic objectives.

Therefore, although Europeans had argued that recognition of Slovene and Croatian sovereignty – and the invitation to recognize Bosnia-Herzegovina and Macedonia – would stop the use of force, its consequence was to up the ante instead. Once it was clear that Yugoslavia was no longer salvageable and that separate states would ensue, the strategic requirements of statehood fuelled war.

In this aspect of the Yugoslav conflict, too, the Slovene case deceived those who thought that the creation of new states, state powers, and foreign relations would be unproblematic and peaceful. Its economy had long been more integrated internationally (especially with Western markets) than domestically. Slovene firms adjusted rapidly to war and international sanctions, maintaining their contracts and markets in Serbia by redirecting routes, through friendly Hungary where necessary, in spite of the UN embargo.[97]

The availability of Austrian capital and the central European trade and tourist organizations such as Alpe-Adria provided Slovenia with a buffer, in the short run, against the collapse of the Yugoslav market. Because Slovenia had the highest proportion of export producers, it could reassure international financial organizations and credit markets that it could reliably assume its portion of the Yugoslav foreign debt and guarantee new loans. Membership in the United Nations for Slovenia came easily and quickly, in May 1992. By December 1992, long before there was any hope of discussion over the economic questions of the Yugoslav succession, Slovenia had been admitted to the IMF and to the Council of Europe.

Slovenia's Alpine terrain provided a natural line of defence as long as the policy it chose during the 1980s to repopulate the uplands could be maintained. It had succeeded in taking control over most of the military assets of the Yugoslav army, establishing a national monopoly over the use of force, and gaining foreign assistance in purchasing supplementary arms even before its declaration of independence. Reconstruction of war damage was minor, in contrast to the effects of the war on its border. With borders and international relations stable, a parliamentary vote of no confidence over failing economic policies brought down the centre-right government that had waged the war, and an election six months later resumed the prewar trend back to the liberals.

In contrast to Slovenia, war in the other republics reflected, in part, the process of creating the coercive instruments and borders of states. Armed clashes began when police forces moved in to challenge local control by national minorities, as in Glina, Plitvice, and Borovo Selo in Croatia in 1990–91. A critical moment in the consolidation of control over Herzeg-Bosnia, the state within Bosnia-Herzegovina being created by the Bosnian Croat branch of the HDZ, occurred when its armed forces succeeded in assassinating Blaž Kraljević, the regional commander of rival Croatian forces, the right-wing HOS, in Trebinje in August 1992. Although the military alliance between the Croatian and Bosnian governments had broken down after September 1992, it did not lead to open warfare between Bosnian Croats and Muslims until the end of January 1993, when Bosnian Croat leader Mate Boban began to disarm Bosnian government police and army personnel in areas of central Bosnia that he claimed for Herzeg-Bosnia. Brutal massacres carried out by both forces in mixed Croat-Muslim towns of central Bosnia beginning with Vitez in April 1993 were triggered when Croatian defence minister Gojko Šušak visited Bosnia and ordered the Croatian state flag raised over these towns.

War in the other republics also concerned strategic assets, in contrast to Slovenia's natural, and largely uncontested, borders and its linkup with European transportation and communication routes. Ethnically defined territories are not by and large defined by natural borders, and the fact of war between ethnically defined armies heightened sensitivity to the need for defensible borders between national states that might be hostile.[98] Access to the sea, ports, and international transportation routes became necessities for landlocked areas which aimed to become independent states. One aspect of the fight for Vukovar was geopolitical, made more immediate by the increasing importance of the Danube River as an international waterway for commerce and defence in the continental expansion of European trade with the end of the Cold War.[99] Although Croatia claimed western Herzegovina on both historicist and ethnodemocratic principles, its importance was strategic: as an essential cordon protecting the Dalmatian coast tourist trade and its thin, long, vulnerable line of north–south communications of an independent state of Croatia.[100]

Montenegro (and therefore Serbia, with which it was allied in one state) could not defend itself without control over the Prevlaka peninsula, and the fishing industry that was critical to its economy could not afford the Croatian claim of territorial waters that it extended from the Prevlaka it controlled. Regardless of international recognition for the former republican borders, the strategic significance of the Prevlaka peninsula for Montenegro, of the Drina and Danube rivers for Serbia, and of the Dalmatian hinterland for Croatia required subsequent negotiation.

Perhaps the greatest confusion for foreign observers was the debate over maps that seemed to derail all political negotiations over Bosnia-Herzegovina. The more war continued in Bosnia-Herzegovina, the more armies fought for routes, defensible corridors, and contiguous territories. Outsiders continued to talk of *percentages* of territory in ethnic terms and of what they considered to be a just solution, including their aim of not 'rewarding aggression.' Neither had much resonance in the behaviour of military forces whose leaders were thinking in strategic terms of independent survival and natural lines of defence and stable borders. Although leaders continued to lay claim to territory on national grounds, including the criterion of the majority ethnic identity of residents in the 1991 census. claims to territory on grounds of national rights did not mean they would be limited to ethnic-majority or historically national territories.

When international mediators, for example, ignored Karadžić's insistence on the cantonization of Bosnia, with his claim of Serbian rights to 65 percent of Bosnian territory on the grounds that Serbs held legal title to this much land in Bosnia even if their percentage in the population was lower, the Bosnian Serb army under General Mladić pushed instead to fill in the patchwork quilt of these landholdings to make contiguous, statelike territory and to build a land corridor between Serbia proper and the Serbian-claimed areas in the Croatian *krajina* that was intended to ensure the survival of Serbs as a nation in this area.[101] Even cities that were considered clearly Muslim territory by population and historical tradition became military targets because of their military assets (airfields, oil depots, hydroelectric power plants, armaments factories, communication lines for supplies).[102] Similarly, when Bosnian government forces took the offensive at the end of 1992, some of the most vicious fighting of the war (in terms of atrocities and ethnic cleansing) occurred in central Bosnia. Whereas journalists argued that this fight between predominantly Muslim forces and their former Croatian allies occurred because the Bosnian government could not penetrate Serbian-held territory, the fact was that Bosnian Muslim goals were strategic: the industrial heartland and above all the armaments factories in towns such as Vitez.

The importance of economic assets to new states, moreover, was behind the prolonged refusal of Bosnian Serbs to sign on to the map part of the Vance-Owen plan. Whereas the international community accused the plan of appeasing aggression (for assigning the Bosnian Serbs majority control over 43 percent of the territory – a rollback from the 70 percent they held militarily at the time of the negotiations but more than their approximately 33 percent of the population), the Bosnian Serbs were calculating not only the percentage of territory given each constituent nation in relation to its percentage of the population, but also the proportional value of industrial and mining sources, energy sources (thermal, coal, hydroelectric power), and railways per province and 'per ethnic group.' In this calculation, the Vance-Owen map was leading to the economic destruction of their territory 'with the stroke of the pen' because it 'deprived them of energy sources and industrial plants' and made them 'dependent in energy and therefore economically submitted [sic]' to Muslim and Croat provinces and 'condemned to permanent economic inferiority and dependence.'[103] The same calculation of economic values by nationality became a key bargaining document of the Bosnian Muslim leadership in the summer of 1994 when the map at issue was one formulated by the Contact Group. A stumbling block in the one in between, the Invincible plan, was the Bosnian government and Bosnian Muslim demand for access to the sea and to the Sava River.

Conclusion

Had the Western view that Yugoslavia was an artificial creation of separate nation-states been correct, there would have been no reason for war. Moreover, the characteristics of the ensuing wars were defined by its causes rather than by some historical predilection to war and to the particular form of brutality witnessed in Yugoslavia. Because the EC left it up to partisans in Yugoslavia to decide which justifications for territory would prevail in defining new states and borders, the constitutional methods of combat during 1989–90 (national claims through constitutional preamble, citizenship rights, and loyalty oaths) were replaced by the methods, social organization, culture, and weapons associated with land and its defence.[104]

Regardless of ethnic differences, the process of justifying a nation's sovereignty over territory became embodied in persons and their rights to live on that land. It was this association, of this link between particular persons and land with past wars, that made historical memories relevant to the conflict and opened thoughts of revenge that had been laid aside. And the EC's insistence on referendums to legitimize those rights, while accepting the validity of only some, provided the impetus – whatever the spontaneous reasons (envy, hatred, competition) – to expel people from their homes and jobs on the basis of their ethnicity and to create ethnically pure areas through population transfers and expulsions as a prelude to a vote. The goal was not territorial acquisition but statehood. For that, only international recognition would complete the task.

Contrary to the distinction made by the international community between humanitarian and political objectives, there can be no distinction between soldier and civilian in such wars. The goal is to claim territories *for* a particular people and to resolve questions of membership and political loyalties through war. As in a referendum, the size of the turnout is as important as the size of the vote – but neutrality is even less of an option. Whatever the methods used, the fight to establish national rights to land has a genocidal aspect. According to the myth of right-wing nationalism, ethnicity is pure and a *natural* basis for state rights. Those who refuse to accept an ethnically defined political loyalty are reclassified as enemies of their people. The conflict is not ethnic, in other words, but national: ethnic Croats who protested exclusive Croatian nationalism or President Tudjman's policies, ethnic Serbs who opposed Slobodan Milošević or argued for intellectual dissent, Serbs and Croats in Bosnia-Herzegovina who identified themselves as Bosnians rather than side with Bosnian Serb or Bosnian Croat nationalists were all classified with the enemy and vulnerable to treatment as traitors.

Moreover, contrary to those who argue that these wars represent a clash of civilizations – between civilized and barbarian, Western and Balkan, Roman Catholic and Eastern Orthodox, Christian and Muslim – the real clash is social and economic. Territorial war for new states does not put an end to the political, economic, and social conflicts raised by the policies of global integration but that lost out to the nationalist juggernaut; they are simply played out under the guise of ethnic conflict. The war became an opportunity for a revolt of the disadvantaged, for individual enrichment, for political aspirations, and for revenge against the communist regime. The character of the fighting itself is best explained by the socioeconomic background of those leading the fight and doing the soldiering. Thus the element of revenge is far more social and generational than historical, although the two can come together. Right-wing nationalists in Serbia and Croatia did revive the names, symbols, and even uniforms of right-wing nationalists from World War II – the monarchist Chetniks and fascist Ustasha – for their paramilitary forces.

The description of the Yugoslav wars as ethnic conflict is most misleading, however, as a predictor of military activity. Military strategy in this case was not driven by ethnic hatred, class conflict, or historical aspirations for territory, but by the geopolitical and institutional preconditions of sovereignty: obtaining the strategic and economic assets and borders of a secure future state, destroying those of one's enemies, and building (in the course of war) the armies and foreign alliances of a new defence. Strategically defensible territories may have little relation to the borders defined by medieval states (as proclaimed by the historicist principle of a nation), by the patterns of migration and settlement of individuals and households (leading to the claim of the democratic principle), or by the administrative units of a former state (and the Helsinki principles); but short of such security, a state is incomplete. Like the social conflicts defining loyalties and fighting, this strategic objective is part of the longer process of the disintegration of one state and transformation of its assets and institutions to new states in the process of formation. The local organization of territorial defence in the previous Yugoslav system, the massive stockpiles of weapons, the armaments factories, and the organization of the federal army contributed substantially to the pattern of fighting. And as an actor in its own right in the constitutional battle, the army also had a political project: first, to hold a Yugoslavia together and to protect its particular assets and people, and then, as the political reality shifted, to create a state (a different state, depending on which officers and conscripts) to serve. Because the multiple elements and conflicts creating the wars in Croatia and Bosnia-Herzegovina were part of a prewar and postwar political continuum encompassing all of former Yugoslavia, however, they also characterized politics and calculation in areas that were not yet at war.

Notes

1. This characterizes much of the commentary on the Yugoslav breakup. An example of a nonparticipant can be found in Paula Franklin Lytle, 'US Policy Toward the Demise of Yugoslavia: The "Virus of Nationalism",' *East European Politics and Societies*, vol. 6 (Fall 1992), pp. 303–18.
2. The Croat writer Slavenka Drakulić captures this essence in 'The Smothering Pull of Nationhood,' *YugoFax*, October 31, 1991, p. 3.
3. The origins of the National Socialist party (Nazis) of Germany are instructive, that the partisan loyalties of people – especially the unemployed – often depend most on who seeks them out and organizes them. See F. L. Carsten, *The Rise of Fascism* (University of California Press, 1982).
4. See discussion and data in Dušan Janjić, 'Gradjanski Rat i Mogućnost Mira u Bosni i Hercegovini' [Civil war and the possibility of peace in Bosnia and Herzegovina], pp. 112–18, and in Vladimir Goati, Politički Život Bosne i Hercegovine 1989–1992 [Political life of Bosnia and Herzegovina 1989–1992],' pp. 55, 57, and 61. Both in *Bosna i Herzegovina Izmedju Rata i Mira* (Belgrade: Institut Društvenih Nauka, 1992).
5. See Mark Thompson, *Forging War: The Media in Serbia, Croatia and Bosnia-Herzegovina* (Article 19, International Centre Against Censorship: May 1994).
6. Janjić, 'Gradjanski Rat,' p. 107, provides a summary for the case of Bosnia-Herzegovina, but the phenomenon was widespread. Mary E. McIntosh, Martha Abele Mac Iver, Daniel G. Abele, and David B. Nolle find, in their empirical study in 1991–92 of attitudes toward ethnic minorities, 'Minority Rights and Majority Rule: Ethnic Tolerance in Romania and Bulgaria,' *Social Forces* (March 1995), that the greatest predictor of ethnic intolerance among a wide range of determinants (education, age, gender, ethnic composition of community, rural/ urban origin, political ideology, democratic values, economic outlook) was the 'perception of threat from the target group . . . to one's state or personal security,' specifically a possible impending attack

from a neighbouring country associated with the ethnic minority. They conclude that the 'importance of actual and imagined irredentist challenges . . . suggests that assurances of secure borders could go a long way toward reducing ethnic tension in both countries.'

7. Svetlana Slapšak, in 'Bestial Words, Bestial War,' *New York Times*, May 25, 1993, p. A23, describes this preparation in Serbia with unusual candour, but wonders therefore whether intellectuals who fought at the time for freedom of expression, for the rights of dissidents regardless of their message (as in the petition-writing campaign among intellectuals to support Vojislav Šešelj, before he became a right-wing radical extremist and stood accused by the international community as a war criminal for his activities in Croatia and eastern Bosnia), should instead have worried about protecting democracy. Which is more harmful to democracy, the expression of racist stereotypes or the measures taken to discourage such expression?
8. On the last part, see Janjić, 'Gradjanski Rat,' p. 107.
9. The charges and countercharges from both sides include numerous instances of actual or rumoured rape, murder, and poisoning. Mark Thompson, A *Paper House* (Pantheon Books, 1992), pp. 129–30, provides needed perspective. The documentary and sensational literature together is huge; an attempt at neutrality can be found in Branko Horvat, *Kosovsko Pitanje* [The Kosovo question], 2d suppl. ed. (Zagreb: Globus, 1989). Documentation of human rights abuses can be found in the publications of Helsinki Watch (a division of Human Rights Watch, New York and Washington): *Increasing Turbulence: Human Rights in Yugoslavia* (October 1989); *Yugoslavia: Crisis in Kosovo*, with the International Helsinki Federation (March 1990); and *Yugoslavia: Human Rights Abuses in Kosovo 1990–1992* (October 1992); and in the Amnesty International Reports: *Yugoslavia: Torture and Deliberate and Arbitrary Killings in War Zones* (November 1991); *Europe: A Compilation Document: Concerns in Europe November 1990–April 1991, Human Rights and the Need for a Fair Asylum Policy* (November 1991); *and Yugoslavia; Further Reports of Torture and Deliberate and Arbitrary Killings in War Zones* (March 1992). See also Thompson, *A Paper House*, p. 128, and Brian Hall, *The Impossible Country: A Journey through the Last Days of Yugoslavia* (Boston: David R. Godine, Publisher, 1994), pp. 235–89.
10. Silva Mežnarić, 'Gender as an Ethnic Marker: Violence, Women and Identity Politics in Albanian-Serbian Conflict,' in V. Moghadam, ed., *Identity, Politics and Women* (Oxford University Press, 1992). On the role of Croatian symbols and the media in both Croatia and Serbia in generating emotions that were 'increasingly hysterical,' and the central role in the 'Belgrade press's campaign of disinformation against the new regime in Zagreb [of] the idea that the latter was preparing genocide against the Serbs,' see Ivo Goldstein, 'Serbs in Croatia, Croatia in Yugoslavia,' *East European Reporter*, Autumn/Winter 1990, pp. 65–66.
11. See Robert M. Hayden, 'Recounting the Dead: The Rediscovery and Re-definition of Wartime Massacres in Late- and Post-Communist Yugoslavia,' in Rubie S. Watson, ed., *Memory, History, and Opposition under State Socialism* (Santa Fe: School of American

Research Press). For similar developments in Serbia, see Bette Denich, 'Dismembering Yugoslavia: Nationalist Ideologies and the Symbolic Revival of Genocide,' *American Ethnologist* (May 1994), pp. 367–90. For evidence that this is not only a Yugoslav phenomenon, see the fascinating analysis by Pamela Ballinger of Italian cave discoveries around Trieste, 'The Politics of Submersion: History, collective memory and ethnic group boundaries in Trieste,' Johns Hopkins University, Department of Anthropology, February 1993.

12. Misha Glenny provides numerous examples in *The Fall of Yugoslavia: The Third Balkan War* (Penguin, 1992), for example, pp. 66, 123. Another good source is *YugoFax/War Report*, a periodical 'critical briefing on the conflict in Yugoslavia' by journalists from all regions of the former country and others concerned to counteract the nationalized and censored flow of information, based in London. In a countrywide public opinion survey in May–June 1990 (a stratified, random sample of 4,232 persons over the age of 18), carried out by a consortium of the primary opinion survey institutions in each republic, television was found to be 'the most popular source of information' about public affairs and government programmes; between 45 percent (in Slovenia) and 64 percent (in Montenegro) used television as a regular source, while only 3 to 8 percent never watched television. 'Public Opinion Survey on the Federal Executive Council's Social and Economic Reform,' *Yugoslav Survey*, vol. 31, no. 3 (1990), pp. 3–5.
13. The newspaper *Oslobodjenje* challenged the constitutionality of the press law in March 1991 and won, but not without substantial and continuing harassment of its editorial board from members of the government.
14. For example, the column in the biweekly *Duga* by Brana Crnčević and the writings of Vojko Djogo and Vojislav Lubarda, who made fortunes on this theme, as did many others. The theme of *tamni vilajet* can be heard among Croats as well.
15. Its editor was given a lifetime achievement award by the Serbian government in 1991; letters of protest or defence from persons identified in its pages were rarely published.
16. Mario Nobilo, in an interview in the presidential palace, Zagreb, July 16, 1991.
17. Tomislav Marčinko, IDF managing editor, and Miroslav Lilić, Croatian Television (HTV) senior programme editor, 'Decree on reporting from war zones.'
18. A good summary for Croatia by Patrick Moore can be found in 'The Media in Eastern Europe,' *Radio Free Europe/Radio Liberty (RFE/RL) Research Report*, May 7, 1993, pp. 25–26. Milan Andrejevich discusses the situation in Slovenia, Serbia, and Montenegro, pp. 33–35, and Louis Zanga in Kosovo, p. 35. The HDZ also exerted its control over the printers to keep *Danas* from publishing until past debts were paid. Then *Danas* tried to publish in Slovenia or Austria, and the HDZ used its control over 80 percent of newsstands and the distribution system to put *Danas* out of business.
19. Slapšak, 'Bestial Words, Bestial War.' On the campaign in Croatia against 'five witches' – women journalists and writers suspected of not being sufficiently nationalist – see Vesna Kesić, 'The High Price of Free Speech: Confessions of a Croatian Witch,' *Women's Review of Books*, June 1993, pp. 16–17.

20. This was not for lack of trying to terrorize opposition media, such as by sending thugs to vandalize the offices of the television station YUTEL and the weekly *Vreme*. Author's interviews with staff at YUTEL and *Vreme*.
21. It would be interesting to speculate what the effect would have been if the normal (constitutional) rotation of the position of president to the HDZ (Croat) or SDS (Serb) had occurred. Was this initial advantage due to the SDA's tenure in that position and the international community's tendency to deal with single, rather than collective, leaders, or was it due to the ambiguity about Serb and Croat commitment to Bosnia and the obvious commitment of the Muslims in Bosnia-Herzegovina to its integrity and sovereignty within its republican borders?
22. Government ministers focused their public speeches abroad on Bosnian history; for example, in a speech entitled 'The Case for Bosnian Recognition,' at The Woodrow Wilson Center, Washington D.C., on January 9, 1992, Haris Silajdžić (at the time minister of international cooperation of the Federal Republic of Bosnia-Herzegovina) gave a discourse instead on Bosnia in the Middle Ages. New histories were written and state symbols, such as a crest and a flag, were created. To what extent this represented a state's creating a nation, as the process in places such as Belarus might more properly be described, depends on one's ideological views toward Bosnia. And as historical and anthropological scholarship shows, this relation between state and nation is always dynamic, a relationship of interaction, and not one represented by unalterable givens. Foreign scholars have contributed to this process also. An example is Noel Malcolm, *Bosnia: A Short History* (New York University Press, 1994). See especially Robert Donia and John Fine, *Bosnia and Herzegovina: A Tradition Betrayed* (Columbia University Press, 1994).
23. Some argue that extreme nationalist leaders in Bosnia-Herzegovina, such as the Serbs Radovan Karadžić and Nikola Koljević and the Croat Mate Boban, were more able to hold to their views that people could not live together because they originated in ethnically pure villages. *WarReport*, June 1993. A representative of the opposing view, architect Bogdan Bogdanović, who was mayor of Belgrade from 1982 to 1986, is 'Murder of the City,' *New York Review of Books*, May 27, 1993, p. 20.
24. Silva Mežnarić, 'Bosnia and Herzegovina: Selected Background Data and Analysis on Refugees, Migration, and Development,' paper prepared for the workshop on Peace in Bosnia and Herzegovina, The Wilson Center, Washington D. C., February 10–12, 1993 (Zagreb, January 1993), p. 12, and subsequent conversations.
25. Secret agreements between Bosnian Serbs and Croats also shaped the military outcome in Vareš, Kiseljak, Kupres, Jajce, and Bosanski/Slavonski Brod, and their mutual cease-fire largely held after the first offensive in 1992.
26. None of the fighting, particularly in Bosnia-Herzegovina, can be understood without placing the political goals of these wars at centre stage, but this is a combination of the classical military tactic of cutting communication lines and of the political objective, including the reformation of loyalties and identities through propaganda. A. Ross

Johnson reports an example from the Croatian wars in the summer of 1991, when the YPA cut local television links between Slavonia and Zagreb and replaced them with feeds solely from Belgrade. 'The Self-Destruction of the Yugoslav People's Army' (November 1991), p. 3.

27. A. D. Smith, 'States and Homelands: the Social and Geopolitical Implications of National Territory,' *Millennium: Journal of International Studies*, vol. 10, no. 3, p. 187.
28. Marcel Fafchamps writes, 'Even in developed economies, the occurrence of war or natural calamities revives solidarity and mutual assistance . . . whenever economic and social conditions are such that individual survival is extremely uncertain without some form of mutual insurance, informal solidarity mechanisms tend to emerge naturally.' 'Solidarity Networks in Preindustrial Societies: Rational Peasants with a Moral Economy,' *Economic Development and Cultural Change*, vol. 41 (October 1992), pp. 148–49.
29. On the origins in patriarchal culture of patriotic loyalty, symbolized by this motto of the British crown, 'Shame on him who thinks evil of it,' see Julian Pitt-Rivers, 'Honour and Social Status' in J. G. Peristiany, ed., *Honour and Shame: The Values of Mediterranean Society* (University of Chicago Press, 1966), pp. 19–78.
30. On rituals about death, see Denich, 'Dismembering Yugoslavia.'
31. The speech of common people caught in the war is not of the ethnic identities commonly asserted by outsiders but of the far stronger personal bonds of *komšije* – neighbours – and *kumstvo* – ritual kinship.
32. Although there is yet insufficient evidence of a deliberate policy, the widespread rape of women – particularly of Muslim women by Serbian soldiers – was a consequence of this explosive combination of mass media campaign, political rhetoric, rural culture, and war, helped along too well by pervasive drunkenness. It is true that fears of the demographic shift as a result of higher Muslim birthrates in Kosovo, Macedonia, and Bosnia-Herzegovina preoccupied nationalists in Slovenia, Croatia, and Serbia in the 1960s and 1980s, but whether this was a motivation for a campaign of rape by Serbian forces needs further analysis. Eyewitness accounts of massive rape in Bosnia-Herzegovina began to appear in Western media in October 1992: see Slavenka Drakulić, 'Rape after Rape after Rape,' *New York Times*, December 13, 1992, section 4, p. 17; and Amnesty International, *Bosnia-Herzegovina: Rape and sexual abuse by armed forces* (London: January 1993). See also Alexandra Stiglmayer, ed., *Mass Rape: The War Against Women in Bosnia-Herzegovina* (University of Nebraska Press, 1994).
33. The president of the third Yugoslavia, from May 1992 to June 1993, Serbian writer Dobrica Ćosić, specialized in novels of World War I and II, for example, and President Tudjman of Croatia wrote a Ph.D. dissertation in history, subsequently published, to revise downward the numbers of dead in concentration camps under fascist Croatia during World War II. For a view on the storm over numbers this caused, see Ljubo Boban, 'Jasenovac and the Manipulation of History,' *East European Politics and Societies* vol. 4 (Fall 1990), pp. 580–92, and the comment by Robert M. Hayden, 'Balancing Discussion of Jasenovac and the Manipulation of History,' and Boban's reply, 'Still

More Balance on Jasenovac and the Manipulation of History' in vol. 6 (Spring 1992), pp. 207–17. 'Like all nationalists of former Yugoslavia, the Serbians exaggerate their losses, sometimes claiming that more than 1 million Serbs were murdered in concentration camps of fascist Croatia alone. (Realistic estimates put the total of Serbian casualties between 500,000 and 600,000. Probably half were civilian victims of Croatian fascism.) Serbian nationalists are, however, right when they point out that Serbian casualties were both absolutely and relatively larger than those of any other Yugoslav group, and that only Serbs, Jews, and Gypsies were the victims of systematic and planned extermination. But Croatian and Muslim casualties were extremely high as well, and a considerable number of them were civilians who fell victim to Serbian extremists.' Aleksa Djilas, 'The Nation that Wasn't,' *The New Republic*, September 20, 1992, p. 30. The most respectable numbers are those from the demographic study of Bogoljub Kočović, Žrtve drugog svetskog rata u Jugoslaviji [World War II victims in Yugoslavia] (Longon: Naše delo, 1985), calculating 487,000 Serb losses in the war.

34. The losses in World War II were greatest in Bosnia. 'Of its 2.8 million people, 400,000 perished – every sixth Serb, eighth Croat, and twelfth Muslim.' Djilas, 'The Nation that Wasn't,' p. 30.
35. This is not to engage in the ethical question, for this seems to become a vicious circle of accusation and redemption, such as the Croatian retort that the murder of 16,000 to 17,000 detainees returned by the British from Bleiburg in 1945 settled whatever question of Croatian guilt there might be and for which certainly Tudjman and contemporary Croats should not be held responsible. In this case also numbers were being inflated under nationalist attention in 1990–92. See, for example, Hall, *The Impossible Country*, pp, 26, 42.
36. 'U šumi,' 'leave for the forests,' was the common expression for joining the Partisan forces.
37. The first question on acquaintance in Slavonia in the 1945–90 period was not 'what do you do?' but 'in whose house do you live?' In an interview with the author, February 5, 1992, in Belgrade, journalist and war correspondent Miloš Vasić argued that the pattern of warfare could be described less by geographic coordinates than by altitude. Paul Shoup concludes from an analysis of the ethnic composition of Serbian-inhabited regions of Croatia that districts most affected by the fighting were 'not those where either Serbs or Croats are in a clear majority but those where the two groups are more or less evenly balanced.' 'The Future of Croatia's Border Regions,' *RFE/RL Report on Eastern Europe*, November 29, 1991, p. 32.
38. 1.3 million Greeks left Asia Minor, and about 400,000 Turks left Greece. The division of India and Pakistan involved about 12 million Hindu and Muslim refugees.
39. According to James Gow in *Legitimacy and the Military: The Yugoslav Crisis* (St Martin's Press, 1992), p. 69, 25,661 Serbs and Montenegrins left Kosovo between 1981 and 1988.

40. Robert M. Hayden refers to this as 'constitutional nationalism' in 'Constitutional Nationalism in the Formerly Yugoslav Republics,' *Slavic Review*, vol. 51 (Winter 1992), pp. 654–73.
41. Misha Glenny describes the pattern of intimidation and arbitrary violence against Serbs in Croatia in 'The Massacre of Yugoslavia,' *New York Review of Books*, January 30, 1992, pp. 30–35. On Serbian ethnic cleansing in Bosnia-Herzegovina, see *The Ethnic Cleansing of Bosnia-Hercegovina*, a staff report to the Committee on Foreign Relations, United States Senate (August 1992).
42. *The Ethnic Cleansing of Bosnia-Hercegovina*, pp. 1–3.
43. On population transfers taking place in Croatia, against Article 49 of the Fourth Geneva Convention, see Žarko Paunović, 'Politics of Transfer,' *YugoFax*, February 3, 1992, p. 3. On the practice of postwar population transfers in the entire region, see Charles Gati, 'From Sarajevo to Sarajevo,' *Foreign Affairs*, Fall 1992, pp. 64–78.
44. For the conflict in Srebrenica, see David B. Ottaway, 'Bosnian Muslims Bar Bid to Evacuate Town; Sarajevo Government Spurns 3-way Talks,' *Washington Post*, April 7, 1993, p. A24. Under persistent criticism from the Bosnian government for assisting ethnic cleansing, the UN forces refused to assist an evacuation from Sarajevo organized by the Red Cross the previous November. See *Financial Times*, November 11, 1992, p. 3.
45. Lt. Colonel Bob Stewart, in his memoir of his days commanding British UN soldiers in central Bosnia in 1993, *Broken Lives: A Personal View of the Bosnian Conflict* (HarperCollins, 1993), pp. 318–19, writes: 'Bosnia is certainly complex beyond anyone's dreams. There are far more than three sides – Serb, Croat and Muslim – we hear about in the media. There are factions within groups and groups within factions. And without an established order, these different elements had created a situation as close to anarchy as I have yet witnessed . . . Even the differentiation between military and civilian is impossible . . . A civilian one minute is a soldier the next . . . the war is mainly being fought by civilians . . . A civilian soldier probably knows little about the established "rules of war". The use of detainees for digging trenches in the front line, where they are liable to be shot by their own side, might make sense to him. But both the ICRC and we were incensed by it. It is strictly against the Geneva Convention, we shout in exasperation. What's the Geneva Convention, comes the reply? How can someone like Commander Leko in Turbe be expected to know all the details of the "civilized" conduct of war? Less than two years ago he was a teacher. He's had very little military training. What he is actually doing, of course, is defending his home, or what is left of it.'
46. 'Akashi Slams Serb Human Rights Violations,' *RFE/RL Daily Report*, July 25, 1994. See also 'Serbs Step Up Ethnic Cleansing,' *RFE/RL Daily Report*, August 2, 1994.
47. Stephen Kinzer, 'Croats Send Back Bosnian Refugees,' *New York Times*, October 31, 1992, p. 3.
48. Aleksandra Mijalković, 'The Vukovar Syndrome,' *East European Reporter*, May/June 1992, p. 16.

49. Especially Zenica, Tuzla, Kakanj, and Vitez, towns that the Vance-Owen Plan for Bosnia-Herzegovina placed in majority 'Muslim provinces' and that Mežnarić describes as 'highly industrialized, ecologically destroyed and densely populated.' 'Bosnia and Hercegovina: Selected Background Data,' p. 8.
50. In the case of Bosnia-Herzegovina, Mešnarić looks for data to answer the question, Were the 'three national groups, at the brink of the war, different to such an extent that the current clash would have been expected?' She finds no evidence in attitudinal data about social differences or tension but strong evidence in regional differences. According to economic and demographic data, there was an 'ever wider developmental gap between specific regions in Bosnia,' which can be linked to ethnic differences if pushed. 'Bosnia and Hercegovina: Selected Background Data,' pp. 4–5. Sociologists and economists in Zagreb warned in 1990 that tensions in Knin, Lika, and other areas subsequently part of the area in which Serbs claimed autonomy were a result of failed industrialization and increasing poverty and unemployed industrial workers that demanded immediate attention. Developmental programmes were drawn up but rejected by the nationalist majority in the Croatian parliament.
51. Austro-Hungarian policy toward Bosnia-Herzegovina after it obtained trusteeship in 1878 was to insist on separate administration so as to prevent its union with either Serbia or Croatia and the creation of a strong south Slav state to its south. This, however, increased the confusion about where Bosnia-Herzegovina lay. Moreover, it left a bitter legacy. See Robert Lee Wolff, *The Balkans In Our Time* (W. W. Norton & Co., 1967), p. 96, on the striking parallel in method with the current period, such as the 1913 statement by the German Kaiser to the Serbs regarding the borders of a new Albanian state: 'When His Majesty Emperor Franz Joseph demands something, the Serbian government must give way, and if it does not then Belgrade will be bombarded and occupied until the will of His Majesty is fulfilled.' Wolff adds, 'It was perhaps little wonder if this incendiary talk encouraged the Austrian Foreign Minister, Berchtold, to think highly of the policy of ultimatums to Serbia. The point is worth stressing, since the outbreak of World War I was then less than a year in the future,' p. 94.
52. Mežnarić, 'Bosnia and Hercegovina: Selected Background Data,' p. 7. More than half of the Bosnian population (58 percent) had not moved, however, but remained in the rural or semirural settlements of less than 2,000 inhabitants in which they were born (p. 12).
53. Dr Srdjan Bogosavljević, 'Bosnia and Hercegovina in the Mirror of Statistics,' p. 13. The fact that Serbs were a minority where they were once a majority (on the basis of which Bosnian Serb nationalists referred to Muslim-inhabited villages and towns in eastern Bosnia, for example, as 'Serb land') was in part due to this economic emigration in 1971–91 and in part the result of the genocidal murders of World War II. In 67 of the total 108 communes in Bosnia-Herzegovina where population declined between 1963 and 1981, the majority had a Serbian majority and were in the *krajina* region and eastern Herzegovina; of those, only seven saw rising income, and of those, four were

among the first targets of Serbian 'cleansing.' Mežnarić, 'Bosnia and Hercegovina: Selected Background Data,' p. 7.

54. Vladimir Goati, 'Politički Život Bosne i Hercegovine,' p. 57. See also the story on Olovo, for example, 'Ethnic Conflicts in Eastern Bosnia Described,' *Borba*, December 8, 1991, p. 11, cited in Foreign Broadcast Information Service, *Daily Report: East Europe*, December 30, 1991, pp. 40–41 (hereafter FBIS, *East Europe*).
55. John Burns's portrait of a 21-year-old Bosnian Serb soldier, Borislav Herak, who admitted and was convicted by a military court (on March 30, 1993) of war crimes, including 'genocide, mass murder, rape and looting,' along with the individual murder of twenty-nine people, provides almost a stereotype. 'A Killer's Tale – a Special Report: A Serbian Fighter's Path of Brutality,' *New York Times*, November 27, 1992, p. Al.
56. On the same type of behaviour and personality in Croatia in April 1991, see the description of anti-Serb, right-wing Croat gangs in Zadar in Thompson, *A Paper House*, pp. 261–64.
57. James Gow, 'The Role of the Military in the Yugoslav War of Dissolution,' *Armed Conflicts in the Balkans and European Security*, an international conference April 20–22, 1993 (Ljubljana, Centre for Strategic Studies, Ministry of Defence, June 1993), p. 74.
58. Gow, 'The Role of the Military'; Janjić, 'Gradjanski Rat,' p. 122; and Milan Vego, 'Federal Army Deployments in Bosnia and Herzegovina,' *Jane's Intelligence Review*, vol. 4 (October 1992), p. 445. Three army corps, totalling 45,000 men, were deployed in Bosnia-Herzegovina: the 17th corps at Tuzla, the 5th at Banja Luka, and the 4th at Sarajevo.
59. Each brigade had several subordinate battalions, composed in turn of four or five eighty-two-man companies, 75 percent of which were ethnic Croats, drawn from the republic internal security police reservists, TDF members, and former YPA officers. It is equipped with light AFVs and ATGMs, and M-84 battle tanks produced in Croatia. MUP forces in Croatia were also in action with APCs and helicopters against Serbs in *krajina* even before the declaration of independence and included a special forces unit, 'Blue Berets,' for counterterrorism. David Isby, 'Yugoslavia 1991 – Armed Forces in Conflict,' *Jane's Intelligence Review*, vol. 3 (September 1991), pp. 401, 403.
60. Janjić discusses the 'close relations between Croat army and proCroatian and proMuslim paramilitary and military formations in Bosnia-Herzegovina,' from shared information and cooperation in propaganda, to the inclusion of actual units of the Croatian army in the war in 'Croat areas' of Bosnia-Herzegovina, and the important role in heightening tensions and worsening relations with the YPA of returning Bosnian citizens, primarily ethnic Croats, who had been living or fighting in Croatia. 'Gradjanski Rat,' p. 120.
61. According to a TANJUG (Yugoslav news agency) report of September 21, 1994, 'Slovenia armed Bosnian Muslims in 1991, months before a civil war broke out in Bosnia-Herzegovina in April 1992. This was evident from classified material of the Slovenian Defence Ministry, said a source which insisted on anonymity because of the

secret nature of the documents . . . In December 1991 and January–February 1992, at least 15 cargo planes carried different arms from Ljubljana to Bosnia . . . intended for Muslim paramilitary preparations to attack the then Yugoslav People's Army and the Bosnian Serbs' with the participation of a 'Slovenian special army and police units.' The arms trade from Slovenia and through Slovene ports had yielded weapons for Croatia as well. By 1994, however, the primary conduit for arms to Bosnia was from Iran through Croatian airports and seaports. According to Roger Cohen of the *New York Times*, Croatian defence minister Gojko Šušak said, 'What I need, I get. . . The arms market is saturated, so saturated you would pay three times the price if you got things legally.' He added that Croatia was providing the Bosnian government army with antitank weapons, cannons, machine guns, and mortar ammunition. See 'Arms Trafficking to Bosnia Goes on Despite Embargo,' *New York Times*, November 5, 1994, p. A1.

62. An exception to joining one's local defence unit, whatever its party allegiance, followed a pattern seen in eastern Croatia: where there was a choice among units, volunteers would tend to choose the better-organized force in hopes of better personal security. Thus, in multiethnic Sarajevo, Bosnian Croats who identified as Sarajevans and Bosnians nonetheless chose to join the HVO rather than the Bosnian army because the HVO's earlier initiative had made it better organized (this was no longer an option after the fall of 1993 when the Bosnian government required HVO units in Sarajevo to integrate into the Bosnian army).
63. Serbia mobilized both police and TDF forces in early July, threatening to join TDF units of Serbs from Bosnia and move to protect Serbs in Croatia if the YPA did not. Isby, 'Yugoslavia 1991 – Armed Forces in Conflict,' p. 403.
64. Ustasha comes from the verb to rebel; it was the name of the stormtroop units of the Croatian fascist state during World War II that were responsible for executing the terror and genocide against Jews, Romany (Gypsies), and Serbs. Four months before the Bosnian war began, 16,000 HOS troops were reported based in western Herzegovina. By mid-March, the HOS had mobilized 45,000. James Gow, 'Military-Political Affiliations in the Yugoslav Conflict,' *RFE/RL Research Report*, May 15, 1992, pp. 19, 25.
65. Janjić, 'Gradjanski Rat,' pp. 124–27.
66. Foreign mercenaries have fought on all sides of the war, the most colourful being the Serb-Australian Captain Dragan, who organized the 'Martićevci' in Croatian *krajina.* West European fascists from Germany, France, and England joined Paraga's Black Legion, Islamic mujahedin from Iran, Saudi Arabia, Egypt, Algeria, Libya, Pakistan, and Morocco, some of whom had fought in the Afghan war, were recruited or volunteered for Bosnia, and 1,000 Russians were on the Serbian side in Bosnia by December 1992 (and Cossack units were forming to go in January 1993).
67. In villages in Bosnia-Herzegovina people report that arms appear out of nowhere, and unconfirmed but persuasive suspicions are that territorial defence forces distributed

weapons to Serb villagers in the second half of 1991. Countless stories from villagers who left Bosnia-Herzegovina report this moment as decisive. They speak of neighbours appearing with arms and finding themselves without, except the random rifle in the barn that had not been fired for who-knows-how-long and which they must learn rapidly how to use. The record suggests, however, that all sides did so. For example, 'Croatian "Pro-Fascist" Party Members in Bosnia,' TANJUG, April 6, 1992, in FBIS, *East Europe*, April 7, 1992, p. 38, reports on weapons being distributed to SDA members in Sarajevo, Bosanski Šamac, Bihać, Vlasenica, and Tuzla. The article adds that a report presented to the Bosnian presidency estimated that there were 'about 600,000 armed people' in the republic.

68. Prime Minister Marković continued his campaign against the army in mid-September 1991, when he demanded the resignations of Kadijević and Stane Brovet on the grounds that they had met secretly with General Yazov in Moscow on March 13 to arrange for the delivery of 'a huge amount of weaponry.' See 'Marković Asks Army to Explain Moscow Arms "Deal",' FBIS, *East Europe*, September 20, 1991, citing TANJUG of September 19, pp. 29–30, and the Defence Ministry's denial of any secret contacts or agreement about arms deliveries, in 'Ministry Denies "Secret Contacts" With Yazov,' FBIS, *East Europe*, September 23, 1991, citing TANJUG of September 20, p. 29.
69. There is some dispute about this event. I accept the version of a reliable informant who was present and knows there was no attack (interview with the author).
70. 'Bosnia, Macedonia Out of Monitoring Cease-Fire,' TANJUG, September 5, 1991, in FBIS, *East Europe*, September 6, 1991, pp. 33–34. The same article reports that that same day, September 4, in Karlobag, the Croatian National Guard Corps (ZNG) 'arrested and maltreated' the presidency's joint cease-fire monitoring group for Lika and northern Dalmatia. 'Croatian Guards Mistreat Cease-Fire Group,' TANJUG, September 5, 1991.
71. Janjić, 'Gradjanski Rat,' pp. 123–24.
72. Between the spring of 1992, when the Yugoslav Army was formed, and August 26, 1993, when the retirement of 42 generals, including the chief of staff, Colonel General Zivota Panić, was announced, 170 generals and admirals were officially retired, leaving only 7 on active duty.
73. Gow, 'The Role of the Military,' p. 71.
74. Citing Col. Jovan Čanak, 'introduction' to a summary of findings on international involvement in the Yugoslav crisis and the Gulf war, in the military theoretical journal, *Vojno Delo*, July–October 1991, vols. 4–5, p. 15 (English translation). Gow, 'The Role of the Military,' pp. 72–75.
75. Miloš Vasić, 'Yugoslav Army's Choice,' *YugoFax*, December 28, 1991, p. 2. A third view comes from Bogdan Denitch, in *Ethnic Nationalism: The Tragic Death of Yugoslavia* (University of Minnesota Press, 1994), p. 164. He suggests that the floundering and change in strategy were linked to events in the former Soviet Union because the

leaders of the army 'were firmly convinced' that 'they had a powerful ally, the Red Army, which faced similar foes in its own country. They and their political allies saw their last chance in the failed coup against Gorbachev in the summer of 1991.' With its defeat, 'both the Yugoslav army and the Milošević government faced total international isolation. In the place of a Yugoslavia that they had sworn to defend they left vast destruction.'

76. In fact, the collapse of The Hague conference with the recognition of Croatia and its admission as a member state of the UN in May 1992 fundamentally altered the political assumptions on which the Vance plan and UN mandate had been based (not to prejudice the political outcome in negotiations) by granting Croatian sovereignty over this territory and beginning a long process of international pressure to get *krajina* Serbs to accept the consequences.

77. The Vance plan compensated Serbs in the UN protected areas (UNPAs) for their loss of protection from the army and their obligation to disarm by restoring their right to representation in local police forces in villages and districts where they were in the majority. One of the reasons for Babić's intransigence against the plan was Croatian president Tudjman's unwillingness to accept this provision, which he revealed in talks with UN negotiators in late January and early February 1992 over the terms of UN deployment when he demanded Zagreb's control over all local police units in the UNPAs (even if mixed, Serb and Croat), the authority of Croatian law in the UNPAs, and the exclusion of all Serb 'rebel leaders' from local councils. Žarko Modrić, 'Croatia denies raising new obstacles to UN peace plan,' Croatian news agency (HINA), February 3, 1992. Another provision of the agreement for the withdrawal of the YPA from Croatia was that the rights of YPA personnel (for example, to their housing, consisting of 37,951 apartments) in Croatia be preserved, but this was violated by the Croatian government – by a law in 1992 that assigned empty, emptied, or abandoned YPA apartments to 'war victims' (allocated by the Ministry of Defence); another law in 1992 that deprived anyone condemned of anti-Croatian activities (applied to all YPA officers who left for Belgrade, even if their families remained in Croatia) of citizenship rights; and a campaign beginning in mid-1991 that escalated to mass proportions in 1994 to evict families from those apartments without notice or right to appeal. (Interviews with the Centre for Human Rights, UN headquarters, Zagreb, October 1994.)

78. United Nations Security Council Resolution 757, S/RES/757, May 30, 1992.

79. On the latter figure, Vego, 'Federal Army Deployments in Bosnia and Herzegovina,' *Jane's Intelligence Review*, p. 445.

80. Many argue that the army was the main defender of the conservative position on economic and political reform within the LCY, actively engaged against the liberal faction, and that this included support in bringing to power such persons as Slobodan Milošević. See, for example, Janjić, 'Gradjanski Rat,' p. 121. However, the policies of the general staff – especially by 1989–91 – suggest that the army was as internally

divided as the republics, at least along economic lines (with a faction favouring export production, technological modernization, and westernization) and that some were attempting to move the army toward civilian control and professionalization. Janjić himself notes that this 'conservative' inclination was also manifest in an extreme nationalism among many officers (the local phrase is 'chauvinism') that led them to desert to the national armies being formed in the republics at the same time that others shifted, with the collapse of the communist regime, to their *own* state-building project of a rump Yugoslavia (pp. 121–22).

81. The distinction for Serbs between Chetniks and Partisans still held in the wars of 1991–95. Many from the *krajina* of Croatia or in mixed villages and towns of Bosnia-Herzegovina were as likely to choose political loyalties, citizenship (where they had a choice), and paths of flight in opposition to Chetniks that was as great as that to Ustasha; rather than memories of ethnic conflict, it was the antifascist character of the World War II struggle that remained decisive.
82. Janjić cites one such example at the time of the incidents in Tuzla that included shots fired at the local mosque. The army response under Colonel Kadić was to deny reports that the Sarajevo Corps had armed only Serbs. Since no one had claimed this, Janjić and others saw it as a trick to test the readiness of Muslims for an armed uprising in support of a rump Yugoslavia. 'Gradjanski Rat,' p. 123.
83. The cause of these events, beginning May 2, 1992, is not clear. The confrontation began when President Izetbegović returned from negotiations in Lisbon and was kidnapped on arrival at Sarajevo airport. In the ensuing negotiations, mediated by UN envoys, the agreement was made to release Izetbegović and to require YPA withdrawal in exchange for unblocked barracks and a secured exodus. Yet Izetbegović did not arrive on the plane he announced to UN forces, which had gone to the airport to provide a safe escort, and instead stopped over in Rome without explanation (and thus arrived to no escort late in the evening). Moreover, despite the commitment to secure YPA exodus, an ambush was staged.
84. Aleksandar Ćirić and Miloš Vasić, 'No Way Out: The JNA and the Yugoslav Wars,' *WarReport*, no. 17 (January 1993), p. 4.
85. Vego, 'Federal Army Deployments,' pp. 445–48, attempts to estimate the number of troops and amount of equipment left when the YPA withdrew. He also cites a dispute over what proportion of troops were actually from Bosnia – 'local Serbs' – between Belgrade, which claimed 80 percent of the 95,000 soldiers there in March 1992, and Sarajevo, which claimed no more than 20 percent, or 19,000. The YPA withdrew 14,000 troops by May 20.
86. Vego, 'Federal Army Deployments,' p. 446. A notable story about Mladić is that members of his immediate family were massacred in front of him by Croat Ustasha in World War II.
87. James Gow, 'The Yugoslav Army – An Update,' *Jane's Intelligence Review*, vol. 4 (November 1992), p. 501. This was not the last of the personnel changes, however, as

Milošević proceeded over the next three years to weaken the army and coopt its best talent with higher salaries and benefits into the internal security police forces, which were, as for Tudjman in Croatia, his base of political power and loyalty.

88. See, for example, 'Yugoslavia: Armament Industry Reportedly Booming,' *Delo* (Ljubljana), September 21, 1993.
89. Tim van Beveren, 'The Anglo-German Connection: Illegal Transfers Made Simple!' pp. 17–18; and Aleksandar Vasović, 'Braced (and Armed) for Confrontation,' *WarReport*, no. 17 (January 1993), p. 19; Zoran Kusovac, 'Stalemate Ended by Crack Troops,' *Jane's Defence Weekly*, November 7, 1992, p. 15; Milan Vego, 'The Croatian Navy,' *Jane's Intelligence Review*, vol. 5 (January 1993), pp. 11–16; Yves Debay and Paul Beaver, 'Croatian Forces Open New Front,' *Jane's Defence Weekly*, June 27, 1992, p. 1133. See also 'Capability, Weapons Supply of Croatian Army,' FBIS, *East Europe*, March 1, 1993, citing Belgrade *NIN* February 5, 1993, p. 15.
90. The Croatian navy was established September 11, 1991. Vego, 'The Croatian Navy,' pp. 11–16.
91. Serbia withheld food especially, a policy it attempted to defend in response to international criticism at the time of the May 1992 decision to impose economic sanctions on Serbia by arguing that Bosnians were making huge profits in selling Serbian food and that food was needed in Serbia. Croatia interrupted transport links, for example, by blowing up the bridge at Bosanski Šamac at the beginning of February 1992 and by putting barricades on the road and rail route connecting the Adriatic harbour at Ploče with Mostar and Sarajevo. In early February 1992, three weeks before the referendum on Bosnian independence, the price of cooking oil in Belgrade was 90 dinars a litre, in Sarajevo, 220 dinars; of milk, 30 dinars in Belgrade and 70 dinars in Sarajevo; of bread, 25 dinars in Belgrade and 50 dinars in Sarajevo. Average monthly salaries were in reverse proportion: 7,000 dinars in Sarajevo, and more than 15,000 in Belgrade. These figures are from the author's observations in both cities.
92. Mikhail Petkovski and others, 'Stabilization Efforts in the Republic of Macedonia,' *RFE/RL Research Report*, January 15, 1993, p. 34, and Hugh Poulton, 'The Republic of Macedonia after UN Recognition,' *RFE/RL Research Report*, June 4, 1993, pp. 23, 27.
93. Gow, 'Military-Political Affiliation,' p. 17; see also Glenny, *The Fall of Yugoslavia*, pp. 108–09. In a confidential report to authorities in Zagreb (the president, prime minister, minister of defence, and minister of internal affairs) on August 18, 1991, a central representative in the government of Vukovar described the activities (and recall, through the intervention of Josip Manolić) of Merčep (who later became head of the influential organization of Croatian Volunteers for the Defence of the Fatherland) and appealed 'for your intervention because the commune of Vukovar is a highly volatile crisis area in which armed conflicts on a large scale can break out any minute, and the city is almost under siege. The newly appointed persons continue the policy of Tomislav Merčep and the city is again victim of terror, armed strife and provocative shoot-outs with potentially unfathomable consequences. The policy pursued so far has

created an atmosphere of terror among the Croatian and Serbian population. The Croatian part of the population unanimously denounces such behaviour and feels disgraced and compromised and no longer wishes to bear responsibility for such a policy. As we do not feel in a position to sort things out with our local resources, we are asking you to urgently send here competent people who would help the legal institutions and authorities bring life back to normal.'

94. In a famous interview in the Belgrade weekly *Ilustrirana Politika* in March 1992, Stefanović admitted flying Šešelj all over the military front in July 1991, while General Aleksandar Vasiljević, former head of military intelligence services, admitted in an interview to *NIN* in 1992 that plans to stage a coup in Belgrade in September 1991 had failed because there were not sufficient military personnel present in the city.
95. Despite the cease-fire negotiated by UN envoy Cyrus Vance in Croatia, Croatian forces retaliated for Vukovar with a counteroffensive on Papuk at the end of November.
96. See Louise Branson, 'Crossing the Line in Bosnia's War,' *Christian Science Monitor*, October 19, 1992, p. 2.
97. Prime Minister Janez Drnovšek admitted September 17, 1992, in a speech at the Centre for Strategic and International Studies, Washington, D.C., that contracts signed with Iraq for tanks before Yugoslavia ended were being fulfilled as before by cooperating Slovene and Serbian firms. In April 1993, John Allcock, a British expert on the former Yugoslavia, told a BBC interviewer that enforcement of the economic sanctions against Serbia was naive because it ignored one of the primary loopholes – Slovene firms.
98. Tihomir Loza illustrates this problem with Kupres, in Herzegovina: the town had a slight Serb majority, followed by Croats and Muslims; it borders a district where Muslims form a small majority, followed by Croats and then Serbs. If division occurred along ethnic lines, 'Kupres must be Serb while Bugojno must be Muslim. But the HDZ has already included Bugojno as part of Herzeg-Bosnia, and in order to join it with Tomislavgrad and Livno all they need is the Kupres plateau.' Croat militias conquered the area in early 1992, the JNA and Serb paramilitaries took it from Croats, and because 'the significance of the Kupres plateau is strategic rather than economic . . . further clashes can be expected.' These occurred in late 1994, when a Bosnian government (Muslim) offensive led Bosnian Serbs to abandon the town to Bosnian Croats (in what appeared to be a secret agreement to prevent Bosnian Muslims from controlling the town). 'Herzegovina: A Key Battleground,' *YugoFax*, May 7, 1992, p. 9.
99. Vukovar is a natural river port for the Sava-Danube basin, and the opening of eastern Europe led Danubian states to hope that links between Atlantic Ocean and Black Sea ports would provide a substantial stimulus for economic recovery. The widening of the Danube with the Gabčikovo/Nagymaros dam – disputed between Slovakia and Hungary in 1992 – was critical, for example, to Slovakia's new development strategy based on Danube transport.

100. This was illustrated powerfully on January 22, 1993, when the government in Zagreb chose to ignore the terms of its signed cease-fire arrangement in the UN protected zones and to retake militarily the area around the Maslenica bridge (the previous structure destroyed by fighting in 1991) which linked Zagreb to the Dalmatian coast at Zadar, and control over the Peruča dam that had been assigned to UN supervision.
101. Jonathan S. Landay, 'A Centuries-Old Serb Enclave Stands Firm,' *Christian Science Monitor*, October 21, 1993, p. 6. One such case is the area of Mt. Ozren, a traditionally Serbian enclave of thirty-five villages surrounding a 500-year-old Serbian Orthodox monastery. Karadžić gave Ozren to the Muslim party at negotiations in August 1993 (the Owen-Stoltenberg plan). It is not economically viable and its communication and transportation lines are more oriented toward towns which the peace plans have put in Muslim-controlled areas. After the failure of this plan, however, the heavy loss of Serbian lives in fighting for Ozren and its religious-historical symbolism made this territorial concession nearly impossible politically for Karadžić in subsequent negotiations.
102. For example, the airfield at Banja Luka and the fuel depot at Bosanski Brod were particularly important, early targets of Serbian forces; the Marshal Tito airforce school at Mostar, the Sokol aircraft factory, and Mostar's position on the Neretva River controlling supply routes from the coast, the hydroelectric plant at Jajce and along the Neretva valley, the coastal shipbuilding industry (with its large military component), and the gunpowder, rocket fuel, and explosives plant at Vitez were Croatian targets; and the industrial heartland of central Bosnia, where most defence plants were located, over which Croat and Muslim forces battled through most of winter-spring 1993.
103. Aleksa Buha, *Basic Information*, January 22, 1993. For example, the north-south rail line that was the 'artery of economic life' in Bosnia-Herzegovina, and most of the hydroelectric plants, thermal energy potential, and coal basins remained outside Serb provinces.
104. On the first, see Hayden, 'Constitutional Nationalism,' pp. 654–73.

10

BOSNIA: PROTOTYPE OF A NATO PROTECTORATE

David Chandler

The Dayton Peace Agreement, the US-sponsored solution to the war for Bosnia concluded in Dayton, Ohio in November 1995, was hailed by US Secretary of State Warren Christopher as a victory for the people of Bosnia: 'Now the Bosnian people will have their own democratic say. This is a worthy goal in and of itself, because the only peace that can last in Bosnia is the peace that the people of the country freely chose.'[1]

According to the Dayton Agreement, there was to be a division of powers between military implementation of the peace agreement, under NATO authority, and civilian implementation, under an international High Representative, including election and media control under the Organisation for Security and Co-operation in Europe (OSCE). During this year of internationally supervised transition, there would be elections and the establishment of two types of joint institutions: the political institutions of the new state, which were to be elected and directly accountable to the people; and the economic, judicial and human rights institutions, which were to be supervised through the appointment of representatives from international institutions for five or six years.[2] This year of transition to, at least partial, self-governing democracy was due to end with the election of state and entity bodies in September 1996, symbolizing 'the democratic birth of the country'.[3] Although these bodies were elected under internationally supervised and ratified elections, the transitional international administration was prolonged for a further two-year 'consolidation period' and then, in December 1997, extended indefinitely. The extension of the time limits for international withdrawal and the creation of new mandates for NATO, the United Nations (UN), and the OSCE since Dayton have been justified by growing reference to the 'spirit' rather than the letter of the Agreement.

The international community has been free to redefine its mandates in Bosnia because the Dayton Agreement, like its successor proposed for Kosovo at Rambouillet, France, in February 1999, only bound the Balkan parties to it, not the international organizations who have given themselves the responsibility for implementing it. Ad hoc international forums such as the international Contact Group of the powers most concerned with Balkan issues (the US, Britain, Germany, France, Italy and Russia), and the Peace Implementation Council (PIC, formerly the International Conference on the Former Yugoslavia) meet to decide policy and then call on international institutions such as the UN, NATO, OSCE, European Union (EU), IMF and World Bank to draw up their own plans. None of these ad hoc forums or international institutions are party to or bound by any clauses of the Bosnia (or Kosovo) agreements.[4]

The lack of constraints on international institutions extending their mandates and powers is revealed by the fact that every international forum on Bosnian policy-making has further extended the network of ad hoc international regulation. The NATO mandate in Bosnia under IFOR (implementation force), due to expire in December 1996, was extended for a further eighteen months under SFOR (stabilization force) and then further extended a year later, this time indefinitely. On similar time-scales, the UN, OSCE and Office of the High Representative (OHR) mandates in Bosnia were temporarily and then indefinitely extended. The powers of these institutions were also expanded, giving them unique scope of authority. Acknowledging the lack of military threat to NATO forces, the new mandate further emphasized the humanitarian economic and policing roles. The OSCE's mandate to regulate elections extended from the organization of the electoral process itself to include novel powers to install post-election administrations and to stipulate the allocation of governing responsibilities, in effect, ratifying elections on the basis of the actions of elected representatives once in post. Along with the official international institutions involved in regulating Bosnia there are also around two hundred international non-governmental organizations involved, on both an official and unofficial basis, in civilian policy implementation. As the *Times* columnist Simon Jenkins notes, the small Bosnian state has become 'the world capital of interventionism'.[5]

The High-Handed Representative

The institution whose powers have extended the most since the Dayton Agreement was signed has been the OHR —the office of international community's High Representative, or Chief of Implementation Mission, in Rambouillet terminology. Under the Dayton provisions, it was envisaged that the role of the High Representative would end once new institutions of government were elected in September 1996. After the elections, the OHR was given authority to draw up two twelve-month 'action plans' for government of the new state. These plans were to be approved by the PIC, not the Bosnian government. In implementing these plans, the international community initially gave lip-service to the democratic mandate of Bosnian politicians, stating that the High Representative could make recommendations to the government and, in case of dispute, make these recommendations public.[6] Six months later, the PIC gave the High Representative the power to set deadlines for compliance with his recommended measures, with the power to impose restrictions on travel abroad for obstructive Bosnian representatives and to impose economic sanctions at a local or regional level in the case of non-compliance. At the same time, he was given the authority to curtail or suspend any media network or programmes which were held to contravene 'either the spirit or the letter' of Dayton.[7]

In December 1997, the High Representative's powers were extended to deciding the time, location and chairmanship of government meetings, enacting measures which had not been accepted by Bosnian authorities, and dismissing non-compliant elected officials at every level of government.[8] The High Representative himself demonstrated the flexibility of international institutional powers over Bosnia, claiming that 'You do not [have] power handed to you on a platter. You just seize it. If you use this power well, no one will contest it. I have already achieved this.'[9] The absence of obstacles to the extension of international regulation means that the High Representative has more autocratic control than even the colonial administrators of the past: 'if you read Dayton carefully . . . [it] gives me the possibility to interpret my own authorities and powers'.[10] Today, the OHR has headquarters both in Brussels and Sarajevo, one for developing policy with other international bodies and the other for implementing policy on the ground. The Sarajevo office, nicknamed 'The Presidency', is staffed by over two hundred international policy-makers, with units responsible for elections, economic reconstruction, humanitarian issues, legal affairs, media issues, refugee return and political affairs.[11]

Far from facilitating autonomy, the transformation of the Dayton mandates has led to the creation of a US-run international protectorate in Bosnia. President Clinton, the Department of Defence and the Joint Chiefs of Staff have, in practice, established the framework of international engagement in the Bosnian state and the UN, OSCE, EU, World Bank, IMF and other international bodies have run their own empire-building projects within this.[12] Compared with the vast international bureaucratic-military machine of around 50,000 international troops and administrators, the elected institutions have little capacity for policy-making or implementation.

Assessments

There is little evidence that international policy is effective in cohering the new Bosnian state and overcoming the divisions of the war. Instead of strengthening the central institutions of the new state and facilitating compromise and negotiation, the international administration has removed policy-making capacity from Bosnian institutions. This has weakened the state and entity institutions which seek to unite society and, at the same time, has reinforced ethnic identification.

The constantly expanding role of the multitude of international organizations has inevitably restricted the capacity of Bosnian people to discuss, develop and decide on vital questions of concern. At state level, the Bosnian Muslim, Croat and Serb representatives can discuss international policy proposals under the guidance of the OHR, but, at most, can make minor amendments or delay the implementation of externally prepared rules and regulations. Even this limited accountability has been diminished by the High Representative, who has viewed democratic consensus-building in Bosnian state bodies such as the tripartite Presidency, Council of Ministers and State Parliament as an unnecessary delay to imposing international policy. Compared to the swift signature of the chief administrator's pen, the working out of democratic accountability through the joint institutions was seen as 'painfully cumbersome and ineffective'.[13] At the Bonn PIC summit in December 1997, the 'cumbersome' need for elected Bosnian representatives to assent to international edicts was removed and the High Representative was empowered both to dismiss elected representatives who obstructed policy and to impose legislation directly. The international community thereby assumed complete legislative and executive power over the formally independent state.

Dayton divided the Bosnian state into two entities, the Muslim-Croat Federation, with 51 per cent of the territory, and the Serb entity, Republika Srpska (RS), with 49 per cent. There was little autonomy for elected representatives at either entity level. In the Federation, policy has been devised by the OHR in close co-operation with US state officials. The ad hoc Federation Forum co-chaired by the Principal Deputy High Representative and Assistant Secretary of State met on a monthly basis with Muslim and Croat representatives, to present international proposals, and Special Groups were set up on a similar ad hoc basis to circumvent elected forums and develop policy in different areas. The lack of support among both sides for imposed Federation policies was dismissed by the Senior Deputy High Representative: 'I don't care. I am simply not interested in who does not want the Federation: this is a concept that we will implement . . . We dictate what will be done.'[14]

In Republika Srpska, the international regulation of policy-making was even more disputed. The seat of government was moved from Pale to Banja Luka and IMF and OHR economic packages prevented the RS régime from raising finances independently of the international community. In July 1997, the international community supported the dissolution of the RS Parliamentary Assembly and overruled the RS constitutional court to force new elections and then organized the selection of a governing coalition which excluded the largest party, the SDS (Serb Democratic Party). In March 1999, before the NATO military campaign over Kosovo, the High Representative took international interference in entity politics further by dismissing the newly elected RS President, Nikola Poplasen.

Consensus versus Consent

At city and local levels, the international community has similarly had a free hand to overrule elected representatives and impose policy under the rubric of multi-ethnic governance. The divided city of Mostar provides a good example of how this works in practice: seats are allocated in advance on the basis of ethnicity and then, under international guidance, 'consensus' politics are enforced against the Croat representatives from West Mostar and Muslim representatives from East Mostar. International regulation marginalizes Mostari voters and removes any local accountability for policy-making. In the disputed region of Brčko, under a Supervisory Order on Multi-Ethnic

Administration, an international administrator regulates the composition of the consultative assembly and issues binding regulations. As the *Washington Post* described, his 'kingly powers' extend 'right down to determining who will live in which house, the list of required attendees at meetings of the local police chiefs, the ethnic composition of the local municipal council and the pace at which privatization will proceed'.[15]

At municipal level, the powers of the international community have also grown since Dayton. In the first two years of international administration, international pressure at this level was limited to the threat of withdrawing reconstruction aid. At the end of 1997, the international community developed two new lines of approach. Firstly, using the post-Bonn powers, the High Representative began to dismiss local mayors who were seen as obstructive. Secondly, following the extension of the OSCE's powers for the municipal elections of September 1997, the international community disregarded election results to impose power-sharing administrations and, in some cases, suspended local assemblies, replacing them with executive boards run by international appointees.[16]

Dayton promised the decentralization of political power and creation of multi-ethnic administrations in Bosnia in order to cohere state institutions and provide security to ethnic minorities and safeguard their autonomy. This has not been delivered under the international administration. At state, entity, city and municipal levels, a clear pattern has emerged where elected majorities have been given little control over policy-making. However, this power has not been decentralized to give minority groups security and a stake in government but, rather, transferred to the international institutions and re-centralized in the hands of the High Representative. Today, the international community regulates Bosnian life, all the way down to the minutiae of local community service provision, employment practices, school admissions and sports.[17] Multi-ethnic administrations exist on paper, but the fact that the consensus attained in these fora is an imposed one, not one autonomously negotiated, is important. Compliance with international edicts imposed by the threat of dismissals or economic sanctions does little to give either majorities or minorities a stake in the process, nor to encourage the emergence of a negotiated accountable solution that could be viable in the long term.

Hollow Democracy

The institutions of Bosnian government are hollow structures, not designed to operate autonomously. The Bosnian state's Council of Ministers, with the nominal role of assenting to pre-prepared policy, has few staff or resources and is aptly described by the OHR as 'effectively, little more than an extended working group'.[18] Muslim, Croat and Serb representatives have all argued for greater ethnic autonomy in policy-making, and have attempted to uphold the rights protected in the 'letter' of the Dayton Agreement against the ad-hoc reinterpretation of international powers under the 'spirit of Dayton'.[19] As an advisor to Bosnian President Izetbegović noted, there is a contradiction between the stated aims of the international protectorate and its consequences: 'A protectorate solution is not good, because the international community would bring all the decisions which would decrease all the functions of Bosnia-Herzegovina institutions. The High Representative's mandate is actually, an opposite one, to strengthen the Bosnia-Herzegovina institutions.'[20]

The frailty of Bosnian institutions has perpetuated the fragmentation of political power and reliance on personal and local networks of support which were prevalent during the Bosnian war. Both Susan Woodward and Katherine Verdery provide useful analyses of the impact on Bosnian society of the external undermining of state and entity centres of power and security.[21] The lack of cohering political structures has meant that Bosnian people are forced to rely on more narrow and parochial survival mechanisms, which has meant that ethnicity has maintained its wartime relevance as a political resource.

It would appear that the removal of mechanisms of political accountability has done little to broaden Bosnian people's political outlook. The removal of sites of accountable political power has, in fact, reinforced general insecurity and atomization which has, in turn, led to the institutionalization of much narrower political relations in the search for individual links to those with influence and power. The narrowing of the political sphere and reliance on individual survival strategies has assumed a generalized pattern across society. The 'new feudalism' noted by some commentators and the continued existence of weak para-state structures in Muslim and Croat areas of the Federation are symptomatic of the vacuum of integrative institutional power at state and entity level, rather than some intrinsically disintegrative dynamic.[22]

The dynamic of the Dayton process has been to institutionalize fears and insecurities through high-handed international rule, disempowering Bosnian people and their representatives. With little influence over, or relationship to, the decision-making process, there is concern that entity boundaries or rights to land, employment and housing can easily be brought into question. The extended mandates of the international institutions have undermined the power of the main political parties and their elected representatives, but have not created the political basis of a unitary Bosnia, except in so far as it is one artificially imposed by, and dependent upon, the international community.

The Anti-Democratic Consensus

There has been little regret over the still-birth of democracy in Bosnia. And there has been even less critical consideration of the role that over-extended international regulation has had in institutionalizing ethnic divisions and weakening political structures. The international institutions running the small state have argued that international mandates make for better democracy than the electoral competition of the ballot box. The Chairman-in-Office of the OSCE has asserted that the 'political level' of the Bosnian voters is 'not very high'.[23] The OHR, equally, has little time for democratic accountability, its representatives alleging that 'Bosnia is a deeply sick society, ill at ease with even the most basic principles of democracy'.[24] The High Representative himself has stated that elected Bosnian representatives are not serving the real interests of their voters and, therefore, have no right to challenge his rulings.[25] These views have been supported by international leaders, the then German Foreign Minister, Klaus Kinkel, openly confirming that the international community had little hesitation in moving to take decisions contrary to the will of the Bosnian people.[26]

Perhaps surprisingly, however, the institution with the lowest opinion of the Bosnian electorate is the Democratisation Branch of the OSCE Mission in Bosnia. Jasna Malkoc, a Senior Co-ordinator, argues that Bosnian people are incapable of handling electoral competition: 'Political parties are a new appearance. People do not know how to cope and neither do their leaders . . . People just follow the flock.'[27] Central to the Branch's approach is the understanding that the Bosnian population, 'damaged' or traumatized by the war and the transition from one-party state regulation, are not capable of acting independently or making choices between 'right' and 'wrong'. Taking over the language of empowerment from the psycho-social counselling work being developed in the war, the new focus is on the capacity of individuals for democracy, as opposed to broader political processes, thereby ignoring the impact of international regulation in shaping the political climate. If anything, the Democratisation Branch work of community education and empowerment is more invidious to democracy than the enforced international administration because it implicitly assumes that Bosnian people are incapable of rational choice. Once the capacity of Bosnian people as rational political actors is negated, there is no reason, in principle, for international administration to be seen as merely temporary or transitional, nor for democracy to be seen as preferable.[28]

Liberal Elitism

This elitist view of the incapacity of Balkan people to cope with democracy has not been challenged by the critics of international engagement in the Balkans. In fact, the most vociferous critics of international policy go further in arguing that there is still too much freedom and autonomy in Bosnia. Ironically, ill-informed liberal critics assert that international institutions have failed to intervene enough to weaken the powers of elected representatives. *The Guardian* argues: 'The West's mistake was to set too much store by holding elections in Bosnia before the conditions were ripe . . . The West allowed Bosnia's politicians too much power over the last three years [since Dayton]'.[29]

Dayton's critics argue that far too much respect has been given to elected representatives, because the West either has a fatalistic view that there is nothing that can be done about ethnic rivalries or is not willing to commit the resources needed to confront Balkan political elites.[30] While the OSCE and the OHR have an ambiguous attitude towards elections, setting them up as democratic enough to legitimize the governing institutions, but not legitimate enough to allow the dominant parties to challenge the OHR's right to impose policy, the liberal critics see elections as highly problematic and bad for democracy in Bosnia. In Britain, some of the campaigning liberal press have called for an end to elections and an 'open-ended occupation' or a '*benign colonial regime*'.[31]

Conclusion

Throughout the international engagement with Bosnia, the powers of the international community have expanded with little criticism. This process has continued through the Kosovo crisis. The *Guardian* boasts that 'we argued from the start . . . for a land war to capture Kosovo and turn it into an international protectorate' and its sister paper, the *Observer*, asserts that 'the only viable course is to use the Bosnian precedent and establish a NATO protectorate in Kosovo'.[32] This liberal-led consensus has facilitated the denial of democracy under international administration in the Balkans. The historically understood meaning of democracy – legitimacy through popular accountability to the electorate, the *demos* – has been replaced by a new and opposite meaning: adherence to regulations laid down by external institutions. The idea that Balkan people are ill-suited to democracy and unable to govern themselves has legitimated the growth of international mandates in the region. This dynamic towards Balkan protectorates is reflected in the increase in powers awarded to NATO and the international community under Rambouillet.

This essay has attempted to question this consensus and suggest that there is an alternative to the cycle of greater and greater international mandates and the establishment of a new set of protectorates in the Balkans. The one alternative that is never advocated by the interventionists is that of allowing people in the region greater autonomy to develop their own solutions. The international experience of Bosnia suggests that any form of international protectorate will intensify and institutionalize ethnic divisions. The trend towards law-making by international edict makes it impossible for any negotiated compromise to arise between Serbs, Croats and Muslims. In turn, this means that there is little capacity for Bosnian institutions to unify society and overcome divisions. The lesson for Kosovo is that more social autonomy, not less, may be the best path to stability and post-conflict peace-building.

Unfortunately this lesson has gone unheeded. Under Rambouillet, elections were to be held within nine months of the agreement although the Chief of the Implementation Mission was to remain the de facto ruler of the province, with the power to remove elected representatives, curtail institutions and close down media organizations, with no right of appeal.[33] Draconian as Rambouillet was, the post-war set-up in Kosovo has accorded even less autonomy to the people of the province. Without any agreed constitutional settlement, the international state-builders are under no pressure to set out clear mandates for the UN, NATO or the OSCE, nor any timescale for the introduction of some form of representative government.

In July 1999, representatives from the G7 powers and 11 other Western states decided Bernard Kouchner, the former French Health Minister, was to be the international governor of the autonomous province. No Kosovars were involved in the selection process. There will be no elections for Kosovar government representatives for at least a year and probably much longer, although a transitional council, hand-picked on the grounds of compliant behaviour, is to be chosen by Kouchner himself.[34]

The ethnic Albanians are discovering that removing Belgrade appointees from positions of influence in the legal system, health, education and the media is not necessarily a step towards greater autonomy or self-rule. There have been protests about high-handed international regulation in each of these spheres as Americans and Europeans have taken on the formerly Serb-held positions. The UN has set up a unique legal system where KFOR, the only recognized police force, arrest people under their own national laws and bring them before panels of UN-appointed judges with the power to make the law as they go, using the Yugoslav penal code as a guide only.[35]

Similarly with the media: the departure of the Serbian local state TV managers meant that the UN took over, not the ethnic-Albanian managerial team.[36] At Priština hospital the UN appointment of a British manager has resulted in ethnic-Albanian doctors organizing a parallel system, similar to that used under the old Serb regime.[37]

Autonomy for Kosovo under the UN and NATO is increasingly looking no more democratic than life under the Yugoslav regime. KFOR clashes with ethnic Albanian KLA supporters indicate that UN rule over the province will similarly have to be enforced through military and police security actions. This highlights a key difference to the Bosnia situation where opposition to UN/NATO regulation was mitigated by the fact that they ostensibly helped guarantee all three communities a certain amount of protection. In Kosovo the limitation of autonomy is a direct attack on the rights of the majority Albanian community.

The destabilizing and fragmentary impact of the international protectorate in Kosovo should not be underestimated. NATO's war to force the province's autonomy has already broken the links that existed between Serb and Albanian communities and destroyed much of the economic basis of Kosovar society. The UN's sidelining of the KLA 'provisional government' has led to faction-fighting and the creation of a plethora of 'alternative governments' as competing ethnic-Albanian elites scramble for the patronage of the international administration.

The lack of democracy in Kosovo and the weakness of new political bodies will make it impossible for Albanian institutions to regulate and re-cohere society; even the parallel institutions that existed under Serb rule will disintegrate under UN pressure and international NGO activity. It seems likely that clan politics will re-emerge to fill the vacuum, as people seek some form of security. Any remaining Serbs, ethnic Turks and Gypsies will bear the full brunt of Albanian frustrations at being marginalized from political decision-making. As in Bosnia, international rule is inevitably institutionalizing inter-communal divisions, setting back any long-term settlement for the region.

Notes

1. 'Statement by Secretary of State Warren Christopher on the Bosnian Elections, released by the Office of the Spokesman 18 September 1996. US Department of State. Available from *http://www.state. gov.* [Accessed 2 February 1998].
2. *The General Agreement for Peace in Bosnia and Herzegovina.* Available from *http://www.ohr.int/gfa/gfa-home.htm.* [Accessed 21 May 1998].
3. *Chairman's Conclusion of the Peace Implementation Council, Florence, 13–14 June,* para. 27. Office of the High Representative. Available from *http:/ohr.int/docu/d960613.htm.* [Accessed 4 February 1997].
4. P. Szasz, 'Current Developments: the Protection of Human Rights through the Dayton/Paris Peace Agreement on Bosnia', *American Journal of International Law,* vol. 90, 1996, p. 304.
5. S. Jenkins, 'Ulster of the Balkans: British Troops Have Been Sent on a Mission Impossible in Bosnia', *The Times,* 17 December 1997.
6. *Conclusions: Guiding Principles of the Civilian Consolidation Plan. Ministerial Meeting of the Peace Implementation Council Steering Board, Paris, 14 November 1996,* para. 6. Office of the High Representative. Available from *http://www.ohr.int/docu/d961114b.htm.* [Accessed 4 February 1997].
7. *Communiqué: Political Declaration from Ministerial Meeting of the Steering Board of the Peace Implementation Council, Sintra, 30 May,* paras 35, 38 & 37. Office of the High Representative. Available from *http://www.ohr.int/docu/d970530a.htm.* [Accessed 19 August 1997].
8. *Summary of Conclusions: Bonn Peace Implementation Conference 1997: 'Bosnia and Herzegovina 1998: Self-Sustaining Structures', Bonn, 10 December,* ix, para. 2. Office of the High Representative. Available from *http://www.ohr.int/docu/d971210b.htm.* [Accessed 12 December 1997].
9. J. Rodriguez, 'Our Man in Sarajevo', *El Pais,* 29 March 1998. Translation available from *http://www.ohr.int/articles/a980329a.htm.* [Accessed 4 May 1998].
10. Interview with Carlos Westendorp, *Slobodna Bosna,* 30 November 1997. Available from *http://www.ohr.int/press/i971130a.htm.* [Accessed 29 May 1998].

11. C. Hedges, 'A Spaniard Rules Bosnia with a Strong Hand', *The New York Times*, 8 December 1998; *Report of the High Representative for Implementation of the Bosnian Peace Agreement to the Secretary-General of the United Nations*, 14 March 1996, para. 5. Available from *http://www.ohr.int/report/r960714a.htm.* [Accessed 29 October 1996].
12. International Crisis Group, 'Changing the Logic of Bosnian Politics: ICG Discussion Paper on Electoral Reform', 10 March 1998. Available from *http://www.intl-crisis-group.org/projects/bosnia/report/bh32rep.htm.* [Accessed 21 May 1998]. 'Address to the Pacific Council on International Policy', Ambassador Robert S. Gelbard, Special Representative of the President and Secretary of State for the Implementation of the Dayton Peace Agreement, Los Angeles, California, 27 January. Available from *http://www.state.gov/www/policy_r...s/1998/980127_gelbard_bosnia.html.* [Accessed 21 May 1998]. 'Statement on Bosnia before the House National Security Committee', Secretary of State Madeleine K. Albright, Washington DC, 18 March 1998. Released by the Office of the Spokesman, US Department of State. Available from *http://secretary.state.gov/www/statements/1998/980318.html.* [Accessed 21 May 1998].
13. *Office of the High Representative Bulletin* 62, 11 October 1997. Available from *http://www.ohr.int/bulletins/b971011.htm.* [Accessed 3 November 1997].
14. E. Suljagic, 'Interview with Senior Deputy High Representative Hanns Schumacher', *Dani*, 11 April 1998. Available from *http://www.ohr.int/press/i980411a.htm.* [Accessed 29 May 1998].
15. L. Hockstader, 'A Bosnian Town in Limbo', *The Washington Post*, 8 October 1998.
16. *Bosnia and Herzegovina TV News Summary*, 15 July 1998. Office of the High Representative e-mail service.
17. *Return and Reconstruction Task Force Report*, December 1997, para. 5.7. Office of the High Representative. Available from *http://www.ohr.int/rrtf/r9712.htm.* [Accessed 1 April 1998].
18. *Report of the High Representative for Implementation of the Bosnian Peace Agreement to the Secretary-General of the United Nations*, 11 July 1997, para. 24. Available from *http://www.ohr.int/reports/r970711a.htm.* [Accessed 19 August 1997].
19. D. Chandler, *Bosnia: Faking Democracy After Dayton*, London 1999, p. 71.
20. *Bosnia and Herzegovina TV News Summary*, 10 November 1997. Office of the High Representative e-mail service.
21. S.L. Woodward, *Balkan Tragedy: Chaos and Dissolution After the Cold War*, Washington, DC 1995; K. Verdery, 'Nationalism, Postsocialism, and Space in Eastern Europe', *Social Research*, vol. 63, no. 1, 1996, pp. 82–3.
22. B. Deacon and P. Stubbs, 'International Actors and Social Policy Development in Bosnia-Herzegovina: Globalism and the "New Feudalism"', *Journal of European Social Policy*, vol. 8 no. 2, 1998, pp. 99–115.
23. 'OSCE Criticises Bosnian Serb Vote', *RFE/RL Newsline*, vol. 1, no. 168, II, 26 November 1997. Available from *http://www.rferl.org/newsline/search.*
24. 'Clearing the Bosnian Air', *The Washington Post*, editorial, 6 October 1997.

25. K. Coleman, 'Sceptic Serbs Doubt the Plavsic Revolution', *Guardian,* 22 November 1997.
26. *Serb Radio Television Banja Luka News Summary,* 10 December 1997. Office of the High Representative e-mail service.
27. Interview by the author with Jasna Malkoc, OSCE Senior Co-ordinator for Democratisation/NGO Development, Sarajevo, 16 June 1997.
28. See further D. Chandler, 'Democratization in Bosnia: the Limits of Civil Society Building Strategies', *Democratization,* vol. 5, no. 4, 1998, pp. 78–102.
29. 'No Retreat: Bosnia Must Keep Dayton Rules', *Guardian,* editorial, 16 September 1998.
30. For example, T. Gallagher, 'A Culture of Fatalism Towards the Balkans: Long-Term Western Attitudes and Approaches', paper presented at the BISA 22nd Annual Conference, Leeds, 15–17 December 1997.
31. M. Woollacott, 'Bosnia's Choice: it's Vote or Die', *Guardian,* 14 September 1996; J. Borger, 'Trials and Error for a Bosnian Solution', *Guardian,* 7 September 1996.
32. 'A Choice That Cannot Wait', *Guardian,* editorial, 7 May 1999; 'There Is No Alternative to this War', *Observer,* editorial, 28 March 1999.
33. Implementation I, Chapter 5, *Interim Agreement for Peace and Self-Government in Kosovo.* Available from *http://www.transnational.org.* [Accessed 24 April 1999].
34. L. Rozen, 'Follow the leader', *Salon,* 2 July 1999.
35. N. Price, 'Judges get to work in Kosovo', *Associated Press,* 3 July 1999.
36. J. Steele, 'UN forces fight to make old foes work together', *Guardian,* 1 July 1999.
37. Ibid., and J. Steele, 'Reversals in workplace leave Albanians on top', *Guardian,* 8 July 1999.

11

THE CRIMINALIZATION OF ALBANIA

Michel Chossudovsky

I. The Historical Background to the Albanian Crisis of 1997

Following the demise of the Communist State in 1991, Western capitalism has come to symbolize for many Albanians the end of an era, as well as the uncertain promise of a better life. In a cruel irony, production and earnings have plummeted under the brunt of the free market reforms inflicted by Western donors and creditors. Since 1991, the national economy has been thoroughly revamped under the supervision of the Bretton Woods institutions. With most of the state-owned enterprises spearheaded into liquidation, unemployment and poverty have become rampant.

President Ramiz Alia, Enver Hoxha's chosen successor, had already initiated an overture to Western capitalism: diplomatic relations had been restored with Bonn in 1987, leading to expanded trade with the European Community. In 1990, at its Ninth Plenum, the Albanian Workers' Party (AWP) adopted an economic reform programme which encouraged foreign investment and provided greater autonomy to managers of state-owned enterprises. These reforms also allowed for the accumulation of private wealth by members of the Communist nomenklatura. In April 1990, Prime Minister Adil Carcani announced confidently that Albania was eager to participate in the Conference on European Cooperation and Security, opening the door to the establishment of close ties with Western defence institutions, including NATO.

President Ramiz Alia was reelected by a multiparty Parliament in May 1991. The defunct Albanian Workers Party was rebaptised, and a coalition government between the new 'Socialists' and the opposition Democratic

Party was formed. Also in 1991, full diplomatic relations with Washington were restored: Secretary of State James Baker visited Tirana, and Albania requested full membership of the Bretton Woods institutions.

Meanwhile, amidst the chaos of hyperinflation and street riots which preceded the 1992 elections, German, Italian and American business interests had carefully positioned themselves, forging political alliances as well as 'joint ventures' with the former Communist establishment. The opposition Democratic Party (in principle committed to Western-style democracy) was led by Sali Berisha, a former Secretary of the Communist Party and a member of Enver Hoxha's inner circle. Berisha's election campaign had been generously funded by the West.

The IMF/World Bank-sponsored reforms

Western capital was anxious to secure a firm grip over the reigns of macroeconomic policy. The IMF/World Bank-sponsored reforms were set in motion immediately after the electoral victory of the Democrats and the inauguration of President Sali Berisha in May 1992. Economic borders were torn down, Albanian industry and agriculture were 'opened up'. Adopted in several stages, the ill-fated IMF-sponsored reforms reached their inevitable climax in late 1996 with the ruin of the industrial sector and the near-disintegration of the banking system. The fraudulent 'pyramid' investment funds which had mushroomed under the Berisha regime closed their doors. The faded promises of the 'free market' evaporated; millions of dollars of life savings had been squandered, the money siphoned out of the country. One third of the population was defrauded with many people selling their houses and land.

Some $1.5 billion had been deposited in the 'ponzi' schemes, with remittances from Albanian workers in Greece and Italy representing a sizeable portion of total deposits. Yet the amounts of money which had transited in and out of the investment funds were significantly larger. The Puglian Sacra Corona Unita and the Neapolitan Camorra mafias had used the pyramids to launder vast amounts of dirty money, part of which was reinvested in the acquisition of state property and land under Tirana's privatization programme. The 'ponzi' schemes were allegedly also used by Italy's crime syndicates as a point of transit – i.e., to reroute dirty money towards safe offshore banking havens in Western Europe. These shady investment funds were an integral part of the economic reforms inflicted by Western creditors.

The application of 'strong economic medicine' under the guidance of the Washington-based Bretton Woods institutions had contributed to wrecking the banking system and precipitating the collapse of the Albanian economy. Since their inception in 1991–92, the free market reforms had also generated an environment which fostered the progress of illicit trade (notably in narcotics and arms sales) and the criminalization of state institutions.

Controlled by the ruling Democratic Party, Albania's largest financial 'pyramid', VEFA Holding, had been set up by the Guëguë 'families' of Northern Albania with the tacit support of Western banking interests. According to one report, VEFA was under investigation in Italy in 1997 for its ties to the Mafia, which allegedly used VEFA to launder large amounts of dirty money.[1] The pyramids helped finance the campaign of the Democratic Party ahead of the June 1996 elections, as well as being used by Party officials to transfer money swiftly out of the country.[2] According to the *Christian Science Monitor*, 'Several of the multi-million-dollar schemes lent their support to the ruling Democratic Party in last year's [1996] parliamentary and local elections . . . To date, no country has investigated the link between governments and the schemes, and critics point to a dearth of fraud-related legislation.'[3]

'Foundation fever' was used in the most blatant manner to bolster Berisha's euphoric 1996 re-election bid. Widely accused of poll-rigging, the Democratic Party had branded the logos of the pyramids in its 1996 campaign posters. Echoing the get-rich-quick frenzy of the 'ponzi' schemes, the Berisha regime had promised: 'With us everybody wins'.

An 'economic success story'

The alleged links of the Albanian state apparatus to organized crime were well known to Western governments and intelligence agencies, yet President Sali Berisha had been commended by Washington for his efforts toward establishing a multiparty democracy 'with legal guarantees of human rights'. Echoing the US State Department, the Bretton Woods institutions (which had overseen the deregulation of the Albanian banking system), had touted Albania as an 'economic success story': 'Albania's performance on macroeconomic policy and structural reforms has been remarkably good since 1992'.[4]

World Bank Director for Central Europe and Asia Jean Michel Severino, on a visit to Tirana in the fall of 1996, had praised Berisha for the country's 'fast growth and generally positive results': the economy 'has bounced back quicker than in other [transition] countries'. A few months later, the scam surrounding the fraudulent 'pyramids' and their alleged links to organised crime was unveiled. As one commentator remarked, 'In all the euphoria about double-digit growth rates, few bothered to notice that the revenue was almost all coming from criminal activity or artificial sources, such as foreign aid and remittances sent home by Albanians working abroad.'[5]

In February 1997, Prime Minister Alekxander Meksi grimly admitted in a statement to Parliament that the country was on 'the brink of macroeconomic chaos . . . a real economic catastrophe . . . even worse than in 1992,' following the initial injection of IMF 'shock treatment'.[6] President Berisha had himself reappointed by Parliament; a state of emergency was in force which 'gave police power to shoot stone-throwers on sight. The main opposition newspaper was set afire, apparently by the secret police, less than 12 hours after the introduction of draconian press censorship laws.'[7] Prime Minister Meksi was sacked in early March 1997; the Commander in Chief of the Armed Forces, General Shemë Kosova, was put under house arrest and replaced by General Adam Copani. The latter – who over the years had established close personal ties to NATO headquarters – was responsible for coordinating with Western governments the activities of the military-humanitarian operation ordered by the UN Security Council.

The economy had come to a standstill, poverty was rampant, the Albanian state was in total disarray leading to mass protest and civil unrest; yet until the formation of an interim government in March 1997, the West's endorsement of the Berisha regime remained impervious.

The bankruptcy programme

The pyramid scam was the direct consequence of economic and financial deregulation. Under the IMF/World Bank-sponsored reforms initiated since the outset of the Berisha regime in 1992, most of the large public enterprises had been earmarked for liquidation or forced bankruptcy, leading to mass unemployment. Under the World Bank programme, budgetary support for the State Owned Enterprises (SOEs) would be slashed while 'clearly identifying which enterprises are to be allowed access to public resources and under which conditions'.[8] This mechanism contributed to rendering inoperative a large part of the nation's productive assets. Credit to state enterprises had already been frozen, with a view to speeding up the bankruptcy process.

A bankruptcy law was also enacted (modelled on that imposed on

Yugoslavia in 1989). The World Bank had demanded that 'restructuring efforts include splitting of SOEs to make them more manageable . . . and prepare them for privatization. The state-owned medium-sized and large enterprises, including public utilities, would be privatized through the mass privatization program (MPP) . . . for which vouchers are being distributed to the citizens.'[9]

The most profitable state enterprises were initially transferred to holding companies controlled by members of the former nomenklatura. State assets within the portfolio of these holding companies were to be auctioned off to foreign capital, according to a calendar agreed upon with the Bretton Woods institutions. The privatization programme had led virtually overnight to the development of a property-owning class, firmly committed to the tenets of neoliberalism. In Northern Albania, this class was associated with the Guëguë 'families' linked to the Democratic Party. According to one report, the traditional Northern tribal clans had also developed links with Italy's crime syndicates.[10]

In turn, this rapid accumulation of private wealth had led to a spurt of luxury housing and imports, including large numbers of shiny Mercedes. Tirana has one of the largest per capita concentrations of Mercedes Benz automobiles in Europe, a large share of which are stolen vehicles, smuggled in; almost every second car in the capital is a Mercedes. The import of cars had of course been boosted by the influx of dirty money. The torrent of hard currency loans granted by multilateral creditors also contributed to fuelling the import of luxury goods. Imports almost doubled from 1989 to 1995. Exports, on the other hand, had dwindled, exacerbating the country's balance of payments crisis.[11]

Financial deregulation

The Albanian Parliament had passed a law in 1992 allowing for the creation (with few or no restrictions) of 'foundations' and 'holding companies' involved in commercial banking activities. The World Bank had insisted on 'an appropriate framework for creating new [small and medium-sized] private banks and encouraging informal money lenders and non-bank financial intermediaries to enter the formal financial intermediation circuit'.[12]

The freeze on commercial bank credit imposed under IMF advice had encouraged the development of the informal banking system. As an Albanian banking expert described the process:

> We observed the development of informal financial schemes . . . the ceilings imposed [by the central bank] on the [state commercial banks] obliged them to freeze credit. Due to IMF restrictions, there was simply no credit available through the formal banking system. The informal banks were allowed to develop; remittances were channelled into 'financial foundations', encouraging the development of a parallel banking system . . . Everybody knew it was a dirty game, nobody was interested in intervening.[13]

The 'pyramids' had thereby become an integral part of the untamed banking environment proposed by the Bretton Woods institutions to the Berisha government. The various funds and 'foundations' were to operate freely alongside the Albanian state banking system, comprising the National Commercial Bank, the Rural Commercial Bank and the Savings Bank. The 1992 law, while supporting the expansion of private financial intermediaries, nonetheless retained certain 'supervisory functions' for the Central Bank authorities. Article 28 of the law provided for the establishment of a Reserve Fund at the Central Bank with a view to 'safeguarding the interests of depositors'.[14] The provisions of Article 28 were later incorporated into a special Article on banks and financial institutions contained in the World Bank-sponsored Draft Law on Bankruptcy, presented to the Albanian Parliament in late 1994. This Article provided for the establishment of a 'deposit insurance fund' under the supervision of the Central Bank.

While the law was being debated in the Legislature, the IMF advisory team at the Central Bank intervened and demanded that this clause be scrapped because it was 'at this time inconsistent with Fund staff advice'. (No other reason was given.) Also, the IMF experts advised, normal bankruptcy procedure should not be applied to banks because that would have meant that the creditors of an insolvent bank could ask that bank to stop operations. This was inadvisable, an IMF expert claimed, because 'in Albania, which has so few banks, this is perhaps a matter solely for the bank regulatory authorities' – and that meant the Central Bank.[15]

In turn, the foreign consultant who had drafted the Bankruptcy Law (on behalf of the government, with the endorsement of the Bretton Woods institutions) had advised the authorities that the removal of the deposit insurance clause from the draft law might result in 'small creditors' rallies in front of closed banks, waving red flags and posters accusing National Bank officials of conspiracy with Western capital, or the Mafia, to exploit and destroy the people.' The IMF experts did not listen. On their advice, the deposit insurance scheme and the full application of insolvency law to banks were scrapped.[16]

Despite this forewarning, the IMF's decision (overruling the government and the World Bank) was to be formally embodied in the draft of a new banking law presented to Parliament in February 1996 'at a time when the danger represented by fraudulent banking enterprises should have been evident to everybody . . .'[17] The new banking law also scrapped the three-tier banking system contained in the 1992 Law:

> It [the 1996 draft law] was written in an Albanian so awful that the poor deputies can hardly have understood it; that may have been the reason why they passed it, certainly very much impressed by its arcane technicality. It evidently was a verbatim translation from an English original, so one may safely assume that this, again, was the work of those IMF experts at the Central Bank everybody believed in – just as, at that same time, nearly everybody believed in those pyramids.[18]

The IMF team at the Albanian Central Bank had thus 'thwarted pending legislation for the safety of depositors . . . The IMF team at the Albanian Central Bank did not use its influence to make the Central Bank carry out its supervisory duties and stop the pyramids in time – perhaps because the IMF experts believed that Albania needed all the banks it could get, honest or fraudulent.'[19] And it was only when the financial scam had reached its climax, in late 1996, that the IMF retreated from its initial position and 'asked President Berisha to act. At that time it was far too late, any sort of soft landing was impossible.'[20]

In parallel with these developments, the World Bank (which was busy overseeing the enterprise restructuring and privatization programme) had demanded in 1995 the adoption of legislation which would transform the state-owned banks into holding companies. This transformation had been included in the 'conditionalities' of the World Bank Enterprise and Financial Sector Adjustment Credit (EFSAC).

The World Bank had carefully mapped out the process of industrial destruction by demanding a freeze of budget support to hundreds of SOEs targeted for liquidation. It had also required the authorities to set aside large amounts of money to prop up SOEs which had been earmarked for privatization. Thus, according to the *Albanian Times*, prior to putting the National

Commercial Bank, the Rural Commercial Bank and the Savings Bank on the auction block, the government (following World Bank advice) was required to 'help restore the banks' balance sheets by assuming their non-performing loan portfolio. This will be done so that they can be really sound banks and be turned into shareholding companies, which will then be sold.'

Making the SOEs (including state-owned public utilities) 'more attractive' to potential foreign investors had predictably contributed to fuelling the country's external debt. This 'strengthening of SOEs in preparation for privatization' was being financed from the gush of fresh money granted by multilateral and bilateral creditors. Ironically, the Albanian state was 'funding its own indebtedness', by providing financial support to SOEs earmarked for sale to Western investors. Moreover, part of the foreign exchange proceeds generated by the influx of overseas remittances and dirty money into the 'foundations' was also being used to prop up the state's debt-stricken enterprises, ultimately to the benefit of foreign buyers who were acquiring state property at rock bottom prices.

In 1996, the Tirana stock exchange was set up with a view to 'speeding up the privatization programme'. In the true spirit of Anglo-Saxon liberalism, only ten players (carefully selected by the regime) would be licensed to operate and 'compete' in the exchange.[21]

The scramble for state property

As the banking system crumbled and the country edged towards disaster, foreign investors (including Italy's crime syndicates) scrambled to take over the most profitable state assets. In February 1997 Anglo-Adriatic, Albania's first voucher-privatization fund, was busy negotiating deals with foreign investors in areas ranging from breweries to cement and pharmaceuticals. The Privatization Ministry, hastily set up in response to Western demands after the rigged June 1996 elections, reaffirmed the government's determination 'to conclude this undertaking to privatise the economy and to do it soundly, steadily and legally. We are determined to go on.' The *Financial Times* advised its readers: 'At midday on March 10, on the third floor of the Albanian Finance Ministry, an auction is due to take place for the sale of a 70 per cent stake in the Elbasan cement plant for cash. A day later, a 70 per cent stake is due to be sold in the associated limestone quarry . . .'[22]

The World Bank had also recommended that all public utilities including water distribution, electricity and infrastructure be placed in private hands.

In turn, civil unrest had served to further depress the book-value of state assets to the benefit of foreign buyers. The *Financial Times* reported '"This is the Wild East", says one Western investor in Tirana. "There is going to be trouble for some time, but that also offers opportunities. We are pressing on regardless."'[23]

Selling off strategic industries

Despite mounting protest from the trade unions, the government had established (in agreement with Western financial institutions) a precise calendar for the sale of its strategic holdings in key industries including oil, copper and chrome. These sales had been scheduled for early 1997. With a modest investment of $3.5 million, Preussag AG, the German mining group, was to acquire an 80 per cent stake in the chrome industry, giving it control over the largest reserves of chrome ore in Europe.

The stakes in the Albanian elections of 1996 were high for both the US and Germany. The Adenauer Foundation had been lobbying in the background on behalf of German economic interests. Berisha's former Minister of Defence, Safet Zhulali (alleged to have been involved in the illegal oil and narcotics trade), had been the architect of the agreement with Preussag against the competing bid of the US-led consortium of Macalloy Inc., in association with RTZ. Several Western oil companies – including Occidental, Shell and British Petroleum – had their eyes riveted on Albania's abundant and unexplored oil-deposits in the regions of Durrës, Patos, and Tirana. Occidental was also drilling off-shore on Albania's Adriatic coastline.

A 'favourable mining law', set up under Western advice in 1994, had enticed several Western mining companies into Mirdita, Albania's main copper producing area. But Western investors were also gawking at Albania's gold, zinc, nickel and platinum reserves in the Kukës, Kacinari and Radomira areas. A spokesman for a major Western mining company had been inspired by the fact that 'Albania [was] stable politically, unlike some of its Balkan neighbours'.[24] In 1996, the government established regulations for the privatization of the entire mining industry.

Foreign control over infrastructure

Under the agreements signed with the Bretton Woods institutions, the Albanian government was in a straitjacket. It was not permitted to mobilize its own productive resources through fiscal and monetary policy. Precise ceilings were imposed on all categories of expenditure – in other words, the state was no longer permitted to build public infrastructure, roads or hospitals without the assent of its creditors. The latter had not only become the 'brokers' of all major public investment projects, they also decided – in the context of the 'Public Investment Programme' (PIP), established under the guidance of the World Bank – on what type of public infrastructure was best suited to Albania.

The grey economy

Alongside the demise of the state-owned corporations, more than 60,000 small-scale 'informal' enterprises had mushroomed overnight. According to the World Bank, this was clear evidence of a buoyant free-enterprise economy: 'The decline of the state sector was compensated by the rapid growth of private, small-scale, often informal, activities in retail trade, handicrafts, small-scale construction, and services.'[25] Yet upon closer scrutiny of official data, it appears that some 73 per cent of total employment (237,000 workers) in this incipient private sector was composed of 'newly created enterprises [which] have only one employee'.[26]

An expansive 'grey economy' had unfolded: most of these so-called 'enterprises' were 'survival activities' (rather than bona fide productive units) for those who had lost their jobs in the public sector.[27] In turn, this 'embryonic' market capitalism was supported by the Albanian Development Fund, a 'social safety net' set up in 1992 by the World Bank, the European Union and a number of bilateral donors with a view to 'helping the development of rural and urban areas by creating new jobs'. The Albanian Development Fund was also to provide support 'with small credits and advice to the unemployed and economically disadvantaged people helping them start their own business'.[28] As in the case of VEFA Holdings, the Albanian Development Fund was managed by appointees of the Democratic Party.

Albania had also become a new cheap-labour frontier, competing with numerous low-wage locations in the Third World: some 500 enterprises and joint ventures (some of them with suspected mafia connections) were involved in cheap-labour assembly in the garment and footwear industries, largely for export back to Italy and Greece. Legislation had also been approved in 1996 to create 'free economic areas' offering foreign investors, among other advantages, a seven-year tax holiday.[29]

Rural collapse

The crisis had brutally impoverished Albania's rural population: food self-sufficiency had been destroyed; wheat production for sale in the domestic market had tumbled from 650,000 tons in 1988 (a level sufficient to feed Albania's entire population) to 271,000 tons in 1996. Local wheat production had declined by 33 per cent in 1996.[30] In turn, the austerity measures imposed by the Bretton Woods institutions at the outset of the Berisha government had led to the destruction of the country's agricultural infrastructure as well as the concurrent collapse of most public works programmes. Cooperative structures in production and marketing were also disbanded.

During the Berisha regime, the World Bank had largely supported a programme which favoured private construction companies, including the outsourcing (through international tender) of most infrastructural programmes to Greek, Italian, German and Austrian construction companies.[31] The World Bank had also financed the purchase of some 4,000 tractors which were purchased by rich farmers with links to foreign capital. With the demise of rural credit, and the hikes of input prices and the fuel prices ordered by the World Bank, the use of farm machinery by the majority of farmers had been abandoned: 'Farm equipment is now rented out by private farmers. But people cannot afford the use of farm machinery, so there is a return to manual farming.'[32]

The dumping of surplus agricultural commodities, alongside the disintegration of rural credit, had contributed to steering Albania's agriculture into bankruptcy. A large chunk of Western financial support was granted in the form of food aid. The United States was supplying the local market with grain surpluses imported under the 1991 'Food for Progress' Act. Dumped on the domestic market, US 'Food for Progress' not only contributed to demobilizing domestic agriculture, it also contributed to the enrichment of a new merchant class in control of the sale of commodity surpluses on the domestic market. The European Union also initiated its food aid programme in 1991–92. By the time it was interrupted in 1996, its destabilizing effects had already led to the demise of local production: minimum tariffs on imported food had been put in place and commercial imports of grain on a significantly larger scale were gradually replacing the influx of food aid. Government trading companies had also entered into shady deals, through Swiss and Greek commodity brokers, involving large shipments of imported wheat.

Locally produced food staples had been replaced by imports; in turn, retail food prices had skyrocketed. In the 1980s, Albania was importing less than 50,000 tons of grain;[33] in 1996, wheat imports were (according to Food and Agricultural Organisation estimates) of the order of 472,000 tons (a more than ten-fold increase in relation to the 1980s). According to official data, the import of wheat and flour (in value terms) increased almost four times: from $32.2 million in 1994 to $123.7 million in 1996. By 1996, more than 60 per cent of the food industry was in the hands of foreign capital.[34] Agro-processing for export to the European Union had developed largely to the detriment of the local market. The World Bank was providing low interest loans, seeds and fertilizers solely in support of non-traditional export crops.

According to one observer, neither credit nor seeds were available to produce grain staples, obliging farmers to 'shift away from wheat and corn into higher value-added products like fruits, vegetables, and pork'.[35] What goes unmentioned, however, is that one of the 'high value crops' for the export market was the illicit production of marijuana, which is grown all over the country. Moreover, Italian intelligence sources have confirmed the establishment of coca plantations in mountainous areas on the border with Greece: 'The Sicilian Mafia, with the support of Colombians, is believed to have set up the plantations.'[36]

The Food and Agricultural Organisation described the situation with regard to grain production as follows:

> [wheat] plantings are estimated to have dropped [in 1996] to only some 127,000 hectares, well below the average 150,000 hectares sown from 1991 to 1995. This reduction was mainly as a result of farmers opting for other crops offering better returns relative to wheat. Yields are also estimated to have dropped further below the previous year's already reduced level. As in the past few years, yield potential was already limited by farmers' limited access to inputs such as fertilizer, crop protection chemicals, and new seeds (farmers have simply been keeping part of the previous season's crop to plant in the next year which has led to a degeneration of the quality of the seed).[37]

Moreover, the production of traditional seeds (reproduced in local nurseries) had been destroyed. Initially, imported seeds were given (free of charge) to the farmers. Then farmers were made to depend largely on seed varieties distributed by international agribusiness; but yet the prices of commercial seeds skyrocketed and, in a cruel irony, the market for imported seeds and farm inputs was totally paralysed. According to a spokesman of the Ministry of Agriculture: 'Some 35,000 tonnes of wheat are needed this year [1996] as seed, which is a great amount and may be ensured through import only. But not a kilogram of seed has been imported until now from private businessmen and the state enterprises.'[38]

This manipulation of the market for seeds and farm inputs heightened Albania's dependence on imported grain to the benefit of Western agribusiness. The dumping of EU and US grain surpluses on domestic markets led to the impoverishment of local producers. Fifty per cent of the labour force in farming now earned a mere $165 per annum. According to the United Nations Development Programme (Albania Human Development Report) average income per peasant household in 1995 was a meagre $20.40 a month, with farms in mountainous areas earning $13.30 per month. Several hundred thousand people have flocked out of the rural areas; Tirana's population has almost doubled since 1990 and a sprawling slum area has developed at Kanza, on the northwestern edge of the city.

Macroeconomic chaos

From 1989 to 1992, Albania's industrial output had declined by 64.8 per cent and its GDP by 41.2 per cent.[39] Recorded GDP later shot up by 7.4 per cent in 1994, 13.4 per cent in 1995 and 10 per cent in 1996.[40] Yet these 'positive results' hailed by the Bretton Woods institutions had occurred against a background of industrial decline supported by the World Bank-sponsored bankruptcy programme. In 1995, industrial output stood at 27.2 per cent of its 1989 level, a decline of more than 70 per cent.[41]

Despite the impressive turnaround in recorded GDP, living standards, output and employment continued to tumble. While domestic prices had skyrocketed, monthly earnings had fallen to abysmally low levels. Real wages stood at an average of $1.50 a day (less than $50 a month) in 1990, declining by 57.1 per cent between 1990 and 1992.[42] This collapse in real earnings continued unabated after 1992. According to recent data, conscripts in the Armed forces are paid $2 a month, old age pensioners receive between $10 and $34 a month. The highest salaries for professional labour were of the order of $100 a month (1996). With the devaluation of the lek in late 1996, real earnings collapsed further (almost overnight) by 33 per cent.

The outbreak of endemic diseases

Such widespread poverty has led to the resurgence of infectious diseases. There was an outbreak of cholera in 1995. In 1996, a polio epidemic spread from the northwestern region to Tirana and the rest of the country.[43] These were all the more devastating in that the economic reforms had also precipitated the disintegration of local health and educational services. The World Bank was assisting the government in slashing social sector budgets through a system of 'cost recovery'. Teachers and health workers were laid off, health spending was squeezed through the adoption of 'new pricing policies and payment mechanisms for outpatient services, hospital services and drugs', devised by the World Bank.[44] In collaboration with the World Bank, the Phare program of the European Union also granted support to the privatization of Albanian health care.

The criminalization of the Albanian state

In parallel with the impoverishment of the industrial and agricultural sectors of the Albanian economy under IMF tuition, a flourishing underground economy had been developing. A triangular trade in oil, arms and narcotics had developed, largely as a result of the embargo imposed by the international community on Serbia and Montenegro, and of the blockade enforced by Greece against Macedonia. In turn, the collapse of industry and agriculture had created a vacuum in the economic system which boosted the further expansion of illicit trade. The latter had become a 'leading sector', an important source of foreign exchange and fertile ground for the criminal mafias.

The influx of overseas remittances from some 400,000 Albanian workers in Greece and Italy had increased (according to official figures) threefold from 1992 to 1996. The actual influx, including unrecorded inflows of dirty money, was much larger. Several reports confirm that the pyramid schemes had been used extensively to launder the proceeds of organized crime as well as channel dirty money towards the acquisition of state assets:

> A Tirana banker, who declined to be named, told Reuters that the last major shipment of dirty money arrived at the start of 1997, with the Mafia paying $1.5 million to a fund which laundered $20 million. He is quoted as saying that: 'The dirty money is plunged into the pyramids and

clean money sent out under the guise of bogus import deals,' adding that 'it is easy to watch the money clear the system.'[45]

The role of Italy's crime syndicates

The Italian mafias were involved in drug-trafficking, cigarette-smuggling and prostitution.

> Pier Luigi Vigna, Italy's chief anti-Mafia prosecutor, confirmed a report by a small business association that Italian-organised crime groups had sunk money into the schemes to raise start-up capital for new ventures. He noted that Albania had become a significant producer of marijuana and was dabbling in the cultivation of coca, the raw material for cocaine.[46]

Local politicians were said to 'benefit from the ambient disorder, they even seem to bank on it, which hardly encourages efforts towards the modernization and restructuring of Albania'.[47] According to one press report (based on intelligence sources), senior members of the government, including cabinet members and members of the state security police, SHIK, were alleged to be involved in drugs trafficking and illegal arms trading.

The allegations were very serious. Drugs, arms, contraband cigarettes were all believed to have been handled by a company run openly by Albania's ruling Democratic Party, Shqiponja. In the course of 1996 Defence Minister Safet Zhulali was alleged to have used his office to facilitate the transport of arms, oil and contraband cigarettes. Drug barons from Kosovo, the Albanian-dominated region controlled by Serbia, operated in Albania with impunity, and much of the transportation of heroin and other drugs across Albania, from Macedonia and Greece en route to Italy, was believed to be organised by SHIK. Intelligence agents were convinced that the chain of command in the rackets went all the way to the top and had no hesitation in naming ministers in their reports.[48] In 1997, amidst massive protests against the government handling of the pyramid schemes, Safet Zhulali fled the country to Italy by boat.

'Guns and ammo for Greater Albania'

The trade in narcotics and weapons was allowed to prosper despite the presence, since 1993, of more than 800 American troops at the Albanian-Macedonian border with a mandate to enforce the embargo. The West had turned a blind eye. The revenues from oil and narcotics were used to finance the purchase of arms (often in terms of direct barter): 'deliveries of oil to Macedonia (skirting the Greek embargo [in 1993–94] can be used to cover heroin, as do deliveries of kalachnikov rifles to Albanian "brothers" in Kosovo.'[49]

These extensive deliveries of weapons were tacitly permitted by the Western powers on geopolitical grounds: both Washington and Bonn had favoured (although not officially) the idea of 'a Greater Albania' encompassing Albania, Kosovo and parts of Macedonia.[50] Not surprisingly, there was a 'deafening silence' on the part of the international media regarding the Kosovo arms-drugs trade: 'the trafficking [of drugs and arms] is basically being judged on its geostrategic implications . . . In Kosovo, drugs and weapons trafficking is fuelling geopolitical hopes and fears.'[51]

Recycling the proceeds of illicit trade

In turn, the financial proceeds of the trade in drugs, oil and arms were recycled towards other illicit activities, including a vast prostitution racket between Albania and Italy. Albanian criminal groups operating in Milan 'have become so powerful running prostitution rackets that they have even taken over the Calabrians in strength and influence'.[52] Dirty money originating from mafia payments for the dispatch of Albanian women to Italy was also deposited in the pyramid funds. According to the Albanian Helsinki Committee, up to one third of Italy's prostitutes are Albanians.[53] Other estimates have placed the number of Albanian prostitutes in Italy at between 4,000 and 7,000.

Organized crime invests in legal business

Legal and illegal activities became inextricably intertwined. The evidence suggests that the involvement of Italy's crime syndicates in Albania was not limited to the mafias' traditional money spinners (drugs, prostitution, arms smuggling, etc.). Organized crime was also suspected to have invested in a number of legal economic activities including the garment industry, tourism and the services economy. According to the *Geopolitical Drug Watch*, 'the pyramid cooperatives of southern Albania mostly invested in medium-sized Italian firms, establishing joint ventures, some of which are being investigated by the Italian authorities'.[54] There is also evidence that Albanian criminal groups have invested in land and real estate in Italy.

The four main Albanian 'pyramid' savings schemes were Sudja, Populli, Xhaferri and VEFA Holding. The latter – upheld by the West during the Berisha regime as 'a model of post-communist free enterprise' – was the country's largest pyramid investment fund, closely controlled by the Democratic Party. It profited extensively from the privatization programme during the Berisha government, buying up a large number of former state-owned enterprises including supermarkets, import-export, transportation and manufacturing companies. By late 1997, VEFA was under investigation in Italy for its alleged ties to the mafia. VEFA had been advised by the Naples-based accounting firm Cecere and Caputo, which was alleged to have connections to the mafia. The brother of the (deceased) founder of the accounting firm, Gennaro Cecere, was arrested in early 1997 on mafia-associated charges.[55] A consultant for the firm, Gianni Capizzi, led a seven-member team to Albania in February 1997 with the mandate to restructure VEFA Holdings and to give a hand to its chairman, Vehbi Alimucaj, a former army supplies manager with no training in economics: 'Capizzi said by telephone that he had no reason to believe that VEFA operated in an illegal way . . . the brother had no connection with the firm . . . Nicola Caputo, the other principal in the Italian firm, has met Alimucaj several times while on business in Albania, Capizzi said.'[56]

Recycling dirty money towards Western creditors

International creditors, anxious to collect interest payments on Tirana's mounting external debt, had their eyes riveted on the growing foreign exchange proceeds of this illegal trade. As Albania fell deeper in debt, and legal industries and agriculture collapsed, income from illicit trade and overseas remittances became the only available source of essential foreign exchange, and creditors and the Tirana government alike shared a vested financial interest in the uninterrupted flow of lucrative contraband.

The gush of remittances and dirty money into the country was being transformed into domestic currency (lek) and funnelled into the pyramid funds (as well as into the acquisition of state assets and land under the privatization programme). In turn, the hard currency proceeds were being funnelled from the inter-bank market towards the Albanian Treasury. In conformity with its agreements with the Bretton Woods institutions, the government would eventually be obligated to use these hard currency reserves to pay the interest and arrears on Albania's external debt. In fact, a large part of the foreign exchange influx (including money of criminal origin) would eventually be used to meet the demands of Tirana's external creditors, leading to a corresponding outflow of resources. According to one report, the creditors had a vested interest in keeping the pyramids afloat as long as possible:

> The IMF waited until October 1996 to raise the alarm. For four years, international institutions, American and European lenders and the foreign ministries of Western countries had been content to back the activities of the Albanian political class, which is an offshoot of the 'fares', a name given the extended family clans without which nothing can be done in Albania.[57]

Western finance capital had relied on Berisha's Democratic Party; the Bretton Woods institutions advising Berisha had insisted on the total deregulation of the banking system. No impediments were to be placed on the development of the pyramids, no restrictions on the movement of money. The conventional wisdom would no doubt argue that this influx of hot and dirty money was helping the country 'improve its balance of payments'. In other words, the West had not only tolerated, during the government of President Berisha, a financial environment in which criminals and smugglers were allowed to prosper; the 'free market' system had also laid the foundations for the criminalization of the state apparatus. The evidence suggests that the 'strong economic medicine' imposed by external creditors contributed to the progress of an extensive criminal economy, feeding on poverty and economic dislocation.

II. The Protest Movement of February 1997

The Albanian protest movement which erupted in February 1997 following the collapse of the 'ponzi' pyramid funds has been badly distorted in the Western press. The financial scam surrounding the 'get-rich-quick schemes' was narrowly depicted by the global media as the sole source of social upheaval. An image of spontaneous street rioting was conveyed, spotlighting the misdeeds of armed gangs and the looting of state property, and citizens' groups opposed to former President Berisha were branded as common criminals; at the same time, the Western media failed to mention the links of the Albanian state to Italy's crime syndicates. Political dissent by civilians, including the formation of the 'salvation committees', was depicted as sabotaging the 'transition' to a 'free market' society. In the words of Italy's foreign minister, the revolt was led by 'delinquent bands incited by far left-activists'. The reality was somewhat different.

The revolt started in February in the southern city of Vlorë, when the police and military headquarters were taken over in February by the local salvation committees. From Vlorë, the insurrection spread to other cities in southern Albania. Students, workers and farmers joined in. The Albanian armed forces and police had become largely inoperative; not only soldiers but officers spontaneously joined the citizens' movement demanding the resignation of President Berisha. As one newspaper put it, 'in southern Albania, the army has gone over to the side of the people'.[58] The commander of the military base of Pasha Limani in the Vlorë region joined the insurrection, and integrated the Vlorë Defence committee with the members of his garrison. In the rebel strongholds of Delvinë and Sarandë, 'the situation [had grown] rapidly out of control as it became apparent that President Berisha's men did not have the support of their police . . .'[59]

Western powers were concerned lest the insurrection get out of hand. US military advisers were rushed to Tirana and a high-tech predator-drone aerial-surveillance system was set up at the Gjader airfield, close to Tirana, with the capability of monitoring the insurgency in southern Albania. In February 1997, the Commander of the Joint Chiefs of Staff, General Shalikashvili, visited US Air Force personnel stationed in Albania. (Not a word was mentioned in the international press concerning Shalikashvili's meetings with government officials and Albania's military establishment.)

In March 1997 a 'Government of National Reconciliation' under a Socialist care-taker prime minister was installed under Western advice. With President Berisha discredited in the eyes of the people, both Europe and America were eager to develop new political alliances with the leadership of the Socialist Party. The latter had committed itself to the adoption of 'sound macroeconomic policies' under the guidance of the Bretton Woods institutions. The interim government's first task was to appease the rebellion in the south, while laying the groundwork for the disarmament of the salvation committees.

Leaders of the Socialist Party (former Communists) held discussions in March with Western governments and the United Nations concerning the dispatch of a so-called Multinational Protection Force (MPF) to Albania. In April, following a UN Security council resolution, the MPF – largely composed of Italian and Greek troops – landed on the beaches of the Adriatic coast. Its mandate was 'to protect the shipments of humanitarian aid'. However, rather than ensuring the delivery of emergency supplies, the first concrete action of the MPF was to provide support to the government's ailing police and military.

The 'hidden agenda' behind the Multinational Protection Force was to bolster the Albanian military and police forces with a view to effectively disarming the civilian population and quelling the rebellion. In the words of the Italian MPF leader General Girolamo Giglio: 'We will help in increasing the efficacy of the police forces, by offering specialized means and professional assistance.'[60] The Council of Europe Parliamentary Assembly provided its rubber stamp to the MPF's de facto mandate by formally condemning the local level 'salvation committees' and demanding their disarmament.[61]

The West's objectives were clear: disarm civilians and ensure the installation of a 'democratically elected' successor regime which would continue to uphold the 'free market' reforms initiated under President Berisha in 1992. Elections were held on 29 June 1997, leading to a landslide victory by the Socialist Party. In August 1997, following the installation of a new president, the last of 7,000 troops of the Multinational Protection Force were withdrawn. Greek and Italian military advisors remained in the country to assist the new authorities in 'rebuilding the country's shattered armed forces'.[62]

The 1997 political protest movement did not identify the role played by international financial institutions and Western business interests in triggering the collapse of the Albanian economy. The salvation committees were made up of people from different sectors of Albanian society, including not only members of the various opposition parties but also members of the Democratic Party who were opposed to Berisha. They did not have a clear political position on the macroeconomic reforms that had served to destroy the national economy and impoverish the Albanian people; neither did they question the role of the West in the implementation of these reforms.

The Socialists (together with the Democrats) were intent upon breaking up these committees, which represented a threat to their authority as 'political brokers' on behalf of foreign capital. Moreover, the West wanted to avoid a situation which would undermine the structure of party politics and the legitimacy of the parliament as a 'rubber stamp'.

The people's movement was largely directed against a corrupt political regime. The Democrats were discredited because society had been impoverished: in the eyes of the people, the Berisha government was to blame. The

West's reputation in Albania remained unscathed; Western interference was not the prime object of political protest. Thus the West was able to enforce its free market reforms via the Berisha government at the same time as it laid the groundwork for Berisha's downfall.

As soon as an interim Government of National Reconciliation had been appointed in March 1997, both Washington and Brussels repudiated President Berisha while forging new alliances with the Socialists. The leader of the Socialist Party Fatos Nano, imprisoned by Berisha in 1994, was released from jail. Nano unequivocally committed himself to continuing the IMF-sponsored macroeconomic reforms initiated under the Democrats in 1992.

III. Transition under the 'Socialist' Coalition Government

By co-opting the Socialist opposition, Western business interests were able to sidetrack political dissent while ensuring the installation of a favourable successor regime. In other words, the West had ensured the replacement of an unpopular, pro-Western government, whose legitimacy was being challenged, by a freshly elected, equally pro-Western 'Socialist' regime formed from the ranks of the opposition. Successive governments have thus borne the brunt of social discontent while shielding the interests of creditors and multinational corporations. Needless to say, therefore, this change of regime did not entail a shift in the direction of macroeconomic policy. On the contrary, it enabled the Bretton Woods institutions to negotiate a fresh wave of economic reforms with the new authorities.

The installation of a pro-Washington 'Socialist' government, however, had changed the geopolitical balance between Europe and America. Several of the new government's key advisors had been trained in the US while the Socialists were in opposition.

The government's commitment to Washington was underscored in the new Albanian Prime Minister's statement to the Rome Conference in July 1997. Washington was invited to actively cooperate in the political, economic and military spheres. The Mining Law adopted under Berisha had largely favoured the German mining consortium, Preussag AG, to the detriment of a competing American mining consortium. Starting in late 1997, the entire mining legislation was revamped with the assistance of a New York based law firm: 'Preussag had been given exclusive rights but now it is a stalemate . . . We are in a transition period. The rules of the game must be defined. The issue is how will we organize the privatization and tendering process.'[63]

Germany had unconditionally backed the Democrats; Sali Berisha had made firm commitments to Preussag AG regarding the privatization of the chrome industry. Under the Socialist coalition government a new generation of officials, firmly committed to American business interests and the Washington consensus, had come into power. The Socialists tended to favour Anglo-American mining interests in the exploration of Albania's huge chrome, nickel and copper reserves. There is also evidence of extensive tar-sand oil fields which are being developed by a Canadian consortium.

The Rome Agreement

Under the arrangement reached with Socialist Party leaders at the Rome Conference on 31 July 1997, a residual contingent of Italian troops would remain in Albania. In the words of Franz Vranitzky, OSCE mediator for Albania, speaking at the final press conference: 'We will continue to fill the framework with substance with regard to the reconstruction of the Albanian police force, of the army, of commerce, of financial systems and of the constitution'. On the economic front, the Bretton Woods institutions would ensure that the Socialists continued to apply 'sound macroeconomic policies'. In the words of Vranitzky, 'the International Monetary Fund and the World Bank would send teams to Tirana in August [1997] to help with economic programmes, including setting up banking systems and advising on how to deal effectively with pyramid schemes'.

The main Albanian government document presented to the Rome Conference had been hurriedly put to the Albanian Parliament on 28 July 1997, just three days before the Conference began, having been rushed together by Albanian officials. It underscored the key objective of 'disarmament of the civilian population' (with the support of Western military and police advisors); the restructuring and modernization of the army with 'guarantee assistance coming by international structures of security and defence, based [on] agreement with Western countries'; and with the objective of integration and 'intensive partnership and a full membership in NATO'.[64]

In his statement to the Rome Conference Prime Minister Fatos Nano fully endorsed the continuation of the macroeconomic reforms initiated under the Democrats (in full conformity with the demands of the Bretton Woods institutions): 'These organisations have put their conditions to help Albania . . . These conditions are fully possible, and this asks good political will from us . . . The agreements with the IMF are under a green light for each programme . . . and we are decided to realise that.' At the close of the Conference he stated triumphantly: 'Our [government] programme has not only received a [parliamentary] vote of confidence but today it has received a vote of confidence from the international community.'

Albania's 'Marshall Plan'

The trusteeship of Western donors and creditors over the Albanian state (as well as the direction of macroeconomic reform under the stewardship of the IMF) was not an object of debate. The rehabilitation programme (although predicated on massive cuts in government expenditure) was labelled a 'Marshall Plan': 'Foreign aid will constitute the basis for the financing of public works through international tender. The immediate objective is for the donors to find in the Albanian [Socialist] government a serious and devoted partner.'[65]

The document proposed a 'reorientation and acceleration' of the privatization programme initiated under the Democrats, including new rules pertaining to the privatization of banking and strategic mineral resources. A comprehensive privatization programme had been demanded by the IMF as a condition for the granting of a three-year structural adjustment loan, to be implemented in 1998. The sectoral ministries were abolished: the jurisdiction over mining, oil and gas, public utilities, etc., was transferred to the Ministry of Privatization. The latter was given the authority to implement the privatization programmes in all sectors of the economy except banking, for which separate procedures had been envisaged.

In turn, the Socialists also began to develop a new framework for the privatization of mineral resources, based on the granting of concessions: 'Our [draft] law is modelled on that applied in Latin America; the purpose is to make it more attractive to foreign investment. Ours [our law] will be the most attractive in the world: the state is prepared to sell 100 per cent of its interests in the mining business.'[66] Prime Minister Nano also confirmed that the privatization programme 'will include any major resources still in public hands . . . They will be offered to the private sector, domestic and international with priorities focusing on mineral resources, telecommunications and transportation.'[67]

The IMF/World Bank-sponsored retrenchment programme

The 1997 Government Programme was translated into English at the last minute for presentation to the Rome Conference. It was put forth alongside another key document, entitled 'Strategy for Recovery and Growth'. The latter had been carefully drafted in Washington by World Bank officials on behalf of the new government. It outlined concrete macroeconomic measures ('conditionalities') to be undertaken by the new authorities.

The World Bank document was adopted verbatim by the Council of Ministers for presentation to the international aid agencies and donors, meeting in Brussels in October 1997. According to a UN official stationed in Tirana, 'The conditionalities [imposed by the donors] were blunt: "You do this by this time . . ." The attitude [within the new Socialist government] was a totally uncritical acceptance of foreign advice: "Please let us know what you want us to do. We want to please the donors."'[68]

Albania's Western donors, meeting in Brussels in October 1997, demanded the retrenchment of surplus personnel in the public sector, with massive lay-offs of health workers and teachers. The retrenchment was to be implemented in three distinct phases, implying an overall compression in the size of the civil service pay-roll (including teachers and health workers) of the order of 25 per cent:

> The number of public sector employees will be reduced by 1,000 before the end of December 1997. The payroll will be then further reduced by 10,000 employees by March 1998 and a further 10–15 per cent [of the total number of remaining employees] during the remainder of 1998. Additional savings will be realised through cuts in operations and maintenance allocations, domestically financed investment and the reserve fund.[69]

Following World Bank guidelines, salary increases would be limited to civil servants in key ministerial positions (*'personnel de confiance'*). Under one proposed scheme the World Bank would 'top up' the salaries of selected individuals in key posts in the ministries, the judiciary and the police. Italy also provided bilateral funding with a view to propping up the police forces, to be reorganized under the guidance of Italian advisors.[70] (Italy has played a vital role in the policing of Albania, as well as supporting Italian business interests there. Opposition journalists in Tirana have pointed to existence of a de facto 'Italian protectorate'.)

The retrenchment programme was applied to public employees whose salaries had fallen to abysmally low levels under the Berisha regime. In December 1997 a young medical doctor, for instance, was earning $45 a month, a registered nurse $30. The maximum wage for a medical doctor in a Tirana hospital with more than 30 years seniority was of the order of $100 a month.[71] In other words, despite the large number of employees targeted for lay-off or dismissal, civil service salaries for those who were fortunate enough to retain their jobs in the public sector remained at very low levels. Moreover, because of this low wage structure, the retrenchment programme – while leading to a further collapse of public services – has not been conducive to a significant reduction in the state's payroll, as demanded by the IMF.

'Fiscal stabilization'

As a means of 'stabilizing' the national economy and 'averting inflationary pressures', the Western donors had imposed a fiscal stabilization programme requiring an immediate hike of the Value Added Tax (VAT) from 12.5 per cent to 20 per cent. Rather than alleviating inflation, as claimed by the IMF, this measure was conducive to an immediate hike in consumer prices (and a corresponding decline in the levels of real earnings). The hike of VAT also backlashed on small producers and farmers.

According to the Recovery Programme for Albania adopted in Brussels in October 1997, 'the final goal of monetary policy will be long-run price stability with the promotion of full employment and growth without inflation'.[72] These objectives would be served by freezing the supply of broad money through the imposition of credit ceilings; the latter would be supervised by the IMF. What this implied in practice was the total destruction of the domestic banking system. Credit to the real economy would be frozen. Local enterprises (both public and private) would be unable to acquire loanable funds from domestic financial institutions. Their only viable alternative would be to set up joint ventures with foreign enterprises that had access to bank financing.

Under the Socialists, the entire state banking system was put up for privatization. The government had already initiated negotiations with several foreign banks. The IMF proceeded to draft (with virtually no input from the government) a comprehensive strategy for the privatization of the commercial banking system.[73] With the Albanian Central Bank virtually paralysed, these foreign banks were given a de facto control over the entire structure of credit with little or no impediment from the monetary authorities. The immediate tendency was towards the provision of short-term loans (import-export trade) with few avenues for the financing of productive investments. The entire credit network was concentrated in Tirana. Money laundering activities, including the drug trade, continued to prosper. Only short-term loans, at 38 per cent in lek and at 3–5 per cent above LIBOR for loans in US dollars, were made available.

The liquidation of the pyramids

'Winding up' the pyramids 'which had stolen the people's money' was one of the main conditions for reaching an agreement with the IMF and the World Bank.[74] But neither the Bretton Woods institutions nor the government were planning on 'giving the money back to the people'. In April 1997, the World Bank had recommended the audit, shut-down and disposal of the remaining pyramid schemes. A $6 million programme (financed under earlier credits granted to the Berisha government) would be made available to the Socialists to pay for the services of a foreign accounting firm.[75]

In consultation with the Western donor community, the Bretton Woods institutions later recommended that the Nano government appoint Deloitte Touche, a British accounting firm, to take over the operations of the pyramids with a view to ultimately selling their assets. Of potential interest were VEFA Holding's mineral and oil deposits. According to the chairman of VEFA, Vehbi Alimucaj:

> The government wants to destroy us. The IMF wants to take over our assets at rock-bottom prices . . . Deloitte Touche has been appointed to keep an eye on us . . . The constitutional court has upheld its judgement in our favour. It decided that the appointment of foreign administrators was unconstitutional, namely that it violated a specific article of the Albanian Constitution. What the government did the following day was to demand an amendment of the Constitution [in the Legislature] with a view to invalidating the Court's decision.[76]

Following these developments, the President of VEFA Holding was put under 'house arrest' in early 1998 for obstructing the activities of Deloitte Touche.

Resurgence of the criminal economy under the 'Socialists'

The dismantling of the pyramids of the Berisha period was largely about collecting debts to reimburse external creditors, as well as transferring assets into the hands of new owners; nor did the administrators appointed under World Bank advice do anything to address the fact that the 'ponzi' schemes had ties to organized crime.

The banking reforms under the Socialists contributed to exacerbating the decline of the national economy. The freeze on credit undermined productive investment while at the same time contributing to the advancement of illicit trade and money laundering. The monetary freeze also affected the prospects for normal regional trade with neighbouring countries including Greece, Italy and the former Yugoslavia. And while the Socialists – under the guidance of the donor community – were busy dismantling the remaining 'ponzi' schemes, the freeze on bank credit ordered by the IMF led to a resurgence of 'informal banking structures' and the sprouting up of new pyramid schemes.[77]

The criminalization of the Albanian economy continued unabated under the Socialists. Part of the proceeds of the drug trade were channelled into new pyramid schemes, and the collapse of domestic agriculture (heightened by the 1997–98 economic reforms) led to a further surge in the production of cannabis in all major regions of the country. In late 1997, the Italian police (in a joint operation with Dutch and German police forces) swooped on a drug-smuggling gang with ties to criminal organizations in Albania and the Puglian region of southern Italy. Lecce police arrested top Puglia mafia boss Mario Tornese and his right hand man Franscesco Santolla:

> Mafia groups from both countries [Albania and Italy] had not yet got together in formal organisations but a frightening integration was taking place . . . There aren't any strict ties yet between the mafias and criminal groups from various countries, but that does not mean there is no cause for alarm, a Lecce police spokesman said.[78]

Albanian criminal groups, in association with their Italian counterparts, were also involved in the transshipment of heroin from Turkey:

> Italy continues to be a transit point for Southwest Asian heroin . . . Trucks drive the Balkans route from Turkey, Greece, Albania and the

> former Yugoslavian countries with ferry boat connections to Southern Italian ports . . . The financial sector in Italy serves as a significant money laundering centre for both narcotics and other illicit funds.[79]

IV. Conclusions

The July 1997 Rome Agreement safeguarded the West's strategic and economic interests in Albania by transforming a country into a territory, and served as a bulwark to block a united resistance by the Albanian people to the plunder of their homeland by foreign capital. Albania's economy has been destroyed and its institutions dismantled under Western supervision. A colonial-style 'protectorate' has been installed. The state budget is overseen by the Bretton Woods institutions; the IMF is in control of monetary policy. Internal security and defence are under Western control; Italian police and military advisors are on hand to assist the government in rehabilitating and re-equipping police facilities with a view to curbing future civilian protest movements.

By the time of the NATO war against Yugoslavia in the spring of 1999, Albania, crippled by 'free market' reforms imposed by Western donors and creditors and transformed into a de facto NATO military base, had been stripped of the last shred of its political and economic sovereignty. Contrary to what has been trumpeted by the global media, the war in Yugoslavia is also a war against Albania and its people. Moreover, in the wake of the war, Albania will be yet again afflicted by external debts contracted with the World Bank and the IMF in order to deal with the plight of the refugees.

The macroeconomic reforms implemented in Albania under the auspices of the Bretton Woods institutions have been conducive to the destruction of the national economy and the impoverishment of the Albanian population, while transferring the control over Albania's extensive mineral deposits into foreign hands. Drug barons in Kosovo, Albania and Macedonia (with links to the Italian mafia) have become the new economic elites, often associated with Western business interests. Albania is the hub of the multi-billion-dollar Balkans drug trade. In turn, the laundering of drug money has played an important role in 'financing the conflict' in Kosovo. The economic reforms have also created an environment in Albania which has favoured the criminalization of state institutions and the development of a flourishing illegal trade in arms and narcotics. And these structures in turn have played an important role in setting the stage for the conflict in Kosovo and for NATO's bombs.

For the war in the Balkans has also been implemented on the economic front, through the imposition of the IMF's deadly reforms. The latter have been implemented in coordination with NATO's strategic and military objectives. Following the pattern set in Bosnia, NATO has been in close liaison with the Bretton Woods institutions and the European Development Bank, which have been called upon to play a crucial role in 'post-war reconstruction'.

The 'post-conflict' reforms envisaged for Kosovo are patterned on those adopted in Albania and Macedonia, implying the setting up of a bogus democracy in an occupied territory. Moreover, with the KLA poised to play a central role in the formation of a 'post-conflict government', the tendency is towards the installation in Kosovo of a state system which maintains pervasive links to organized crime. In this regard, the US State Department's position (contained in the May 1999 G8 proposal) is that the KLA would 'not be allowed to continue as a military force but would have the chance to move forward in their quest for self government'; by which (according to US State Department spokesman James Foley, quoted in the *New York Times*) one can only understand the inauguration of a new 'narco-democracy', under NATO control.[80]

Notes

1. Andrew Gumbel, 'The Gangster Regime We Fund', *Independent*, 14 February 1997, p. 15.
2. 'Albania, More than a Bankruptcy, the Theft of a Century', *Geopolitical Drug Watch*, Paris, no. 66, April 1997, p. 1.
3. *Christian Science Monitor*, 13 February 1997.
4. World Bank Public Information Department, Washington, 5 December 1995.
5. Gumbel, 'The Gangster Regime We Fund', p. 15.
6. *Albanian Daily News*, Tirana, 28 February 1997.
7. Jane Perlez, 'Albania Tightens Grip, Cracks Down on Protests', *New York Times*, 4 March 1997.
8. World Bank Public Information Department, 5 December 1995.
9. Ibid.
10. 'Albania, More than a Bankruptcy', *Geopolitical Drug Watch*, p. 4.
11. United Nations Economic Commission for Europe (UNECE), *Economic Survey of Europe 1996*, Geneva 1996, pp. 188–89.

12. World Bank Public Information Department, 5 December 1995.
13. Interview with the author, Tirana, December 1997.
14. See F. Münzel, 'IMF Experts Partially Responsible for Albanian Unrest', Kosova Information Office, Stockholm, 13 March 1997.
15. Ibid.
16. Ibid.
17. Ibid.
18. Ibid.
19. Ibid.
20. Ibid.
21. *Albanian Times*, vol. 2, no. 18, May 1996.
22. Kevin Done, *Financial Times*, London, 19 February 1997.
23. Ibid.
24. *Albanian Times*, Tirana, vol. 2, no. 19, 1996.
25. World Bank Public Information Department, 5 December 1995.
26. *Albanian Times*, vol. 1, no. 8, Tirana, December 1995.
27. World Bank Public Information Department, 5 December 1995.
28. *Albanian Times*, vol. 2, no. 19, Tirana, 1995.
29. *Albanian Times*, vol. 2, no. 7, Tirana, February 1996.
30. *Statistical Yearbook*, Ministry of Agriculture and Food, Tirana, 1996, p. 25; see also Food and Agricultural Organisation press release, 8 October 1996.
31. Interview by the author with a senior official of the Ministry of Agriculture, Tirana, December 1997.
32. Ibid.
33. World Bank, World Development Report 1992.
34. *Albanian Times*, vol. 2. no. 15.
35. *Albanian Times*, vol. 1, no. 2, 1995.
36. Helena Smith, 'Italy fears Influx will set back War on Mafia', *Guardian*, London, 25 March 1997.
37. Food and Agricultural Organisation press release, 8 October 1996.
38. *Albanian Observer*, vol. 2, no. 1.
39. United Nations Economic Commission for Europe (UNECE), *Economic Survey of Europe 1996*, Geneva, 1996, p. 184.
40. Ibid. The 1996 figure is an estimate.
41. Ibid., p. 185.
42. *Statistical Yearbook of Albania*, Tirana 1991, p. 131.
43. World Health Organisation press release WHO/59, 18 September 1996; *Albanian Times*, vol. 2, no. 40.
44. World Bank Public Information Department, 'Albania – Health Financing and Restructuring Project', Washington, January 1994.
45. Fabian Schmidt, 'Is There A Link Between The Albanian Government And

Organized Crime?', *Bulletin of the Open Media Research Institute,* 17 February 1997, vol. 1, no. 553.

46. Gumbel, 'The Gangster Regime We Fund', p. 15.
47. *Geopolitical Drug Watch,* no. 35, September 1994, p. 3.
48. Gumbel, 'The Gangster Regime We Fund', p. 15.
49. *Geopolitical Drug Watch,* no. 35, p. 3.
50. *Geopolitical Drug Watch,* no. 32, June 1994, p. 4.
51. Ibid.
52. *Guardian,* 25 March 1997.
53. Ismije Beshiri and Fabian Schmidt, 'Organized Criminal Gangs Force Albanian Women Into Prostitution Abroad', Open Media Research Institute brief, 14 August 1996.
54. *Geopolitical Drug Watch,* no. 66, April 1997, p. 3.
55. Daniel J. Wakin, Associated Press Dispatch, 19 February 1997.
56. Ibid.
57. *Geopolitical Drug Watch,* no. 66, p. 2.
58. *La Vanguardia,* Barcelona, 10 March 1997.
59. *The Times,* London, 10 March 1997.
60. ATA dispatch, 21 April 1997.
61. ATA dispatch, 26 April 1997.
62. *Jane's Defence Weekly,* vol. 28, no. 7, 20 August 1997.
63. Interview by the author with an Albanian expert on the mining industry, Tirana, December 1997.
64. Government Programme: Fatos Nano, Prime Minister of Albania's presentation to the Rome Conference, Republic of Albania, Tirana, 28 July 1997, p. 6.
65. Government Programme, 28 July 1997, p. 28.
66. Interview by the author with an Albanian mining expert, Tirana, December 1997.
67. Richard Murphy, 'Prime Minister Plans Privatisation Drive', *Albanian Observer,* vol. 3, no. 11, p. 3.
68. Interview by the author with UN official stationed in Tirana, December 1977.
69. 'Reform and Recovery, Current Developments and Priority Needs', Brussels, 22 October 1997, p. 4.
70. *Albanian Daily News,* Tirana, 9 December 1997, p. 8.
71. Interviews by the author in a Tirana hospital, December 1997.
72. 'Reform and Recovery, Current Developments and Priority Needs', p. 4.
73. *Albanian Daily News,* Tirana, 9 December 1997, p. 7.
74. *Albanian Observer,* no. 9, 1997, p. 22.
75. Carlos Elbirt, 'Albania under the Shadow of the Pyramids', World Bank, Washington, 1997. In 1997, Elbirt was head of the World Bank's Representative Office in Albania.
76. Interview by the author with the Chairman of VEFA Holding, Tirana, December 1997.

77. Interviews by the author with representatives of foreign banks, Tirana, December 1997.
78. Reuters dispatch, 'Police Swoop on Italy, Albania Mafia Drug Network', Lecce, 29 November 1997.
79. US Department of State, International Narcotics Control Strategy Report on Italy, Washington, March 1997.
80. US State Department spokesman James Foley, quoted in the *New York Times*, 2 February 1999.

PART IV

Dispatches from the Time of War

12

OPEN LETTER FROM A TRAVELLER TO THE PRESIDENT OF THE REPUBLIC

Régis Debray

On returning from Macedonia, Serbia and Kosovo I feel morally bound to pass my impression on to you: I am afraid, Monsieur le Président, that we are taking a wrong turning. You are a practical man. You have little time for the intellectuals who fill the media with grandiloquent and peremptory near-misses. And that is good, for neither have I. So I will stick to facts. Everyone has their own version of those, you will say; to each his own. Certainly those I was able to observe on the spot during a short visit – a week in Serbia (taking in Belgrade, Novi Sad, Niš and Vramje and including four days in Kosovo visiting Priština, Prej, Prizren and Produjevo) between 2 and 9 May 1999 – do not seem to correspond with the words you have been using, in good faith but from a distance.

I hope you will not think me biased. I had spent the previous week in Macedonia, watched refugees arriving, listened to their testimony which horrified me along with many others. I wanted at all costs to go and see 'from the other side' how such an outrageous crime was possible. Having a rooted distrust of Intourist-style journeys and journalistic bus trips, I asked the Serbian authorities if I could have my own translator, my own vehicle and the right to go and talk to anyone I wanted. They agreed to these conditions and respected them.

The question of the interpreter is an important one. For I had already discovered, somewhat to my cost (and how could it be otherwise?), that in Macedonia and Albania it is possible to fall into the hands of local dragomen, mostly members or sympathisers of the KLA, who make their network and expertise available to newly-arrived foreigners. The accounts of exactions are too numerous for anyone to be able to doubt some basis of truth for them.

Nevertheless some of the accounts I recorded turned out, when later checked in the places where they had happened, to be exaggerated or even inaccurate. Of course that makes no difference to the scandal and ignominy of this exodus.

What is it you keep telling us?

> We are not making war on the Serbian people but on a dictator, Milošević, who has refused to negotiate and has cold-bloodedly programmed the genocide of the Kosovars. We are limiting ourselves to destroying his repressive apparatus, a task which is already well advanced. And the reason why we are still making air strikes despite regrettable targeting errors and involuntary collateral damage, is that the Serbian forces are continuing their ethnic cleansing operation in Kosovo.

I have grounds for fearing, Monsieur le Président, that all of these words are misleading in the extreme.

1. 'Not making war on the Serbian people . . .'

You may not know that the Dušan-Radević children's theatre adjoins the television building in the heart of old Belgrade, and the missile that destroyed the one damaged the other. Three hundred schools, altogether, have been damaged by bombs. Children are left to their own devices and not attending classes. In the country there are even some who collect toy-like yellow explosive tubes (model CBU87). The Soviets used to scatter similar fragmentation bombs in Afghanistan.

Demolition of factories has left a hundred thousand workers kicking their heels, and living on an income of 230 dinars – about £10 – a month. Nearly half the population is unemployed. If you are hoping to turn people against the régime by these means, you are making a mistake. Despite the lassitude and shortages I did not notice any real fissures in the sacred union. A young girl in Priština said to me: 'When four Chinese are killed, citizens of a great power, the whole world is up in arms; but when it's four hundred Serbs it doesn't seem to count at all. Strange, wouldn't you say?'

I certainly did not witness any of the carnage wrought by NATO bombers on buses, refugee columns, trains, the hospital at Niš and other places. Nor the raids on Serbian refugee camps (Majino Maselje, 21 April 1999, four dead, twenty injured. The refugees I mean are the four hundred thousand-odd Serbs whom the Croatians deported from Krajina unseen by cameras and unheard by microphones).

To stick to the places and incidents of my stay in Kosovo, the NATO spokesman, General Wertz, declared: 'We have not attacked any convoys and we have never attacked civilians.' This is a lie. In the hamlet of Lipjan on Thursday 6 May, three kilometres from any military target in any direction, I saw a private house that had been demolished by a missile, causing the death of three small girls and their grandparents. The next day, in the Gypsy quarter of Prizren, I saw two other civilian cottages which had been reduced to rubble two hours earlier, with several victims buried in the ruins.

2. 'The dictator Milošević . . .'

My contacts in the opposition – the only politicians with whom I conversed – reminded me of the harsh realities. Autocratic, swindling, manipulative and populist, Mr Milošević has nevertheless been elected three times: dictators only need to get elected once. He respects the Yugoslav constitution. There is no single party, and his own does not have a parliamentary majority. No political prisoners, just changing coalitions. He is virtually absent from the everyday landscape. People can criticize him in public, and they do, but on the whole nobody pays much attention to him. There is no 'totalitarian' charisma weighing on people's minds. The West seems a hundred times more befogged by Mr Milošević than his fellow-countrymen.

To mention Munich in connection with him is to overturn the relationship between the weak and the strong; to imagine that a poor and isolated country of ten million inhabitants, one that covets nothing outside the frontiers of the former Yugoslavia, can be compared to Hitler's overbearing and overequipped Germany. If you hide your face too thoroughly you become unable to see.

3. 'Genocide of the Kosovars . . .'

A terrible business. I only came across two accessible Western eyewitnesses. One, Aleksander Mitić, admittedly of Serbian origin, is the Agence France Presse correspondent in Priština. The other, Paul Watson, an Anglophone Canadian, is the central Europe correspondent of the *Los Angeles Times*. Having covered Afghanistan, Somalia, Cambodia, the Gulf war and Rwanda, he is not what you would call green. Somewhat anti-Serb, he had followed the

Kosovo civil war for two years and knew every road and village. A hero, so modest. When all the foreign journalists were expelled from Priština on the first day of the bombing, he had gone to ground and stayed there, continuing to move about and observe.

His testimony is therefore balanced and, taken in combination with other evidence, convincing. The worst exactions were committed in the first three days of the deluge of bombs – 24, 25 and 26 March 1999 – with burning, looting and murders. Some thousands of Albanians were then ordered to leave. He assures me that since that time he has not found any trace of crimes against humanity. Of course these two scrupulous observers cannot have seen everything. And I myself, still less. I can only testify to Albanian peasants returning to Pudajevo, to Serbian soldiers standing guard outside Albanian bakeries – ten of which had reopened in Priština – and people wounded in the bombing, Albanians and Serbs side by side, in the 2,000-bed Priština hospital.

So what happened? According to the two eyewitnesses, the sudden superimposition of an international air war on a local civil war (and an extremely cruel one at that). Let me remind you that during 1998, 1,700 Albanian combatants were killed, along with 180 Serbian police and 120 Serbian soldiers; the KLA kidnapped 380 people and released 103, the rest (including two journalists and 14 workers) having either disappeared or been killed, sometimes after being tortured. The KLA said it had 6,000 clandestine members in Priština, and its snipers (I was told) went into action as soon as the first bombs fell. Judging that they could not fight on two fronts, the Serbs then seem to have decided to expel *manu militari* NATO's 'fifth column' or 'land forces', in other words the KLA, especially in the villages where it was impossible to distinguish its members from the rest of the population.

Localized but undeniable, these evacuations are described by Serb forces as 'Israeli-style' and would certainly be recognized by an old Algeria hand like yourself (from the days when a million Algerians were rounded up by us and shut in camps surrounded by barbed wire in order to 'drain the water from around the fish'). As in Algeria, obvious traces were left here and there: empty villages, houses burned to the ground. These military clashes caused civilians – mostly, I am told, combatants' families – to flee before the bombing started. According to the AFP correspondent their numbers were very limited. 'People took refuge in other neighbouring houses,' he told me. 'No one was dying of hunger, getting killed on the road or fleeing into Albania or Macedonia. There isn't the slightest doubt that it was the NATO attack that started the humanitarian catastrophe snowballing. Until that moment, in fact, there was no need for reception camps at the frontiers.' Everyone agrees that in the first few days reprisals were unleashed by so-called 'uncontrolled elements', with the probable complicity of the local police.

Mr Vuk Drasković, the deputy prime minister who has now started to distance himself from the régime, is among those who told me that they have subsequently arrested and charged three hundred persons with exactions committed in Kosovo. Cover-up? Excuse? Apology? Nothing is out of the question. Later the exodus continued, but on a smaller scale: on orders from the KLA which wanted to group its supporters; for fear of being thought 'collaborators' (with the Serbs); for fear of the bombs (since no one can tell the difference between Serbs, Albanians and others from 20,000 feet); to join relations who had already left; because the livestock had been killed; because America was going to win; because it was the ideal moment to emigrate to Switzerland, Germany or anywhere. All these reasons were given to me on the spot. I bring them to your attention, but do not guarantee their truth.

Is it possible that I have listened too attentively to the 'people over there'? To do the opposite would be racist. To define a whole people – Jewish, German or Serbian – *a priori* as criminal is unworthy of a democrat. After all, during the occupation France made the acquaintance of SS divisions manned by Albanians, Muslims and Croats, but never by Serbs. The Serbs are a pro-Semitic and stubborn people; ten nationalities coexist in Serbia itself; could they really have gone Nazi fifty years too late? In any case a number of Kosovar refugees told me they had only escaped the repression through the help of Serb neighbours and friends.

4. 'The destruction of the Serb forces, which is well advanced . . .'

Sorry, but in fact the Serb forces seem very fit indeed. A young sergeant picked up hitchhiking on the Niš–Belgrade motorway asked me what was the strategic reason for NATO's furious attacks on civilians. 'When we soldiers go to town we have to drink warm Coca-Cola because there's no electricity. It's a nuisance, but we can live with it.' I imagine army units have their own generators.

In Kosovo, you have damaged bridges (easily bypassed using nearby fords, when they are not still usable); destroyed an airport of no importance; demolished empty barracks; burned discarded army lorries; bombed helicopter mock-ups and wooden artillery pieces artistically scattered about the fields. This is all very well for battlefield video images and indoor press briefings, but what happens later? Remember that the Yugoslav armed forces, formed by Tito and his partisans, are not like most regular armies: scattered and omnipresent, with underground command and storage centres, set up to meet a long-term conventional military threat (for some time a Soviet one). This is an army that moves cattle about with its artillery to baffle infra-red detection devices.

It is no secret that in Kosovo there are 150,000 men under arms, aged between twenty and seventy (no age limit for reservists), of whom only 40–50,000 are in General Pavković's Third Army. Messages are relayed effectively by walkie-talkie radio, and the Yugoslavs are themselves jamming telephone frequencies, as the KLA had been using mobiles to pinpoint targets for US bombers.

As for the expected demoralization, do not believe in it. I am afraid that in Kosovo they are awaiting our troops with equanimity and even with a certain impatience. A Priština reservist buying bread, AK over shoulder, told me: 'Land intervention by all means! At least in a real war there are dead on both sides.' The NATO planners' war game is taking place 15,000 feet above reality. I beg you, do not send our sensitive and intelligent Saint-Cyr graduates into territory they know nothing about. Their cause may possibly be just but they will not be waging the defensive war (let alone the sacred one) that – rightly or wrongly – the Serb volunteers of Kosovo and Metohija will be fighting.

5. 'They are continuing with their ethnic cleansing . . .'

I was angered by the accumulation of car number plates and identity documents – taken from people leaving – at the frontier post on the Albanian border. The reply given me was that it was feared the 'terrorists' would use them to disguise their own and their vehicles' identities to re-infiltrate Kosovo. Much may have escaped my own modest investigations, but the German defence minister was lying when he said on 6 May 1999 that 'between 600,000 and 900,000 displaced persons have been located inside Kosovo'. In a territory of only 10,000 square kilometres that would certainly have been visible to an observer travelling on that same day from north to south and from east to west. In Priština, where tens of thousands of Kosovars are still living, it is possible to dine at an Albanian pizzeria in the company of Albanians.

Could not our ministers visit the terrain to question unexcitable witnesses, people like the Greek doctors with Médecins sans frontières, like priests and ecclesiastics? I am thinking particularly of Fr Stephen, the Prior of Prizren, who is singularly level-headed. For this civil war is not a religious war: the innumerable mosques are intact, with only two exceptions according to what I was told.

You can buy a country's foreign policy – as the United States is doing with various countries in the region – but not its dreams or its memory. If you could see the looks of hatred on the faces of Macedonian police and customs officers when the nightly convoys of tanks from Salonika to Skopje are passing, driven by arrogant escorts wholly unaware of what surrounds them, you would understand without difficulty how much easier it will be to enter this 'theatre' than to get out of it. Would you then, like the Italian president, have the courage or the intelligence to abandon unrealistic postulates, to seek with Ibrahim Rugova what he has called 'a political solution on realistic foundations'?

If you do, a number of realities will force themselves on your attention. The first is that there is no solution without a *modus vivendi* between Albanians and Serbs, as Mr Rugova insists, for there are two or more communities in Kosovo, not just one. Without getting entangled in the war of statistics caused by the absence of trustworthy census figures, my understanding is that there are a million or more Albanians, a quarter of a million Serbs and another quarter of a million members of other communities: Islamized Serbs, Turks, Gorans or montagnards, Romanies, 'Egyptians' or Albanian-speaking gypsies – these last having taken the Serbian side for fear of what a Greater Albania would mean to them. The second reality is the high probability of a resurgence of fierce internal warfare, an episode in a secular to-and-fro, the Act I without which the present Act II is incomprehensible, but which was itself the result of earlier oppression.

At the moment, politicians seem to be seeing everything in terms of analogies with the past. It is still a good idea to find the least bad analogies possible. You have chosen the Hitlerian analogy, with the Kosovars as persecuted Jews. Allow me to suggest a different one: Algeria. Mr Milošević is certainly no de Gaulle. But the civilian government is confronted with an army that has had enough of losing and dreams of waging war in earnest. And this regular army rubs shoulders with locally-born militias that might one day come greatly to resemble a sort of OAS.

And suppose the problem did not arise in Belgrade but in the streets, the cafés and grocers' shops of Kosovo? The fact is that the men I am talking about are far from reassuring. On one or two occasions I found myself the object of fierce criticism verging on the ugly. I owe it to the truth to say that each time this happened it was Serbian officers who came to the rescue and saved my bacon.

You remember de Gaulle's definition of NATO: 'An organization imposed on the Atlantic Alliance which is no more and no less than the military and political subordination of Western Europe to the United States of America.' One day perhaps you will explain the reasons that have led you to modify this assessment. In the meantime I must confess to feeling a bit humiliated when, on asking a member of the Serbian democratic opposition why his president had rushed to receive some American personality before a French one, I received the answer: 'Look, it's always a better idea to talk to the organ-grinder than his monkey.'

This 'Open Letter' was first published on the front page of Le Monde, 13 May 1999.

13

THE NATO ACTION IN SERBIA

Harold Pinter

The NATO action in Serbia had nothing to do with the fate of the Kosovan Albanians; it was yet another blatant and brutal assertion of US power.

The bombing was not only an action taken in defiance of international law and in contempt of the United Nations, it was also totally unnecessary. The negotiation process at Rambouillet is said to have been exhausted but this was not in fact the case. At the start of the crisis there were two main objectives: to restore substantive autonomy to Kosovo and to ensure that the Yugoslav government respected the Kosovars' political, cultural, religious and linguistic freedoms. The plan at the Rambouillet conference was to achieve these two aims by peaceful means. The Serbs had specifically agreed to grant Kosovo a large measure of autonomy. What they would not accept was NATO as the international peace keeping force, or rather, an occupying force, a force whose presence would extend throughout Yugoslavia. They proposed a protectorate under United Nations auspices. NATO would not agree to this and the bombing started immediately. It's worth remembering that the bombing of Iraq last December followed a similar pattern. The United Nations was saying: 'Now wait a minute, surely we can work something out,' when the US and Great Britain said it was too late to work anything out and started the bombing. They're still doing it, by the way. And the sanctions upon Iraq continue, from which thousands of Iraqi children are dying every month.

The United States has finally agreed to a resolution of the Serbian conflict which differs in no significant respect from that which the Yugoslav parliament was ready to accept before the violence started. Why therefore was this action taken? I believe the United States wanted to make Kosovo into a NATO – or rather American – colony. This has now been achieved. I shall return to this in due course.

Nothing else has been achieved. NATO gave Milošević the excuse he needed to escalate his atrocities, thousands of civilians, both Kosovan and Serbian, have been killed, the country has been poisoned and devastated. The Serbian atrocities are savage and disgusting but there is little doubt that the vast escalation of these atrocities took place after the bombing began. To cite 'humanitarian' reasons, in any event, as NATO originally did, really doesn't bear scrutiny. There are just as many 'moral' and 'humanitarian' reasons, for example, to intervene in Turkey. The Turkish government has been waging a relentless war against the Kurdish people since 1984. The repression has claimed 30,000 lives. Not only does the United States not intervene, it actively subsidises and supports what is effectively a military dictatorship and of course Turkey is an important member of NATO. The revelations of the Serbian police torture chambers are horrific but the Turkish police torture chambers practise exactly the same techniques and bring about exactly the same horror. So did the Guatemalan and El Salvadoran and Chilean torture chambers before them. But these were *our* torture chambers so they never reached the front pages. Those torture chambers were defending democracy against the evil of subversion, if you remember. Turkey is still doing it, with our full support, our weapons and our money.

In 1975 Kissinger and Ford gave the nod to the Indonesian government to invade East Timor. 200,000 East Timorese people, a third of the population, were murdered. The West has maintained a very active business relationship with Indonesia ever since. The arms trade has flourished. Israel's oppression of the Palestinian people continues while Israeli settlement of the West Bank goes on in contravention of international agreements and UN resolutions. In all these cases humanitarian considerations are not exactly at the forefront of US foreign policy. Human life – or human death – means little to Blair and certainly nothing to Clinton. Don't let us forget that Clinton ensured his presidential candidacy by going to Arkansas to witness the execution of a mentally deficient eighteen-year-old.

NATO has claimed that the bombing of civilians in Serbia were accidents. I suggest that the bombing of civilians was part of a deliberate attempt to terrorise the population. NATO's supreme commander, General Wesley K. Clark, declared just before the bombing began: 'Unless President Milošević accepts the International Community's demands we will systematically and progressively attack, disorganise, ruin, devastate and finally destroy his forces.' Milošević's 'forces', as we now know, included television stations, schools, hospitals, theatres, old people's homes. The Geneva Convention states that no civilian can be targeted unless he is taking a direct part in the hostilities, which I take to mean firing guns or throwing hand grenades. These civilian deaths were therefore acts of murder.

A body of lawyers and law professors based in Toronto in association with the American Association of Jurists, a non-government organisation with consultative status before the United Nations, has laid a complaint before the War Crimes Tribunal charging all the NATO leaders (headed by President Clinton and Prime Minister Blair) with war crimes committed in its campaign against Yugoslavia. The list of crimes include: 'wilful killing, wilfully causing great suffering or serious injury to body or health, extensive destruction of property, not justified by military necessity and carried out unlawfully and wantonly, employment of poisonous weapons or other weapons to cause unnecessary suffering, wanton destruction of cities, towns or villages, devastation not justified by military necessity, bombardment of undefended towns, villages, dwellings or buildings, destruction or wilful damage done to institutions dedicated to religion, charity and education, the arts and sciences, historic monuments.' The charge also alleges 'open violation of the United Nations Charter, the NATO Treaty itself, the Geneva Conventions and the principles of International Law.'

It is worth remarking here that the enormous quantities of high explosives dropped on Serbia have done substantial damage to irreplaceable treasures of Byzantine religious art. Precious mosaics and frescos have been destroyed. The thirteenth-century city of Peć has been flattened. The sixteenth-century Hadum mosque in Djakovica, the Byzantine Basilica in Niš and the ninth-century church in Prokuplje have been badly damaged. The fifteenth-century rampart in the Belgrade fort has collapsed. The Banovina palace in Novi Sad, the finest work of art-deco architecture in the Balkans, has been blown up. This is psychotic vandalism.

Why were cluster bombs used to kill civilians in Serbian marketplaces? The NATO high command can hardly have been ignorant of the effect of these weapons. They quite simply tear people to pieces. The effect of depleted uranium in the nose of missile shells cannot be precisely measured. Jamie Shea, our distinguished NATO spokesman, would probably say, 'Oh come on lads, a little piece of depleted uranium never did anyone any harm.' It can be said, however, that Iraqi citizens are still suffering serious effects from depleted uranium after nine years, not to mention the Gulf War syndrome experienced by British and American soldiers. What is known is that depleted uranium leaves toxic and radioactive particles of uranium oxide that endanger human beings and pollute the environment. NATO has also targeted chemical and pharmaceutical plants, plastics factories and oil refineries, causing substantial environmental damage. Last month the Worldwide Fund for Nature warned that an environmental crisis is looming in the lower Danube, due mainly to oil slicks. The river is a source of drinking water for 10 million people.

Tony Blair said the other day 'Milošević has devastated his own country'. This statement reminds me of the story of the English actress and the Japanese actor. The Japanese actor couldn't understand why the English actress was so cold towards him, so unfriendly. Finally he appealed to the director. He said, 'We have a love scene to do tomorrow but she simply won't smile at me, she never looks at me, she won't speak to me. How can we play the love scene?' The director said to the actress, 'Now what's the trouble, darling? Kobo is really an extremely nice man.' The actress looked at the Japanese actor and said, 'He may be – but some of us haven't forgotten Hiroshima.'

This is standing language – and the world – on its head. There is indeed a breathtaking discrepancy between, let us say, US government language and US government action. The United States has exercised a sustained, systematic and clinical manipulation of power worldwide since the end of the last World War, while masquerading as a force for universal good. Or to put it another way, pretending to be the world's Dad. It's a brilliant – even witty – stratagem and in fact has been remarkably successful. But in 1948 George Kennan, head of the US State Department, set out the ground rules for US foreign policy in a 'top secret' internal document. He said 'We will have to dispense with all sentimentality and day dreaming and our attention will have to be concentrated everywhere on our immediate national objectives. We should cease to talk about vague and unreal objectives such as human rights, the raising of living standards and democratisation. The day is not far off when we will have to deal in straight power concepts. The less we are hampered by idealistic slogans the better.' Kennan was a very unusual man. He told the truth.

I believe that the United States, so often described – mostly by itself – as *the* bastion of democracy, freedom and Christian values, for so long accepted as leader of the 'free world', is in fact and has in fact been for a very long time a profoundly dangerous and aggressive force, contemptuous of international law, indifferent to the fate of millions of people who suffer from its actions, dismissive of dissent or criticism, concerned only to maintain its economic power, ready at the drop of a hat to protect that power by military means, hypocritical, brutal, ruthless and unswerving.

But US foreign policy has always been remarkably consistent and entirely logical. It's also extremely simple. 'The free market must prevail, big business must be free to do business and nobody – but nobody – can get in the way of that.'

A banker I know addressed a meeting of potential US investors on the complex political and economic structure of Mexican society, attempting to place this in an historical context. An American investor stood up and said 'Listen, we don't give a damn about any of that, all we want to know is – what do we get for our dollar?'

NATO is America's missile. As I think I indicated earlier, I find nothing intrinsically surprising in what is essentially an American action. There are plenty of precedents. The US did tremendous damage to Iraq in the Gulf War, did it again last December and is still doing it. Earlier this year it destroyed a pharmaceutical factory in Khartoum, declaring that chemical weapons were made there. They were not. Baby powder was. Sudan asked the United Nations to set up an international enquiry into the bombing. The United States prevented this enquiry from taking place. All this goes back a very long way. The US invaded Panama in 1990, Grenada in 1983, the Dominican Republic in 1965. It destabilised and brought down democratically elected governments in Guatemala, Chile, Greece and Haiti, all acts entirely outside the parameters of international law. It has supported, subsidised and in a number of cases engendered every right-wing dictatorship in the world since 1945. I refer again to Guatemala, Chile, Greece and Haiti. Add to these Indonesia, Uruguay, the Philippines, Brazil, Paraguay, Turkey El Salvador, for example. Hundreds upon hundreds of thousands of people have been murdered by these regimes but the money, the resources, the equipment (all kinds), the advice, the moral support as it were, has come from successive US administrations. The devastation the US inflicted upon Vietnam, Laos and Cambodia, the use of napalm, agent orange, was a remorseless, savage, systematic course of destruction, which however failed to destroy the spirit of the Vietnamese people. When the US was defeated it at once set out to starve the country by way of trade embargo. Its covert action against Nicaragua was declared by the International Court of Justice in The Hague in 1986 to be in clear breach of international law. The US dismissed this judgement, saying it regarded its actions as outside the jurisdiction of any international court. Over the last six years the United Nations has passed six resolutions with overwhelming majorities (at the last one only Israel voting with the US) demanding that the US stop its embargo on Cuba. The US has ignored all of them.

Milošević is brutal. Saddam Hussein is brutal. But the brutality of Clinton (and of course Blair) is insidious, since it hides behind sanctimony and the rhetoric of moral outrage. Very little moral outrage is expressed in the United States about its own prison system. There are nearly two million people in prison in the United States.

These are some of the devices used in these prisons.

The restraint chair is a steel-framed chair in which the prisoner is immobilised with four-point restraints securing both arms and legs and straps which are tightened across the shoulders and chest. The prisoner's arms are pulled down towards his ankles and padlocked and his legs secured in metal shackles. Prisoners are often left strapped in restraint chairs for extended periods in their own urine and excrement.

A stun gun is a hand-held weapon with two metal prongs which emits an electrical shock of roughly 50,000 volts. The use of stun guns and stun belts is widespread. The belt on the prisoner is activated by a button on the stun gun held by a prison guard. The shock causes severe pain and instant incapacitation. This has been described as torture by remote control.

Mentally disturbed prisoners have been bound, spread-eagled on boards for prolonged periods in four-point restraints without medical authorisation or supervision.

It is common practice for prisoners to be shackled during transportation by leg irons or chains. Pregnant women are not excluded.

Sexual abuse and rape by guards and inmates in these prisons are commonplace.

In 1997 thirty-six states operated fifty-seven 'supermax' facilities housing 13,000 prisoners. More are under construction. These are super maximum security facilities. They are designed for isolation of dangerous prisoners but in fact prisoners may be assigned to 'supermax' units for relatively minor disciplinary infractions, such as insolence towards staff or, in the case of both men and women, complaints about sexual abuse. Severely disturbed prisoners are held within these facilities receiving neither appropriate evaluation or treatment.

Prisoners spend between 22 and 24 hours a day in claustrophobic and unhealthy conditions. The concrete cells have no natural light. The doors are solid steel. There is no view of and no contact with the outside world.

United Nations Human Rights Committee stated in 1995 that conditions in these prisons were 'incompatible' with international standards. The UN special Rapporteur on torture declared them inhuman in 1996.

Thirty-eight states out of fifty employ the death penalty. Lethal injection is the most popular method, followed by electrocution, the gas chamber, hanging and the firing squad. Lethal injection is regarded as the most humane method. But in fact some of the case histories of injections that go wrong are as grotesque as they are grisly.

Mental deficients and people under eighteen do not escape the death penalty. However, the assistant attorney-general of Alabama did make the following observation: 'Under Alabama law you cannot execute someone who is insane. You have to send him to an asylum, cure him up real good, then execute him.'

Amnesty International stated that all these practices constitute cruel, inhuman and degrading treatment. But the 'international community' has not been invited to comment on a system at one and the same time highly sophisticated and primitive, shaped in every respect to undermine the dignity of man.

Why is NATO in Yugoslavia? This question is related to another. Why has NATO, which was effectively made redundant at the end of the Cold War, in fact expanded? Why are Czechoslovakia, Poland and Hungary members of NATO? The answer appears to lie in the considerable potential oil wealth in the Caspian Sea region. One of the *Guardian* newspaper intellectuals had this to say the other day: 'How absurd it is,' he jeered, 'to refer to the oil in the Caspian Sea region as having anything to do with the NATO operation. The Caspian Sea is over a thousand miles from Yugoslavia.' It is indeed. But to get the oil from the Caspian Sea into the hands of the West you can't use buckets. You need pipelines and those pipelines have to be installed and protected. The oil reserves in the Caspian Sea are vast. The pipelines mean that the security in the Balkans is of concrete economic and strategic importance. The US Energy Secretary, Bill Richardson, has explained it quite clearly: 'This is about America's energy security. It's also about preventing strategic inroads by those who don't share our values. We are trying to move these newly independent countries toward the West. We would like to see them reliant on Western commercial and political interests. We've made a substantial political investment in the Caspian and it's important that both the pipeline map and the politics come out right.'

I'm now going to use the term imperialism, which some of you might think no longer means anything. I believe that imperialism remains an active and vibrant force in the world today.

Using the vehicle of financial institutions such as the International Monetary Fund and the World Bank, imperialism is in a position to dictate policy to smaller states which rely on their credit. Through their domination of the world market, the imperialist powers drive down prices for raw materials and keep the smaller states impoverished. The more these countries borrow, the more destitute and dependent they become. Palmerston said of the British Empire, 'It has neither permanent friends nor permanent enemies. It has only permanent interests.'

There was a time, by the way, when I thought Tony Blair would do well to consult one – or even two – of you ladies and gentlemen here tonight. I was struck by the demented light of battle in his eyes. But now I'm not at all sure that he's actually gone round the bend. I've come to the conclusion that his moral fervour and fanaticism is a masquerade. There's a big financial cake to be cut somewhere in the centre of all of this. And this government would like a nice thick slice of it.

I suggest that it was in the interest of the imperialist states – the USA, the United Kingdom and Germany – to fragment what was an effectively, if precariously, unified Yugoslavia. The way to do this was to demand the break-up of nationalised industries and to impose austere neo-liberal policies which exacerbated simmering ethnic tensions. The economic pressure exerted upon Yugoslavia laid the objective foundations for the dissolution of the Balkan State. The break-up was accelerated by Germany which abruptly recognised the independence of Croatia and Slovenia in 1991 and the US which gave its approval to Bosnian succession in 1992. Naturally to break up a state into many parts is to reduce the strength of that state.

The dismantling of the USSR has created a power vacuum in Eastern Europe, Russia and Central Asia. The principal significance of Yugoslavia at this critical juncture is that it lies on the Western periphery of a massive swathe of territory on to which the major world powers aim to expand. This process expresses the most profound requirements of the profit system. Today's trans-national companies, as we know, measure their success in global terms. No market in the world can be ignored by General Motors, Toyota, Airbus, or Coca-Cola. These immense operations compete across continents to achieve dominance. For them, the penetration of one-sixth of the globe newly opened to capitalistic exploitation is a life-and-death question. The greatest untapped oil reserves in the world are located in the former Soviet Republics bordering the Caspian Sea (Azerbaijan, Kazakhstan and

Turkmenistan). These resources are now being divided between the major capitalist countries. This is the fuel that is feeding militarism and which threatens to lead to new wars of conquest by imperialist powers against local powers. Brzezinski, the former national security chief under Carter, stated in 1997: 'America's status as the world premier power is unlikely to be contested by any single challenger for more than a generation. No state is likely to match the United States in the four key positions of power – military, economic, technological and cultural – that confer global political clout.'

Having consolidated its power in its base in the Western Hemisphere, the US, Brzezinski argues, must make sustained efforts to penetrate the two continents of Europe and Asia. 'America's emergence as the sole global superpower' he continues, 'now makes an integrated and comprehensive strategy for Eurasia imperative. A power that dominated Eurasia would exercise decisive influence over two of the world's most economically productive regions, Western Europe and East Asia. A glance at the map also suggests that the country dominant in Eurasia would almost automatically control the Middle East and Africa. In Eurasia the immediate task is to ensure that no state or combination of states gains the ability to expel the United States or even diminish its decisive role. An enlarged NATO will serve the short term and long term interests of US policy.'

The US House Committee on International Relations has begun holding hearings on the strategic importance of the Caspian region. Doug Bereutter, the committee chairman, spoke as follows: 'Stated US policy goals regarding energy resources in this region include fostering the independence of the new states and their ties to the West, breaking Russia's monopoly over oil and gas transport routes, encouraging the construction of East/West pipelines that do not transit Iran and denying Iran dangerous leverage over the central Asian economies.' Mortimer Zuckerman, the editor of *US News* and *World Report* said last month that the 'Central Asian resources may revert back to the control of Russia or to a Russian-led alliance. This would be a nightmare situation. We had better wake up to the dangers or one day the certainties on which we base our prosperity will be certainties no more. The potential prize in oil and gas riches in the Caspian sea, valued up to 4 trillion dollars, would give Russia both wealth and strategic dominance. The potential economic rewards of Caspian energy will draw in their train Western military forces to protect our investment if necessary.' It could be argued that the significance of the military action against Yugoslavia rests in the fact that Kosovo was a testing ground for wars that might follow in the former Soviet region – to protect the interests of the United States.

The nuclear 'balance' in the world, if there is such a thing, has been severely disturbed by recent events. The Ukrainian parliament has voted unanimously to return the country to its former nuclear status. The Russian National Security Council recently approved the modernisation of all strategic and tactical nuclear warheads. It decided to develop strategic low-yield nuclear missiles capable of pinpoint strikes anywhere in the world. In Beijing, the bombing of the Chinese Embassy in Belgrade has resulted in a shift away from the no-first-strike principle. I believe it is not fanciful to conclude that the United States is on course to bring about a Third World War which will be the end of us all, with the possible exception of Bill Clinton, Madeleine Albright, Tony Blair and all the generals and all the presidents of multinational companies eating baked beans and hamburgers in their McDonald's nuclear bunker deep down in Arizona.

This speech was delivered to the Confederation of Analytical Psychologists in London on 25 June 1999.

14

BE MORE CAREFUL WITH THE BALKANS!

Yevgeny Yevtushenko

Not long ago, I received a letter from the parents in Israel of a boy they had named 'Babi Yar'. From the photograph of their son, two dark eyes stared out at me like the smoking coals we see on TV today from Kosovo and Belgrade. The parents wanted people to remember what happened at Babi Yar [*the massacre-site of Jews which was the title of Yevtushenko's 1961 poem*] and, if they didn't know, they would ask what the name means and would remember these two words forever. But today, as I look at this photograph, it seems to me that this Israeli boy has either an Albanian or a Serb face.

Like Raskolnikov, history returns to the scene of its crime. And right now it has returned to the Balkans where at the beginning of the century the first world war began with a shot fired at Archduke Ferdinand. People have reduced the astonishingly beautiful Balkans into a place bewitched, concealing in its crevice-filled rocky crags a serpent's nest of future wars.

Be more careful with the Balkans! If into this nest we too arrogantly start to poke either the toe of a soldier's boot or a colonial master's riding crop, or winged rockets, then the awakened serpents may crawl far afield and one of them, like a cobra, puffing out from a local war into a world war, may possibly destroy the entire globe.

Of course it is amoral to contemplate a fire in a neighbour's house with indifference. But can it be that the only solution is to put the fire out with bombs? It seems the leaders of NATO countries, in taking the decision to bomb Serbs in order to save Albanians, have inexcusably not thought out many factors.

Not everyone in America, and far from everyone in Europe, likes a surgical operation on a purulent ethnic cancer to be carried out with an axe rather than a delicate scalpel.

It may dangerously complicate the relationship of the US and the west with Russia and provoke the future birth of an alternative military alliance, say of China, India, and Russia: and incidentally, what might happen if Texan separatists who wanted independence from the US were some day to turn to this Chinese-Indian-Russian military union with a request for assistance?

In my childhood, all my generation were engrossed in reading *The Fairy Tales of Montenegro,* which became a classic for Russians. During the Second World War, the feats of Yugoslav partisans in their struggle against fascism inspired not only our soldiers but also our famous poets. A whole anthology could be compiled of Russian poetry about Yugoslavia.

When I heard in the placid, icy commentary of a smarmy NATO spokesman the name of the city of Kraguevat as one of their targets, I shuddered, because this name was a symbol of the heroic confrontation of the Yugoslav nation with Hitler's occupation. Yugoslavia manifested no less heroic opposition towards Stalin's regime. But this was never transformed into hatred towards Russians. And when Moscow newspapers began to call Tito no longer a hero but a traitor, it never took root with the Russian people.

I remember my father and I went to the Moscow Circus in 1948. A clown brought an enormous dog into the arena wearing a Yugoslav marshal's peaked cap. The dog had a bundle of gigantic faked stage dollars in his teeth. 'Hey Tito you mongrel, let go of them,' the clown screamed, shrill and laughing. But the audience kept deadly silent. 'How disgusting . . . Let's get out of here,' my father said loudly as he got up. And suddenly from every seat fathers and mothers got up and led their children out. The circus hall was empty. I was told later they had to remove that scene from the circus programme.

For a long time Yugoslavia was the most prosperous and the most independent socialist country – at least that is how it appeared to us. Only later, after the death of Tito, upon seeing the collapse of the Yugoslav federation that was held together only by his 'anti-Stalin Stalinist will', we began to understand that not everything was so pure and just in the land of our Yugoslav 'brothers-in-arms', whose lives seemed to us so free in comparison with our own, and whom we so greatly envied. But nonetheless, we didn't stop loving the Yugoslavs. That war meant so much to us and we cannot abandon when they are in trouble those who had to struggle just as much as we did.

Have today's NATO countries, who also fought with the Yugoslavs against fascism, forgotten this? Just recently Russia and the US celebrated the demise of the Cold War between them. But no sooner had the NATO bombs begun to fall on Yugoslavia, than the skeleton of the Cold War, awakened by the explosions, lifted the lid and, as it appears, jumped out of its grave on to the ground of Russia.

It pulls on to its skull first the nationalist politician Zhirinovsky's pug-dog mask – beaming crudely at the lucky opportunity to bark at the NATO elephant – then the bellicose whiskers of the president of Belarus; then the ski-mask of an unknown would-be terrorist trying to shoot a bazooka at the US embassy.

For all these remarkable people, a better gift than the bombs couldn't be imagined. Politicians who have often deceived their own populace promptly used the occasion to pound a fist threateningly on the table, at the same time putting out their other palm for an expected handout. The Speaker of the Duma, who brought back from Milošević the science-fantasy project of a union of Russia, Yugoslavia, and Belarus, has taken heart.

I can hardly believe in the knee-jerk solidarity with the Serbian people of some of our politicians of doubtful sincerity, because real solidarity is never a politically convenient paroxysm. And how can one believe them when many members of our parliament do not manifest any kind of elementary solidarity whatsoever with their own people, even with war veterans standing with their hands out in subways, with teachers and physicians who for six months haven't received a salary, with miners pounding their helmets on the pavement without response?

In my opinion the only correct position is simultaneously pro-Serb and pro-Albanian – that is pro-humanity.

We must not confuse people with extremists. During the conflict in Bosnia one charming Serbian woman, who teaches philosophy in an American college, ceased being intelligent in my eyes as soon as she began to speak about Bosnians. 'These dirty Bosnians are like wild animals . . . They must all be destroyed.' Wolf fangs seemed to show from her beautifully modelled lips. But within a month I talked with a Bosnian graduate student at another university and wolf fangs appeared when she began speaking about Serbs . . .

Do not demonise any nation because somebody might start to demonise your own. The endless procession of completely innocent Albanian refugees moving across the television screen appeals to the mercy of humanity. But so do the burning houses of completely innocent Serbs. It is tragic that Russia and America watch two completely different wars on television, although it is one and the same war. In the American TV version the Serbs are guilty of everything, and in the Russian version the Americans.

Previously, when Solzhenitsyn spoke out against the Soviet authorities, his every half-word was printed in the top columns of American newspapers. But now no one in the US is rushing to print what he says about the bombing of Yugoslavia. 'A beautiful European country is being destroyed and civilised governments brutally applaud.' (*Argumenty I fakty*, no. 15, April 1999.)

The truth is summed up not only in this, but also in the barely alive old Albanian woman being pulled over the snow in a plastic garbage bag, just to drag her out of the Kosovo hell into Montenegro; and in the old Serbian woman who stands at night on a bridge with a target on her sunken chest inviting bombs from the sky; and in the three American military prisoners with their little-boy faces beaten and bloody . . . Be more careful with the Balkans!

15

THE TREASON OF THE INTELLECTUALS

Edward Said

No one at all can doubt that what has transpired in Kosovo as a result both of Slobodan Milošević's brutality and the NATO response has made matters a good deal worse than they were before the bombing. The cost in human suffering on all sides has been dreadful, and whether it is in the tragedy of the refugees or the destruction of Yugoslavia, no simple reckoning or remedy will be available for at least a generation, perhaps longer. As any displaced and dispossessed person can testify, there is no such thing as a genuine, uncomplicated return to one's home; nor is restitution (other than simple, naked revenge, which sometimes gives an illusory type of satisfaction) ever commensurate with the loss of one's home, society, or environment. Through a combination whose exact proportions we will never know, despite NATO as well as Serbian propaganda, Kosovo has been purged forever of any hopes that coexistence between different communities is soon going to be possible. A number of honest reporters here and there have admitted that what exactly took place so far as the ethnic cleansing of Albanians by Serbs was concerned is still mostly unknown, since the NATO bombings of Kosovo, the actions of the Kosovo Liberation Army, and the actual brutality of individual or collective Serb actions took place all at once: trying to determine the blame and responsibility in such a chaos, except to score self-justifying debating points, is pretty difficult, if not impossible.

But that the illegal bombing increased and hastened the flight of people out of Kosovo cannot be doubted. How the NATO high command, with Bill Clinton and Tony Blair leading the pack, could ever have assumed that the number of refugees would have decreased as a result of the bombing fairly beggars the imagination. Neither leader, significantly, has ever experienced the horrors of war; neither man fought, neither has any direct knowledge of what it means to search desperately for survival, to protect and feed one's family. For those reasons alone, both leaders deserve the strongest moral condemnation and, given Clinton's appalling record in Sudan, Afghanistan, Iraq and the White House corridors, he should be indicted as a war criminal as much as Milošević. In any event, even according to US law, Clinton violated the constitution by fighting a war without congressional sanction. That he also violated the UN Charter simply adds to the felony.

Morality teaches that, if one wants to intervene to alleviate suffering or injustice (this is the famous idea of humanitarian intervention which so many Western liberals have dragged out as an excuse for the bombing war), then one must make sure first of all that by doing so the situation will not be made worse. That lesson seems to have eluded the NATO leaders, who plunged in ill-prepared, poorly informed and heedless, and therefore cold-bloodedly sealed the fate of hundreds of thousands of Kosovars who, whether they had to bear the brunt of Serbian vengeance on them, or because the sheer volume and density of the bombing (despite ludicrous claims about precision-guided ordinance) made it imperative for them to flee the province, became victims twice over.

There is now the colossal job of trying to restore a million people to their homes with no clear idea of what, once they return, is to be their fate. Self-determination? Autonomy under Serbia? Military occupation under NATO? Partition? Shared sovereignty? According to what sort of timetable? Who is going to pay? These are only some of the questions that remain unanswered, if the agreement brokered by Russia actually works and goes through. What does it mean that (according to the agreement) some Serb police or military personnel will be allowed back in? Who will protect them against Albanian violence, and who will regulate their actions? Who will protect the Serbian Kosovars? Add to that the exorbitant cost of re-building Kosovo and Serbia, and you have a web of problems that simply defies the limited powers of understanding and political sophistication possessed by any or all of the present NATO leaders.

What concerns me most, though, as an American and a citizen, is what the Kosovo crisis portends for the future of the world order. 'Safe' or 'clean' wars, in which American military personnel and their equipment are almost totally invulnerable to enemy retaliation or attack, are profoundly troubling things to think about. In effect, as the distinguished international jurist Richard Falk has argued, such wars share the same structure as torture, with the investigator-torturer having all the power to choose and then employ whatever method he wishes; the victim, who has none, consequently is left to the whim of his persecutor. America's status in the world today is at its lowest, that of a stupid bully capable of inflicting much more damage than any power in history.

The US military budget is 30 per cent higher than that of the total budget spent by all the other NATO countries combined. Over half the countries of the world today have felt either the threat or the actuality of US economic or trade sanctions. Pariah states like Iraq, North Korea, Sudan, Cuba and Libya (pariahs because the US has labelled them so) bear the brunt of US unilateral anger; one of them, Iraq, is in the process of genocidal dissolution, thanks to US sanctions which go on well past any sensible purpose other than to satisfy the US's feelings of righteous anger. What is all this supposed to accomplish, and what does it say to the world about US power? This is a frightening message bearing no relationship to security, national interest, or well-defined strategic aims. It is all about power for its own sake. And when Clinton takes to the airwaves to inform Serbs or Iraqis that they will get no help from the country that destroyed theirs unless they change their leaders, arrogance simply knows no bounds. The International Tribunal that has branded Milošević a war criminal cannot in the present circumstances have either viability or credibility unless the same criteria are applied to Clinton, Blair, Albright, Sandy Berger, General Clark and all the others whose murderous purpose completely overrode any notion of decency and the laws of war. In comparison with what Clinton has done to Iraq alone, Milošević, for all his brutality, is a rank amateur in viciousness. What makes Clinton's crimes worse is the sanctimony and fraudulent concern in which he cloaks himself and, worse, which seem to fool the neo-liberals who now run the Natopolitan world. Better an honest conservative than a deceptive liberal.

Adding to this unhealthy situation, making it worse in fact, is the media, which has played the role not of impartial reporter but of partisan and partial witness to the folly and cruelty of the war. During the 79 days of bombing I must have watched at least 30 days of NATO briefings, and I cannot recall more than five or six reporters' questions that even remotely challenged the bilge put out by Jamie Shea, George Robertson and, worst of all, Javier Solano, the NATO honcho who has simply sold his 'socialist' soul to US global hegemony. There was no scepticism in evidence at all from the media, no attempt to do anything more than 'clarify' NATO positions, using retired military men (never women) to explicate the niceties of the terror bombing. Similarly liberal columnists and intellectuals, whose war in a sense this was, simply looked away from the destruction of Serbia's infrastructure (estimated at $136 billion) in their enthusiasm for the idea that 'we' were doing something to stop ethnic cleansing. Worst of all, the media only half-heartedly (if at all) reported on the war's unpopularity in the US, Italy, Greece, and Germany. No memory of what happened in Rwanda four years ago, or in Bosnia, or the displacement of 350,000 Serbs at the hands of Tudjman, or the continuing Turkish atrocities against the Kurds, the killing of over 560,000 Iraqi civilians, or – to bring it back to where it all started – Israel's ethnic cleansing of Palestine in 1948, which continues, with liberal support, until today. In what essential ways are Barak, Sharon, Netanyahu and Eitan different in their views and practices toward different and 'inferior' races from Milošević and Tudjman?

In the post-Cold War era, the question remains: is the US and its sordid military-economic policy, which knows only profit and opportunism, to rule the world, or can there develop a sufficiently powerful intellectual and moral resistance to its policies? For those of us who live in its sphere or are its citizens, the first duty is to demystify the debased language and images used to justify American practices and hypocrisy, to connect US policies in places like Burma, Indonesia, Iran and Israel with what it is now doing in Europe – making it safe for US investments and business – and to show that the policies are basically the same, though they are made to seem different. There can be no resistance without memory and universalism. If ethnic cleansing is evil in Yugoslavia – as it is, of course – it is also evil in Turkey, Palestine, Africa, and elsewhere. Crises are not over once CNN stops covering them. There can be no double standards. If war is cruel and deeply wasteful, then it is cruel whether or not American pilots bomb from 30,000 feet and remain unscathed. And if diplomacy is always to be preferred over military means, then diplomacy must be used at all costs.

Finally, if innocent human life is sacred, then it must not cynically be sacrificed if the victims happen not to be white and European. One must always begin one's resistance at home, against power that as a citizen one can influence; but alas, a fluent nationalism masking itself as patriotism and moral concern has taken over the critical consciousness, which then puts loyalty to one's 'nation' before everything. At that point there is only the treason of the intellectuals, and complete moral bankruptcy.

16

NATO'S BALKAN CRUSADE

Tariq Ali

In 1908, when hardly anyone in Europe was thinking of war and only eccentrics were dreaming of aeroplanes, a quaint British socialist, H.G. Wells, wrote a chilling futuristic fiction entitled, *War in the Air*, a book I first read four decades ago. Something must have remained in my sub-conscious. As I watched the deadly daily routines of NATO warplanes bombing the cities of the Yugoslav federation during NATO's Balkan crusade, I recalled H.G. Wells. Here are a few prophetic lines from this forgotten writer:

> Everywhere went the airships dropping bombs . . . And everywhere below were economic catastrophe, starving workless people, rioting and social disorder . . . towns and cities with the food supply interrupted and their streets congested with starving unemployed . . . crises in administration and states of siege . . . Money vanished into vaults, into holes, into walls of houses, into ten million hiding places. Money vanished, and at its disappearance trade and industry came to an end. The economic world staggered and fell dead . . . It was like water vanishing out of the blood of a living creature, it was a sudden, universal coagulation of intercourse . . . Everywhere there are ruins and unburied dead, and shrunken yellow-faced survivors in a mortal apathy . . .

In another novel, *The World Set Free*, Wells saw a world war brought about by an attack on the Slav Confederacy by Central European Powers, with Britain and France coming to the aid of the Confederacy. Not this time. The decision to bomb Belgrade was taken by Madeleine Albright and her advisers. When the New Labour government in Britain were informed as to what was required of them, they were, unsurprisingly, eager and willing to help pressure

France, Germany and Italy. These three countries had hitherto resisted attempts by Albright to embark on unilateral missions without UN sanction.

Albright convinced her European allies that (a) Milošević would capitulate abjectly after a few days of bombing and (b) that under no circumstances could the Russians be permitted to veto the operation. This meant that no appeal to the UN Security Council was possible. NATO would take international law into its own claws.

The pretext for this whole sordid affair was the refusal by the Serb leadership to accept the ultimatum thrown in its face at the Rambouillet talks where NATO (read Albright) insisted both that the peace-keeping force proposed for Kosovo would be limited to NATO troops (i.e. no Russians or Irish or Austrians) and that these forces would have the power to inspect any part of Serbia, and not simply Kosovo. This was the equivalent of putting a revolver to the head of Milošević. He walked out, as any other leader of a country would have done in similar circumstances. Hardly surprising then, given these facts, that Mikhail Gorbachev, on a visit to Britain at the beginning of the war, told anyone prepared to listen that negotiations might have become prolonged, but they could have succeeded if the United States had not so desperately wanted a war.

Albright wanted a quick NATO victory to show the world that NATO, under US leadership, was so much more effective than the United Nations. In the 14 June 1999 issue of the US liberal weekly *The Nation*, George Kenney, a former State Department Yugoslav desk officer, wrote: 'An unimpeachable press source who regularly travels with Secretary of State Madeleine Albright told this writer that, swearing reporters to deep-background confidentiality at the Rambouillet talks, a senior State Department official had bragged that the United States "deliberately set the bar higher than the Serbs could accept". The Serbs needed, according to the official, a little more bombing to see reason.'

This strategy lay in ruins the week after its implementation. Why?

The NATO campaign unleashed against Yugoslavia on 24 March 1999 was undermined by a fatal flaw, which soon threatened to undermine the alliance. They had either to negotiate a peace deal or get involved in a wider conflict, which could have led to a humanitarian mega-disaster and compelled the Russians to think seriously about creating their own security alliance: CRUVIS (China, Russia, Ukraine, Vietnam, India, Serbia). If the Ukraine agreed to such a plan, as it could have done, then the new alliance would be in a permanent confrontation with NATO on the Polish-Ukrainian border.

The flaw in the Albright strategy can be simply stated. Operation Allied Force was designed to win the Yugoslav government over to NATO's side through the operations of Western (Weberian) rationality, mediated by smart weaponry and a threat to bomb Yugoslavia back into the Stone Age. The idea was simple. Albright believed that the response of the government of Yugoslavia would be 'rational'. In other words it would adapt its ends to its means. Once the West destroyed these means by a blitzkrieg from the skies, the Yugoslav government, it was hoped, would begin the process of adjusting its ends until they ended up being virtually the same as those of NATO. It was hoped that two days of bombing might be sufficient. This did not happen.

The main concerns of the United States in this war had very little to do with the suffering of the Kosovan Albanians. If they had, the Western powers would have made a joint démarche with Russia, thus making it clear to Milošević that he had nowhere to turn to. Such a joint approach would have meant Russian participation in any peace-keeping force and it was this that the Pentagon rejected. The launching of NATO aerial bombardment was a calculated demonstration that NATO can resolve problems like this by itself. The risk that it would unleash Serb paramilitary terror on Kosovo was manifest. That is why most critics of the war believed that the US motives in this operation were sordid from the very outset.

The American decision to violate the sovereignty of a European state by ordering NATO air strikes against Serbia – the first time since Brezhnev launched the Warsaw Pact invasion of Czechoslovakia over three decades ago – posed two basic questions. What could justify this blatant disregard of international law and what future did NATO intend for the region? The answer to the first seems obvious. The American President, his English factotum and various European politicians, not to mention the overwhelming majority of the media, provide us with the reason every day: Milošević is Hitler. Yesterday Saddam Hussein was Hitler and who knows which Hitler tomorrow has in store for the trusting citizens of Europe. This infantilisation of European politics is a dangerous strategy and could well threaten the long-term functioning of liberal democracy itself. The use of the 'Hitler-genocide-holocaust' thesis to justify the new human rights imperialism rests on a lie. The notion that Britain and France (and later, the United States) declared war on Hitler in order to save the Jews is a grotesque re-writing of history. Media-idiocy is now so pronounced that nothing surprises, but social-democratic politicians and war-mongering academics who espouse such nonsense need detoxification.

The use of the Hitler analogy reflects the ideological weakness of human-rights imperialists. It appears to be the only way to convince the citizens of Western Europe that war is necessary. Anything else would be 'appeasement'. In order to crush such a leader, who refuses to listen to reason, it is necessary to wage war. That Milošević is a brutal leader has never been in doubt, and that the present Republic of Yugoslavia is based on the national oppression of the Albanians of Kosovo is equally true. But this was already true in 1991, when Milošević's rump Federation was recognised by every Western power, and it was still true at the time of the Dayton negotiations of 1995, when no attempt was made by any party to raise the question of Kosovo. That Milošević's forces have committed crimes against the Kosovars is undeniable. But is he alone? The West's highly selective pattern of concern for human rights continues today, as we all know. Israel's Netanyahu was an even more brutish politician, a violent and racist demagogue who defied UN resolutions with impunity and regularly bombed targets in Lebanon. In fact, the very foundation of Israel was accompanied by massacres and the ethnic cleansing of Palestinians, who were swept off their land in a fashion not dissimilar to what is taking place in Kosovo today.

And what of Milošević's counterpart in Croatia, the ailing Franjo Tudjman? He may be approaching his end now, but he, too, in his time, authorised the ethnic cleansing of Serbs and, on occasion, Bosnians. When he ethnically cleansed the Krajina of just under 200,000 Serbs in 1995, his action was actually in concert with NATO's Bosnian campaign. He presided over a regime which rehabilitated the leaders of Croatian fascists who collaborated with the Nazi occupiers during the Second World War. His government behaved thuggishly towards dissenters. But Netanyahu and Tudjman were on 'our side' and nothing else mattered. The only function of the Hitler analogy has been to obfuscate political discourse and to incite a stampede to reckless military action.

Plenty of crimes against humanity have been committed since Hitler. The Anglo-Saxon powers have fostered atrocities on a large scale in the second half of the century. Hitler's crimes should never be forgotten, but should we ignore US crimes in Latin America or southeast Asia simply because Washington emerged as the victor in the global civil war that began in 1917? In the name of freedom and democracy, they have backed dictators much worse than Milošević – who, we should remember, has been repeatedly elected by the Serbs in the course of elections which have been far less rigged than Yeltsin's referendum on the Constitution, so cravenly backed at the time by Western apologists – and helped them to power on every continent. This was usually done after great massacres. The Indonesian dictator, Suharto, was being armed by Britain and America right up to the day he was toppled by the popular uprising of May 1998, which received no support from either Washington or London. Indonesia, admittedly, is a faraway country, not visible (to paraphrase Tony Blair) from a Tuscan beach, but what about Turkey? It might certainly be sighted by a New Labour MP sunbathing on a Greek island. What successive governments in Ankara have inflicted on their Kurdish citizens has been as bad, if not worse, than the treatment meted out to the Kosovars. The argument used by the Turkish authorities is exactly the same as that employed by the Serb leadership. In torturing, maiming, killing and denying autonomy to the Kurds, they were simply defending the unity of the Turkish state. How many TV viewers are aware of the fact that this is still taking place, or that Turkey is an important member of NATO?

It is this blatant double standard that compels any critical observer to look for the deeper reasons that underlie this conflict. The need to protect the Kosovars served as the pretext for NATO's bombardment, but its real aim was to secure its control of this strategic region and to fortify an extensive NATO bridgehead in the heart of the Balkans. This action must be seen in the context of the expansion of NATO to include the larger, Western-oriented East European states. This expansion was never envisaged as including Russia, which remains the potential foe against which NATO measures itself. Nevertheless, until fairly recently, the NATO strategists hoped that Russia could be brought to accept a symbolic role as a 'Partner for Peace' under Western, actually US, hegemony. To soothe Russian sensibilities, NATO also established a Joint Council with Russia which would supposedly discuss difficult problems of mutual interest. In a keynote address given as late as 23 June 1998, the NATO Secretary General Javier Solana argued that it was essential, when tackling difficult issues such as Kosovo, that 'Russia . . . be on board'. He urged that it would be folly to exclude Russia completely when addressing any problem of European security, or to present a hostile front. He urged that the Permanent Joint Committee of NATO and Russian personnel should address not only Kosovo – described as the critical security challenge – but also such issues as NATO–Russian co-operation in SFOR, disarmament, terrorism and 'the retraining of retired military personnel'. Solana also spoke of the need for a 'European Security Identity' within NATO.

The NATO aerial bombardment of March 1999 broke completely with this earlier approach. Indeed, the prior six months of pressure and negotiations with Milošević had almost completely excluded Russia and entities such as the so-called Contact Group, which included Russia. Mikhail Gorbachev repeatedly pointed out that agreement on Kosovo could have been reached if the West had been willing to use the international machinery set up with great effort and fanfare to tackle issues such as this by the Organisation for Security and Co-operation in Europe (OSCE). The decision to exclude the approach most likely to secure a negotiated settlement meant that those who had determined NATO's strategy wanted a war. The decision of the Russian premier to abort his visit to the United States at the start of the air war made it perfectly plain that Washington was denying Russia's new government the earlier-envisaged role as partner. No doubt this was because the Primakov government no longer adhered to the abject stance associated with Kozyrev, the Russian Foreign Minister, described by Gorbachev as the 'former US Consul in Moscow'.

The NATO assault on Serbia thus marked a watershed in European politics. It reflected a decision by the United States to abandon all notions of a 'norm-based system of collective security' in Europe. This may have been wistful piety in any case, given a world ruled by capital under US hegemony, but it is something that the Russians have been demanding ever since Gorbachev came to power and it is a demand that was echoed by a number of EU states, including Kohl's Germany, following the end of the Cold War in 1989. The central reason why the NATO operation has taken place is that the West believes that Russia is still too weak to prevent such actions, and that a network of bases and fortified positions must be constructed now in order to contain Russia in the future, plugging the gap in the Balkans from Greece in the south to Hungary in the north.

Some supporters of the war, such as the *Guardian*'s egregious Jonathan Freedland, have argued that we should not worry about the ulterior motives of the Americans so long as they were doing the right thing – namely, defending the Kosovars. And, likewise, we should welcome it if the Western powers take against an oppressor they have indulged in the past – arguing that, having sorted out Milošević, the logic of their action now required an equally tough line against Turkey and Israel. But the fact is that the NATO approach has been a disaster for all the inhabitants of Kosovo – and the plight of the Kurds and Palestinians would hardly be improved by NATO bombardment of Israel or Turkey.

With the exception of the British, all European governments have hitherto refused to sanction any act of unilateral aggression, whatever the provocation, unless it had prior UN sanction. This was Germany's policy throughout the 1990s. The day after the bombardment started, Volker Rühe, the former German Defence Minister, insisted that German soldiers in Macedonia had been sent as 'peacekeepers' and 'not to make war' and therefore should be immediately withdrawn. It has also now emerged that a major reason for the dramatic resignation of Oskar Lafontaine was his total opposition to the NATO plan. He told the German Cabinet that it was reckless to follow the Americans in Kosovo (a German minister informed the *New York Times* that: 'In the end, it was Kosovo, that made him go'). The former German Chancellor, Helmut Schmidt, has launched a blistering attack on NATO's adventure and it is clear that the ruling SPD in Germany is seriously split. The bombers' faction in the Greens, too, might soon find themselves confronted by a rank-and-file rebellion.

A silent, behind-the-scenes war is being fought across Western Europe to determine the leadership of the EU. The US has used its old British Trojan Horse to lead a neo-liberal drive in the EU. Kosovo is a neat operation from the Anglo-American point of view to drag the EU behind NATO/US world leadership, and to get rid of the notion that Russian sensibilities should be catered for. American strategists, desperate to retain NATO as their battering-ram in the new Europe, manoeuvred Europe into a war in order to prove that NATO had a permanent function, that it was the ultimate arbiter and could act alone, presenting the rest of the world with a fait accompli. Action through the OSCE would have been more laborious, but it would have favoured a negotiated solution and would have meant obliging the Yugoslav government to honour an agreement which it had itself accepted.

Of course, a negotiated settlement would not have helped the market a great deal. The war certainly appears to have boosted stocks, as noted slightly defensively in the *Financial Times* of 12 April 1999:

> It may seem a little macabre to look for beneficiaries of the Kosovo conflict, but then the stock market is not sentimental. Since NATO started its bombing raids on March 24, shares in British Aerospace and Smiths Industries have climbed nearly 9 per cent, while GKN is up 8 per cent and Raytheon by 7 per cent. There is cold-blooded logic in this. Jane's, a military research group, estimates that NATO has spent close to $1bn in less than three weeks, most of it on armaments and fuel. The US, for

> example, has fired off over 150 cruise missiles, made by Lockheed and Boeing at a cost of $1.2m each, as well as losing a $35m Stealth fighter, also built by Lockheed. Matra's missiles and Raytheon's laser-guided bombs have also been in action, while the heavy use of warplanes should benefit BAE, Rolls-Royce and the big US defence groups that service them and supply spare parts. Further out, there may be a 'war dividend' if countries reassess their military needs in light of the conflict. Speculation that NATO will be forced to send in ground troops equipped with fighting vehicles and helicopters has helped buoy GKN, which manufactures both.

If the NATO assault eventually forces the Serbs to accept a NATO peacekeeping force, it will be hailed as a major victory and will strengthen the Anglo-American alliance in the EU. But, if the air war fails to bring Milošević to the negotiating table, then NATO will have to decide whether to commit ground troops – with all the hazards and difficulties entailed – or to abandon the unilateral approach and invite Russian mediation. If NATO splits, the results would be catastrophic for the Alliance, but good for Europe as a whole. That is why what is important for NATO planners is not how many Kosovars die in the process or become refugees, but how these deaths and displacements are perceived. If NATO is blamed for them, then they will have failed and moves towards a European Security Council, which includes the non-NATO states, might be revived. This is what the German and Russian states really want and they might yet succeed. In fact, the very existence of NATO has been an anachronism since the collapse of the Soviet Union and the dissolution of the Warsaw Pact. NATO is, essentially, nothing more than an instrument to secure US hegemony in Europe and, if the Kosovo operation is successful, the world.

Just before the bombing began, the Kosovan and Serb leaderships had agreed a three-year period of autonomy, after which the issue could be rediscussed. The discussions broke down on the presence of a 'peacekeeping force'. The Serbs, not unreasonably, regarded the composition of this force as NATO-in-disguise. The Russians could have persuaded them that this was not the case if NATO had agreed to a Russian complement under UN auspices, but, before matters could proceed further, the United States said 'enough'. The Serbs left the table, the monitors were withdrawn and the bombs began to fall. Negotiations will have to begin again. It is unlikely that the Serbs will accept the presence of any NATO soldiers on their soil. The

Kosovars, on their part, will refuse to tolerate Milošević's special police units or soldiers. Both will be right and a solution might lie in a neutral UN or OSCE peacekeeping force, which does not contain soldiers from armies that have attacked either side.

Many despairing liberals and kind-hearted social democrats, understandably upset by the images of fleeing Kosovan refugees on television, have become keen warmongers. The Europe that is backing the American war in Serbia is the liberal, social-democratic half of the continent. In a simplistic political culture dominated by life politics, the shedding of tears for one set of victims is coupled with dropping bombs on their oppressors – even if the process means both creating new victims and bringing horrendous reprisals upon those on whose behalf military action was undertaken. Sadly, the distorted news values of the main Western media allow both for much popular confusion and ignorance and for a ludicrous imbalance in presentation, such that the fate of three US soldiers is given as much prominence as the enforced exodus of 250,000 Kosovan refugees.

Even the most servile NATO apologists, who fervently claimed that the bombing of Serbia was designed to help the Kosovars, must surely be able to see the scale of the humanitarian disaster that this has unleashed. Were NATO's political leaders really surprised by the brutal reaction of the Serbian Government? The Defense Department spokesman in Washington was clear where his own organisation stood: 'In the Pentagon, in this building, we were not surprised by what Milošević has done. I think there is historical amnesia here if anyone says they are surprised by the campaign.' In that case, why was more not done to prepare for the flood of refugees? New Labour's Minister for Overseas Development, Ms Clare Short, explained on British television that, if the West had been seen to prepare for the refugees, people might have assumed this to be 'the inevitable effect of NATO's bombing action'. Here we have the grotesque logic of this entire operation in a nutshell. We knew the Kosovars would be victimised because of our bombing, but we could not acknowledge this in advance. The bombing, as most serious observers on Right and Left had predicted, has utterly failed either to help the Kosovars or to weaken support for Milošević.

Interestingly, in Britain, the most sustained critique of the war has come from commentators associated with the Right: Corelli Barnett, Andreas Whittam-Smith, William Rees-Mogg, Alan Clark and Norman Stone, to name but the most prominent. Most of the traditional liberal, social-democratic and anti-war Left, as well as their newspapers and journals, backed the NATO action. Since the bombing has failed, the liberal warmongers, who think nothing these days of violating national sovereignty – a crime for which Galtieri was crushed and Saddam is still being punished – began to call loudly for ground troops. This option was not favoured from the outset because NATO soldiers are willing to kill but not to die. Since this remains the NATO approach, there is likely to be a search for proxy warriors. One is tempted to suggest that those on the Left calling for ground troops should, if they are serious, set an example and volunteer to create International Brigades to fight alongside the Kosovo Liberation Army to establish the independence of Kosovo. This at least would be in harmony with the internationalist tradition: socialists and liberals fought against Franco during the 1930s and some of us active against the Vietnam war discussed the question of volunteers quite seriously with the North Vietnamese leadership. The principle is a basic one. You do not call on others to fight in what you regard as a just war unless you are prepared to do so yourself. In these 'third way' times, such brigades, no doubt, could be sponsored by companies such as Sandline, Somerfield and so on. The new warmongers want NATO's armies to fight their war for them, willingly accepting the perversion of the Kosovan cause by Western strategic obsessions that will follow.

The Kosovo Liberation Army is not the military wing of a political movement. It is a very recent creation and has no connection with the parties that have won Kosovan votes in the past, such as that led by Ibrahim Rugova. A recent report in the *Los Angeles Times* quoted in the *Guardian* claimed that the KLA was linked to organised crime, to drug traffickers and to Osama Bin Laden. It added: 'Ivo Daalder, until recently the National Security Council's top expert on the Balkans in the White House, said: "If what we are proposing here is starting a major guerrilla campaign to regain Kosovo, that is the Afghan syndrome".' Afghanistan today is certainly a grim reminder of where the West's anti-Russian obsession can all too easily lead. Daalder went on to say 'We won't be able to control these guys . . . they may not turn out to be a force that is in our interest'. However, it would be foolish to accept these comments at face value. The US has a long record of using organisations when it suits their purposes and later discarding them without ceremony.

What is taking place is one of the last scenes in the tragedy which was the break-up of Yugoslavia. The West bears a central responsibility for encouraging this process. The claim that it is all Milošević's fault is one-sided and erroneous, indulging those Slovenian, Croatian and Western politicians who allowed him to succeed. It could be argued, for instance, that it was Slovene egoism, throwing the Bosnians and Albanians, as well as non-nationalist Serbs and Croats, to the wolves, that was a decisive factor in triggering the whole disaster of disintegration. Once the collapse of the old Federation became unstoppable, then it was obvious that Kosovo had an equal if not greater right to independence than Croatia and Macedonia, let alone Bosnia. None of the latter have 90 per cent of the population belonging to one ethnic group. The Western powers refused to countenance Kosovan self-determination, because it was committed to a Bosnian protectorate based on exactly the opposite principle, the inviolability of the old republican frontiers. The entire record of the West in Yugoslavia is a long series of cynical and hypocritical manoeuvres, of which the bombing of Serbia is only the most recent, but will surely not be the last.

NATO bombing was designed, or so we were led to believe, to halt the flow of refugees. It has increased it a hundredfold. Pre-bombing spin had also implied that Milošević wanted his country bombed so that he could quickly capitulate and isolate the more hardline nationalists. This turned out to be pure fantasy. Another reason was to weaken political support for Milošević within Serbia. Instead, as the Belgrade correspondent of the *New York Times* reported during the second week of the bombing, it has strengthened him. The bombing of Belgrade and the bridge in Novi Sad is hardly designed to win over the population. The citizens of Serbia were either angry and prepared for a prolonged resistance, or in a state of sullen despondency.

The old Yugoslavia was unique in the sense that it was founded twice this century. After the Treaty of Versailles, imposed by the victors of the First World War, it was conceived of as a Serb-dominated kingdom, a buffer carefully designed to exclude Soviet influence in the Balkans. The second Yugoslavia was born after a long resistance struggle against German fascism and its indigenous relays. Its leader, Tito, a communist of Croatian origin, devised a federation based on a model equality between constituent nationalities and minorities, with the exception of Kosovo, which should have been, but never was, granted equal status within the Federation. He was also fierce in defending Yugoslav independence against both Stalin and NATO. The second Yugoslavia did not survive its creator by too many years, but it does represent the most tranquil period this region has enjoyed. It would be difficult to recreate. We cannot live by yesterday's clock, nor by today's, but by tomorrow's. During the sea voyages of old, a man was sent aloft a mast from where he could see icebergs and maelstroms and foundering ships which were invisible from the deck. Is the West going to repeat its mistakes in Yugoslavia or think creatively ahead?

The break-up of Yugoslavia has already cost the EU and the USA tens of billions of dollars. This war alone has been costed at $12 billion and the figure will rise. If half this amount of money had been publicly offered for the economic development of all of former Yugoslavia, as part of a OSCE-brokered compromise, we might have been spared the traumas of the last decade. Today, the EU could still underwrite a reconstruction plan based on the experience of Marshall Aid, and encourage, if not the rebirth of a third Yugoslavia, then a new Balkan confederation of states which would deal as a whole with the EU. Such an arrangement would have to include an independent Kosovo. There are only two serious alternatives for this region: either a series of NATO protectorates imposed by war and bloody battles, leading to the re-militarization of Europe and a new Cold War with Russia, or a serious attempt to create a new regional framework and to engage Russia in constructive negotiations on all outstanding issues.

The long-term future of the region should be decided within the framework of the OSCE, equipped, as the Russians have long demanded, with a Secretariat and Security Council. Within such a forum, the European powers could raise issues of repression in Chechnya and the Russians could table policing in Northern Ireland, Corsica or Southern Turkey.

In the end it became clear that NATO couldn't go it alone. The 'once in, we've gotta win' approach failed. NATO needed the Russians in order to avoid a ground war and casualties. The Germans and Russians ultimately brokered a deal. Under US pressure, Yeltsin had removed Primakov as Prime Minister. Moscow told Belgrade that unless Milošević accepted the new compromise, which was better than Rambouillet, they would consider cutting off oil supplies. Milošević agreed to withdraw. Most of his army and their equipment in Kosovo was intact. So much for NATO propaganda which claimed that the Serb army in the province had been well and truly 'degraded'.

Those who paid a heavy price in this war were ordinary Kosovans and Serbs alike. If one takes NATO at face value and accepts that the aim had been to protect the Kosovan Albanians, then the war was a monumental failure. It created a much worse humanitarian catastrophe. NATO-occupied Kosovo will be ethnically pure. Serbs and gypsies are being driven out by the KLA under NATO's protection. But the war has been a major political failure. NATO is seriously divided. It could not secure its goal without involving

Russia and the UN, and the Germans, Italians and Greeks will think long and hard before agreeing to a similar adventure in the future.

An early indication of this was a signed editorial headed 'Madeleine's War' by Rudolf Augstein, the influential publisher of the German weekly *Der Spiegel*, published on 31 May 1999, in which Augstein rejected suggestions that this was a humanitarian war and insisted that it was much more a 'colonial war'. He argued that 'The strategic meaning, from Washington's point of view, was to make clear to the Europeans that NATO could no longer be what it had successfully been for fifty years: a defensive alliance. It would have to have different goals and different structures and that had to be made clear to the Europeans.'

Albright's policy was short-sighted and foolish. It created the basis for new conflicts. The Ukraine, for instance, was the only country in the world to renounce nuclear weapons and unilaterally disarm. During the war its Parliament voted unanimously to revert to its former nuclear status. The deputies claimed that they had foolishly believed the United States when it had promised a new norm-based and inclusive security system. NATO's war on Yugoslavia had destroyed all their illusions and belated attempts to woo them back into the fold by promising EU membership 'in the future' may not work.

If Kiev was angry, Moscow was incandescent. Mikhail Gorbachev mocked the EU leaders: 'Yes, you are strong economically, but politically you are pygmies.' The military-industrial complex is one of the best-preserved institutions in the country. Its leaders have been arguing with the politicians for nearly two years, pleading that they be allowed to upgrade Russia's nuclear armoury. Till 24 March 1999 they had not made much headway. On 30 April, a meeting of the National Security Council in Moscow approved the modernisation of all strategic and tactical nuclear warheads. It gave the green light to the development and manufacture of strategic low-yield nuclear missiles capable of pin-point strikes anywhere in the world. Simultaneously the Defence ministry authorised a change in nuclear doctrine. First use is no longer excluded. In the space of several weeks, Javier Solana and Robin Cook, former members of European Nuclear Disarmament, had re-ignited the nuclear flame.

In Beijing, too, the bombing of the Chinese Embassy has resulted in a shift away from the no-first-strike principle. The Chinese refuse to accept that the bombing of their embassy was an accident. Rightly or wrongly, they believe that it was a Machiavellian ploy by the war-party in Washington to raise the stakes and make a settlement more difficult. When Beijing insisted that 'We want those responsible to be severely punished', they were not referring to the pilots who simply obeyed orders. The Chinese have long memories. They were hoping that Clinton would sack either Albright or Berger, just as President Truman had sacked MacArthur for suggesting a land invasion of China during the Korean War of the 1950s. There are also indications that Moscow and Beijing are discussing new security arrangements to counter NATO. The bombs that fell on Belgrade and other cities may well come to be seen as the first shots of a new Cold War.

This is something that was ignored by liberal and social-democratic warmongers. Why? Partially, I think, it is the carefully controlled images on television. We live in an atomised world where, ironically, the internationalisation of the market has led to a cultural and political insularity, especially in the United States and Britain. But there are deeper and other causes. In France, for instance, the human rights hysteria reached irrational proportions. The verbal violence used against Régis Debray, who, in his inimitable fashion, dared to challenge French involvement in the war was, to put it mildly, disproportionate – a literary version of the NATO bombing. Parisian intellectual fashions have never been the same since the 'new philosophers' took over the pages of *Le Monde* during the Reagan era, mimicking the crude anti-communism of the White House while trying to render it more profound. It is the same old gang at work again. They want more war, more bombs and a ground invasion. *Libération* has become their house-journal.

In the United States there is a general indifference to the war, but the liberal warmongers were hard at work. In the *New York Review of Books* Tony Judt, a Cold War academic, penned a ferocious attack on Clinton, comparing him to Neville Chamberlain and accusing him of betraying the cause of human rights by refusing to send in ground troops.

Ever since the collapse of the Soviet Union in 1991 and the triumph of capital, the international left has been in a state of great demoralisation. This is only natural. The scale of the defeat was enormous and its effects have been disorienting. Some on the left have lost confidence in the capacity of people to emancipate themselves. This loss of self-confidence makes them desperate. They want others to accomplish what they cannot do themselves. The problem here is that US interests in the world have very little to do with human rights. True, human rights, freedom and democracy are usually used to justify sanctions, bombings and invasions, but it was always thus. The European powers partitioned Africa, claiming that their purpose was to wipe out the slave trade. In the end they spread forced labour systems of a horrendous nature, which reached a climax in the Congo where King Leopold's colonisers killed between six and eight million people in the name of a superior civilisation.

Times have changed and with them the mode of exploitation has also become different. The experience of Bosnia as a NATO protectorate is not a happy one. In effect, Western rule has extinguished democracy in the region. NATO makes the political decisions and a local *mafia* runs the economy in accord with the dictates of the IMF. This is not a model that a human rights fundamentalist should seek to impose on any country but that could be Kosovo's future; it does not work.

In the bad old days when the United States was implanting dictators in every continent, the left was content to rely on the people to topple tyrants. We never pleaded with Moscow to invade Chile and topple Pinochet or with Beijing to invade Indonesia and get rid of Suharto. The human rights fundamentalists have a positive preference for the use of force and a naked display of power. Some of them may not be aware of it, but they are playing the role of imperial foot soldiers in the new struggle for hegemony that will mark the next century.

NATO's first Secretary General, the late Lord Ismay, once remarked that their aim was 'to keep the Americans in, the Russians out and the Germans down'. Fifty years later, the world has changed but NATO's logic appears to be the same. The dissolution of NATO might be the first step on the long road to world peace.

17

KOSOVO: THE WAR OF NATO EXPANSION

Robin Blackburn

NATO has established a Kosovo protectorate at the cost of great suffering for the peoples of the region and in a way that is likely to further poison the relations between different communities. The bombing by NATO set the scene for the expulsion of around one million Albanian Kosovans and devastated social infrastructure throughout Yugoslavia. The death toll after 24 March 1999 in Kosovo itself was about ten thousand, with some five thousand killed in the rest of Yugoslavia; those wounded or rendered homeless are very much more numerous. Most of the victims were civilians and refugees, not soldiers. Despite the claims for precision weapons, errors claimed many lives.

Some critics of the air war argued that a ground assault should have been mounted from the beginning. On this point the NATO high command had a more realistic grasp. The Serb army was well dug in and possessed thousands of rocket launchers, mortars and artillery pieces. While the ultimate outcome would never have been in doubt, the casualties arising from an immediate invasion would have been very high, civilian as well as military. No sane commander would prefer a contested entry in such circumstances, amongst some of the most inhospitable terrain imaginable, to the prior destruction of the enemy's hardware, supply dumps, communications and morale. Advocates of a ground assault might claim that it would have avoided sorties against civilian targets, the use of cluster bombs, and some of the errors. But the prior aerial bombardment had a perfect military logic, and it was the first week of bombing that precipitated the escalation of violence on the ground as hundreds of thousands were driven from their homes by enraged and murderous Serb soldiers and paramilitaries.

As the conflict developed both sides were frustrated at their inability to hit and hurt the enemy's military capacity so they hit civilian targets instead. As it turned out the NATO bombardment was, in fact, militarily even less effective than was realised at the time, with many of the targeted tanks, artillery pieces and the like being plastic decoys while the real military assets were hidden in underground bunkers. Unfortunately the bridges, power plants, refineries, hospitals and schools destroyed were the real thing. The war was undertaken by NATO in the name of human rights but the conflict itself hardened ethnic animosity and blindness, ending with the terrorisation and forced expulsion of the great majority of Kosovo's Serbs and Gypsies. The desire for revenge instilled in the minds of many Kosovan Albanians was, of course, very understandable. But the role of outsiders in perpetuating and aggravating the cycle of communal conflict is quite another matter, especially when the supposed champions of human rights are silent as women, children and old people are driven from their homes.

The West has a heavy responsibility for the bloody break-up of former Yugoslavia and for its prolonged neglect of the oppression of the Kosovo Albanians. But even as late as December 1998 or March 1999 it could have played a crucial part in promoting a peaceful settlement. The disastrous air war was wrong not because there was another military option but because, from the outset, a deal was available providing for the withdrawal of Serb forces and their replacement by a UN or OSCE security force. This alternative foundered because it did not give NATO the protectorate it wanted. The Russian government, eager to please its Western creditors and play what it saw as its rightful part on the international scene, was amenable to a joint approach to Belgrade.[1] The UN Contact Group could have reached an agreement on a withdrawal of Serb forces from Kosovo at any time from March to December 1998 so long as the leading Western powers had lined up the Russians first. The Yugoslav government was on the brink of signing up to such a package at Rambouillet but when details of the provisions of the Agreement were imposed by the United States, it became clear that Russia had been by-passed. The provisions stipulated that the international security force would be NATO-led, that it would have the right of inspection throughout the Yugoslav republic and that its members would be exempt from responsibility for their actions before local courts. Moscow attacked the proposal for a NATO-led occupation force and the Russian negotiator declined to be present when the Agreement embodying it was signed by the Kosovan delegation on 15 March 1999. When news of the bombing came through the Russian prime minister cancelled in mid-flight a visit to Washington. Milošević was never going to accept an agreement rejected by the Russians, especially one which provided for a provocative expansion of NATO's sphere of operations. To do so would deprive him of vital support and make him vulnerable to internal opponents. But by the same token a settlement supported by Russia would be very difficult for him to reject even if it meant wholesale evacuation from Kosovo.

An item on the failed Rambouillet negotiations in the *New York Times* for 8 April 1999 observed: 'In a little-noted resolution of the Serbian Parliament just before the bombing, when that hardly independent body rejected NATO troops in Kosovo, it also supported the idea of UN forces to monitor a political settlement there.' The Serbian delegation, under duress, had been willing to accept the principles of the Rambouillet package save for the very detailed twenty-fifth chapter on the NATO-led occupation force.[2] When Milošević made a deal at Dayton he implemented it punctiliously, accepting the forced expulsion of hundreds of thousands of Serbs from lands they had long inhabited. Even if implementation of a Kosovo deal had been more difficult, the relationship of forces, both in Kosovo and in the world, would have ensured compliance without the horrendous cost the war had entailed.

In late April and early May a new round of diplomatic mediation assisted by the governments of Russia and Finland again foundered on NATO insistence that the proposed security force should be built around a NATO 'core'. Following a meeting of the G8 the Russian Foreign Minister, Igor Ivanov, made it clear no agreement had been reached on this issue because Russia could not accept the transformation of Kosovo into a NATO protectorate. The Western insistence on a controlling role for NATO thus precluded a combined approach to Belgrade and doomed the prospects for a Security Council resolution on the question. This phase of negotiation was brought to an end by the bombing of the Chinese Embassy in Belgrade without the West having made any concession on NATO's role.

Of course the willingness of Milošević to strike a deal did not come from the goodness of his heart but because of his fear of NATO striking power, his wish for an end to sanctions and a craving for international respectability, precisely the motives which brought him to endorse the agreement at Dayton in 1995. It might be thought that the fear element in the Serbian leader's motivation itself justified the air assault. But this would only have been the case if the bombardment had produced a result for the Kosovans very much better than that already available at Rambouillet in February, and after the carnage of the war that could scarcely be the case. The settlement eventually reached, notwithstanding the token Russian role, meant that NATO acquired a better strategic emplacement in the region, but the Kosovans have still paid a heavy price.

The composition of the security force was the stumbling block in March and in early May 1999 because NATO opposed any security force in Kosovo that it did not wholly control. In public both sides were bound to overstate their position but the composition of the security force was always the sticking point. At all times the Russian stance was bound to be critical to Belgrade, not only because a Serbian dominated Yugoslavia would always find it easier to go along with Russian mediation, enforced with the help of Russian troops, or because Russia had the resources to help Yugoslavia with fuel, arms and diplomatic comfort, but because any Belgrade government authorising a NATO protectorate in Kosovo would earn the enmity of Russia. Milošević was always sure in the knowledge that all sectors of Russian opinion would oppose the conversion of Kosovo into a NATO protectorate.

Some Kosovans and their supporters argued that anything less than immediate and full self-determination for the people of Kosovo was unacceptable. But at Rambouillet the Kosovan delegation, after much pressure and agonising, declared that they accepted a NATO protectorate and that the security force must be NATO-led. Of course, the composition and leadership of this delegation had been carefully vetted by NATO – the veteran KLA leader Adem Demaci was excluded and an inexperienced 29-year-old, Hashim Thaqi, was recognised as leader of the delegation while the veteran Ibrahim Rugova was sidelined. NATO did not to allow the Kosovans to dictate its strategy. At no point did NATO ask Belgrade to renounce all claim to Kosovo. The Kosovan delegation was eventually persuaded to sign up to Rambouillet despite this fact.[3]

NATO was willing to allow a token Yugoslav presence at some border points as a sop to the notion that, in some loose way, Kosovo was still, like Montenegro, part of Yugoslavia. The justification offered for this was that the key issue was the replacement of Serb occupation by an international security force that would allow refugees to return and would lay the basis for some new political structure. If it were not for the fact that NATO insisted that such a process required a NATO protectorate, the proposal for a purely transitional, face-saving formula would be a reasonable compromise, permitting an orderly withdrawal of Serb forces.

The UN or OSCE alternative to a NATO-led security force would almost certainly have included a large contingent from some NATO states but it would also have had significant Russian and neutral participation. If the European powers were prepared to pay the greater part of the cost of such a force, which is only fair considering their large contribution to the escalation of the Yugoslav wars, there is every reason to suppose that such a broader security force would do a more disinterested job than a NATO-led force. So long as their wages are paid, armies are structured to obey orders; this is as true for the Russian, Irish and Finnish armies as it is for NATO forces. And because it would not provoke the Russians, it would contribute to regional security rather than undermining it. In terms of the practicality of inserting such a force into Kosovo it should be borne in mind that in February 1999 there were already a few thousand OSCE monitors in place; instead of withdrawing them, an act which undoubtedly encouraged the Serb paramilitaries to do their worst, the number of monitors could have been sharply increased as the occupation force was assembled.

Some saw any countenancing of a Russian role as naïve or treacherous; it was to ignore Russia's brutal attempt in 1994–96 to suppress the Chechen republic or to underestimate how reckless and bloody Russian politicians and the Russian military can be. The fact is that a very similar objection could be made to the leading NATO states. For example in 1998 the US appointed William Walker, a man responsible for working with a murderous military regime in Guatemala, to lead the OSCE monitoring force in Kosovo; on a recent trip to Central America President Clinton publicly apologised for the US contribution to the campaign of military terror unleashed by Rios Montt and the Guatemalan military and para-military forces in the 1980s. The British government has publicly apologised for the Bloody Sunday shootings and its soldiers in Northern Ireland have been found guilty of torture of suspects. The French security services blew up the 'Rainbow Warrior' and actively collaborated with the Hutu militia in Rwanda. And so on. In all these cases the misdeeds of the Western security forces and advisers primarily reflected the character of the mission entrusted to them by the politicians. Likewise in Chechnya.[4] The West itself has not banned Russia from any military role outside its borders. Indeed there is a Russian contingent in the Bosnia security force. If the Kosovo security force had excluded all NATO powers then it could certainly have excluded Russia as well without aggravating the already lop-sided military stand-off in East-Central Europe, but this has never been proposed.

The prolonged occupation of Kosovo by troops of any foreign power – Russian, US, or for that matter Finnish and Irish – will be likely to lead to abuse, corruption and repression which is why any such arrangement should be strictly limited to the period of time required to allow self-determination for the people of Kosovo to become a reality. At all times it was clear that the negotiated withdrawal of the Serbian paramilitaries, police and army units was the pre-condition for lifting the afflictions of the Kosovan Albanians. The unleashing of the bombardment and the wave of Serb reprisals made the task of peace and reconciliation vastly more difficult. But a Serb withdrawal was still required to create the best conditions for a return of refugees and for recuperation from the ordeal of occupation and war. A large force of mixed foreign troops would then be needed to keep the peace and this force would undoubtedly face the very difficult task of preventing further revenge attacks. The UN or the Council of Europe were far more suitable sponsors of such an occupation than NATO but even they should have had the urgent goal of recruiting and training a local police force drawn from all sections of society. Advocates of the war sought to discredit any UN role by intoning the word Srebrenica as if the deployment of a UN force in Kosovo *after the withdrawal of Serbian forces* would invite the disasters that attended UN 'peace-keeping' efforts in Bosnia where there were large Serb military formations and where, unlike Kosovo, the Serbs were the largest national group. The group most at risk in Kosovo after a Serb withdrawal was obviously going to be the local Serbs, a fact which the war party wilfully ignored.

I have argued that the war was unleashed, and was allowed to become a protracted assault on the whole social infrastructure of Yugoslavia, for one reason, and one reason only; that nothing less than a 'NATO-led' solution and NATO-protectorate status for Kosovo was acceptable to the US and Britain, and that other alliance members went along with this, whatever their public or private reservations. In other words the war had a strategic dimension which blighted early prospects of settlement, precipitated a humanitarian catastrophe and is likely to continue to poison East–West relations.

When former President Mikhail Gorbachev visited King's College, Cambridge, in March 1999 he expressed astonishment that the West was prepared to follow up the expansion of NATO by making a bonfire of all the international accords and organisations that had been put in place to safeguard peace and human rights. Those who went to war treated the Helsinki agreements as a scrap of paper and shunted aside the OSCE. They denied Russia a real say in the crisis, notwithstanding the obvious contribution which the Russian government could make to a settlement. Those who heard

Gorbachev, and had the opportunity to speak with him, could not fail to be impressed by his alarm nor fail to be shocked by the failure of many commentators even to address the wider issues raised by the war. On this issue Gorbachev was evidently speaking for nearly every strand of Russian opinion.

From the outset the Russian government denounced unilateral NATO military action, warning that it would provoke a new Cold War, bring instability to a wide arc of countries and lead to the final burial of both nuclear and conventional disarmament. It saw the insistence that Kosovo become a NATO protectorate as part of a wider scene of encirclement.

Advocates of a NATO-led ground war proposed a further escalation of the provocation. Given the huge difficulties of landing a significant force in Kosovo the NATO commanders would be tempted to move against Belgrade directly from their bases in Macedonia, Bosnia and Hungary, with the help of allied local forces. A military plunge into Serbia could well have detonated the political minefields in Macedonia, Bosnia and Montenegro. If Hungary, Rumania or Croatia had been given any role, then territories such as the Voyvodina and Moldova could also be dragged in, as could Russia, the Ukraine, and their respective borderlands. A NATO-occupied Yugoslavia would complete Russia's encirclement.

So, had the NATO leaders forgotten about Russia's possession of 3,500 intercontinental ballistic missiles, with their nuclear warheads? Did the fragility of the political order in Russia need to be pointed out to them? Did it require the Chinese reaction to the bombing of their Belgrade embassy to notice that Russia, the military giant, and China, the rising economic power, are exploring economic and military cooperation?

For whatever reason most Western commentators rarely refer to such matters preferring to maintain the comfortable illusion of an end to the Cold War. But it would be absurd to suppose that Pentagon or State Department strategists do not think about them the whole time. The Kosovo operation was a further evolution of the new policy of enlarging NATO, projecting NATO power and containing Russia. US Secretary of State Madeleine Albright and National Security Adviser Sandy Berger, with encouragement from veteran cold warriors like Zbigniew Brzezinski and Senator Jesse Helms, have certainly focused on the global strategic dimension even if the US President, Congress and public were engrossed in the Lewinsky affair. When justifying the size of the US military budget complicated formulas have been put forward about the need to confront two major regional crises at the same time; thinly veiled hints then make it clear that the US military establishment is designed to be able to confront and contain both Russia and China. Two former senior officials at the Defense Department recently noted: 'For obvious reasons, the administration would like to avoid having to explain why it regards these countries (i.e. Russia and China) as potential adversaries in its defense analyses.'[5] But is a new show-down with Russia inevitable or could it be avoided by constructive engagement? Should the emphasis be upon carrying through already-negotiated disarmament agreements, such as START-2, or should these be abandoned in favour of discreet preparations for a new confrontation with what William Cohen, the Defense Secretary, has called the potential 'global peer competitor'. Should Russia be invited to join NATO or should the alliance give Russia a demonstration of the fate that awaits it if it steps out of line?

In a new book, *Preventive Defense,* Ashton Carter and William Perry, who stepped down as Secretary of Defense in early 1997, have explained their own fears that the US, in overreacting to manageable problems like Kosovo, may actually re-create a mortal threat to US security. Paraphrasing their argument in a review of this work Lawrence Freedman writes:

> Unfortunately the fund of goodwill between Washington and Moscow with which the 1990s started has now largely been spent, and has not been replenished. A large part of the problem is economic as the Russians blame the West for the failure of their bowdlerised version of capitalism to deliver the goods. The major strain in political relations, however, has come from NATO enlargement, a policy that was bound to be seen in Moscow as reneging on past pledges not to take advantage of the collapse of the Warsaw Pact to strengthen the Western Alliance. The authors make it clear as delicately as they can that they opposed the advocates of this move in the Clinton administration, precisely because of the negative Russian reaction it predictably generated.[6]

Other opponents of enlargement have included George Kennan, Jeff Matlock and many other senior diplomats and former ambassadors, including virtually all of those who have been posted to Moscow. The fullest statement of the case against by a US strategic analyst was Michael Mandelbaum's book, *The Dawn of Peace in Europe.*[7]

Brzezinski on the other hand has consistently claimed that NATO expansion was not only a wise but an essential policy. In 1996 he was quoted as saying that the Russian Federation was 'redundant'. He explained: 'Russia is viable as a nation state. I don't think, however, it has much future as an empire. I don't think the Russians can re-establish their empire. If they're stupid enough to try, they'll get themselves into conflicts that'll make Chechnya and Afghanistan look like a picnic.'[8] He believed that Russia was menacing and over-centralised: 'Given the country's size and diversity, a decentralised political system and free-market economics would be most likely to unleash the creative potential of the Russian people and Russia's vast natural resources.' He looked forward to a 'loosely confederated Russia – composed of a European Russia, a Siberian republic and a Far Eastern republic'.[9] Brzezinski advocated economic and military measures to boost the independence of each of the states on Russia's borders. Indeed he himself helped to promote the formation of a new alliance between Georgia, Ukraine, Azerbaijan, and Moldova (GUAM). Following the financial crisis in Russia in August 1998 Brzezinski observed that the events in Moscow signalled 'the end of this rather naïve spin . . . namely that Russia has been successful at privatising and that Russia has been successful at democratising. I'm afraid neither is true.'[10]

As a former National Security Adviser Brzezinski, who is still based on Washington, gave needed strategic weight to the policy of NATO enlargement. For his part Clinton adopted the policy prior to the last Presidential election having found that it would play well with many Polish Americans, Baltic Americans, Czech Americans and so forth, as well as enhancing his image as a tough leader. NATO enlargement was one more issue on which the incumbent could wrongfoot the Republicans. This was politics rather than thoroughgoing backing for the Brzezinski vision and efforts were still made to help Yeltsin, including a very mild response to the repression in Chechnya. For its part the Russian government was almost pathetically anxious to do the West's bidding. Brzezinski discounts this on the grounds that it is the power structure that matters; for him the Russian Federation is a chip off the old block and its politics and armed forces are insufficiently de-sovietised. The Secretary of State is obliged to be more cautious but basically Madeleine Albright remains in thrall to the outlook of her old mentor and contemptuous of those who would indulge Russia. In an article published in November 1998 she curtly observed that 'Russia is wrestling with severe economic and military challenges' and lectured its leaders on the need for disarmament.[11]

With Kosovo, and with the President distracted, NATO enlargement moved from diplomacy and budget planning to fait accompli and unilateral military initiative. It is unlikely that Tony Blair, Britain's callow and histrionic premier, grasped the larger picture or understood that he was helping the hawks to prevail. On the eve of the war *Foreign Affairs* published articles by Garry Wills and Samuel P. Huntington expressing alarm at the course of events. Wills proclaimed that it was a great error for the US to play the role of the 'bully of the free world' while Huntington urged that 'the core state of a civilisation can better maintain order among the members of its extended family than an outsider'.[12] But such advice had already been flouted by the time it appeared.

It was at US insistence that Russia was cut out of the process that led to the war, and excluded from its implementation. The humiliation of the Russians was the more intense because they had played a central role in diplomatic contacts before and during the Rambouillet conference. The notion that bombing would be effective, even without Russian support, and that Milošević would quickly crumble, was sold to the lesser allies by the Anglo-Saxon powers. But the dominant faction in Washington was anyway persuaded that the best way to deal with the Russian threat was by encircling that country with military bases, client states and NATO protectorates. Some British foreign policy advisers urged that it was unwise to forgo the possible contribution of Russian good offices in the attempt to impose an agreement on Milošević, but were told that Russian involvement was not acceptable to the Americans. The crassly provocative exclusion of Russia eventually had its opponents in NATO counsels but to begin with they tamely followed where the US and Britain led, sending out pathetic little signals of concern as the military juggernaut headed for the abyss.

The rigorous exclusion of Russia from any other than a messenger-boy role represented a clear departure from previously announced doctrine. Javier Solana, the NATO Secretary General, declared in a speech on 23 June 1998 that it was essential that 'Russia must be on board' if the West was to tackle the critical issue of Kosovo.[13] At this time it was obvious to Solana that Russia should be involved both because that would maximise the chances of a successful settlement and because to leave Russia out would be a colossal strategic snub. The Russian financial collapse of August 1998, leading to the advent of the Primakov government, may help to explain a hardening of the US stance and the eventual abandonment of the position so recently adopted by Solana.

The reading offered here might seem to be at odds with the well-informed account written by Tim Judah in the *New York Review of Books* in its issue dated 10 June 1999, after discussions with Chris Hill, the US Ambassador to Macedonia. Judah wrote:

> What of the then-current theory that Milošević was prepared to accept a military force so long as it was not overtly a NATO one? Hill says that this is simply not the case. The Rambouillet negotiators – Hill himself, Wolfgang Petritsch for the EU and Boris Mayorski for Russia – would have been happy to agree to any suitable disguise for the force, but the Serbs simply 'would not engage' on the question. He adds: 'If the Serbs had said yes to the force but no to the independent judiciary – and insisted on all sanctions relief (i.e. on the West dropping all sanctions) – do you think we could have bombed?'

This account at least takes us to the crux of the question. But the direct and indirect quotes from Ambassador Hill only seem to allow for a 'suitable disguise' not for a genuinely non-NATO force. It is also certainly the case that the Russian government expected to participate in implementation, notwithstanding the view curiously attributed to the Russian negotiator here – Ambassador Mayorski boycotted the Kosovan signing ceremony because of the NATO-led formula. Naturally Russia resents its exclusion just as keenly as Serbia, if not more so. And the purpose of getting Russia on board would always have been to maximise the pressure on Serbia.

If the United States rather than Russia had been excluded from the negotiating process then the chances of a peaceful outcome would have been much greater. US involvement may gratify the hawks in Washington but overseas military adventures, with limitless prospects of further entanglements, are of no interest to the great mass of US citizens. It serves to distract the US public from such alarming problems as the growth of its prison population, and the expense of NATO enlargement, and the sustenance of a string of protectorates, could erode those budget surpluses which make possible Clinton's surprisingly bold approach to the problem of social security retirement funding. No country should arrogate to itself the role of global bully and the US is particularly unsuited to it because the structure of its politics makes it so vulnerable to special-interest lobbies.[14] The reluctance of US political leaders to envisage casualties to their own forces might be a gain for restraint but it is largely cancelled out by Washington's ability and preparedness to launch destruction from afar.

On 24 May 1999 Clinton used the columns of the *New York Times* to re-state

US terms, to signal a small change, and backhandedly to acknowledge criticism of the policy adopted. After reiterating that the security force for Kosovo should 'have NATO command and control and NATO rules of engagement, with special arrangements for non-NATO countries, like our force in Bosnia' he added: 'Our military campaign will continue until these conditions are met, not because we are stubborn or arbitrary but because they are the only conditions under which the refugees go home in safety and the KLA will have any incentive to disarm – the basic requirements of a resolution that will work.' In point of fact the US roles in Bosnia and Somalia simply did not bear out this claim; many refugees have not returned to Bosnia and in Somalia, US troops under US command proved very bad at handling a difficult and delicate situation.[15] Whoever entered Kosovo after a Serb withdrawal was going to have a difficult task preventing new communal conflicts and a new wave of refugees but there was no basis for claiming that only NATO had the answer. Obliquely referring to critics of the dump-on-Russia approach, Clinton continued: 'This strategy gives us the best opportunity to meet our goals in a way that strengthens, not weakens, our fundamental interest in a long term relationship with Russia. Russia is now helping to work out a way for Belgrade to meet our conditions. Russian troops should participate in the force that will keep the peace in Kosovo, turning a source of tension into an opportunity for cooperation, like our joint effort in Bosnia.' No doubt the new willingness to contemplate a Russian role in both mediation and implementation – under NATO command and control – reflected Yeltsin's willingness to accommodate Washington and his success in removing Primakov. But an item on the front page of that day's *Herald Tribune* showed the damage being done – it reported that the START-2 disarmament agreement had completely stalled, since it needed the approval of the Duma. Far from being ready to implement either conventional or nuclear disarmament the Russian high command had taken the decision to modernise their nuclear arsenal.

Public opinion in the NATO countries only gradually became aware of the costs of the air war to the many refugees still inside Kosovo, to Yugoslav civilians and to regional tension. The Italian and German governments came out against a ground offensive. Unhappy coalition partners called for an immediate cessation of the air bombardment and encouragement for Russian mediation efforts. Some realised that NATO's supposed objective of 'degrading' the 'control and command' function of the Yugoslav forces only made sense to those bent on a wider war since, if successful, it would prevent

Belgrade from ordering its forces to withdraw and release Serb units in Kosovo from any remaining restraint. And the relentless air assault actually strengthened Milošević's control over his own population. Only the advent of peace could expose Milošević to the attacks of all those Serbs who had good cause to rue his long history of disastrous leadership. (Significantly the strong Serb opposition movement of 1996–97 occurred during a time of peace.)

The principles enunciated by the Council of Europe, the Organisation for Security and Cooperation in Europe, and the United Nations could have furnished the appropriate basis for conducting negotiations with Yugoslavia. Past and present Yugoslav governments have subscribed to them, as have the NATO powers. Intervention by these bodies would have a legitimacy which NATO lacked and would thus have subjected the Serbian leader to greater pressure. Right up to the end the method of NATO diktat simply prolonged the agony. The other bodies had been established by arduous international agreement, and subsequently ratified by parliaments and assemblies, for the very purpose of regulating relations between states and monitoring their observance of human and civil rights. When the new Yugoslav Federation was established it vociferously insisted that it assumed all the international obligations of the old Federation. Of the previously-mentioned organisations the Council of Europe, a body specifically established to safeguard human rights and civil liberties, would have been by far the most appropriate for dealing with the Kosovan crisis, so long as it was given appropriate facilities by its member states. The Council represents the region threatened by the crisis and, as a body, had no responsibility for the recent chapter of disasters. It would also be a suitable vehicle for channelling much-needed economic assistance from the EU to the whole region.

The international organisations referred to are far from perfect and their mode of operation is open to improvement. Both in principle and in practice the Western powers, as important member states, have had every opportunity to obtain improvements in the operating principles of these organisations. In the past they have used their influence to block the emergence of more effective systems for making and executing decisions, notably Russian proposals for an OSCE secretariat and Security Council. The OSCE and the Council of Europe do include Russia and would ensure its participation in both negotiation and implementation of any agreement.

For two decades the West had ignored or even aggravated the plight of the Kosovars. In the 1970s it had seemed that the people of Kosovo were at last emerging from a semi-colonial condition but, following Tito's death, the growing strength of the racist variant of Serbian nationalism led to a worse subjugation than before. The Western powers aided and abetted the disorderly disintegration of the old Yugoslav Federation which had acted as a restraint on the Serb authorities. The IMF greatly aggravated a desperate economic crisis and denied the last Yugoslav government the money to pay its soldiers.[16] Without a squeak from the West Milošević imposed a brutal and arbitrary regime on the so-called province.[17] Kosovan self-determination was a more justified and urgent cause than the secessions of Slovenia, Croatia or Bosnia which were so precipitately and fatally recognised by the Western powers. The Kosovan cause should have been supported throughout the 1990s in appropriate diplomatic and material ways, much as, say, Sweden, the Soviet Union and, belatedly, the United States supported the cause of the African National Congress in South Africa. The armed actions by the KLA in 1998 created a situation with all the elements of a classic anti-colonial struggle, as in Algeria, with guerrilla attacks and military repression, with some localised but not large-scale massacres – up to Rambouillet. According to NATO, up to February 1999 about one thousand Serb soldiers and functionaries had been killed and two thousand Albanian Kosovans; two hundred thousand Kosovans had left their homes but, up to this point, most remained in Kosovo.

The bombing transformed a vicious colonial conflict into ethnic cleansing on a large scale, a phenomenon which in the twentieth century has so often required the cover of war to carry through – as the wartime fate of Armenians, Jews, Palestinians, Germans, Bosnians and, most recently, Serbs in the Krajina, demonstrates.[18] The glib analogy that has been so often made between Hitler and Milošević forgets that Britain and France did not declare war on Nazi Germany because of its practice of genocide; the Holocaust was the product of war not the casus belli. War was declared against Germany because it broke treaties and invaded neighbouring countries in the name of defending German minorities from persecution.

According to the classic Augustinian theory of the 'just war' the means should be proportionate to the ends and the decision for war should be made only after all prospects of mediation have been exhausted and as an act of legitimate authority. A war which causes massive harm to those on whose behalf it is undertaken, where a vital prospect of mediation has been shunned, which is in violation of treaties, and not put to the prior sanction of elected bodies, cannot be a just war. Those who brandish crusading causes, like Tony Blair, can be the most dangerous militarists of all. There is a world of difference between a just war and a holy war. The carnage of the First World War was held to be justified by the wrong done to Belgium. The colonial partition of Africa was undertaken in the name of the suppression of the slave trade. In pursuing a justified cause we should always be alert to the ulterior motives and vested interests which might distort it, seeking, so far as may be possible, to favour approaches which stymie those interests and motives. Thus the more principled and effective abolitionists found it quite possible to support resistance to slavery and international covenants against the slave trade without endorsing wars of colonial conquest.

Both the UN and the OSCE have been involved in the peaceful or negotiated resolution of difficult cases of national oppression, decolonisation and conflict containment in the past. They have had their failures but the US has contributed to these too. The Council of Europe and European Union could have aimed to improve on their record. They would at least have been able to do better than NATO which furnished a dangerous precedent of unilateral action, shed much innocent blood and stoked local and global tensions.

But would not such a negotiated approach have delivered the Kosovan cause to cynical exploitation by great power interests? An alert public opinion and active peace movement could have acted as one safeguard against such an outcome. But potentially so might an inclusive network of international and regional agreement. The pressures of international negotiation, agreement and military disengagement can help to neutralise or restrain both great power interests and reckless emotional spasms. It obliges participants to justify themselves in terms of international norms and public opinion. In a context of structured negotiation and cooperation the whole is just a bit better than the parts since the participating states hold one another in check. We should not forget or discount the appalling role of Serb security forces in Kosovo or much of former Yugoslavia, nor of Russian forces in Chechnya, nor of Turkish forces in Kurdish areas, nor of US-backed and advised military regimes in Central America. We should press for a world where the special military units responsible for death squads are disbanded. But faced by the Kosovo crisis we cannot ignore the reality that Western military power acts as a potential check on Serbia and that Russian military capacity acts as a check on NATO. Without endorsing either military establishment we should be able to see the merit of pressing for a pacific accommodation between them, one which leads to a further programme of disengagement and disarmament.

And without romantic illusions in the KLA we can see that it offered a means of self-defence to the major national group in Kosovo and that its armed methods drew away support from the pacific parties which had previously won elections there. It accordingly deserved a measure of recognition but not a monopoly of de facto control. In any settlement there had to be a transitional role for the Yugoslav armed forces – though not for the paramilitaries and police battalions which were specially created to carry out the lawless terror and ethnic cleansing which the regular army found distasteful. If it was always true that only an agreement could produce a peaceful Serbian withdrawal from Kosovo, as actually happened, then the cooperation of the Yugoslav armed forces was essential to this. Those who wish for peace in the Balkans and in Europe cannot simply wish away the various bodies of armed men that are in contention but must rather seek to disengage them in the most effective way possible.

The Council of Europe should have been convened to consider action on Kosovo in March 1998 when the armed struggle commenced, or at any later time. It was the best body to convene a wider conference to consider the fate of the region and to furnish security guarantees. At such a conference there should have been a range of representatives of the people of Kosovo, including the party of Ibrahim Rugova, the KLA and representatives of minority groups. The KLA might well have demanded full and immediate self-determination for the people of Kosovo. While the KLA should have had every right to put its point of view, the Conference would not have been bound to accept it. Given the situation in Kosovo an immediate vote on the future of this territory was not possible anyway. As it was NATO used its huge leverage to manipulate Kosovan organisations – for example by excluding the veteran Kosovan leader Adem Demaci and by promoting a former general in the Croatian army, who had participated in the cleansing of the Krajina Serbs, to a key position in the KLA structure in April 1999. After June the NATO occupation forces gave great leeway to the KLA while denying them the immediate self-determination they demanded – indeed the June agreement did not even contain the promise of a referendum in three years' time which had been part of the Rambouillet accords.

While the Albanian Kosovans have suffered greatly we should be wary of understandable but misguided attempts to absolutise their cause. The exercise of self-determination by the people of any state should itself be pursued by proportionate means and with due account taken of wider implications of the action. While large nations are given to hegemonism small ones can also be, in their own way, oblivious and self-centred. Thus the precipitate haste with which Slovenia exited from the Yugoslav Federation in 1991 actually assisted Milošević in his oppression of the Kosovars. The European Community of the time should have delayed recognition of the break-up of the Yugoslav Federation until the Kosovans had been conceded their own republic. That Slovenian leaders gave overwhelming priority to Slovenian interests – regardless of the consequences – was, no doubt, as inevitable as it was unfortunate. The real culpability here resided with those Western powers, above all Germany and Britain, who went along with Slovenian secession despite the warnings they had received.[19] Another case of small nation egoism would be the response of Fidel Castro and Che Guevara to the Cuban missiles crisis of 1962. The defence of Cuba against the United States was an entirely just cause, but risking nuclear war was not justified; fortunately Khrushchev was prepared to back down. As it turns out Cuba was secured from direct invasion by the results of the crisis. Some Kosovan leaders have insisted – very much at Western prompting – that only a NATO-led force is acceptable to them. But even if all Kosovans agreed, it would still not be right to ignore the larger context. And some Kosovans are aware that NATO's tutelage may be indefinite. An international occupation force may have been needed to ensure the evacuation of the Serb forces and to insure the safety of all inhabitants of Kosovo – including the Serb minority. But its aim should always have been to make itself redundant as speedily as possible.

Those who rightly called for an immediate halt to the bombing knew that Belgrade would still have an incentive to settle to prevent any resumption. Does this mean that the policy of the doves was covertly complicit with that of the hawks and thus proves that the latter were right all along? No, because the situation would have been better for the Kosovars at every stage if their case had been strongly pressed by all means short of war – in 1991–92 at the time of the break-up, in 1995 at Dayton, and in 1998–99 when hostilities began. If the Western governments who now pose as champions of human rights had been genuinely concerned with the fate of the Kosovars on any of these occasions they could have achieved a decent settlement and avoided the humanitarian catastrophe we face. On each of these occasions it would have been better to act with Russia and without the United States.

In the end settlement was reached with Russia's good offices. Indeed the Chernomyrdin–Ahtisarri mission which produced the basis for the agreement was the first joint Russian–European approach to Belgrade. By this time, after much arm-twisting, the Russians had been brought to accept a mainly NATO occupation force. However, it would still be better for the Kosovars, and better for Europe and the world, if NATO announced a schedule for its withdrawal from Kosovo and encouraged the Council of Europe to convene a conference to address the need for a new and democratic Balkan settlement.

John Lloyd, reporting from Moscow in the *Financial Times* for 27 May 1999, explained two important points relating to the Russian role, whether military or diplomatic, in a solution. Firstly that Chernomyrdin was seen as a corrupt, compromised and pro-Western figure in Russia and consequently a settlement endorsed only by Chernomyrdin and Yeltsin would have little credibility. On the other hand Lloyd also reported that the plan for a settlement proposed by Igor Ivanov, the Foreign Minister, envisaged a complete Serb withdrawal and not a partition of Kosovo.[20] Not surprisingly, the concern of Russian political circles was always with whether there was to be a huge NATO force in Kosovo and not with any other details of the settlement. The inclusion of a token force of Russian soldiers in a NATO-led operation was the eventual price of the settlement but was so modest and grudging that it will not allay this concern and will simply store up problems for the future.[21]

The dramatic Russian arrival at the airport at Priština in June 1999 helped to highlight the dangers courted by Western policy. Later reports indicated that General Wesley Clark ordered General Jackson to contest this action, with the latter declining to do so. (In fact a more assertive Russian government could have used control of the airport to fly in a sizeable force – after all Russia still has very capacious troop-carrying aircraft and no shortage of oil.) The British commander of K-FOR and the British chief of the defence staff also gave it as their opinion that the Russian mediation had been decisive in ending the conflict and that, by implication, the air war had been misconceived. General Jackson told the *Sunday Telegraph*: 'The event of June 3rd [when Moscow urged Milošević to surrender] was the single event that appeared to me to have the greatest significance in ending the war.' Asked about the air war he replied: 'I wasn't responsible for the air war, you're talking to the wrong person.' A *Guardian* interview with General Sir Charles Guthrie, chief of the defence staff, also acknowledged that the war ended 'thanks to the Russian intervention'.[22]

The eventual decision to settle with Milošević, rather than send NATO's forces smashing into Yugoslavia, was welcome, cheating the Western ground assault party of the reckless further slaughter and provocation they craved. In allowing many refugees to return it at least undid some of the damage inflicted in late March 1999. But despite many months of notice, no police forces were on hand to prevent looting and revenge killing, or to prevent gangsterism or to begin training a mixed, locally-recruited force. Those

Kosovan Albanians who still supported Ibrahim Rugova, perhaps a majority, were also treated with hostility by the KLA. The continuing danger of Albanian revenge attacks has been used to justify protectorate status and, effectively, to deny the rights of Kosovans to run their own affairs. It seems likely that, before long, Kosovo will become one more ethnically-cleansed statelet, joining such other shards of former Yugoslavia as Croatia and the three Bosnias. And as the Bosnian statelets show, protectorate status encourages criminal networks rather than the capacity for self-government.[23] More generally, the reluctance to engage constructively with Russia and China bequeaths confrontation and the makings of a new Cold War.

In the short run NATO's war for NATO expansion looks like being claimed as a huge success for the hawks. Not only has its Balkan sphere of action been greatly enlarged – probably permanently – but the intimidation of war has produced a far-reaching reordering of regional and global politics. In Germany Oskar Lafontaine has been ousted and the Social Democrat–Green coalition blooded by combat. Lionel Jospin has declared himself happy with the new order of things and José Borrell, the Spanish Socialist leader, has been induced to resign. Hungary, the Czech Republic and Poland have been kept in line, and Rumania and Bulgaria prepared for the next round of expansion. Last, but not least, NATO itself, after some bad moments, looks set to preside over a world in which it can act more freely than ever before. If they were unwise the hawks might add Primakov's scalp to their trophy list. They might like to reflect that he was brought down thanks to a new yellow/brown alliance of Yeltsin, Zhirinovsky and Chernomyrdin, men who were the architects of the Chechen war and who have, with Western help, imposed on the Russian people a dreadful toll of misery. Indeed Primakov's successor, Putin, saw NATO's onslaught on Serbia as a green light for a renewed attack on Chechnya, complete with horrendous aerial bombardments. Meanwhile, and in sharp contrast, international pressure through the UN secured Indonesian withdrawal from East Timor without resort to war.

Notes

1. Jonathan Steele, a knowledgeable and seasoned observer of the pre-war diplomacy, later argued that 'NATO has achieved its aims in Yugoslavia but the war need never have been. The deal extracted from Milošević last week could probably have been

obtained twelve months ago without the horror of bombing at all.' 'NATO's Russian Roulette', *Guardian*, 9 June 1999. The strapline on this piece read: 'The West's contempt for its former Cold War enemy caused estrangement during the Kosovo crisis just when they needed to work together.'

2. This emerges even from an account written by the legal adviser to the Kosovan delegation: Marc Weller, 'The Rambouillet Conference', *International Affairs*, vol. 75, April 1999.
3. See ibid.
4. See the conclusion to Anatol Lieven, *Chechnya, Tombstone of Russian Power*, London 1998. Paradoxically, while the West allowed only a minimal Russian role in Kosovo, where it would have been positive, it was later to indulge a new Russian assault upon Chechnya in the autumn of 1999.
5. Zlamy Khalilzad and David Ochmanek, 'Rethinking US Defense Planning', *Survival* (IISS London), vol. 39, no. 1, Spring 1997, p. 49, quoted in Gilbert Achcar, 'The Strategic Triad: the United States, Russia and China', *New Left Review*, 228, March–April 1998, pp. 91–128, pp. 102–3.
6. Lawrence Freedman, 'On the C List', *Times Literary Supplement*, 30 April 1999. This is a review of Asthenia B. Carter and William J. Perry, *Preventive Defense: a New Security Strategy for America*, Washington, DC: Brookings Institute.
7. Michael Mandelbaum, *The Dawn of Peace in Europe*, New York 1996. I cite this work and that by Ashton and Perry because it shows that the recklessness of current US policy arouses disquiet even within the political establishment. For an informative critique of NATO enlargement see *The Expansion of NATO*, Campaign Against the Arms Trade, London 1999, available from 11 Goodwin St, London N4 3HQ.
8. *Transition*, 15 November 1996.
9. Zbigniew Brzezinski, 'A Geostrategy for Asia', *Foreign Affairs*, November–December 1997.
10. Interview, CNBC, 'Power Lunch', 27 August 1998. Sternly critical of Russia's democracy, Brzezinski is, however, known for favouring close links to Azerbaijan. He is a consultant to Amoco and the Azerbaijan International Operating Company, a cartel whose projected oil pipe-lines and agreements help to cement the GUAM alliance. Freedom House, of which Brzezinski is a board member, recently pronounced that political conditions in Geidar Aliev's Azerbaijan were improving (Aliev was a member of Brezhnev's Politburo and responsible for the ethnic cleansing of Armenians from Nagorno-Karabak). For material on Brzezinski and Azerbaijan see the website of counterpunch.org and the article by Christopher Hitchens in web magazine *Salon*, 29 September 1997. While Brzezinski's links with the oil companies are evidently close it is not necessarily the case that he is doing their bidding; some observers believe that the oil concerns are being dragged into Brzezinski's politically inspired machinations through a combination of naiveté and greed.
11. Madeleine Albright, 'The Testing of American Foreign Policy', *Foreign Affairs*, November/December 1998, pp. 50–68.

12. Garry Wills, 'Bully of the Free World', *Foreign Affairs*, March–April 1999, pp. 50–60; and Samuel P. Huntington, 'The Lonely Superpower', ibid., pp. 35–49.
13. Tariq Ali, 'Springtime for NATO', *New Left Review*, 234, March–April 1999. The text of Solana's speech can be found on the website Kosova.newsroom.
14. See Daniel Lazarre, *The Frozen Republic*, New York 1996.
15. See Alex de Waal, 'US War Crimes in Somalia', *New Left Review*, 230, July–August 1998, 131–44, p. 135.
16. Robin Blackburn, 'The Break-up of Yugoslavia', *New Left Review*, 199. For the role of economic 'landslides' in precipitating ethnic violence, see Tom Nairn, 'Reflections on Nationalist Disasters', *New Left Review*, 230, July–August 1998.
17. See Branka Magaš, 'The Balkanization of Yugoslavia', *New Left Review*, 174, 1989.
18. See Michael Mann, 'The Dark Side of Democracy: the Modern Tradition of Ethnic and Political Cleansing', *New Left Review*, 235, May–June 1999, pp. 18–45.
19. For a trenchant indictment of Western policy towards Yugoslavia see Susan Woodward, *The Balkan Tragedy*, Washington 1995. As Woodward points out, most Western statesmen and diplomats gave absolute priority to self-determination within each of the republics of the Federation, neglecting the ways in which this prejudiced the rights of individuals and nationalities within the republics.
20. John Lloyd, 'Russians Doubt Chernomyrdin's Kosovo Chances', *Financial Times*, 27 May 1999.
21. Brzezinski's comment on 15 June 1999 on the CSIS website was: 'It is really the strategic task of the US to create a situation through its relationships with Europe and China whereby Russia really has a single, constructive option, that is to say, accommodation with Europe and the West.' He went on: 'In the last several days, three countries in southeastern Europe [Romania, Bulgaria, Hungary], one of which is a member of NATO [Hungary], have refused overflight rights to the Russians, and they have been and remain the object of intense pressure to yield these rights, including now some threats. We have actually encouraged Romania and Bulgaria to refuse these rights. That de facto creates a special security relationship with them, which introduces a new element into the NATO enlargement process. Romania and Bulgaria are now in a relationship with NATO which is quite special, and puts them in a special category as candidates for membership.'
22. See Richard Norton-Taylor, Analysis and Comment page, *Guardian*, 3 August 1999; interview with General Jackson, *Sunday Telegraph*, 1 August 1999.
23. The dismal record of the Bosnia protectorate is surveyed in David Chandler, 'Rise of the Balkan Protectorate', *New Left Review*, 235, May–June 1999, pp. 124–34.

18

MAY DAY SPEECH AT SAARBRÜCKEN

Oskar Lafontaine

Oskar Lafontaine, who resigned from his post as finance minister in the German government at the beginning of March 1999, made his first public appearance following his resignation at the May Day rally organised by the DGB (German Trade Union Federation) in Saarbrücken. We print below extracts from his speech that dealt with the war in Yugoslavia.

In taking a position on the war in Yugoslavia today, we should first remember that this is not the only war in our world. Poverty and misery, death and expulsion are sadly present in quite a few countries: I'm thinking of Africa, of Algeria, Ethiopia, Sudan, Rwanda, the Congo. I'm thinking of Asia and of the persecuted Kurds in Turkey, a member state of NATO. I'm thinking of Tibet, Afghanistan and of many other countries where we find gross injustice and large-scale human misery.

But it is of the war in Yugoslavia that I want to speak today. I don't want to simplify because none of us have simple answers. But what has to stand in the forefront of all our thinking is, in my view, this: How can we alleviate, as quickly as possible, the suffering of the people there? How can peace be established as quickly as possible? And the issue is not one of saving face, as some suggest it is. The sole issue is the suffering of people and the preservation of human life.

Of course, all of us are concerned about the people of Kosovo who are being expelled and killed. We are also concerned about the people in Serbia who are afraid and who are suffering from bombardment. We are thinking of the people in Serbia who have been the victims of the bombing. And we are thinking of the deserters from the armies who are also persecuted and who are suffering because they don't want to take part in the war. As I have already said, there are no simple answers to these terrible events. And I don't want to give the impression that I have any simple answer. And I would like, right from the beginning, to distance myself from the placard against the Chancellor. This style of argument leads nowhere. The issues that we are facing are too serious for this kind of argument.

We know now that mistakes have been made with respect to Yugoslavia and some of these mistakes were made some years ago. I often hear it said that German shouldn't go its own way, but I must remind you that, at the very beginning of all this, Germany did indeed go its own way in pushing through the official recognition of the independence of Yugoslavia's constituent republics, against the resistance of Paris, London and Washington, and on the basis of a false understanding of the concepts of freedom and self-determination. Freedom and self-determination are not compatible with national exclusion and ethnic exclusion. Freedom and self-determination are only imaginable and can only be lived and experienced when they are linked with solidarity and human fellowship. That's why it was wrong to give recognition to this small-state nonsense (*Kleinstaaterei*) based on ethnic differences. It was also a mistake when NATO bombardment made it possible for Croatia to drive the Serbs from Krajina. I want to bring this to your attention today when we speak about the war in Yugoslavia.

It would be a mistake to believe that only one of the nations in the multi-national Yugoslavia suffered expulsion. The Serbs have suffered expulsion. I'm saying this because it is important that we don't adopt a one-sided view. I believe, I am firmly convinced, that we cannot advance one step when we demonise one particular national group and see the others as the good side. The reasonable thing to do is to recognise that there are many people in that country, and not just people from one group, who have suffered unjustly, who have been unjustly persecuted, and it is therefore false to divide the people there into good and bad national groups. Peace will never be achieved in this manner. Serbian men also have wives and children who weep for them, they also have friends who weep for them. We shouldn't forget this. We too have had our experience with dictatorships and we know that many soldiers follow orders but their hearts are not in what they are doing. We know that and that's why I mentioned the deserters.

With regard to the present situation I want to distinguish political from military considerations. First, the political reasoning of recent weeks and months. There is no doubt whatever that Milošević is pursuing a criminal policy that we must all condemn. And there is also no doubt that we must do everything possible to bring this criminal policy to a halt. And we should recognise that the Western states did attempt to do this, that they did make this effort, but in spite of this we still are obliged to consider critically whether the decisions made up to now have been correct.

With respect to the decisions of recent weeks and months, two serious errors have been made that will have long-term consequences. Firstly, the UN was pushed aside. That was a serious error that we have to learn from. If we want peace, then we have to strengthen the law. And if we want international peace then we have to strengthen international law. There is no other way. And international law can be constituted only by the United Nations, not by any other bodies that are self-mandating. It is good, therefore, that an attempt is now being made to bring in the United Nations. We can learn from our mistakes and we should learn from this one, and here I appeal not just to the German government. I appeal to the European governments. We have to make clear to our American allies that pushing the UN aside was a mistake, that, in the long term, we can have a politics that is reasonable and right, just and peaceful, only if we base ourselves on the rules of international law, however difficult that may be in any particular case.

The second big mistake, and here I appeal to the governments of Europe to take a stand against it, was to take advantage of the present weaknesses of Russia in order to exclude her. We cannot achieve peace in this world without Russia. And we cannot bring about peace in Europe without Russia. And we Germans should never forget what Gorbachev did for this nation, for Germany. We have a duty to be fair to Russia, to bring Russia on board, and I welcome the fact that the attempt is now being made to involve Russia more strongly.

Sometimes the organs of the UN and the Security Council are justly criticised when what is at stake are proposals that we consider right but, in this respect, I would like to remind you that some very good proposals have been put forward for the reform of the UN. The UN, created after the war, is in need of reform today. The right of veto over international law enjoyed by certain individual powers is questionable. So let us reform the UN but let us not push it aside.

It isn't possible today to pass judgement on whether everything was done to use peaceful means to achieve a solution and to stop the killing and the exclusion. I wasn't part of many of the negotiations and, as I have said, these efforts and decisions go back over many years. I would like to make clear, however, how the recent decisions were arrived at: following the victory of the red-green coalition last year, and at a time when the Schröder government had not yet been formed, the Kohl government invited us to find out if we could agree with a decision of the German parliament, the old German parliament, that in the event of a state of alert (*Alarmbereitschaft*) for the NATO allies, German troops would be made available.

I feel it is my duty here today, once again, to point to the fact that, as leader of the German Social Democratic Party in these negotiations, I posed the question whether such a decision of the German parliament and the German government would set an automatic process in motion which would require no further consultation before a military attack. The answers given by the defence and foreign ministers of the then government were not consistent. I got a written confirmation from the foreign ministry at that time that a positive decision by the German parliament would not set an automatic process in motion . . . [speech interrupted by medical emergency in the audience] As I was explaining, the decision of the German parliament in October [1998] did not set up an automatic process; it would be possible beforehand, before any military attack, to enter again into a political discussion in which a decision would be made, a political decision, about whether the state of alarm would lead to a command to intervene militarily.

On this basis I gave my agreement as leader of the German Social Democratic Party because it would not have been responsible, after all the preparations, and after all that had been achieved by the governments of Europe and by the United States, to stop it or even to change it in just a few days. However, I insisted in the cabinet during the days of the Rambouillet negotiations that, before the cabinet came to a decision that would involve German approval of a military intervention, there would have to be a detailed discussion of the military plans, because it is my view that it is not possible to agree to a military intervention without knowing and carefully considering the plans and their effects.

Up to the time of my resignation as finance minister, there were no further discussions on the military question, so I can only judge after the event. It is my view that the present military operation could only be justified if the goal were, following these attacks, to get Milošević's signature to an agreement to end the war, as happened a few years ago. Only if there were solid reasons for believing that this would happen would the military attacks be justified and understandable.

If, however, there were no firm reasons for believing this, if, as the later discussion indicated, the most important goal of the military intervention was the protection of the Kosovo population, then the military intervention plans were not justifiable from any point of view.

Every metaphor limps. But what would we think of a police force which, discovering that a group was on the way from A to B in order to expel and murder the people at B, decided to bomb the bridges, refineries, railways, etc. in A? A country would not accept for a minute this behaviour on the part of the police. I know that things are not as simple as the metaphor suggests. But it does make clear that the military planning was inadequate because it did not take into its calculations the possibility that Milošević would not capitulate and because it is now, in my view, in a dead-end street . . .

Regardless of what army generals or politicians may say, bombing is a form of collective punishment. All the talk about systematic attacks on the enemy, about degrading his capacity, about wearing him down and eventually destroying him, only serves to cover over the fact that the innocent are also being hit. This is the problem that the bombing had led us to: increasing numbers of innocent people are the victims of our bombs. And that is why today, here from the Deutsch-Französischer Garten [in Saarbrücken], I call on the responsible authorities to call a halt to the bombing, and to find a way at the conference table to end the killing and expulsions in Yugoslavia, by bringing in the United Nations and Russia and also by consulting with the Chinese . . .

I welcome the fact that the Chancellor has brought a Marshall Plan into the discussion and that some thought is being given to the reconstruction of what has been destroyed. But when we look at the television in the evening and see the bridges that have been destroyed and think how they will now need to be built again, we ask ourselves what is the sense of this bombing, what is it leading too, and in what kind of reason is this activity based. What is needed is a lot of diplomacy, not megaphone diplomacy because, as all of us familiar with international mechanisms are aware, this only creates resistance. I hope that the European governments and, following the decisions of the American Congress, the Clinton administration will recognise that they have reached a dead end and that what they have to do is return to the negotiating table.

I hear it said quite often now that NATO can't lose face. It has no choice; it has to win. In *Thus Spoke Zarathustra*, Nietzsche wrote, 'Let your peace be a victory'. In the present case I ask, whose victory would the victory be? And what does victory mean in the context of the human suffering from this war? The important point is not victory or face-saving, the important point is saving lives and ending the misery in Yugoslavia . . .

No one can offer simple solutions and no one is in the position today to offer a solution that is guaranteed to take us out of this situation. But we should hold on to what we have achieved over many years. And I say this to my friends in the German Social Democratic Party, what we need to do is to carry on the peace and détente policies of Willy Brandt, the best tradition of social democratic foreign policy since the war.

19

THE KOSOVO PEACE ACCORD

Noam Chomsky

On March 24, US-led NATO air forces began to pound the Federal Republic of Yugoslavia (FYR, Serbia and Montenegro), including Kosovo, which NATO regards as a province of Serbia. On June 3, NATO and Serbia reached a Peace Accord. The US declared victory, having successfully concluded its '10-week struggle to compel Mr. Milošević to say uncle,' Blaine Harden reported in the *New York Times*. It would therefore be unnecessary to use ground forces to 'cleanse Serbia' as Harden had recommended in a lead story headlined 'How to Cleanse Serbia'. The recommendation was natural in the light of American history, which is dominated by the theme of ethnic cleansing from its origins to the present day, achievements celebrated in the names given to military attack helicopters and other weapons of destruction. A qualification is in order, however: the term 'ethnic cleansing' is not really appropriate: US cleansing operations have been ecumenical; Indochina and Central America are two recent illustrations.

While declaring victory, Washington did not yet declare peace: the bombing would continue until the victors could determine that their interpretation of the Kosovo Accord had been imposed. From the outset, the bombing had been cast as a matter of cosmic significance, a test of a New Humanism, in which the 'enlightened states' (Foreign Affairs) would open a new era of human history guided by 'a new internationalism where the brutal repression of whole ethnic groups will no longer be tolerated' (Tony Blair). The enlightened states are the United States and its British associate, perhaps also others who enlist in their crusades for justice.

Apparently the rank of 'enlightened states' is conferred by definition. One finds no attempt to provide evidence or argument, surely not from their history. The latter is in any event deemed irrelevant by the familiar doctrine of 'change of course', invoked regularly in the ideological institutions to dispatch the past into the deepest recesses of the memory hole, thus deterring the threat that some might ask the most obvious questions: with institutional structures and distribution of power essentially unchanged, why should one expect a radical shift in policy – or any at all, apart from tactical adjustments?

But such questions are off the agenda. 'From the start the Kosovo problem has been about how we should react when bad things happen in unimportant places,' global analyst Thomas Friedman explained in the *New York Times* as the Accord was announced. He proceeded to laud the enlightened states for pursuing his moral principle that 'once the refugee evictions began, ignoring Kosovo would be wrong . . . and therefore using a huge air war for a limited objective was the only thing that made sense'.

A minor difficulty is that concern over the 'refugee evictions' could not have been the motive for the 'huge air war'. The United Nations Commissioner for Refugees (UNHCR) reported its first registered refugees outside of Kosovo on March 27 (4,000), three days after the bombings began. The toll increased until June 4, reaching a reported total of 670,000 in the neighbouring countries (Albania, Macedonia), along with an estimated 70,000 in Montenegro (within the FYR), and 75,000 who had left for other countries. The figures, which are unfortunately all too familiar, do not include the unknown numbers who have been displaced within Kosovo, some 2–300,000 in the year before the bombing according to NATO, a great many more afterwards.

Uncontroversially, the 'huge air war' precipitated a sharp escalation of ethnic cleansing and other atrocities. That much has been reported consistently by correspondents on the scene and in retrospective analyses in the press. The same picture is presented in the two major documents that seek to portray the bombing as a reaction to the humanitarian crisis in Kosovo. The most extensive one, provided by the State Department in May 1999, is suitably entitled 'Erasing History: Ethnic Cleansing in Kosovo'; the second is the Indictment of Milošević and associates by the International Tribunal on War Crimes in Yugoslavia after the US and Britain 'opened the way for what amounted to a remarkably fast indictment by giving [prosecutor Louise] Arbour access to intelligence and other information long denied to her by Western governments,' the *New York Times* reported, with two full pages devoted to the Indictment. Both documents hold that the atrocities began 'on or about January 1'; in both, however, the detailed chronology reveals that atrocities continued about as before, until the bombing led to a very sharp escalation. That surely came as no surprise. Commanding General Wesley Clark at once described these consequences as 'entirely predictable' – an exaggeration of course; nothing in human affairs is that predictable, though ample evidence is now available revealing that the consequences were anticipated, for reasons readily understood without access to secret intelligence.

One small index of the effects of the 'huge air war' was offered by Robert Hayden, director of the Center for Russian and East European Studies of the University of Pittsburgh: 'The casualties among Serb civilians in the first three weeks of the war are higher than all of the casualties on both sides in Kosovo in the three months that led up to this war, and yet those three months were supposed to be a humanitarian catastrophe.' True, these particular consequences are of no account in the context of the jingoist hysteria that was whipped up to demonize Serbs, reaching intriguing heights as bombing openly targeted the civilian society and hence required more fervent advocacy.

By chance, at least a hint of a more credible answer to Friedman's rhetorical question was given in the *Times* on the same day in a report from Ankara by Stephen Kinzer. He writes that 'Turkey's best-known human rights advocate entered prison' to serve his sentence for having 'urged the state to reach a peaceful settlement with Kurdish rebels.' A few days earlier, Kinzer had indicated obliquely that there is more to the story: 'Some [Kurds] say they have been oppressed under Turkish rule, but the Government insists that they are granted the same rights as other citizens.' One may ask whether this really does justice to some of the most extreme ethnic cleansing operations of the mid 1990s, with tens of thousands killed, 3,500 villages destroyed, some 2.5 to 3 million refugees, and hideous atrocities, which easily compare to those recorded daily in the front pages for selected enemies, reported in detail by the major human rights organizations but ignored. These achievements were carried out thanks to massive military support from the United States, increasing under Clinton as the atrocities peaked, including jet planes, attack helicopters, counterinsurgency equipment and other means of terror and destruction, along with training and intelligence information for some of the worst killers.

Recall that these crimes have been proceeding through the 1990s within NATO itself, and under the jurisdiction of the Council of Europe and the European Court of Human Rights, which continues to hand down judgements against Turkey for its US-supported atrocities. It took real discipline for participants and commentators 'not to notice' any of this at the celebration of NATO's 50th anniversary in April. The discipline was particularly impressive in light of the fact that the celebration was clouded by sombre concerns over ethnic cleansing – by officially designated enemies, not by the enlightened states that are to rededicate themselves to their traditional mission of bringing justice and freedom to the suffering people of the world, and to defend human rights, by force if necessary, under the principles of the New Humanism.

These crimes, to be sure, are only one illustration of the answer given by the enlightened states to the profound question of 'how we should react when bad things happen in unimportant places.' We should intervene to escalate the atrocities, not 'looking away' under a 'double standard,' the common evasion when such marginalia are impolitely adduced. That also happens to be the mission that was conducted in Kosovo, as revealed clearly by the course of events, though not the version refracted through the prism of ideology and doctrine, which do not gladly tolerate the observation that a consequence of the 'the huge air war' was a change from a year of atrocities on the scale of the annual (US-backed) toll in Colombia in the 1990s to a level that might have approached atrocities within NATO/Europe itself in the 1990s had the bombing continued.

The marching orders from Washington, however, are the usual ones: Focus laser-like on the crimes of today's official enemy, and do not allow yourself to be distracted by comparable or worse crimes that could easily be mitigated or terminated thanks to the crucial role of the enlightened states in perpetuating them, or escalating them when power interests so dictate. Let us obey the orders, then, and keep to Kosovo.

A minimally serious investigation of the Kosovo Accord must review the diplomatic options of 23 March 1999, the day before the 'huge air war' was launched, and compare them with the agreement reached by NATO and Serbia on 3 June 1999. Here we have to distinguish two versions: (1) the facts, and (2) the spin – that is, the US/NATO version that frames reporting and commentary in the enlightened states. Even the most cursory look reveals that the facts and the spin differ sharply. Thus the *New York Times* presented the text of the Accord with an insert headed: 'Two Peace Plans: How they Differ'. The two peace plans are the Rambouillet (Interim) Agreement presented to Serbia as a take-it-or-be-bombed ultimatum on March 23, and the Kosovo Peace Accord of June 3. But in the real world there are three 'peace plans', two of which were on the table on March 23:

the Rambouillet Agreement and the Serb National Assembly Resolutions responding to it.

Let us begin with the two peace plans of March 23, asking how they differed and how they compare with the Kosovo Peace Accord of June 3, then turning briefly to what we might reasonably expect if we break the rules and pay some attention to the (ample) precedents.

The Rambouillet Agreement

The Rambouillet Agreement called for complete military occupation and political control of Kosovo by NATO, and effective NATO military occupation of the rest of Yugoslavia at NATO's will. NATO is to 'constitute and lead a military force' (KFOR) that 'NATO will establish and deploy' in and around Kosovo, 'operating under the authority and subject to the direction and political control of the North Atlantic Council (NAC) through the NATO chain of command'; 'the KFOR commander is the final authority within theater regarding interpretation of this chapter [Implementation of the Agreement] and his interpretations are binding on all Parties and persons' (with an irrelevant qualification). Within a brief time schedule, all Yugoslav army forces and Ministry of Interior police are to redeploy to 'approved cantonment sites', then to withdraw to Serbia, apart from small units assigned to border guard duties with limited weapons (all specified in detail). These units would be restricted to defending the borders from attack and 'controlling illicit border crossings', and not permitted to travel in Kosovo apart from these functions.

'Three years after the entry into force of this Agreement, an international meeting shall be convened to determine mechanisms for a final settlement for Kosovo.' This paragraph has regularly been construed as calling for a referendum on independence, not mentioned.

With regard to the rest of Yugoslavia, the terms for the occupation are set forth in Appendix B: Status of Multi-National Military Implementation Force. The crucial paragraph reads:

> 8. NATO personnel shall enjoy, together with their vehicles, vessels, aircraft, and equipment, free and unrestricted passage and unimpeded access throughout the FRY including associated airspace and territorial waters. This shall include, but not be limited to, the right of bivouac, maneuver, billet, and utilization of any areas or facilities as required for support, training, and operations.

The remainder spells out the conditions that permit NATO forces and those they employ to act as they choose throughout the territory of the FRY, without obligation or concern for the laws of the country or the jurisdiction of its authorities, who are, however, required to follow NATO orders 'on a priority basis and with all appropriate means'. One provision states that 'all NATO personnel shall respect the laws applicable in the FRY . . .,' but with a qualification to render it vacuous: 'Without prejudice to their privileges and immunities under this Appendix, all NATO personnel . . .'

It has been speculated that the wording was designed so as to guarantee rejection. Perhaps so. It is hard to imagine that any country would consider such terms, except in the form of unconditional surrender.

In the massive coverage of the war one will find little reference to the Rambouillet Agreement that is even close to accurate, notably the crucial article of Appendix B just quoted. The latter was, however, reported as soon as it had become irrelevant to democratic choice. On June 5, after the peace agreement of June 3, the *New York Times* reported that under the annex to the Rambouillet Agreement 'a purely NATO force was to be given full permission to go anywhere it wanted in Yugoslavia, immune from any legal process,' citing also the wording. Evidently, in the absence of clear and repeated explanation of the basic terms of the Rambouillet Agreement – the official 'peace process' – it has been impossible for the public to gain any serious understanding of what was taking place, or to assess the accuracy of the preferred version of the Kosovo Accord.

The Serbian National Assembly Resolutions

The second peace plan was presented in resolutions of the Serbian National Assembly on 23 March 1999. The Assembly rejected the demand for NATO military occupation, and called on the OSCE (Organization for Security and Cooperation in Europe) and the UN to facilitate a peaceful diplomatic settlement. It condemned the withdrawal of the OSCE Kosovo Verification Mission ordered by the United States on March 19, in preparation for the March 24 bombing. The resolutions called for negotiations leading 'toward the reaching of a political agreement on a wide-ranging autonomy for Kosovo and Metohija [the official name for the province], with the securing of a full equality of all citizens and ethnic communities and with respect for the sovereignty and territorial integrity of the Republic of Serbia and the Federal Republic of Yugoslavia.' Furthermore, though 'The Serbian Parliament does not accept the presence of foreign military troops in Kosovo and Metohija,' the Serbian Parliament is ready to review the size and character of the international presence in Kosmet [Kosovo/Metohija] for carrying out the reached accord, immediately upon signing the political accord on the self-rule agreed and accepted by the representatives of all national communities living in Kosovo and Metohija.

The essentials of these decisions were reported on major wire services and therefore certainly known to every news room. Several database searches have found scarce mention, none in the national press and major journals.

The two peace plans of 23 March 1999 thus remain unknown to the general public, even the fact that there were two, not one. The standard line is that 'Milošević's refusal to accept . . . or even discuss an international peacekeeping plan [namely, the Rambouillet Agreement] was what started NATO bombing on March 24' (Craig Whitney, *New York Times*), one of the many articles deploring Serbian propaganda – accurately no doubt, but with a few oversights.

As to what the Serb National Assembly Resolutions meant, the answers are known with confidence by fanatics – different answers, depending on which variety of fanatics they are. For others, there would have been a way to find out the answers: to explore the possibilities. But the enlightened states preferred not to pursue this option; rather, to bomb, with the anticipated consequences.

The Kosovo Accord

Further steps in the diplomatic process, and their refraction in the doctrinal institutions, merit attention, but I will skip that here, turning to the Kosovo Accord of June 3. As might have been expected, it is a compromise between the two peace plans of March 23. On paper at least, the US/NATO abandoned their major demands, cited above, which had led to Serbia's rejection of the ultimatum. Serbia in turn agreed to an 'international security presence with substantial NATO participation [which] must be deployed under unified command and control . . . under UN auspices.' An addendum to the text stated 'Russia's position [that] the Russian contingent will not be under NATO command and its relationship to the international presence will be governed by relevant additional agreements.' There are no terms permitting access to the rest of the FYR for NATO or the 'international security presence' generally. Political control of Kosovo is not to be in the hands of NATO but of the UN Security Council, which will establish 'an interim administration of Kosovo'. The withdrawal of Yugoslav forces is not specified in the detail of the Rambouillet Agreement, but is similar, though accelerated. The remainder is within the range of agreement of the two plans of March 23.

The outcome suggests that diplomatic initiatives could have been pursued on March 23, averting a terrible human tragedy with consequences that will reverberate in Yugoslavia and elsewhere and which are, in many respects, quite ominous.

To be sure, the current situation is not that of March 23. A *Times* headline the day of the Kosovo Accord captures it accurately: 'Kosovo Problems Just Beginning.' Among the 'staggering problems' that lie ahead, Serge Schmemann observed, are the repatriation of the refugees 'to the land of ashes and graves that was their home,' and the 'enormously costly challenge of rebuilding the devastated economies of Kosovo, the rest of Serbia and their neighbors.' He quotes Balkans historian Susan Woodward of the Brookings Institution, who adds 'that all the people we want to help us make a stable Kosovo have been destroyed by the effects of the bombings,' leaving control in the hands of the KLA (Kosovo Liberation Army). The US had strongly condemned the KLA as 'without any question a terrorist group' when it began to carry out organized attacks in February 1998, actions that Washington condemned 'very strongly' as 'terrorist activities,' probably giving a 'green light' thereby to Milošević for the severe repression that led to the Colombia-style violence before the bombings precipitated a sharp escalation.

These 'staggering problems' are new. They are 'the effects of the bombings' and the vicious Serb reaction to them, though the problems that preceded the resort to violence by the enlightened states were daunting enough.

Turning from facts to spin, headlines hailed the grand victory of the enlightened states and their leaders, who compelled Milošević to 'capitulate,' to 'say uncle,' to accept a 'NATO-led force,' and to surrender 'as close to unconditionally as anyone might have imagined,' submitting to 'a worse deal than the Rambouillet plan he rejected.' Not exactly the story, but one that is far more useful than the facts. The only serious issue debated is whether this shows that air power alone can achieve highly moral purposes, or whether, as the critics allowed into the debate allege, the case still has not been proven. Turning to broader significance, Britain's 'eminent military historian' John Keegan 'sees the war as a victory not just for air power but for the "New World Order" that President Bush declared after the Gulf War,' military expert Fred Kaplan reports. Keegan wrote that 'If Milošević really is a beaten man, all other would-be Miloševićs around the world will have to reconsider their plans.'

The assessment is realistic, though not in the terms Keegan may have had in mind: rather, in the light of the actual goals and significance of the New World Order, as revealed by an important documentary record of the 1990s that remains unreported, and a plethora of factual evidence that helps us understand the true meaning of the phrase 'Miloševićs around the world.' Merely to keep to the Balkans region, the strictures do not hold of huge ethnic cleansing operations and terrible atrocities within NATO itself, under European jurisdiction and with decisive and mounting US support, and not conducted in response to an attack by the world's most awesome military force and the imminent threat of invasion. These crimes are legitimate under the rules of the New World Order, perhaps even meritorious, as are atrocities elsewhere that conform to the perceived interests of the leaders of the enlightened states and are regularly implemented by them when necessary. These facts, not particularly obscure, reveal that in the 'new internationalism . . . the brutal repression of whole ethnic groups' will not merely be 'tolerated,' but actively expedited – exactly as in the 'old internationalism' of the Concert of Europe, the US itself, and many other distinguished predecessors.

While the facts and the spin differ sharply, one might argue that the media and commentators are realistic when they present the US/NATO version as if it were the facts. It will become The Facts as a simple consequence of the distribution of power and the willingness of articulate opinion to serve its needs. That is a regular phenomenon. Recent examples include the Paris Peace Treaty of January 1973 and the Esquipulas Accords of August 1987. In the former case, the US was compelled to sign after the failure of the Christmas bombings to induce Hanoi to abandon the US–Vietnam agreement of the preceding October. Kissinger and the White House at once announced quite lucidly that they would violate every significant element of the Treaty they were signing, presenting a different version which was adopted in reporting and commentary, so that when North Vietnam finally responded to serious US violations of the accords, it became the incorrigible aggressor which had to be punished once again, as it was. The same tragedy/farce took place when the Central American Presidents reached the Esquipulas Accord (often called 'the Arias plan') over strong US opposition. Washington at once sharply escalated its wars in violation of the one 'indispensable element' of the Accord, then proceeded to dismantle its other provisions by force, succeeding within a few months, and continuing to undermine every further diplomatic effort until its final victory. Washington's version of the Accord, which sharply deviated from it in crucial respects, became the accepted version. The outcome could therefore be heralded in headlines as a 'Victory for US Fair Play' with Americans 'United in Joy' over the devastation and bloodshed, overcome with rapture 'in a romantic age' (Anthony Lewis, headlines in *New York Times,* all reflecting the general euphoria over a mission accomplished).

It is superfluous to review the aftermath in these and numerous similar cases. There is little reason to expect a different story to unfold in the present case – with the usual and crucial proviso: If we let it.

20

THE CHINA CARD

John Gittings

The bombing of the Chinese embassy in Belgrade during the Kosovo war has refocused attention on the unstable strategic dynamics of Asia after a decade in which the subject was mostly shrugged aside. Suddenly, the warm sentiments of friendship exchanged between Presidents Bill Clinton and Jiang Zemin a year before in Beijing seemed to belong to an earlier age. After the anti-US demonstrations in China had ended, it became clear that the embassy bombing had crystallised a deeper formation of mistrust towards US intentions which was already embedded in Chinese strategic thinking. Publication soon afterwards of the Cox Committee report in Washington, with its sweeping allegations of Chinese nuclear spying, illustrated the same contrary strands in US thinking.

A cluster of events around the region highlighted the simple fact – long brushed aside by those claiming a new era in Asia – that geo-economics cannot supplant geo-politics. It is not just a question of having to deal with a 'rogue state' in North Korea. Japan has signed up to a new set of defence arrangements to deal with unspecified future 'military contingencies'. The Philippines has allowed US ships back into its ports while squabbling with Beijing over the suitably named Mischief Reef in the South China Sea. Taiwan is advertising its alarm (with support from Pentagon hawks) at the missiles pointing at it from the mainland coast. Beijing responds by reminding the US that it had 'never renounced the use of force' to deal in the last resort with an independent Taiwan. Meanwhile US plans for a Theater Missile Defence (TMD) – a sort of mini-Star Wars package for Asia – have gone ahead. China expresses its strong opposition as Taiwan flirts with the idea.

None of these tensions are exactly new: some were advertised three years before during the Taiwan Straits crisis. But the global marketeers had dominated the argument until now. The notion that economic activity between Asian states could make strategic tensions redundant seemed more plausible during the great regional boom of the earlier 1990s. The moment that it collapsed in 1997, exposing the fragile social basis on which it was constructed, the deep fissures became apparent. This is after all a region where three great powers (the US, China and Japan) rub shoulders, together with a fourth former one (Russia); while the Korean peninsula contains the embryo of a fifth. It is also a region where two major issues – Taiwan and the divided Korea – have been left over from the Cold War.

China has its own marketeers who have dominated the policy argument in recent years. Indeed the idea of an economically strong China, sharing the fruits of international trade with the capitalist world, was suggested early on by Mao Zedong. In 1945 he attempted to win US neutrality in the coming civil war with Chiang Kai-shek by offering the lure of a limitless Chinese market, under Communist rule, for American investors. But the dominant feature of Mao's thinking, and that of a whole generation of Chinese brought up in the shadow of the foreign powers, was strategic. It was embodied in Mao's 'theory of contradictions' as applied to foreign policy: the overriding task was to decide whether hostile or friendly forces in the outside world had the upper hand, and to make common cause with those who could at least be temporary allies. This was a strategy based upon weakness: the central thrust of Chinese policy was to make the country sufficiently strong not to need alliances of convenience. (The Sino-Soviet alliance had demonstrated the dangers of relying on outside friends.) This pursuit of great-power status has again become explicit: its military implications were spelt out by President Jiang Zemin in a well-publicised speech to an armed forces' research academy on 28 June 1999: 'In the face of worldwide military developments,' he said, 'China's armed forces must sharpen their high-tech edge to cope with regional wars.' There are persistent reports of some sort of timetable within which China should become more than a regional power – and that this has now been speeded up. Hardliners in Beijing may have taken advantage of the Belgrade embassy bombing, but mainstream leaders already regarded US policy towards China as equivocal. Even before the bombing – and while Premier Zhu Rongji headed for the US to pursue friendship diplomacy – President Jiang Zemin was setting out a harsher analysis of the world scene. He denounced NATO's 'gunboat diplomacy' in Yugoslavia and told China's military leaders that 'The world is not safe', warning them to prepare for the possibility of 'regional warfare' in the face of US 'hegemonism'. Indeed the concept of 'hegemonism' had never been discarded throughout the 1990s although the identity of the potential hegemonic power was usually left unsaid.

Some Western analysts have drawn comfort from the domestic purposes allegedly served by Beijing's 'instigation' of nationalist outrage among its population. The timing of the embassy bombing – less than a month before the tenth anniversary of the crushing of the Democracy Movement in Tiananmen Square – certainly allowed the government to channel public protest in an acceptable direction. It also put pro-democracy protestors in an impossible position if they attempted to mobilise public support. But with or without the demonstrations, the Chinese shift in strategic outlook was already taking place. In fact the tone and extent of the demonstrations was far from uniform. In Shanghai the movement assumed a less aggressive tone; in Chengdu it turned into a near-riot which probably alarmed the Chinese as much as the US government. Nor was there universal support for the more aggressive forms of protest. Bulletin boards on Chinese public websites carried a number of vigorous arguments by critics who asked what purpose they served.

Western analysts have also focused on the potential parallel drawn by Beijing with Tibet. If the primacy of national sovereignty is eroded, and the West claims the authority to intervene in the defence of human rights (and without UN sanction) in Europe, how long will it be before it claims the same authority in Asia? The argument is certainly current in China but it goes much further than the borders of the People's Republic. Japan's new 'defence guidelines', now approved by the Diet, have long been seen by Chinese analysts as fitting into a disturbing global picture. Again, the embassy bombing translated this into starker terms. The US, said the *China Daily*, was seeking 'to turn NATO and the US–Japan alliance into a fortress over Europe and Asia'. The guidelines, explicitly directed at improving US–Japan 'defence co-operation', could not have come at a worse time. It has long been an open secret in Tokyo that they have been revised with the prospect of a stronger China in mind. The new rules say that Japan is now entitled to back up US action in 'surrounding areas' – a concept said to be 'not geographical but situational'. Does this mean, Beijing was already asking, that Japan would support the US to stop the mainland from regaining Taiwan? There are also Chinese concerns, encouraged by military interests, over the defence of its claims to the disputed islands (Paracels and Spratlys) in the South China Sea.

To explain the Chinese position in terms of domestic politics, anxiety over Tibet or simple 'paranoia' – a term often used by Western analysts – evades these larger issues highlighted by the crisis. Just as Chinese strategic thinking had prefigured the sharper conclusions reached after the embassy bombing, so there was also a darker side to the US strategic outlook however much this was obscured at times of free market euphoria. The hand-shaking and toast-drinking obscured the fact that American policy has always faced a hard choice in Asia: whether to regard China or Japan as its primary ally. Washington's trade tensions with Tokyo also obscured the fact that, in the last analysis, Japan was and is the preferred partner. This was clearly spelt out in the US Department of Defense's annual East Asia Strategy Report issued in November 1998. US aims in the region included (in the following order):

- 'to maintain a robust overseas military presence of approximately 100,000 in the region';
- 'strengthening the US alliance with Japan' (described later on as 'the linchpin' of our security strategy in Asia);

and, sixth in the list after 're-affirming the US security alliance with Australia':

- 'building the foundation for a long-term relationship with China based on comprehensive engagement.'

Notably absent was the concept of a 'strategic co-operative partnership' with China which featured in the rhetoric of US–Chinese presidential exchanges – but was never clearly defined. The State Department would prefer to put matters differently, stressing the joint role of China and the US in guaranteeing regional peace and helping to build a 'dynamic Asia–Pacific community'. But the underlying view is shared by US diplomats and defence experts. Beijing may no longer be a 'rogue state' – but it has been one before. The task is to find ways of tying in China to US strategy in a situation where (as the Pentagon report put it) 'lasting security in the Asia–Pacific region is not possible without a constructive role played by China'. Trade in the 1990s had replaced anti-Sovietism as the most binding force in this relationship. (From this perspective, the US trade deficit could even be seen as a price worth paying.) The rhetoric of friendship also fostered some illusions that in some undefinable way, US and Chinese leaders shared a sense of togetherness which would see them through hard as well as good times. From the Kissinger era onwards – one might even say from missionary times onwards, a century before – many Americans shared the same illusion that they were 'foreign friends' in a very special sense. Less explicitly, there was also an assumption that the US could assist forces of change in China which were already working towards a more pluralistic society which would fully 'join the world community'. No one mentioned the collapse of communism but it was implicit in Clinton's repeated references on his China trip to the spread of the Internet which proved that 'the information age (is) . . . another argument for democracy'. Clinton and the advocates of engagement are in this sense the new missionaries who seek to win China. But at the back of their minds is the historical memory that if China can be 'won', it can also be 'lost'.

The return of Hong Kong and Macau to mainland China will now shift the focus to Taiwan. No one can be sure whether Chinese leaders will accept indefinitely the implicit humiliation of the island's de facto independence, and yet re-unification is now rejected as much by the ruling Guomindang party as by the opposition. Trade and cultural links may be extensive but they cannot obliterate the strategic uncertainties. Speaker after speaker at a May 1999 conference in Kaohsiung, organised by Taiwan's Airforce Academy, invoked the magic figure 'seven' – the number of minutes it takes a Chinese missile to cross from the mainland. 'They are well dug in with many dummy exits,' says Taiwanese defence analyst Chang Jen-fu. 'Even satellite intelligence will never spot a launch in time.'

For strategic commentator Alex Kao, the missiles are not the real threat. The mainland troops would come by sea, he says, and it would take much less than 10 hours – the time on which all Taiwan defence planning is based. 'They could be building a fleet of super-fast landing boats. They'll get here first, and present the US with a fait accompli: escalate the war, or abandon Taiwan!' But why, after decades of stalemate, should armed conflict even be an option? China's insistence that it has 'never renounced the use of force' is surely nothing new. The reason to be more worried now, says Mr Kao, is precisely because 'China will not wait another 50 years'. With Hong Kong and Macau 'rejoining the motherland', no self-respecting Beijing leadership can let the Taiwan situation drag on.

A perceptive Taiwanese diplomat sees it more as a problem of impatience in Taipei than in Beijing. 'The real danger is that our pro-independence people will do something stupid, like buying a stake in the American TMD. Beijing has already said this would provoke "military counter-measures".' Current Taiwanese President Lee Teng-hui himself could be tempted to do something provocative. He has just published a book advocating a 'Great China' concept with full autonomy for Taiwan, Tibet, Xinjiang, Mongolia and former Manchuria. It did not go down at all well in Beijing.

After the Belgrade crisis, other Asian countries could only hope that before too long the emotive pendulum of US–China relations would start swinging back the other way. There is a minority view that discord between Washington and Beijing will be to the region's advantage, impelling China to attach a higher priority to good relations with its neighbours. This may be tested before long by the issues of the disputed reefs and islets in the South China Sea where China has so far said that it will only talk on a bilateral basis and refuses a multilateral approach. Southeast Asia has taken a relatively relaxed attitude so far towards China's rise to become a major military power. But in the majority view, any instability in the relations between the three big powers, the US, China and Japan, makes the region more vulnerable. A rise in tension also increases pressure – especially in Japan – for TMD-type measures which heighten Chinese suspicions, creating a vicious circle of mistrust.

No row can go on at the same intensity for ever. Beijing started talking about 'friendly co-operation' within a month of the embassy bombing, while the White House urged Congress to renew China's trade privileges. But the Clinton–Jiang rhetoric of building a strategic partnership has failed its first test, leaving a legacy of suspicion: the Asian vision of long-term stability into the twenty-first century seems outdated before the new millennium has begun.

21

WAR IN KOSOVO – CONSEQUENCES AND LESSONS FOR EUROPEAN SECURITY ARRANGEMENTS

Dieter S. Lutz

War has broken out in Europe. The outcome of the situation in the Balkans is still uncertain and the follow-up work there will occupy us for years, even decades. But this should not mean that Europe delays serious discussion about the consequences and lessons of the war in Kosovo. Already looming on the horizon are new hostilities that threaten to turn into wars; as the Kurdish conflict shows, these may also be associated with the danger of war on German streets.

What lessons for the structure of today's peace and security arrangements in – and for – Europe can be learnt from Bosnia, Kosovo and all the other military conflicts since the so-called epochal change of 1989–90? What would be the shape of a peace and security arrangement in Europe, and for Europe, that would be truly worthy of the name – i.e. that would ensure both peace in Europe, and peace for Europe? To answer this, we must first examine the present arrangement. It is marked by a series of important paradoxes.

Paradoxes of the Present Peace and Security Arrangements in – and for – Europe

One of the paradoxes of the current European security arrangement is the vociferously proclaimed commitment of all political powers to crisis prevention, on the one hand, while, on the other, whenever it is confronted with discernible or indeed escalating conflict scenarios, the European community of states remains oblivious and inactive. The 'prevention is better than cure' credo is given only lip service.

For example, intentionally or not, Kosovo was forgotten at Dayton. Year after year the Kosovan-Albanians obtained barely a hearing amongst the European community of nations. Only once Kosovan-Albanians' social defence had turned into armed struggle, once the freedom fighters had become terrorists, once the Serbs had begun to massacre Albanian civilians, and Albanian nationalists had threatened to drag the whole of the Balkans into a war over a greater Albania, only then did Europe wake from its lethargy in order to force Serbs and Kosovan-Albanians to the negotiating table of Rambouillet. By then, of course, it was too late; prevention is no longer possible after the eleventh hour.

Another of the important paradoxes of current European security arrangements concerns the whole sphere of armaments in relation to disarmament and arms limitation. Public consensus seems to imagine that the past decade since the end of the East–West conflict has been a 'decade of disarmament'. The NATO states are supposed to have disarmed to an extraordinary degree – and, indeed, over-proportionally. Such a view is a dangerous fallacy. It would be more accurate to say that the worldwide decline in military spending and supplies of soldiers has been the result, first and foremost, of reductions in Russia, or rather in the former Soviet Union. Russia's military spending is presently set at only $20 to $40 billion. The US and the European NATO states, in comparison, still spend around $270 and $180 billion respectively. NATO not only spends ten to twenty times what Russia spends: concomitantly, the 19 NATO states alone, with their huge spending of over $450 billion, are responsible for more than half the total arms spending of the world's states, which number almost two hundred. In stark contrast to the official picture, the members of NATO, the 'most powerful military alliance of all time', are currently involved in an absurd and expensive arms race – largely between themselves! But in spite of all this, the arms colossus NATO proved unable to deter Serbia from its repression of the Kosovan-Albanians in Yugoslavia; nor could the deployment of its huge war machine bring about the declared goal of preventing the 'humanitarian catastrophe' in Kosovo from taking place.

A third paradox involves the assumption of a *European* peace and security arrangement, when, in fact, Europe as an active, independent or coequal actor in matters of security policy does not exist at all. During the Cold War, (Western) Europe delegated its security policy interests either to the USA directly or to the US-dominated military pact, NATO. The USA *was* the solution to the problem of European security. Today – ten years after the epochal change – the Warsaw Pact, the Soviet Union and the deterrence system may no longer exist, but little or nothing has changed in terms of the structural dependence of Europe on America. In his book *The Grand Chessboard*, former US presidential adviser Zbigniew Brzezinski pinpoints this state of affairs in accurate, if not exactly flattering terms (from the German translation): 'There are no two ways about it: Western Europe and, increasingly, Central Europe too will largely remain an American protectorate, whose allied states are reminiscent of the vassals and tributaries of long ago.'

It is indeed the case that, at the current moment, peace and security in Europe can only be enforced by the USA. The Dayton process, the Aegean conflict and the Kosovo conflict all underline this. However, the enforcement of peace by military means must not be confused with a *preventive* peace policy within the framework of a functioning and effective security arrangement. Such a preventive peace policy is urgently needed in Europe. Its specific effect would be to make the deployment of military means superfluous, and so to help prevent wars. But as long as recourse to the military means and capabilities of the USA is a possibility, Europeans will not be able to agree on a common peace and security arrangement. As long as the Europeans cannot agree, America will retain its dominant, indeed hegemonic, influence in Europe. It is in the interests of the US, not of Europe, that this vicious circle sets itself in motion again and again. Were it to be ended, then the unthinkable would have to be thought: either the USA accommodates and subordinates itself to the vision of a security arrangement based on the principle of the force of law; or the security architecture of Europe must, at least for the time being, renounce the inclusion of America.

The fourth and final paradox of the present security system involves the fact that the years 1989–90 brought with them a 'once in a lifetime' opportunity to create stable and lasting peace and security arrangements in, and for, Europe, along the lines of a regional system of collective security, as provided for in chapter VIII of the UN charter and also article 24 of the Law Code of the German Federal Republic. This opportunity has still not been taken up.

Measured against this 'opportunity of a lifetime', the perpetuation of NATO is a fundamental mistake. This conclusion is all the more valid in the context of NATO's expansion eastwards. Military alliances such as NATO or the West European Union (WEU) – with or without their expansion eastwards – only ever include one part of the European continent. They serve to perpetuate the division of Europe into secure and insecure, stable and unstable zones. They are unable to deal preventively with conflicts outside their borders, as the example of the former Yugoslavia demonstrates. Unlike a genuine system of collective security, they do not possess the means and mechanisms to so do. But even problems between the partners can barely be sorted out by military alliances, as the Aegean conflict between Turkey and Greece or the decade-long Cyprus conflict illustrate. Military alliances are neither created nor equipped for such work. Furthermore, states excluded from membership perceive themselves to be isolated or threatened simply through the existence of these alliances. The result can be counter-alliances, arms' escalations, deterrence mentality and, as experience shows repeatedly, the breakout of war.

A system of collective defence cannot replace a system of collective security, as NATO's apologists maintain. It is also not sufficient to simply redesignate NATO as a system of collective security – as the German Federal Constitutional Court did in a paradoxical *obiter dictum* of 12 July 1994.

Reform the OSCE

If the historic opportunity that arose from the 'epochal change' of 1989–90 is not to be completely wasted European peace and security arrangements must be reformed. NATO, whose members comprise only one tenth of the state community of this world, yet whose military spending accounts for nearly five-eighths of the world's total, has nevertheless proved itself incapable of preventing genocide and war in Europe. What Europe urgently needs is a regional system of collective security, as foreseen in the German Law Code under article 24GG, and as anticipated as a regional organisation in the UN charter. Such a European peace and security arrangement, then, would rest on a system of law requiring no further mandate. It would possess adequate and efficient instruments for crisis prevention, and peaceful and civil conflict resolution. It could pursue aggressors and war criminals and put them on trial, and it would have (in co-operation with NATO and the WEU) military means of enforcement, which as *ultima ratio* do not open the way to political arbitrariness, but follow the system of law and, if need be, reinstate it.

Without a doubt these and similar considerations appear fanciful right now. However, a number of starting points and demands, as found in the coalition pacts of the present German governing parties, as well as in election manifestos, prove that they are neither unrealistic nor utopian. One of the consequences of the lessons of the Kosovo war should be, therefore, to draft conceptional and operative contributions to the question of reform of the OSCE along the lines of a regional system of collective security. Amongst other things, these suggestions should include:

- creation of a foundation for the OSCE that is bound by international law;
- establishment of a structure of decision making in the OSCE according to majority principle and without veto rights;
- founding of a pan-European security council;
- strengthening of the position and expansion of the remit of the OSCE general secretary;
- reformation of the OSCE law court along the lines of a compulsory and legally binding court of arbitration as laid out in article 24, paragraph 3 GG;
- stationing of appropriate peacekeeping troops, including troops at the disposal of the general secretary, as well as the equipping of a military command;
- introduction and legal anchoring of the principle 'OSCE first', before NATO and UNO.

Of course, the considerations and suggestions outlined here are in need of further discussion and expansion. Precisely for that reason the German federal parties should conduct this discussion as a major debate, for it affects the whole society and has significance beyond national borders. In addition, after the debacle in Kosovo, such a debate would help to cleanse society morally and politically, in the best sense, while bringing people together.

PART V

The Last Word

22

'TRAITORS' OF ALL BALKAN LANDS: UNITE!

Gazi Kaplan

In my building, back in Albania, there lived two convinced 'patriots'. We other residents were all afraid of them, because they could grass you up. They were police informers. It was a time when we lived with the watchword: He who doesn't love the Party doesn't love the motherland; he who doesn't love the motherland doesn't love the Party.

Scattered through the district were still more informers. I remember that when we were adolescents we insulted one of the most notorious, the snitch of snitches so to speak (for we knew several others), by bawling 'Grass!' after him and quickly dodging out of sight. For although there were a lot of informers, this term had remained an insult. But the one we had picked on was an informer through conviction. He became annoyed and insulted us back, shouting louder than we had and saying something that, I suppose, expressed my own convictions on the motherland and patriots: 'Listen, children of shit! Better an informer for the motherland than a puppet of the Americans!' We laughed, but the heart of one of our group was touched, and he suggested that we stop doing it – insulting informers by calling them informers – because in the final analysis these people were doing what they were doing for the good of the motherland and the country and they were true patriots.

So in my building, in my district, in my town, in my country there were a lot of patriots, on the alert to uncover potential secret agents, internal enemies, traitors. They were constantly on the lookout for evidence of the great conspiracy that was being mounted against the motherland, and that threatened to deprive us of the earthly paradise in which we lived.

For myself, I wondered (in the fastness of my mind, needless to say!) if it was really necessary for the good of the motherland that Visar should be shut in prison, at the age of thirty, for having written poems dangerous to the motherland and the Party, that Emiliano should have been sent into exile with his family because his brother had been killed at the frontier while attempting to escape from Albania, that there should be villages of exiles, forced labour camps and people who were said not to have 'good CVs'. And I wondered if it was necessary for the good of my motherland to have to lower my voice when suggesting we might be taking a wrong direction, to have to draw the curtains when looking at foreign TV, to have to not bother too much about careful critical thought, to have to try to believe that this state of things was eternal (one of the consequences of tyranny is that very conviction), to have to tolerate an utterly barmy xenophobia directed against everyone and everything, or to have to lock myself away to read any of the legion of banned authors and poets, terrified of the ear or eye of the 'patriot' who could turn up anywhere, even in your own house.

The patriots were there to consolidate this order of things, to serve the motherland. To not be, as they constantly trumpeted, 'puppets of the Americans', to try to transform my country into a space inhabited by servile and unhappy souls, in which paranoia would pass for love of country. To help the government's propaganda convince my fellow-citizens that on this planet absolute truth reigned only on a patch measuring 28,000 square kilometres: the area of Albania.

Everything outside this area was suspect, unacceptable, false, rotten, uncivilized, barbaric. The 'patriots', those lovers of all that was ours, were always there ready to serve the government, their own government and that of their cronies with their misery, their perversion, their brainwashing. After the fall of the regime I saw one or two of these old-time patriots. They didn't radiate the same glitter now. They were no longer characters who provoked a feeling of fear. Many had even forgotten their profession through lack of practice. Sometimes they lived next door to their victims, 'traitors' together in a ravaged motherland.

Others no longer serve the Party but still serve the motherland. The age of pluralism has arrived and these two notions have become dissociated to a certain extent. Some of the old patriots have become new patriots. They have changed eras. And they have started denouncing traitors and secret agents once more, this time not in the name of the Party but only of the motherland. All the same, their vocabulary has hardly changed at all. Nowadays they discover agents, not of America which they profess to adore, but of the Greeks or the Serbs. Only the names have changed.

The saddest thing in all this story is the fact that among those baying with the wolves one sometimes sees people who have themselves been condemned in the past as traitors and agents. One might say they had been infected by the disease of their persecutors.

The reason I have said all this is to sketch a little of the prehistory of my allergy to 'patriots' (and to tell the truth the latent or open sympathy I have had for traitors ever since that time).

In my view, based on my experience, there are three stages (which also blend into one another) in obtaining a certificate of excellence in the profession of 'patriot'. To acquire this reputation you do not need any specific ability. All you need is goodwill, a loud shouting voice and a decent measure of hypocrisy. Then you start extolling the glory of the national virtues that make your own nation unique in the world, different and better than all the others, repeating all the historical myths surrounding the motherland, and rejoicing (either secretly or moderately) when members of another religion or race look askance, for that is a sign of healthy national unity. Generally speaking, the good 'patriot' adores purity. He may arrive at the conclusion that xenophobia is a sign of self-respect, but without necessarily becoming aware of it. Be that as it may, a measure of hatred for the Other, for the person who has a different religion or belongs to another race, is needed for a successful performance in the role of 'patriot'. We might call this first stage that of the *general and specific discourse on the motherland and xenophobia*. When you start to discover and denounce foreign and indigenous agents, traitors to purity, traitors to the national idea or to national integration, you are moving towards the second stage of 'patriotism'.

At this stage you often notice an impressive improvement in the patriot's relations with his country's Secret Services. This is necessary not only for ethical reasons, but also because at this stage the need for a conspiracy against the nation becomes imperative.

This stage could be called that of the *conspiracy discourse*. And lastly, when you have discovered that ours is the chosen people, constantly victimized and threatened with even greater loss, you reach the highest stage of patriotism. This might be called the *paranoid discourse* stage.

Obviously one could add hundreds if not thousands of other qualities characteristic of the 'patriot'. I must say that as I am from the Balkans, anything that signifies patriotism and the patriot is a subject close to my heart. How could it be otherwise, when in the Balkans the notions of patriotism and treason are on everyone's lips from morning to night? If by some miracle 'patriotic' (nationalist) discourse were to disappear for say six months, at least half the parliamentarians (along with journalists, writers, singers and public orators in general) would be technically unemployed. The KLA, to prevail in the political arena, is obliged to call Ibrahim Rugova a traitor. It would not be thought sufficient to reject him as an incapable political leader or something like that; he has to be a traitor. Because here in the Balkans, where we don't clown around, the treason discourse is the most effective means of getting power. Even Kadaré (the greatest Albanian writer ever) declares that he is disappointed in Rugova, having found him to be too pacifist. My own view is that while a military officer, or in extreme cases a Minister of Defence, might justifiably claim to be disappointed in someone because of his pacifist attitude, the remark is inappropriate coming from a poet, and still more so from a great poet.

That said, I am afraid the new image that has been forged of the patriot corresponds to the first of the three stages described above. And the greater the accumulation of hatred (justified or not) and insecurity, the closer the notion of patriot comes to the next stage.

But what, really, is the patriot? What does patriotism mean? Is the patriot perhaps one who demystifies, who deconstructs, the image of the hero? I would say, Yes, that is mostly what he is. Perhaps because I have lived with deadly myths. But also because, looking around me, I see the criminal weight of myths pressing down on the Balkans. I don't see this job of deconstructing myths solely as a scientific experiment. I see it much more as a change in our way of thinking. So that we don't have to live the future as prisoners of our past.

Many say that the situation of the Balkans is determined by outside forces. I won't say this view is altogether off target. But my own opinion is that the main cause is the fact that the Balkans are still a supermarket, a whole industry, of nationalist myths. It is on these myths that 'specialists' like Milošević draw when they are leading the nation into crime or suicide.

On our own side, to prevent the nationalist myth of the Other from being accepted, we are constructing our own nationalist myth. To oppose the Other's nationalist dream, we are constructing our own. Still in the name of History, whose victims we all are, without exception.

So, what is patriotism? Perhaps it means knowing how to love your motherland in every possible way, in the manner of Homer and Archilochus, Socrates and Sappho (personally I rather favour Archilochus, Sappho and Socrates). The other day one of my friends was telling me that nationalism offers us a good opportunity to acquire the national unity and social cohesion we lack.

My own view is that the only thing nationalism can do for us is turn us into cretins and, with the help of a 'specialist', drive us to national suicide. God help us if social cohesion is the fruit of nationalism instead of democracy. For we will be governed once again by people whose only concern is to hunt down and root out treason.

The patriot, according to the Serb traitor Stevanović, is one who fights his own nationalism. But if you fight your own nationalism, how can you prevent yourself from dying of solitude? How can you organize fabulous concerts, become a poet, singer, hero or national statue, or just generally participate in the national spirit?

'Traitors' of All Balkan Lands: Unite!

ACKNOWLEDGEMENTS

'The Strategic Triad: USA, China, Russia', by Gilbert Achcar, and versions of the essays in this volume by Robin Blackburn, Tariq Ali and David Chandler were first published in *New Left Review*. Ellen Meiksins Wood's article is a slightly revised version of the original which appeared in *Monthly Review*. Robert Redeker's essay was first published in *Les Temps Modernes*. Oskar Lafontaine's May Day speech was translated by Gus Fagan from *Junge Welt* and first published in English in *Labour Focus on Eastern Europe*. Yevgeny Yevtushenko's article appeared in the *Guardian* and Régis Debray's 'Open Letter' in *Le Monde*. Edward Said's 'Treason of the Intellectuals' first appeared in the Cairo daily, *al-Ahram*. Susan L. Woodward's essay is extracted from her classic work, *Balkan Tragedy: Chaos and Dissolution After the Cold War*, The Brookings Institute, Washington, DC 1995. We would like to thank them all for their kind permission to reprint in this volume.

The texts by Gilbert Achcar, Régis Debray and Robert Redeker were translated from the French by John Howe. Dieter Lutz's essay was translated from the German by Esther Leslie and Gazi Kaplan's from the Greek by Riki Van Boeschoten.

The editor of this book would also like to thank Sebastian Budgen and Susan Watkins from Verso, for their editorial help and suggestions.

INDEX